mummers pp 143-

THE SCHOLAR'S LIBRARY

General Editor:—Guy Boas, M.A.

THE RETURN OF THE NATIVE

Thomas Hardy's WESSEX
Fictitious names as Exonbury
Real names as Portsmouth
0 5 10 15 Miles
Cliff without name
Targan Bay
Dundagel
Nallency Vale
St. Launce's
Plymouth
OFF WESSEX
Trufal
Penzephyr
Lands End
Channel
Bristol
Stancey Castle
Mendip Hills
Bath
Exon Moor
Dunkery Beacon
Quantock Hills
Tountall
Glaston
OUTER WESSEX
Sedgemoor
Downstaple
Toneborough
LOWER WESSEX
Tinworthy
Exonbury
Well
Christminster
Lumsdon
NORTH WESSEX
Alfredstone
Marygreen
Castle Royal
Aldbrickham
MID WESSEX
Marlbury Downs
Batton Castle
Kennetbridge
Inkpen Beacon
Stoke Barehills
Quartershot
Weydon Priors
Icenway House
The Great Plain
Stonehenge
Stour Head
Melchester
UPPER WESSEX
Wintoncester
Deansleigh
Southampton
Shaston
Wingreen
The Chase
Trantridge Cross
Shottsford Forum
Chaseborough
Lornton Inn
Sherton Abbas
Stourcastle
Vale of Blackmore
Kings Hintocks
High Stoy
Bulbarrow
Emminster
Flintcombe Ash
Pilsdon
Chalk Newton
SOUTH WESSEX
Casterbridge
Egdon Heath
Wurborne
Chene Manor
Havenpool
The Great Forest
Sandbourne
Solentsea
Portsmouth
The Island
River Axe
Port Bredy
Blackon
Talbothays
R. Frome
Anglebury
Overcombe
Wellbridge
Knollsea
Budmouth
Idmouth
Deadmans Bay
Isle of Slingers
The Beal
The Race
Lightship
Tor-upon-Sea
The Channel
0 5 10 15 Miles
Septentrio
Oriens
Meridies
Occidens

THE RETURN OF THE NATIVE

By

THOMAS HARDY

Edited by

CYRIL ALDRED

With an Introduction

by

SYLVIA LYND

To sorrow
I bade good morrow,
And thought to leave her far away behind
But cheerly, cheerly,
She loves me dearly;
She is so constant to me, and so kind.
I would deceive her,
And so leave her,
But ah! she is so constant and so kind.

LONDON
MACMILLAN & CO LTD
NEW YORK · ST MARTIN'S PRESS
1955

—

First printed in The Scholar's Library 1935
Reprinted 1936, 1937, 1938, 1942, 1943, 1945, 1946
1948, 1949, 1952, 1953, 1954, 1955

MACMILLAN AND COMPANY LIMITED
London Bombay Calcutta Madras Melbourne

THE MACMILLAN COMPANY OF CANADA LIMITED
Toronto

ST MARTIN'S PRESS INC
New York

PRINTED IN GREAT BRITAIN

INTRODUCTION

HARDY is a writer who has, for our generation, a dual interest: he must be regarded not only as a great figure in literature, but as a figure who marks the boundary between nineteenth-century literature and our own. In technique he is a Victorian; in mind, a modern man. His view of life is shared by far more people at the present day than it was when he expressed it. To find how wholly modern he is, how immediate his opinions, it is necessary only to glance at *The Dynasts* with its preface, written in 1903, which speaks of the Napoleonic Wars as a "Great Historical Calamity, or Clash of peoples artificially brought about," with its exposition of the motives of war, which would almost satisfy a Disarmament pamphleteer; and its "Phantom Intelligences," Spirits of the Years, the Pities and the Ironies and, not to be discounted, the Spirit Sinister, all of whom might be presiding presences in the War literature of our own generation. Or we may take the description of Clym Yeobright at the beginning of the Third Book of the present novel as a plain indication of what Hardy himself believed:—

"In Clym Yeobright's face could be dimly seen the typical countenance of the future. Should there be a classic period to art hereafter, its Pheidias may produce such faces. The view of life as a thing to be put up with, replacing that zest for existence which was so intense in early civilisations, must ultimately enter so thoroughly into the constitution of the advanced races that its facial expression will become accepted as a new artistic departure.

People already feel that a man who lives without disturbing a curve of feature, or setting a mark of mental concern anywhere upon himself, is too far removed from modern perceptiveness to be a modern type. . . . That old-fashioned revelling in the general situation grows less and less possible as we uncover the defects of natural laws, and see the quandary that man is in by their operation."

This is a statement of the disillusioned view upon which nowadays we pride ourselves. There is certainly little "revelling in the general situation" in vogue at the present day. Probably the complacency of Victorian times has been much exaggerated in retrospect (complacency, we may suspect, is never much more than a refuge in which men try to hide from themselves and from one another); but Hardy was unusual in that he did not try to hide. He spoke his griefs and fears aloud to people who preferred to forget them.

Almost alone among English novelists, he takes the tragic view of life. George Eliot, to some extent shared it, but outfaced it with the fortitude of her spirit; Meredith met it with his customary swagger; Emily Brontë, having her faith, could escape from it with wings. To Hardy alone it was the complete and final truth. In his day it was the custom glibly to call him a pessimist, as if an entirely cheerful opposite opinion could easily be held, and old age and disease and the fading of love and all the ironic misfortunes, misunderstandings, conflicts, follies, cruelties, and prides with which life abounds, regarded as mournful and rather crack-brained fancies. It was the custom for authors in his day to contrive better lives for their characters than Destiny, as discoverable by human experience, could reasonably be expected to contrive. Bad people were easily distinguishable from good people, wickedness was punished, virtue rewarded, and what further knowledge emerged from the pageant of existence was successfully concealed. Hardy, however, rejected these simplicities, not without a certain grim satisfaction, perhaps, in doing so. He writes of a race of men who cannot be classified and petted or punished like children in a nursery. He demands, if we are to enjoy his novels, that we shall use the full range of our emotions and intelligence. The people whom he sets before us are beautiful and erroneous and self-defeated, and what they themselves do not contribute to their own unhappiness is contributed by the petty spite of chance. Yet, however exact Hardy may be in his attention to melancholy detail, we are never allowed to forget that in addition to being a realist he is a poet. This is very important. It is because he is a poet, contradictory as this may seem, that Hardy is a realist. Poets cannot fail to be serious critics of life. They cannot help perceiving the sad unchanging pattern behind the charmingly varied surface. It was because he did not fail to acknowledge this pattern that Hardy is a great novelist—that he is also for many people a depressing novelist is because he happened to be a man without any counterbalancing animal spirits—and it is because he is a poet that Hardy's novels contain some of the most beautiful descriptive passages in literature.

As a descriptive writer, Hardy belongs to his own century, though in what he chose to describe we may again claim him as belonging to ours—"The new Vale of Tempe may be a gaunt waste in Thule . . ." he says. "The time seems near, if it has not actually arrived, when the chastened sublimity of a moor, a sea, or a mountain will be all of nature that is absolutely in keeping with the moods of the more thinking among mankind." We may smile a little at his choice of words and at that rather priggish phrase, "the more thinking among mankind"; but we must admit the correctness of the prophecy. Loneliness, in an overcrowded world, has come to delight us. In the manner of his descriptions, however, Hardy is emphatically a Victorian. The chief contribution to literature of the nineteenth century was its descriptive writing. Scene, atmosphere, the look of imagined events, had till then been left to the poets. The early novelists approached life as if they were making a catalogue rather than painting a picture. They relied on their readers' imaginations to fill in the appropriate emotional or decorative effects. They stated facts about life rather than made copies of it. Roderick Random crosses the South Atlantic without once mentioning the appearance of the sea, and in the pages of Jane Austen we are trusted to build and furnish our own Regency mansions and villas.

It was left to the Victorians to discover the art of painting in words ; of doing more than this, of transporting the reader out of his arm-chair into the world of the writer's imagination. With them we no longer read a story, we live a story.

Such a discovery, it is interesting to observe, may have been made in obedience to the law of compensation. The Victorians, though as unlimited in their actual experience as other generations of men, were extraordinarily limited as to what they might relate of it. Much might be known, but little might be told. This was a revolutionary state of affairs in literature. Eighteenth-century writers knew no such restriction. There was nothing that they were not permitted to mention in their matter-of-fact, exquisitely tidy prose. The words into which they translated life reduced it at once to seemliness and order. The Victorians laid their hands upon new modes of expression. Deprived of one supremely interesting subject, they found a way of escape for their genius in a new art, the art of making interesting the less intrinsically interesting things. They seized upon the panorama of the whole visible world —landscapes and seascapes, towns, farms, fogs, storms, slums, gaols, sunlight, candlelight, and a range of emotions that make the novels of the eighteenth century seem trivial in comparison. Those long peregrinations through the follies of a heartless world, in which heroes lose their simplicity and heroines do not always succeed in retaining theirs, are not profoundly interesting : they do not exercise the emotions ; they are a spectacle seen through a window. If we compare Fielding's heroes and rogues and gaols, with those of Dickens ; or Clarissa Harlowe in her yellow paduasoy, with Beatrix Esmond with her red-heeled shoes and lighted candle ; above all, if we compare Defoe's account of adventure with Conrad's or Mr. Tomlinson's, we shall have no doubt as to our gain in riches. Whatever excites us, moves us, makes us forgetful of ourselves in modern literature, we owe to the Victorians. The eighteenth-century writers teach us to be observant and shrewd, and very pleasant and urbane is their company ; the Victorians teach us to see and feel and think.

It is as a great writer of this kind that Hardy takes his place in literature. That he shared some of the faults of the writing of his day as well as its supreme virtues was, perhaps, inevitable. We find throughout his prose a curiously pompous choice of words, an ungainliness only to be paralleled in the prose of Charlotte Brontë, and a fondness for classical allusions which is now old-fashioned pedantry. So intense is the vision that he makes us share with him, however, that these faults matter little. When we open a novel of Hardy's, we put ourselves into a great story-teller's power. We must listen and attend to whatever he has to tell us until he bids us cease. His eyes, his brain, and his emotions take the place of our own. Until the book is closed we share his wisdom, his insight, his vision, and his charity.

It is Hardy's charity—that observant, comprehending tolerance of his—which is his outstanding characteristic. Thackeray had something of the same virtue ; but with Thackeray it was part of his urbanity rather than a spiritual quality. He was polite to error, as it were, in spite of himself. Mentally he was full of the primmest disapprovals. Dickens had within him a spouting well of pity, but its waters were kept well dammed back from any save the obviously pitiful object. Tennyson may fairly be regarded as the perfect representative of his age.

Hardy extends his pity to those who are, by every commonplace standard of good conduct, deplorable. He is far more akin to Dostoevsky—from whom and from the psychologists our modern tolerance is largely derived, I think—than to any earlier island novelist. There are few human conditions and follies for which Hardy does not make the heart bleed. Discontents and failures which pettier minds would dismiss or jeer at—Jude's longing for learning, Eustacia's longing for cities, Tess's disastrous lie, Sue's defeated courage—he awards these their full dignity of pain, no less than to the forsaken, the betrayed, the despised.

That Hardy does this is all the more remarkable because he accepted the Christian standard of virtues and vices. His charity is not of the kind which denies the existence of sin. He believes in its existence in the ethical sense as firmly as did his fellow Victorians, or as did, for that matter, Shakespeare. Only Hardy perceives that the commission of a sin may have more to do with virtue than its avoidance. The gross Arabella and the delicate Sue, though one a wife and the other a mistress, are different as fine weather from foul. This is a discovery which only a writer with the courage to originate doctrine could have made. Until Hardy's day no serious flaw was to be found in heroines. They were immune from crime and folly and ignoble desires and they all held marriage as of more importance than love—very sensibly and perhaps rightly. With Hardy, they ceased to be perfect ; but did not cease to be good. He was ready, indeed, on their behalf to defy and deny every social and religious convention of his time.

To do this frankly in so many words was a revolutionary proceeding. It had the effect of making the better-behaved heroines of his contemporaries look like dolls, as women in fiction are too apt to do unless they breathe only the rarefied, delightful air of comedy. Yet Hardy, in this new presentation of good and bad, was being merely honest. He was simply acknowledging a fact that everyone in actual experience sooner or later acknowledges. He was reflecting life and compelling his readers to draw their own disconcerting conclusions, instead of telling them a well-pointed, moral tale. He was pointing out that here were faulty human beings who did shocking things, and who yet were triumphantly insistent upon being loved, admired, and respected. These elements of Hardy's genius have come to be overlooked, his purpose forgotten, in our admiration of the art with which he states it. The purpose having been achieved, the art alone remains of importance.

The Return of the Native

The Return of the Native belongs to Hardy's middle period. In the earlier novels he moves easily enough within the Victorian convention. Its limitations do not hamper him, because they do not conflict with what he has to tell. For this reason *Far from the Madding Crowd*, in which the convention is accepted, may be held to share the highest pinnacle of his achievement with *Tess of the D'Urbervilles* and *Jude the Obscure*, in which the convention is defied.

The Return of the Native, glorious as it is, must be given a lower place among Hardy's writings than any of these three. It is a novel with a peculiar magnificence of scene, a magnificence which has never been excelled perhaps in fiction ; but it is a novel which suffers markedly from the Victorian convention. If we consider the story as it is actually told, with no further implications, we find that it is an insufficient ground for the towering tragedy that is based upon it. Wildeve has philandered with Eustacia and with Thomasin, but there is no convincing reason for Thomasin's distress at the delay of her marriage to Wildeve, while Mrs. Yeobright's disapproval of the whole affair seems unreasonable, as does her opposition to her son's marriage to Eustacia. So it is with Clym's jealousy, nor is there any sound explanation of the hostility of her country neighbours to Eustacia, nor yet of her final despair. It is not that the story makes the emotions seem exaggerated ; but that the emotions call our attention to the insufficiency of the story. Had Hardy defied his age here as in his later novels, *The Return of the Native* might well have been his masterpiece. As it is, we are conscious of some slight disappointment in his "big scenes." The things that his characters say to one another are never quite natural, we never feel that they are really speaking their minds : their stilted phrases increase this impression. (Unless when his rustic characters use their racy vernacular, Hardy is always at his least admirable in "conversation.") In fact we may say that at these points in the story the illusion is shattered, and instead of sharing in life we find ourselves watching a theatrical performance.

This is the flaw of the book, its only flaw. Beyond this it has a majestic beauty that seems to wrap it in a sunset splendour unsurpassed in fiction. In his description of Egdon Heath Hardy follows Dickens's scheme of great descriptive openings, and the beginning of *The Return of the Native* is worthy to be put beside the opening pages of *Great Expectations* or *Our Mutual Friend*. From the moment that we set foot on Egdon Hardy has us in his power. We are in the Elf King's country and under a spell. Let us try for a moment to find the secret of that magic. It is to be discovered in the exact precision of Hardy's observation and the words with which he has matched it. Egdon is not any heath at any time. It is a very particular and special heath at very particular and special times. We see it from the depths of its fern, from its roads and valley footpaths ; or we look down upon it as if from a height and see human faces glimmer upon its darkness like pearls. We know it in spring when its birch trees are in leaf, or we share its "curious microscopic" life with Clym Yeobright, when, driven from his books by failing eyesight, he lives the humble life of a furze-cutter:—

"His familiars were creeping and winged things, and they seemed to enrol him in their band. Bees hummed around his ears with an intimate air, and tugged at the heath and furze-flowers at his side in such numbers as to weigh them down to the sod. The strange amber-coloured butterflies which Egdon produced, and which were never seen elsewhere, quivered in the breath of his lips, alighted upon his bowed back, and sported with the glittering point of his hook as he flourished it up and down. Tribes of emerald-green grasshoppers leaped over his feet, falling awkwardly on their backs, heads, or hips, like unskilful acrobats, as chance might rule ; or engaged themselves in noisy flirtations under the fern-fronds with silent ones of homely hue. Huge flies, ignorant of larders and wire-netting, and quite in a savage state, buzzed about him without knowing that he was a man. In and out of the fern-dells snakes glided in their most brilliant blue and yellow guise, it being the season immediately following the shedding of their old skins, when their colours are brightest. Litters of young rabbits came out from their forms to sun themselves upon hillocks, the hot beams blazing through the delicate tissue of each thin-fleshed ear, and firing it to a blood-red transparency in which the veins could be seen. None of them feared him."

But it is Egdon as we first see it, the Egdon of winter and darkness, that is the supreme masterpiece of the book. It is the heath in all its changing moods and unchanging majesty that is Hardy's chief character. With consummate skill we are given our first impressions of its inhabitants, meeting them one by one reduced to pygmy size against its sombre background: the Reddleman and Thomasin and Captain Vye, each gaining from us the required measure of sympathy, interest, or indifference ; then the solitary figure of Eustacia Vye standing on the summit of Rainbarrow " like the spike upon a helmet " and conveying in that brief moment an impression of her importance in the story and of someone romantic, ill-starred, and sinister; then again, as with the vitality of the silhouettes in one of those little old books of moving figures, forerunners of the cinema, that were used long ago to amuse children, the minor characters of the story swarm upon the sky-line and perform their antics. They are purely comic figures, these yokels whose mouths close "like the two halves of a muffin," but how racy and on occasion how touching their talk when they open them. With admirable ease the story is unfolded before us as we leave the glowing ashes of the villagers' fire to attend that other blazing beacon where Eustacia Vye resumes her old sway over Wildeve. Eustacia is the only figure in the book who is in any sense a rival to Egdon. In her dark beauty Hardy has painted one of his most memorable portraits. The black-velvet ribbon that binds her forehead, the long, romantic cloak, the sigh that shakes her "whenever a flash of reason darted like an electric light upon her lover—as it sometimes would—and showed his imperfections," belong to a real person, and all her passionate romanticism and her ill-luck are indicated in that single sentence. Eustacia had "the passions and instincts which make a model goddess" and had therefore "those which make not quite a model woman." With what insight and understanding it is said; and was it by intent, or by one of the lucky accidents which seem to attend upon art, that the sound of a stone thrown into a pond with which her lover signals his arrival should be the sound that Eustacia herself must have made as she flung herself out of life in storm and darkness into the swift river? Everything about her seems to have the significance not only of reality but of a symbolic thing. She and Egdon together produce the inevitable atmosphere for a story of violent passions, treachery, hatred, failure and despair.

It is not the true Egdon which wears so cheerful a face in the final pages. We should know this even if we had not Hardy's own word for it in a footnote. The Reddleman, with his constant watchfulness and benign interferences, is a figure drawn from fairy tales rather than from life, and that he should persist in his courtship and Thomasin finally accept him is a conclusion of his story in the fairy-tale tradition. He mingles a little strangely with reality. How different is his simple and faithful love for Thomasin, for instance, from that of Charley, the Vyes' serving man, for Eustacia. The one leaves us indifferent, the other moves us. Perhaps we know, instinctively, that a story-book happiness is in store for Diggory Venn. We are quite certain that it cannot be contrived for Charley.

It is not only by deep feeling that the tragic atmosphere is contrived, but by that exquisitely exact gift for noticing things which was part of Hardy's poetic endowment. The flapping of a child's pinafore in the wind is not too unimportant a thing to receive a certain value at his hands. He can give weight to a goose-feather, as in that delightful scene in his final chapter where Granfer and Christian Cantle are filling a feather-bed for Thomasin. And how miraculous is his gift for creating ominous detail we realise in such a passage as that in which Captain Vye is deterred from sleep by seeing in the sudden light from Eustacia's window "the white pole of the flag-staff flash into existence like a streak of phosphorus drawn downwards across the shade of night without"; or in the last touch to the description of Clym's unlucky cottage, "a small apple tree, of the sort called Ratheripe, grew just inside the gate, the only one which throve in the garden, by reason of the lightness of the soil; and among the fallen apples on the ground beneath were wasps rolling drunk with juice, or creeping about the little caves in each fruit which they had eaten out before being stupefied by its sweetness." It is a tragic return that Clym Yeobright makes to Egdon and Eustacia, and yet, perhaps because the male characters in the book are less distinctly drawn than the female, or because Eustacia's beauty, like the beauty of Egdon, triumphs over its sombreness, we cannot feel him wholly desolate in his blindness and solitude. He has had, after all, his summer upon Egdon.

Life of Thomas Hardy

Thomas Hardy was born in 1840 near Dorchester in the West of England. Dorchester is a characteristic English town and must have been a wholly beautiful one in Hardy's childhood. It has still its ancient main street in which seventeenth and eighteenth-century architecture mingle, but is now surrounded with a wide band of haphazard streets and villas. Hardy was educated at local schools and at the age of sixteen was articled to an architect. At the age of nineteen he began to write verse and essays, but his first short story was not published until 1865. Meantime he had enjoyed some success in his architectural career, becoming the assistant in London of Sir Arthur Blomfield and winning several prizes at the Royal Institution of British Architects.

His first novel, *Desperate Remedies,* was written at the instigation of George Meredith, who had, as reader to Chapman and Hall, rejected an earlier MS. of Hardy's—a novel which has never been published. *Desperate Remedies* was followed in 1872 by *Under the Greenwood Tree,* which is still, for many people, the most pleasing of Hardy's novels. It contains a charming picture of rural England and no indication of the author's tragic genius. In 1873 came *A Pair of Blue Eyes* ; but Hardy's first popular success was made with *Far from the Madding Crowd,* which was published in 1874 and is held by general consent to be the most delightful of all his writings. In that year also (1874) he married his first wife, Emma Lavinia Gifford.

After this, in the following order, he published : *The Hand of Ethelberta* (1876) ; *The Return of the Native* (1878); *The Trumpet Major* (1880) (of which the scene is laid at Weymouth, where at this time he was living) ; *A Laodicean* (1881) ; *Two on a Tower* (1882) ; *The Mayor of Caster-*

bridge (1886); *The Woodlanders* (1888); *A Group of Noble Dames* (1891); *Tess of the D'Urbervilles* (1891); *Life's Little Ironies* (1894); *Jude the Obscure* (1895); *The Well Beloved* (1897); *Wessex Poems* (1898); *The Dynasts* (1904–1906); *Time's Laughing Stocks, and Other Verses* (1909); and *Collected Poems* (1919). Nearly all these books can still be read with as intense an interest as when they first appeared. It is advisable, however, to read them in their historical order if possible, because it may be disappointing after reading *Jude the Obscure* to read others that are less impressive. Hardy died in 1928 at Max Gate, the house he built for himself on the outskirts of Dorchester in 1883. His body was buried with great ceremony in Westminster Abbey; but his heart is buried at Stinsford Church in Dorset.

S. L.

CONTENTS

BOOK FIRST

THE THREE WOMEN

BOOK SECOND

THE ARRIVAL

BOOK THIRD

THE FASCINATION

BOOK FOURTH

THE CLOSED DOOR

BOOK FIRST

THE THREE WOMEN

A FACE ON WHICH TIME MAKES BUT LITTLE IMPRESSION

I

A SATURDAY afternoon in November was approaching the time of twilight, and the vast tract of unenclosed wild known as Egdon Heath embrowned itself moment by moment. Overhead the hollow stretch of whitish cloud shutting out the sky was as a tent which had the whole heath for its floor.

The heaven being spread with this pallid screen and the earth with the darkest vegetation, their meeting-line at the horizon was clearly marked. In such contrast the heath wore the appearance of an instalment of night which had taken up its place before its astronomical hour was come: darkness had to a great extent arrived hereon, while day stood distinct in the sky. Looking upwards, a furze-cutter would have been inclined to continue work; looking down, he would have decided to finish his faggot and go home. The distant rims of the world and of the firmament seemed to be a division in time no less than a division in matter. The face of the heath by its mere complexion added half an hour to evening; it could in like manner retard the dawn, sadden noon, anticipate the frowning of storms scarcely generated, and intensify the opacity of a moonless midnight to a cause of shaking and dread.

In fact, precisely at this transitional point of its nightly roll into darkness the great and particular glory of the Egdon waste began, and nobody could be said to understand the heath who had not been there at such a time. It could best be felt when it could not clearly be seen, its complete effect and explanation lying in this and the succeeding hours before the next dawn: then, and only then, did it tell its true tale. The spot was, indeed, a near relation of night, and when night showed itself an apparent tendency to gravitate together could be perceived in its shades and the scene. The sombre stretch of rounds and hollows seemed to rise and meet the evening gloom in pure sympathy, the heath exhaling darkness as rapidly as the heavens precipitated it. And so the obscurity in the air and the obscurity in the land closed together in a black fraternization towards which each advanced half-way.

The place became full of a watchful intentness now; for when other things sank brooding to sleep the heath appeared slowly to awake and listen. Every night its Titanic form seemed to await something; but it had waited thus, unmoved, during so many centuries, through the crises of so many things, that it could only be imagined to await one last crisis—the final overthrow.

It was a spot which returned upon the memory of those who loved it with an aspect of peculiar and kindly congruity. Smiling champaigns of flowers and fruit hardly do this, for they are permanently harmonious only with an existence of better reputation as to its issues than the present. Twilight combined with the scenery of Egdon Heath to evolve a thing majestic without severity, impressive without showiness, emphatic in its admonitions, grand in its simplicity. The qualifications which frequently invest the façade of a prison with far more dignity than is found in the façade of a palace double its size lent to this heath a sublimity in which spots renowned for beauty of the accepted kind are utterly wanting. Fair prospects wed happily with fair times; but alas, if times be not fair! Men have oftener suffered from the mockery of a place too smiling for their reason than from the oppression of surroundings oversadly tinged. Haggard Egdon appealed to a subtler and scarcer instinct, to a more recently learnt emotion, than that which responds to the sort of beauty called charming and fair.

Indeed, it is a question if the exclusive reign of this orthodox beauty is not approaching its last quarter. The new Vale of Tempe may be a gaunt waste in Thule: human souls may find themselves in closer and closer harmony with external things wearing a sombreness distasteful to our race when it was young. The time seems near, if it has not actually arrived, when the chastened sublimity of a moor, a sea, or a mountain will be all of nature that is absolutely in keeping with the moods of the more thinking among mankind. And ultimately, to the commonest tourist, spots like Iceland may become what the vineyards and myrtle-gardens of South Europe are to him now; and Heidelberg and Baden be passed unheeded as he hastens from the Alps to the sand-dunes of Scheveningen.

The most thorough-going ascetic could feel that he had a natural right to wander on Egdon: he was keeping within the line of legitimate indulgence when he laid himself open to influences such as these. Colours and beauties so far subdued were, at least, the birthright of all. Only in summer days of highest feather did its mood touch the level of gaiety. Intensity was more usually reached by way of the solemn than by way of the brilliant, and such a sort of intensity was often arrived at during winter darkness, tempests, and mists. Then Egdon was aroused to reciprocity; for the storm was its lover, and the wind its friend. Then it became the home of strange phantoms; and it was found to be the hitherto unrecognized original of those wild regions of obscurity which are vaguely felt to be compassing us about in midnight dreams of flight and disaster, and are never thought of after the dream till revived by scenes like this.

It was at present a place perfectly accordant with man's nature—neither ghastly, hateful, nor ugly: neither commonplace, unmeaning, nor tame; but, like man, slighted and enduring; and withal singularly colossal and mysterious in its swarthy monotony. As with some persons who have long lived apart, solitude seemed to look out of its countenance. It had a lonely face, suggesting tragical possibilities.

This obscure, obsolete, superseded country figures in Domesday. Its condition is recorded therein as that of heathy, furzy, briary wilderness—'Bruaria.' Then follows the length and breadth in leagues; and, though some uncertainty exists as to the exact extent of this ancient lineal measure, it appears from the figures that the area of Egdon down to the present day has but little diminished. 'Turbaria Bruaria'—the right of cutting heath-turf—occurs in charters relating to the district. 'Overgrown with heth and mosse,' says Leland of the same dark sweep of country.

Here at least were intelligible facts regarding landscape—far-reaching proofs productive of genuine satisfaction. The untameable, Ishmaelitish thing that Egdon now was it always had been. Civilization was its enemy; and ever since the beginning of vegetation its soil had worn the same antique brown dress, the natural and invariable garment of the particular formation. In its venerable one coat lay a certain vein of satire on human vanity in clothes. A person on a heath in raiment of modern cut and colours has more or less an anomalous look. We seem to want the oldest and simplest human clothing where the clothing of the earth is so primitive.

To recline on a stump of thorn in the central valley of Egdon, between afternoon and night, as now, where the eye could reach nothing of the world outside the summits and shoulders of heathland which filled the whole circumference of its glance, and to know that everything around and underneath had been from prehistoric times as unaltered as the stars overhead, gave ballast to the mind adrift on change, and harassed by the irrepressible New. The great inviolate place had an ancient permanence which the sea cannot claim. Who can say of a particular sea that it is old? Distilled by the sun, kneaded by the moon, it is renewed in a year, in a day, or in an hour. The sea changed, the fields changed, the rivers, the villages, and the people changed, yet Egdon remained. Those surfaces were neither so steep as to be destructible by weather, nor so flat as to be the victims of floods and deposits. With the exception of an aged highway, and a still more aged barrow presently to be referred to—themselves almost crystallized to natural products by long continuance—even the trifling irregularities were not caused by pickaxe, plough, or spade, but remained as the very finger-touches of the last geological change.

The above-mentioned highway traversed the lower levels of the heath from one horizon to another. In many portions of its course it overlaid an old vicinal way, which branched from the great Western road of the Romans, the Via Iceniana, or Ikenild Street, hard by. On the evening under consideration it would have been noticed that, though the gloom had increased sufficiently to confuse the minor features of the heath, the white surface of the road remained almost as clear as ever.

HUMANITY APPEARS UPON THE SCENE, HAND IN HAND WITH TROUBLE

II

ALONG the road walked an old man. He was white-headed as a mountain, bowed in the shoulders, and faded in general aspect. He wore a glazed hat, an ancient boat-cloak, and shoes; his brass buttons bearing an anchor upon their face. In his hand was a silver-headed walking-stick, which he used as a veritable third leg, perseveringly dotting the ground with its point at every few inches' interval. One would have said that he had been, in his day, a naval officer of some sort or other.

Before him stretched the long, laborious road, dry, empty, and white. It was quite open to the heath on each side, and bisected that vast dark surface like the parting-line on a head of black hair, diminishing and bending away on the furthest horizon.

The old man frequently stretched his eyes ahead to gaze over the tract that he had yet to traverse. At length he discerned, a long distance in front of him, a moving spot, which appeared to be a vehicle, and it proved to be going the same way as that in which he himself was journeying. It was the single atom of life that the scene contained, and it only served to render the general loneliness more evident. Its rate of advance was slow, and the old man gained upon it sensibly.

When he drew nearer he perceived it to be a spring van, ordinary in shape, but singular in colour, this being a lurid red. The driver walked beside it ; and, like his van, he was completely red. One dye of that tincture covered his clothes, the cap upon his head, his boots, his face, and his hands. He was not temporarily overlaid with the colour : it permeated him.

The old man knew the meaning of this. The traveller with the cart was a reddleman—a person whose vocation it was to supply farmers with redding for their sheep. He was one of a class rapidly becoming extinct in Wessex, filling at present in the rural world the place which, during the last century, the dodo occupied in the world of animals. He is a curious, interesting, and nearly perished link between obsolete forms of life and those which generally prevail.

The decayed officer, by degrees, came up alongside his fellow-wayfarer, and wished him good evening. The reddleman turned his head, and replied in sad and occupied tones. He was young, and his face, if not exactly handsome, approached so near to handsome that nobody would have contradicted an assertion that it really was so in its natural colour. His eye, which glared so strangely through his stain, was in itself attractive—keen as that of a bird of prey, and blue as autumn mist. He had neither whisker nor moustache, which allowed the soft curves of the lower part of his face to be apparent. His lips were thin, and though, as it seemed, compressed by thought, there was a pleasant twitch at their corners now and then. He was clothed throughout in a tight-fitting suit of corduroy, excellent in quality, not much worn, and well-chosen for its purpose ; but deprived of its original colour by his trade. It showed to advantage the good shape of his figure. A certain well-to-do air about the man suggested that he was not poor for his degree. The natural query of an observer would have been, Why should such a promising being as this have hidden his prepossessing exterior by adopting that singular occupation?

After replying to the old man's greeting he showed no inclination to continue in talk, although they still walked side by side, for the elder traveller seemed to desire company. There were no sounds but that of the booming wind upon the stretch of tawny herbage around them, the crackling wheels, the tread of the men, and the footsteps of the two shaggy ponies which drew the van. They were small, hardy animals, of a breed between Galloway and Exmoor, and were known as 'heath-croppers' here.

Now, as they thus pursued their way, the reddleman occasionally left his companion's side, and, stepping behind the van, looked into its interior through a small window. The look was always anxious. He would then return to the old man, who made another remark about the state of the country and so on, to which the reddleman again abstractedly replied, and then again they would lapse into silence. The silence conveyed to neither any sense of awkwardness; in these lonely places wayfarers, after a first greeting, frequently plod on for miles without speech; contiguity amounts to a tacit conversation where, otherwise than in cities, such contiguity can be put an end to on the merest inclination, and where not to put an end to it is intercourse in itself.

Possibly these two might not have spoken again till their parting, had it not been for the reddleman's visits to his van. When he returned from his fifth time of looking in the old man said, 'You have something inside there besides your load?'

'Yes.'

'Somebody who wants looking after?'

'Yes.'

Not long after this a faint cry sounded from the interior. The reddleman hastened to the back, looked in, and came away again.

'You have a child there, my man?'

'No, sir, I have a woman.'

'The deuce you have! Why did she cry out?'

'Oh, she has fallen asleep, and not being used to travelling, she's uneasy, and keeps dreaming.'

'A young woman?'

'Yes, a young woman.'

'That would have interested me forty years ago. Perhaps she's your wife?'

'My wife!' said the other bitterly. 'She's above mating with such as I. But there's no reason why I should tell you about that.'

'That's true. And there's no reason why you should not. What harm can I do to you or to her?'

The reddleman looked in the old man's face. 'Well, sir,' he said at last, 'I knew her before to-day, though perhaps it would have been better if I had not. But she's nothing to me, and I am nothing to her; and she wouldn't have been in my van if any better carriage had been there to take her.'

'Where, may I ask?'

'At Anglebury.'

'I know the town well. What was she doing there?'

'Oh, not much—to gossip about. However, she's tired to death now, and not at all well, and that's what makes her so restless. She dropped off into a nap about an hour ago, and 'twill do her good.'

'A nice-looking girl, no doubt?'

'You would say so.'

The other traveller turned his eyes with interest towards the van window, and, without withdrawing them, said, 'I presume I might look in upon her?'

'No,' said the reddleman abruptly. 'It is getting too dark for you to see much of her; and, more than that, I have no right to allow you. Thank God she sleeps so well: I hope she won't wake till she's home.'

'Who is she? One of the neighbourhood?'

'’Tis no matter who, excuse me.'

'It is not that girl of Blooms-End, who has been talked about more or less lately? If so, I know her; and I can guess what has happened.'

'’Tis no matter. . . . Now, sir, I am sorry to say that we shall soon have to part company. My ponies are tired, and I have further to go, and I am going to rest them under this bank for an hour.'

The elder traveller nodded his head indifferently, and the reddleman turned his horses and van in upon the turf, saying, 'Good night.' The old man replied, and proceeded on his way as before.

The reddleman watched his form as it diminished to a speck on the road and became absorbed in the thickening films of night. He then took some hay from a truss which was slung up under the van, and, throwing a portion of it in front of the horses, made a pad of the rest, which he laid on the ground beside his vehicle. Upon this he sat down, leaning his back against the wheel. From the interior a low soft breathing came to his ear. It appeared to satisfy him, and he musingly surveyed the scene, as if considering the next step that he should take.

To do things musingly, and by small degrees, seemed, indeed, to be a duty in the Egdon valleys at this transitional hour, for there was that in the condition of the heath itself which resembled protracted and halting dubiousness. It was the quality of the repose appertaining to the scene. This was not the repose of actual stagnation, but the apparent repose of incredible slowness. A condition of healthy life so nearly resembling the torpor of death is a noticeable thing of its sort; to exhibit the inertness of the desert, and at the same time to be exercising powers akin to those of the meadow, and even of the forest, awakened in those who thought of it the attentiveness usually engendered by understatement and reserve.

The scene before the reddleman's eyes was a gradual series of ascents from the level of the road backward into the heart of the heath. It embraced hillocks, pits, ridges, acclivities, one behind the other, till all was finished by a high hill cutting against the still light sky. The traveller's eye hovered about these things for a time, and finally settled upon one noteworthy object up there. It was a barrow. This bossy projection of earth above its natural level occupied the loftiest ground of the loneliest height that the heath contained. Although from the vale it appeared but as a wart on an Atlantean brow, its actual bulk was great. It formed the pole and axis of this heathery world.

As the resting man looked at the barrow he became aware that its summit, hitherto the highest object in the whole prospect round, was surmounted by something higher. It rose from the semi-globular mound like a spike from a helmet. The first instinct of an imaginative stranger might have been to suppose it the person of one of the Celts who built the barrow, so far had all of modern date withdrawn from the scene. It seemed a sort of last man among them, musing for a moment before dropping into eternal night with the rest of his race.

There the form stood, motionless as the hill beneath. Above the plain rose the hill, above the hill rose the barrow, and above the barrow rose the figure. Above the figure was nothing that could be mapped elsewhere than on a celestial globe.

Such a perfect, delicate, and necessary finish did the figure give to the dark pile of hills that it seemed to be the only obvious justification of their outline. Without it, there was the dome without the lantern; with it the architectural demands of the mass were satisfied. The scene was strangely homogeneous, in that the vale, the upland, the barrow, and the figure above it amounted only to unity. Looking at this or that member of the group was not observing a complete thing, but a fraction of a thing.

The form was so much like an organic part of the entire motionless structure that to see it move would have impressed the mind as a strange phenomenon. Immobility being the chief characteristic of that whole which the person formed portion of, the discontinuance of immobility in any quarter suggested confusion.

Yet that is what happened. The figure perceptibly gave up its fixity, shifted a step or two, and turned round. As if alarmed, it descended on the right side of the barrow, with the glide of a water-drop down a bud, and then vanished. The movement had been sufficient to show more clearly the characteristics of the figure, and that it was a woman's.

The reason of her sudden displacement now appeared. With her dropping out of sight on the right side, a new-comer, bearing a burden, protruded into the sky on the left side, ascended the tumulus, and deposited the burden on the top. A second followed, then a third, a fourth, a fifth, and ultimately the whole barrow was peopled with burdened figures.

The only intelligible meaning in this sky-backed pantomime of silhouettes was that the woman had no relation to the forms who had taken her place, was sedulously avoiding these, and had come thither for another object than theirs. The imagination of the observer clung by preference to that vanished, solitary figure, as to something more interesting, more important, more likely to have a history worth knowing than these new-comers, and unconsciously regarded them as intruders. But they remained, and established themselves; and the lonely person who hitherto had been queen of the solitude did not at present seem likely to return.

THE CUSTOM OF THE COUNTRY

III

HAD a looker-on been posted in the immediate vicinity of the barrow, he would have learned that these persons were boys and men of the neighbouring hamlets. Each, as he ascended the barrow, had been heavily laden with furze-faggots, carried upon the shoulder by means of a long stake sharpened at each end for impaling them easily—two in front and two behind. They came from a part of the heath a quarter of a mile to the rear, where furze almost exclusively prevailed as a product.

Every individual was so involved in furze by his method of carrying the faggots that he appeared like a bush on legs till he had thrown them down. The party had marched in trail, like a travelling flock of sheep ; that is to say, the strongest first, the weak and young behind.

The loads were all laid together, and a pyramid of furze thirty feet in circumference now occupied the crown of the tumulus, which was known as Rainbarrow for many miles round. Some made themselves busy with matches, and in selecting the driest tufts of furze, others in loosening the bramble bonds which held the faggots together. Others, again, while this was in progress, lifted their eyes and swept the vast expanse of country commanded by their position, now lying nearly obliterated by shade. In the valleys of the heath nothing save its own wild face was visible at any time of day; but this spot commanded a horizon enclosing a tract of far extent, and in many cases lying beyond the heath country. None of its features could be seen now, but the whole made itself felt as a vague stretch of remoteness.

While the men and lads were building the pile, a change took place in the mass of shade which denoted the distant landscape. Red suns and tufts of fire one by one began to arise, flecking the whole country round. They were the bonfires of other parishes and hamlets that were engaged in the same sort of commemoration. Some were distant, and stood in a dense atmosphere, so that bundles of pale strawlike beams radiated around them in the shape of a fan. Some were large and near, glowing scarlet-red from the shade, like wounds in a black hide. Some were Mænades, with winy faces and blown hair. These tinctured the silent bosom of the clouds above them and lit up their ephemeral caves, which seemed thenceforth to become scalding caldrons. Perhaps as many as thirty bonfires could be counted within the whole bounds of the district; and as the hour may be told on a clock-face when the figures themselves are invisible, so did the men recognize the locality of each fire by its angle and direction, though nothing of the scenery could be viewed.

The first tall flame from Rainbarrow sprang into the sky, attracting all eyes that had been fixed on the distant conflagrations back to their own attempt in the same kind. The cheerful blaze streaked the inner surface of the human circle—now increased by other stragglers, male and female—with its own gold livery, and even overlaid the dark turf around with a lively luminousness, which softened off into obscurity where the barrow rounded downwards out of sight. It showed the barrow to be the segment of a globe, as perfect as on the day when it was thrown up, even the little ditch remaining from which the earth was dug. Not a plough had ever disturbed a grain of that stubborn soil. In the heath's barrenness to the farmer lay its fertility to the historian. There had been no obliteration because there had been no tending.

It seemed as if the bonfire-makers were standing in some radiant upper storey of the world, detached from and independent of the dark stretches below. The heath down there was now a vast abyss, and no longer a continuation of what they stood on ; for their eyes, adapted to the blaze, could see nothing of the deeps beyond its influence. Occasionally, it is true, a more vigorous flare than usual from their faggots sent darting lights like aides-de-camp down the incline to some distant bush, pool, or patch of white sand, kindling these to replies of the same colour, till all was lost in darkness again. Then the whole black phenomenon beneath represented Limbo as viewed from the brink by the sublime Florentine in his vision, and the muttered articulations of the wind in the hollows were as complaints and petitions from the 'souls of mighty worth' suspended therein.

It was as if these men and boys had suddenly dived into past ages, and fetched therefrom an hour and deed which had before been familiar with this spot. The ashes of the original British pyre which blazed from that summit lay fresh and undisturbed in the barrow beneath their tread. The flames from funeral piles long ago kindled there had shone down upon the lowlands as these were shining now. Festival fires to Thor and Woden had followed on the same ground and duly had their day. Indeed, it is pretty well known that such blazes as this the heathmen were now enjoying are rather the lineal descendants from jumbled Druidical rites and Saxon ceremonies than the invention of popular feeling about Gunpowder Plot.

Moreover to light a fire is the instinctive and resistant act of man when, at the winter ingress, the curfew is sounded throughout Nature. It indicates a spontaneous, Promethean rebelliousness against the fiat that this recurrent season shall bring foul times, cold darkness, misery and death. Black chaos comes, and the fettered gods of the earth say, Let there be light.

The brilliant lights and sooty shades which struggled upon the skin and clothes of the persons standing round caused their lineaments and general contours to be drawn with Dureresque vigour and dash. Yet the permanent moral expression of each face it was impossible to discover, for as the nimble flames towered, nodded, and swooped through the surrounding air, the blots of shade and flakes of light upon the countenances of the group changed shape and position endlessly. All was unstable; quivering as leaves, evanescent as lightning. Shadowy eye-sockets, deep as those of a death's head, suddenly turned into pits of lustre: a lantern-jaw was cavernous, then it was shining; wrinkles were emphasized to ravines, or obliterated entirely by a changed ray. Nostrils were dark wells; sinews in old necks were gilt mouldings; things with no particular polish on them were glazed; bright objects, such as the tip of a furze-hook one of the men carried, were as glass; eyeballs glowed like little lanterns. Those whom Nature had depicted as merely quaint became grotesque, the grotesque became preternatural; for all was in extremity.

Hence it may be that the face of an old man, who had like others been called to the heights by the rising flames, was not really the mere nose and chin that it appeared to be, but an appreciable quantity of human countenance. He stood complacently sunning himself in the heat. With a speäker, or stake, he tossed the outlying scraps of fuel into the conflagration, looking at the midst of the pile, occasionally lifting his eyes to measure the height of the flame, or to follow the great sparks which rose with it and sailed away into darkness. The beaming sight, and the penetrating warmth, seemed to breed in him a cumulative cheerfulness, which soon amounted to delight With his stick in his hand he began to jig a private minuet, a bunch of copper seals shining and swinging like a pendulum from under his waistcoat: he also began to sing, in the voice of a bee up a flue—

'The king' call'd down' his no-bles all',
By one', by two', by three';
Earl Mar'-shal, I'll' go shrive' the queen',
And thou' shalt wend' with me'.

'A boon', a boon', quoth Earl' Mar-shal',
And fell' on his bend'-ded knee',
That what'-so-e'er' the queen' shall say',
No harm' there-of' may be'.'

Want of breath prevented a continuance of the song; and the breakdown attracted the attention of a firm-standing man of middle age, who kept each corner of his crescent-shaped mouth rigorously drawn back into his cheek, as if to do away with any suspicion of mirthfulness which might erroneously have attached to him.

'A fair stave, Grandfer Cantle; but I am afeard 'tis too much for the mouldy weasand of such a old man as you,' he said to the wrinkled reveller. 'Dostn't wish th' wast three sixes again, Grandfer, as you was when you first learnt to sing it?'

'Hey?' said Grandfer Cantle, stopping in his dance.

'Dostn't wish wast young again, I say? There's a hole in thy poor bellows nowadays seemingly.'

'But there's good art in me? If I couldn't make a little wind go a long ways I should seem no younger than the most aged man, should I, Timothy?'

'And how about the new-married folks down there at the Quiet Woman Inn?' the other inquired, pointing towards a dim light in the direction of the distant highway, but considerably apart from where the reddleman was at that moment resting. 'What's the rights of the matter about 'em? You ought to know, being an understanding man.'

'But a little rakish, hey? I own to it. Master Cantle is that, or he's nothing. Yet 'tis a gay fault, neighbour Fairway, that age will cure.'

'I heard that they were coming home to-night. By this time they must have come. What besides?'

'The next thing is for us to go and wish 'em joy, I suppose?'

'Well, no.'

'No? Now, I thought we must. *I* must, or 'twould be very unlike me—the first in every spree that's going!

"Do thou′ put on′ a fri′-ar's coat′,
And I'll′ put on′ a-no′-ther,
And we′ will to′ Queen Ele′anor go′,
Like Fri′ar and′ his bro′ther."

I met Mis'ess Yeobright, the young bride's aunt, last night, and she told me that her son Clym was coming home a' Christmas. Wonderful clever, 'a believe—ah, I should like to have all that's under that young man's hair. Well, then, I spoke to her in my well-known merry way, and she said, "Oh that what's shaped so venerable should talk like a fool!"—that's what she said to me. I don't care for her, be jowned if I do, and so I told her. "Be jowned if I care for 'ee," I said. I had her there—hey?'

'I rather think she had you,' said Fairway.

'No,' said Grandfer Cantle, his countenance slightly flagging. ''Tisn't so bad as that with me?'

'Seemingly 'tis; however, is it because of the wedding that Clym is coming home a' Christmas—to make a new arrangement because his mother is now left in the house alone?'

'Yes, yes—that's it. But, Timothy, hearken to me,' said the Grandfer earnestly. 'Though known as such a joker, I be an understanding man if you catch me serious, and I am serious now. I can tell 'ee lots about the married couple. Yes, this morning at six o'clock they went up the country to do the job, and neither vell nor mark have been seen of 'em since, though I reckon that this afternoon has brought 'em home again, man and woman—wife, that is. Isn't it spoke like a man, Timothy, and wasn't Mis'ess Yeobright wrong about me ?'

'Yes, it will do. I didn't know the two had walked together since last fall, when her aunt forbad the banns. How long has this new set-to been in mangling then ? Do you know, Humphrey ?'

'Yes, how long ?' said Grandfer Cantle smartly, likewise turning to Humphrey. 'I ask that question.'

'Ever since her aunt altered her mind, and said she might hae the man after all,' replied Humphrey, without removing his eyes from the fire. He was a somewhat solemn young fellow, and carried the hook and leather gloves of a furze-cutter, his legs, by reason of that occupation, being sheathed in bulging leggings as stiff as the Philistine's greaves of brass. 'That's why they went away to be married, I count. You see, after kicking up such a nunny-watch and forbidding the banns 'twould have made Mis'ess Yeobright seem foolish-like to have a banging wedding in the same parish all as if she'd never gainsaid it.'

'Exactly—seem foolish-like ; and that's very bad for the poor things that be so, though I only guess as much, to be sure,' said Grandfer Cantle, still strenuously preserving a sensible bearing and mien.

'Ah, well, I was at church that day,' said Fairway, 'which was a very curious thing to happen.'

'If 'twasn't my name's Simple,' said the Grandfer emphatically. 'I ha'n't been there to-year ; and now the winter is a-coming on I won't say I shall.'

'I ha'n't been these three years,' said Humphrey ; 'for I'm so dead sleepy of a Sunday ; and 'tis so terrible far to get there ; and when you do get there 'tis such a mortal poor chance that you'll be chose for up above, when so many bain't, that I bide at home and don't go at all.'

'I not only happened to be there,' said Fairway, with a fresh collection of emphasis, 'but I was sitting in the same pew as Mis'ess Yeobright. And though you may not see it as such, it fairly made my blood run cold to hear her. Yes, it is a curious thing; but it made my blood run cold, for I was close at her elbow.' The speaker looked round upon the bystanders, now drawing closer to hear him, with his lips gathered tighter than ever in the rigorousness of his descriptive moderation.

''Tis a serious job to have things happen to 'ee there,' said a woman behind.

'"Ye are to declare it," was the parson's words,' Fairway continued. 'And then up stood a woman at my side—a-touching of me. "Well, be damned if there isn't Mis'ess Yeobright a-standing up," I said to myself. Yes, neighbours, though I was in the temple of prayer that's what I said. 'Tis against my conscience to curse and swear in company, and I hope any woman here will overlook it. Still what I did say I did say, and 'twould be a lie if I didn't own it.'

'So 'twould, neighbour Fairway.'

'"Be damned if there isn't Mis'ess Yeobright a-standing up," I said,' the narrator repeated, giving out the bad word with the same passionless severity of face as before, which proved how entirely necessity and not gusto had to do with the iteration. 'And the next thing I heard was, "I forbid the banns," from her. "I'll speak to you after the service," said the parson, in quite a homely way—yes, turning all at once into a common man no holier than you or I. Ah, her face was pale! Maybe you can call to mind that monument in Weatherbury church—the cross-legged soldier that have had his arm knocked away by the school-children? Well, he would about have matched that woman's face, when she said, "I forbid the banns."'

The audience cleared their throats and tossed a few stalks into the fire, not because these deeds were urgent, but to give themselves time to weigh the moral of the story.

'I'm sure when I heard they'd been forbid I felt as glad as if anybody had gied me sixpence,' said an earnest voice—that of Olly Dowden, a woman who lived by making heath brooms, or besoms. Her nature was to be civil to enemies as well as to friends, and grateful to all the world for letting her remain alive.

'And now the maid have married him just the same,' said Humphrey.

'After that Mis'ess Yeobright came round and was quite agreeable,' Fairway resumed, with an unheeding air, to show that his words were no appendage to Humphrey's, but the result of independent reflection.

'Supposing they were ashamed, I don't see why they shouldn't have done it here-right,' said a widespread woman whose stays creaked like shoes whenever she stooped or turned. ''Tis well to call the neighbours together and to hae a good racket once now and then; and it may as well be when there's a wedding as at tide-times. I don't care for close ways.'

'Ah, now, you'd hardly believe it, but I don't care for gay weddings,' said Timothy Fairway, his eyes again travelling round. 'I hardly blame Thomasin Yeobright and neighbour Wildeve for doing it quiet, if I must own it. A wedding at home means five and six-handed reels by the hour; and they do a man's legs no good when he's over forty.'

'True. Once at the woman's house you can hardly say nay to being one in a jig, knowing all the time that you be expected to make yourself worth your victuals.'

'You be bound to dance at Christmas because 'tis the time o' year; you must dance at weddings because 'tis the time o' life. At christenings folk will even smuggle in a reel or two, if 'tis no further on than the first or second chiel. And this is not naming the songs you've got to sing. . . . For my part I like a good hearty funeral as well as anything. You've as splendid victuals and drink as at other parties, and even better. And it don't wear your legs to stumps in talking over a poor fellow's ways as it do to stand up in hornpipes.'

'Nine folks out of ten would own 'twas going too far to dance then, I suppose?' suggested Grandfer Cantle.

''Tis the only sort of party a staid man can feel safe at after the mug have been round a few times.'

'Well, I can't understand a quiet lady-like little body like Tamsin Yeobright caring to be married in such a mean way,' said Susan Nunsuch, the wide woman, who preferred the original subject. ''Tis worse than the poorest do. And I shouldn't have cared about the man though some may say he's good-looking.'

'To give him his due he's a clever, learned fellow in his way—a'most as clever as Clym Yeobright used to be. He was brought up to better things than keeping the Quiet Woman. An engineer—that's what the man was, as we know; but he threw away his chance, and so 'a took a public-house to live. His learning was no use to him at all.'

'Very often the case,' said Olly, the besom-maker. 'And yet how people do strive after it and get it! The class of folk that couldn't use to make a round O to save their bones from the pit can write their names now without a sputter of the pen, oftentimes without a single blot: what do I say?—why, almost without a desk to lean their stomachs and elbows upon.'

'True: 'tis amazing what a polish the world have been brought to,' said Humphrey.

'Why, afore I went a soldier in the Bang-up Locals (as we was called), in the year four,' chimed in Grandfer Cantle brightly, 'I didn't know no more what the world was like than the commonest man among ye. And now, jown it all, I won't say what I bain't fit for, hey?'

'Couldst sign the book, no doubt,' said Fairway, 'if wast young enough to join hands with a woman again, like Wildeve and Mis'ess Tamsin, which is more than

Humph there could do, for he follows his father in learning. Ah, Humph, well I can mind when I was married how I zid thy father's mark staring me in the face as I went to put down my name. He and your mother were the couple married just afore we were, and there stood thy father's cross with arms stretched out like a great banging scare-crow. What a terrible black cross that was—thy father's very likeness in en! To save my soul I couldn't help laughing when I zid en, though all the time I was as hot as dog-days, what with the marrying, and what with the woman a-hanging to me, and what with Jack Changley and a lot more chaps grinning at me through church window. But the next moment a strawmote would have knocked me down, for I called to mind that if thy father and mother had had high words once, they'd been at it twenty times since they'd been man and wife, and I zid myself as the next poor stunpoll to get into the same mess. . . . Ah—well, what a day 'twas!'

'Wildeve is older than Tamsin Yeobright by a good-few summers. A pretty maid too she is. A young woman with a home must be a fool to tear her smock for a man like that.'

The speaker, a peat or turf-cutter, who had newly joined the group, carried across his shoulder the singular heart-shaped spade of large dimensions used in that species of labour; and its well-whetted edge gleamed like a silver bow in the beams of the fire.

'A hundred maidens would have had him if he'd asked 'em,' said the wide woman.

'Didst ever know a man, neighbour, that no woman at all would marry?' inquired Humphrey.

'I never did,' said the turf-cutter.

'Nor I,' said another.

'Nor I,' said Grandfer Cantle.

'Well, now, I did once,' said Timothy Fairway, adding more firmness to one of his legs. 'I did know of such a man. But only once, mind.' He gave his throat a thorough rake round, as it it were the duty of every person not to be mistaken through thickness of voice. 'Yes, I knew of such a man,' he said.

'And what ghastly gallicrow might the poor fellow have been like, Master Fairway?' asked the turf-cutter.

'Well, 'a was neither a deaf man, nor a dumb man, nor a blind man. What 'a was I don't say.'

'Is he known in these parts?' said Olly Dowden.

'Hardly,' said Timothy; 'but I name no name. . . . Come, keep the fire up there, youngsters.'

'Whatever is Christian Cantle's teeth a-chattering for?' said a boy from amid the smoke and shades on the other side of the blaze. 'Be ye a-cold, Christian?'

A thin jibbering voice was heard to reply, 'No, not at all.'

'Come forward, Christian, and show yourself. I didn't know you were here,' said Fairway, with a humane look across towards that quarter.

Thus requested, a faltering man, with reedy hair, no shoulders, and a great quantity of wrist and ankle beyond his clothes, advanced a step or two by his own will, and was pushed by the will of others half a dozen steps more. He was Grandfer Cantle's youngest son.

'What be ye quaking for, Christian?' said the turf-cutter kindly.

'I'm the man.'

'What man?'

'The man no woman will marry.'

'The deuce you be!' said Timothy Fairway, enlarging his gaze to cover Christian's whole surface and a great deal more; Grandfer Cantle meanwhile staring as a hen stares at the ducks she has hatched.

'Yes, I be he; and it makes me afeard,' said Christian. 'D'ye think 'twill hurt me? I shall always say I don't care, and swear to it, though I do care all the while.'

'Well, be damned if this isn't the queerest start ever I know'd,' said Mr. Fairway. 'I didn't mean you at all.

There's another in the country, then! Why did ye reveal yer misfortune, Christian?'

''Twas to be if 'twas, I suppose. I can't help it, can I?' He turned upon them his painfully circular eyes, surrounded by concentric lines like targets.

'No, that's true. But 'tis a melancholy thing, and my blood ran cold when you spoke, for I felt there were two poor fellows where I had thought only one. 'Tis a sad thing for ye, Christian. How'st know the women won't hae thee?'

'I've asked 'em.'

'Sure I should never have thought you had the face. Well, and what did the last one say to ye? Nothing that can't be got over, perhaps, after all?'

'"Get out of my sight, you slack-twisted, slim-looking maphrotight fool," was the woman's words to me.'

'Not encouraging, I own,' said Fairway. '"Get out of my sight, you slack-twisted, slim-looking maphrotight fool," is rather a hard way of saying No. But even that might be overcome by time and patience, so as to let a few grey hairs show themselves in the hussy's head. How old be you, Christian?'

'Thirty-one last tatie-digging, Mister Fairway.'

'Not a boy—not a boy. Still there's hope yet.'

'That's my age by baptism, because that's put down in the great book of the Judgment that they keep in church vestry; but mother told me I was born some time afore I was christened.'

'Ah!'

'But she couldn't tell when, to save her life, except that there was no moon.'

'No moon: that's bad. Hey, neighbours, that's bad for him!'

'Yes, 'tis bad,' said Grandfer Cantle, shaking his head.

'Mother know'd 'twas no moon, for she asked another woman that had an almanac, as she did whenever a boy was born to her, because of the saying, "No moon, no man," which made her afeard every man-child she had. Do ye really think it serious, Mister Fairway, that there was no moon ? '

' Yes ; " No moon, no man." 'Tis one of the truest sayings ever spit out. The boy never comes to anything that's born at new moon. A bad job for thee, Christian, that you should have showed your nose then of all days in the month.'

' I suppose the moon was terrible full when you were born ? ' said Christian, with a look of hopeless admiration at Fairway.

" Well, 'a was not new,' Mr. Fairway replied, with a disinterested gaze.

' I'd sooner go without drink at Lammas-tide than be a man of no moon,' continued Christian, in the same shattered recitative. ' 'Tis said I be only the rames of a man, and no good for my race at all ; and I suppose that's the cause o't.'

' Ay,' said Grandfer Cantle, somewhat subdued in spirit ; ' and yet his mother cried for scores of hours when 'a was a boy, for fear he should outgrow hisself and go for a soldier.'

' Well, there's many just as bad as he," said Fairway. ' Wethers must live their time as well as other sheep, poor soul.'

' So perhaps I shall rub on ? Ought I to be afeard o' nights, Master Fairway ? '

' You'll have to lie alone all your life ; and 'tis not to married couples but to single sleepers that a ghost shows himself when 'a do come. One has been seen lately, too. A very strange one.'

' No—don't talk about it if 'tis agreeable of ye not to ! 'Twill make my skin crawl when I think of it in bed alone. But you will—ah, you will, I know, Timothy ; and I shall dream all night o't ! A very strange one ? What sort of a spirit did ye mean when ye said, a very strange one, Timothy ?—no, no—don't tell me.'

'I don't half believe in spirits myself. But I think it ghostly enough—what I was told. 'Twas a little boy that zid it.'

'What was it like?—no, don't——'

'A red one. Yes, most ghosts be white; but this is as if it had been dipped in blood.'

Christian drew a deep breath without letting it expand his body, and Humphrey said, 'Where has it been seen?'

'Not exactly here; but in the same heth. But 'tisn't a thing to talk about. What do you say,' continued Fairway in brisker tones, and turning upon them as if the idea had not been Grandfer Cantle's—'what do you say to giving the new man and wife a bit of a song to-night afore we go to bed—being their wedding-day? When folks are just married 'tis as well to look glad o't, since looking sorry won't unjoin 'em. I am no drinker, as we know, but when the womenfolk and youngsters have gone home we can drop down across to the Quiet Woman, and strike up a ballet in front of the married folks' door. 'Twill please the young wife, and that's what I should like to do, for many's the skinful I've had at her hands when she lived with her aunt at Blooms-End.'

'Hey? And so we will!' said Grandfer Cantle, turning so briskly that his copper seals swung extravagantly. 'I'm as dry as a kex with biding up here in the wind, and I haven't seen the colour of drink since nammet-time to-day. 'Tis said that the last brew at the Woman is very pretty drinking. And, neighbours, if we should be a little late in the finishing, why, to-morrow's Sunday, and we can sleep it off?'

'Grandfer Cantle! you take things very careless for an old man,' said the wide woman.

'I take things careless; I do—too careless to please the women! Klk! I'll sing the "Jovial Crew," or any other song, when a weak old man would cry his eyes out. Jown it; I am up for anything.

"The king′ look'd o′-ver his left′ shoul-der′,
And a grim′ look look′-ed hee′,
Earl Mar′-shal, he said′, but for′ my oath′
Or hang′-ed thou′ shouldst bee′."'

'Well, that's what we'll do,' said Fairway. 'We'll give 'em a song, an' it please the Lord. What's the good of Thomasin's cousin Clym a-coming home after the deed's done? He should have come afore, if so be he wanted to stop it, and marry her himself.'

'Perhaps he's coming to bide with his mother a little time, as she must feel lonely now the maid's gone.'

'Now, 'tis very odd, but I never feel lonely—no, not at all,' said Grandfer Cantle. 'I am as brave in the night-time as a' admiral!'

The bonfire was by this time beginning to sink low, for the fuel had not been of that substantial sort which can support a blaze long. Most of the other fires within the wide horizon were also dwindling weak. Attentive observation of their brightness, colour, and length of existence would have revealed the quality of the material burnt; and through that, to some extent the natural produce of the district in which each bonfire was situate. The clear, kingly effulgence that had characterized the majority expressed a heath and furze country like their own, which in one direction extended an unlimited number of miles: the rapid flares and extinctions at other points of the compass showed the lightest of fuel—straw, beanstalks, and the usual waste from arable land. The most enduring of all—steady unaltering eyes like planets—signified wood, such as hazel-branches, thorn-faggots, and stout billets. Fires of the last-mentioned materials were rare, and, though comparatively small in magnitude beside the transient blazes, now began to get the best of them by mere long-continuance. The great ones had perished, but these remained. They occupied the remotest visible positions—sky-backed summits rising out of rich coppice and plantation districts to the north, where the soil was different, and heath foreign and strange.

Save one ; and this was the nearest of any, the moon of the whole shining throng. It lay in a direction precisely opposite to that of the little window in the vale below. Its nearness was such that, notwithstanding its actual smallness, its glow infinitely transcended theirs.

This quiet eye had attracted attention from time to time ; and when their own fire had become sunken and dim it attracted more ; some even of the wood fires more recently lighted had reached their decline, but no change was perceptible here.

'To be sure, how near that fire is ! ' said Fairway. 'Seemingly, I can see a fellow of some sort walking round it. Little and good must be said of that fire, surely.'

'I can throw a stone there,' said the boy.

'And so can I ! ' said Grandfer Cantle.

'No, no, you can't, my sonnies. That fire is not much less than a mile off, for all that 'a seems so near.'

''Tis in the heath, but not furze,' said the turf-cutter.

''Tis cleft-wood, that's what 'tis,' said Timothy Fairway. 'Nothing would burn like that except clean timber. And 'tis on the knap afore the old captain's house at Mistover. Such a queer mortal as that man is ! To have a little fire inside your own bank and ditch, that nobody else may enjoy it or come anigh it ! And what a zany an old chap must be, to light a bonfire when there's no youngsters to please.'

'Cap'n Vye has been for a long walk to-day, and is quite tired out,' said Grandfer Cantle, 'so 'tisn't likely to be he.'

'And he would hardly afford good fuel like that,' said the wide woman.

'Then it must be his grand-daughter,' said Fairway. 'Not that a body of her age can want a fire much.'

'She is very strange in her ways, living up there by herself, and such things please her,' said Susan.

'She's a well-favoured maid enough,' said Humphrey the furze-cutter; 'especially when she's got one of her dandy gowns on.'

'That's true,' said Fairway. 'Well, let her bonfire burn an't will. Ours is well-nigh out by the look o't.'

'How dark 'tis now the fire's gone down!' said Christian Cantle, looking behind him with his hare eyes. 'Don't ye think we'd better get home-along, neighbours? The heth isn't haunted, I know; but we'd better get home. . . . Ah, what was that?'

'Only the wind,' said the turf-cutter.

'I don't think Fifth-of-Novembers ought to be kept up by night except in towns. It should be by day in outstep, ill-accounted places like this!'

'Nonsense, Christian. Lift up your spirits like a man! Susy, dear, you and I will have a jig—hey, my honey?—before 'tis quite too dark to see how well-favoured you be still, though so many summers have passed since your husband, a son of a witch, snapped you up from me.'

This was addressed to Susan Nunsuch; and the next circumstance of which the beholders were conscious was a vision of the matron's broad form whisking off towards the space whereon the fire had been kindled. She was lifted bodily by Mr. Fairway's arm, which had been flung round her waist before she had become aware of his intention. The site of the fire was now merely a circle of ashes flecked with red embers and sparks, the furze having burnt completely away. Once within the circle he whirled her round and round in a dance. She was a woman noisily constructed; in addition to her enclosing framework of whalebone and lath, she wore pattens summer and winter, in wet weather and in dry, to preserve her boots from wear; and when Fairway began to jump about with her, the clicking of the pattens, the creaking of the stays, and her screams of surprise, formed a very audible concert.

'I'll crack thy numskull for thee, you mandy chap!' said Mrs. Nunsuch, as she helplessly danced round with him, her feet playing like drumsticks among the sparks. 'My ankles were all in a fever before, from walking through that prickly furze, and now you must make 'em worse with these vlankers!'

The vagary of Timothy Fairway was infectious. The turf-cutter seized old Olly Dowden, and, somewhat more gently, poussetted with her likewise. The young men were not slow to imitate the example of their elders, and seized the maids; Grandfer Cantle and his stick jigged in the form of a three-legged object among the rest; and in half a minute all that could be seen on Rainbarrow was a whirling of dark shapes amid a boiling confusion of sparks, which leapt around the dancers as high as their waists. The chief noises were women's shrill cries, men's laughter, Susan's stays and pattens, Olly Dowden's 'heu-heu-heu!' and the strumming of the wind upon the furze-bushes, which formed a kind of tune to the demoniac measure they trod. Christian alone stood aloof, uneasily rocking himself as he murmured, 'They ought not to do it—how the vlankers do fly! 'tis tempting the Wicked one, 'tis.'

'What was that?' said one of the lads, stopping.

'Ah—where?' said Christian, hastily closing up to the rest.

The dancers all lessened their speed.

''Twas behind you, Christian, that I heard it—down there.'

'Yes—'tis behind me!' Christian said. 'Matthew, Mark, Luke, and John, bless the bed that I lie on; four angels guard——'

'Hold your tongue. What is it?' said Fairway.

'Hoi-i-i-i!' cried a voice from the darkness.

'Halloo-o-o-o!' said Fairway.

'Is there any cart-track up across here to Mis'ess Yeobright's, of Blooms-End?' came to them in the same voice, as a long, slim, indistinct figure approached the barrow.

'Ought we not to run home as hard as we can, neighbours, as 'tis getting late?' said Christian. 'Not run away from one another, you know; run close together, I mean.'

'Scrape up a few stray locks of furze, and make a blaze, so that we can see who the man is,' said Fairway.

When the flame arose it revealed a young man in tight raiment, and red from top to toe. 'Is there a track across here to Mis'ess Yeobright's house?' he repeated.

'Ay—keep along the path down there.'

'I mean a way two horses and a van can travel over?'

'Well, yes; you can get up the vale below here with time. The track is rough, but if you've got a light your horses may pick along wi' care. Have ye brought your cart far up, neighbour reddleman?'

'I've left it in the bottom, about half a mile back. I stepped on in front to make sure of the way, as 'tis night-time, and I han't been here for so long.'

'Oh, well, you can get up,' said Fairway. 'What a turn it did give me when I saw him!' he added to the whole group, the reddleman included. 'Lord's sake, I thought, whatever fiery mommet is this come to trouble us? No slight to your looks, reddleman, for ye bain't bad-looking in the groundwork, though the finish is queer. My meaning is just to say how curious I felt. I half thought 'twas the devil or the red ghost the boy told of.'

'It gied me a turn likewise,' said Susan Nunsuch, 'for I had a dream last night of a death's head.'

'Don't ye talk o't no more,' said Christian. 'If he had a handkerchief over his head he'd look for all the world like the Devil in the picture of the Temptation.'

'Well, thank you for telling me,' said the young reddleman, smiling faintly. 'And good night t'ye all.'

He withdrew from their sight down the barrow.

'I fancy I've seen that young man's face before,' said

Humphrey. 'But where, or how, or what his name is, I don't know.'

The reddleman had not been gone more than a few minutes when another person approached the partially revived bonfire. It proved to be a well-known and respected widow of the neighbourhood, of a standing which can only be expressed by the word genteel. Her face, encompassed by the blackness of the receding heath, showed whitely, and without half-lights, like a cameo.

She was a woman of middle-age, with well-formed features of the type usually found where perspicacity is the chief quality enthroned within. At moments she seemed to be regarding issues from a Nebo denied to others around. She had something of an estranged mien: the solitude exhaled from the heath was concentrated in this face that had risen from it. The air with which she looked at the heathmen betokened a certain unconcern at their presence, or at what might be their opinions of her for walking in that lonely spot at such an hour, thus indirectly implying that in some respect or other they were not up to her level. The explanation lay in the fact that though her husband had been a small farmer she herself was a curate's daughter, who had once dreamt of doing better things.

Persons with any weight of character carry, like planets, their atmospheres along with them in their orbits; and the matron who entered now upon the scene could, and usually did, bring her own tone into a company. Her normal manner among the heathfolk had that reticence which results from the consciousness of superior communicative power. But the effect of coming into society and light after lonely wandering in darkness is a sociability in the comer above its usual pitch, expressed in the features even more than in the words.

'Why, 'tis Mis'ess Yeobright,' said Fairway. 'Mis'ess Yeobright, not ten minutes ago a man was here asking for you—a reddleman.'

'What did he want?' said she.

'He didn't tell us.'

'Something to sell, I suppose; what can it be I am at a loss to understand.'

'I am glad to hear that your son Mr. Clym is coming home at Christmas, ma'am,' said Sam, the turf-cutter. 'What a dog he used to be for bonfires!'

'Yes. I believe he is coming,' she said.

'He must be a fine fellow by this time,' said Fairway.

'He is a man now,' she replied quietly.

''Tis very lonesome for 'ee in the heth to-night, mis'ess,' said Christian, coming from the seclusion he had hitherto maintained. 'Mind you don't get lost. Egdon Heth is a bad place to get lost in, and the winds do huffle queerer to-night than ever I heard 'em afore. Them that know Egdon best have been pixy-led here at times.'

'Is that you, Christian?' said Mrs. Yeobright. 'What made you hide away from me?'

''Twas that I didn't know you in this light, mis'ess; and being a man of the mournfullest make, I was scared a little, that's all. Oftentimes if you could see how terrible down I get in my mind, 'twould make 'ee quite nervous for fear I should die by my hand.'

'You don't take after your father,' said Mrs. Yeobright, looking towards the fire, where Grandfer Cantle, with some want of originality, was dancing by himself among the sparks, as the others had done before.

'Now, Granfer,' said Timothy Fairway, 'we are ashamed of ye. A reverent old patriarch man as you be—seventy if a day—to go hornpiping like that by yourself!'

'A harrowing old man, Mis'ess Yeobright,' said Christian despondingly. 'I wouldn't live with him a week, so playward as he is, if I could get away.'

''Twould be more seemly in ye to stand still and welcome Mis'ess Yeobright, and you the venerablest here, Grandfer Cantle,' said the besom-woman.

'Faith, and so it would,' said the reveller, checking himself repentantly. 'I've such a bad memory, Mis'ess Yeobright, that I forget how I'm looked up to by the rest of 'em. My spirits must be wonderful good, you'll say? But not always. 'Tis a weight upon a man to be looked up to as commander, and I often feel it.'

'I am sorry to stop the talk,' said Mrs. Yeobright. 'But I must be leaving you now. I was passing down the Anglebury Road, towards my niece's new home, who is returning to-night with her husband; and seeing the bonfire and hearing Olly's voice among the rest I came up here to learn what was going on. I should like her to walk with me, as her way is mine.'

'Ay, sure, ma'am, I'm just thinking of moving,' said Olly.

'Why, you'll be safe to meet the reddleman that I told ye of,' said Fairway. 'He's only gone back to get his van. We heard that your niece and her husband were coming straight home as soon as they were married, and we are going down there shortly, to give 'em a song o' welcome.'

'Thank you indeed,' said Mrs. Yeobright.

'But we shall take a shorter cut through the furze than you can go with long clothes; so we won't trouble you to wait.'

'Very well—are you ready, Olly?'

'Yes, ma'am. And there's a light shining from your niece's window, see. It will help to keep us in the path.'

She indicated the faint light at the bottom of the valley which Fairway had pointed out; and the two women descended the tumulus.

THE HALT ON THE TURNPIKE ROAD

IV

DOWN, downward they went, and yet further down—their descent at each step seeming to outmeasure their advance. Their skirts were scratched noisily by the furze, their shoulders brushed by the ferns, which, though dead and dry, stood erect as when alive, no sufficient winter weather having as yet arrived to beat them down. Their Tartarean situation might by some have been called an imprudent one for two unattended women. But these shaggy recesses were at all seasons a familiar surrounding to Olly and Mrs. Yeobright; and the addition of darkness lends no frightfulness to the face of a friend.

'And so Tamsin has married him at last,' said Olly, when the incline had become so much less steep that their footsteps no longer required undivided attention.

Mrs. Yeobright answered slowly, 'Yes: at last.'

'How you will miss her—living with 'ee as a daughter, as she always have.'

'I do miss her.'

Olly, though without the tact to perceive when remarks were untimely, was saved by her very simplicity from rendering them offensive. Questions that would have been resented in others she could ask with impunity. This accounted for Mrs. Yeobright's acquiescence in the revival of an evidently sore subject.

'I was quite strook to hear you'd agreed to it, ma'am, that I was,' continued the besom-maker.

'You were not more struck by it than I should have been last year this time, Olly. There are a good many sides to that wedding. I could not tell you all of them, even if I tried.'

'I felt myself that he was hardly solid-going enough to mate with your family. Keeping an inn—what is it? But 'a's clever, that's true, and they say he was an engineering gentleman once, but has come down by being too outwardly given.'

'I saw that, upon the whole, it would be better she should marry where she wished.'

'Poor little thing, her feelings got the better of her, no doubt. 'Tis nature. Well, they may call him what they will—he've several acres of heth-ground broke up here, besides the public-house, and the heth-croppers, and his manners be quite like a gentleman's. And what's done cannot be undone.'

'It cannot,' said Mrs. Yeobright. 'See, here's the waggon-track at last. Now we shall get along better.'

The wedding subject was no further dwelt upon; and soon a faint diverging path was reached, where they parted company, Olly first begging her companion to remind Mr. Wildeve that he had not sent her sick husband the bottle of wine promised on the occasion of his marriage. The besom-maker turned to the left towards her own house, behind a spur of the hill, and Mrs. Yeobright followed the straight track, which further on joined the highway by the Quiet Woman Inn, whither she supposed her niece to have returned with Wildeve from their wedding at Anglebury that day.

She first reached Wildeve's Patch, as it was called, a plot of land redeemed from the heath, and after long and laborious years brought into cultivation. The man who had discovered that it could be tilled died of the labour: the man who succeeded him in possession ruined himself in fertilizing it. Wildeve came like Amerigo Vespucci, and received the honours due to those who had gone before.

When Mrs. Yeobright had drawn near to the inn, and was about to enter, she saw a horse and vehicle some two hundred yards beyond it, coming towards her, a man walking alongside with a lantern in his hand. It was soon evident that this was the reddleman who had inquired for her. Instead of entering the inn at once, she walked by it and towards the van.

The conveyance came close, and the man was about to pass her with little notice, when she turned to him and said, 'I think you have been inquiring for me? I am Mrs. Yeobright of Blooms-End.'

The reddleman started, and held up his finger. He stopped the horses, and beckoned to her to withdraw with him a few yards aside, which she did, wondering.

'You don't know me, ma'am, I suppose?' he said.

'I do not,' said she. 'Why, yes, I do! You are young Venn—your father was a dairyman somewhere here?'

'Yes; and I knew your niece, Miss Tamsin, a little. I have something bad to tell you.'

'About her—no? She has just come home, I believe, with her husband. They arranged to return this afternoon—to the inn beyond here?'

'She's not there.'

'How do you know?'

'Because she's here. She's in my van,' he added slowly.

'What new trouble has come?' murmured Mrs. Yeobright, putting her hand over her eyes.

'I can't explain much, ma'am. All I know is that, as I was going along the road this morning, about a mile out of Anglebury, I heard something trotting after me like a doe, and looking round there she was, white as death itself. "O, Diggory Venn!" she said, "I thought 'twas you: will you help me? I am in trouble."'

'How did she know your Christian name?' said Mrs. Yeobright doubtingly.

'I had met her as a lad before I went away in this trade. She asked then if she might ride, and then down she fell in a faint. I picked her up and put her in, and there she has been ever since. She has cried a good deal, but she has hardly spoke; all she has told me being that she was to have been married this morning. I tried to get her to eat something, but she couldn't; and at last she fell asleep.'

'Let me see her at once,' said Mrs. Yeobright, hastening towards the van.

The reddleman followed with the lantern, and, stepping up first, assisted Mrs. Yeobright to mount beside him. On the door being opened she perceived at the end of the van an extemporized couch, around which was hung apparently all the drapery that the reddleman possessed, to keep the occupant of the little couch from contact with the red materials of his trade. A young girl lay thereon, covered with a cloak. She was asleep, and the light of the lantern fell upon her features.

A fair, sweet, and honest country face was revealed, reposing in a nest of wavy chestnut hair. It was between pretty and beautiful. Though her eyes were closed, one could easily imagine the light necessarily shining in them as the culmination of the luminous workmanship around. The groundwork of the face was hopefulness; but over it now lay like a foreign substance a film of anxiety and grief. The grief had been there so shortly as to have abstracted nothing of the bloom, and had as yet but given a dignity to what it might eventually undermine. The scarlet of her lips had not had time to abate, and just now it appeared still more intense by the absence of the neighbouring and more transient colour of her cheek. The lips frequently parted, with a murmur of words. She seemed to belong rightly to a madrigal—to require viewing through rhyme and harmony.

One thing at least was obvious: she was not made to be looked at thus. The reddleman had appeared conscious of as much, and, while Mrs. Yeobright looked in upon her, he cast his eyes aside with a delicacy which well became him. The sleeper apparently thought so too, for the next moment she opened her own.

The lips then parted with something of anticipation, something more of doubt; and her several thoughts and fractions of thoughts, as signalled by the changes on her face, were exhibited by the light to the utmost nicety. An ingenuous, transparent life was disclosed; as if the flow of her existence could be seen passing within her. She understood the scene in a moment.

'O yes, it is I, aunt,' she cried. 'I know how frightened you are, and how you cannot believe it; but all the same, it is I who have come home like this!'

'Tamsin, Tamsin!' said Mrs. Yeobright, stooping over the young woman and kissing her. 'O my dear girl!'

Thomasin was now on the verge of a sob; but by an unexpected self-command she uttered no sound. With a gentle panting breath she sat upright.

'I did not expect to see you in this state, any more than you me,' she went on quickly. 'Where am I, aunt?'

'Nearly home, my dear. In Egdon Bottom. What dreadful thing is it?'

'I'll tell you in a moment. So near, are we? Then I will get out and walk. I want to go home by the path.'

'But this kind man who has done so much will, I am sure, take you right on to my house?' said the aunt, turning to the reddleman, who had withdrawn from the front of the van on the awakening of the girl, and stood in the road.

'Why should you think it necessary to ask me? I will, of course,' said he.

'He is indeed kind,' murmured Thomasin. 'I was once acquainted with him, aunt, and when I saw him to-day I thought I should prefer his van to any conveyance of a stranger. But I'll walk now. Reddleman, stop the horses, please.'

The man regarded her with tender reluctance, but stopped them.

Aunt and niece then descended from the van, Mrs. Yeobright saying to its owner, 'I quite recognize you now. What made you change from the nice business your father left you ?'

'Well, I did,' he said, and looked at Thomasin, who blushed a little. 'Then you'll not be wanting me any more to-night, ma'am ?'

Mrs. Yeobright glanced around at the dark sky, at the hills, at the perishing bonfires, and at the lighted window of the inn they had neared. 'I think not,' she said, 'since Thomasin wishes to walk. We can soon run up the path and reach home : we know it well.'

And after a few further words they parted, the reddleman moving onwards with his van, and the two women remaining standing in the road. As soon as the vehicle and its driver had withdrawn so far as to be beyond all possible reach of her voice, Mrs. Yeobright turned to her niece.

'Now, Thomasin,' she said sternly, 'what's the meaning of this disgraceful performance ?'

PERPLEXITY AMONG HONEST PEOPLE

V

THOMASIN looked as if quite overcome by her aunt's change of manner. 'It means just what it seems to mean: I am—not married,' she replied faintly. 'Excuse me—for humiliating you, aunt, by this mishap: I am sorry for it. But I cannot help it.'

'Me? Think of yourself first.'

'It was nobody's fault. When we got there the parson wouldn't marry us because of some trifling irregularity in the licence.'

'What irregularity?'

'I don't know. Mr. Wildeve can explain. I did not think when I went away this morning that I should come back like this.' It being dark, Thomasin allowed her emotion to escape her by the silent way of tears, which could roll down her cheek unseen.

'I could almost say that it serves you right—if I did not feel that you don't deserve it,' continued Mrs. Yeobright, who, possessing two distinct moods in close contiguity, a gentle mood and an angry, flew from one to the other without the least warning. 'Remember, Thomasin, this business was none of my seeking; from the very first, when you began to feel foolish about that man, I warned you he would not make you happy. I felt it so strongly that I did what I would never have believed myself capable of doing—stood up in the church, and made myself the public talk for weeks. But having once consented, I don't submit to these fancies without good reason. Marry him you must after this.'

'Do you think I wish to do otherwise for one moment?' said Thomasin, with a heavy sigh. 'I know how wrong it was of me to love him, but don't pain me by talking like that, aunt! You would not have had me stay there with him, would you?—and your house is the only home I have to return to. He says we can be married in a day or two.'

'I wish he had never seen you.'

'Very well; then I will be the miserablest woman in the world, and not let him see me again. No, I won't have him!'

'It is too late to speak so. Come with me. I am going to the inn to see if he has returned. Of course I shall get to the bottom of this story at once. Mr. Wildeve must not suppose he can play tricks upon me, or any belonging to me.'

'It was not that. The licence was wrong, and he couldn't get another the same day. He will tell you in a moment how it was, if he comes.'

'Why didn't he bring you back?'

'That was me!' again sobbed Thomasin. 'When I found we could not be married I didn't like to come back with him, and I was very ill. Then I saw Diggory Venn, and was glad to get him to take me home. I cannot explain it any better, and you must be angry with me if you will.'

'I shall see about that,' said Mrs. Yeobright; and they turned towards the inn, known in the neighbourhood as the Quiet Woman, the sign of which represented the figure of a matron carrying her head under her arm, beneath which gruesome sign was written the couplet so well known to frequenters of the inn:—

SINCE THE WOMAN'S QUIET
LET NO MAN BREED A RIOT.[1]

The front of the house was towards the heath and Rainbarrow, whose dark shape seemed to threaten it from the sky. Upon the door was a neglected brass plate, bearing the unexpected inscription, 'Mr. Wildeve, Engineer'—a useless yet cherished relic from the time when he had been started in that profession in an office at Budmouth by those who had hoped much from him, and had been disappointed. The garden was at the back, and behind this ran a still deep stream, forming the margin of the heath in that direction, meadow-land appearing beyond the stream.

But the thick obscurity permitted only sky-lines to be visible of any scene at present. The water at the back of the house could be heard, idly spinning whirlpools in its creep between the rows of dry feather-headed reeds which formed a stockade along each bank. Their presence was denoted by sounds as of a congregation praying humbly, produced by their rubbing against each other in the slow wind.

The window, whence the candlelight had shone up the vale to the eyes of the bonfire group, was uncurtained, but the sill lay too high for a pedestrian on the outside to look over it into the room. A vast shadow, in which could be dimly traced portions of a masculine contour, blotted half the ceiling.

'He seems to be at home,' said Mrs. Yeobright.

'Must I come in, too, aunt?' asked Thomasin faintly. 'I suppose not; it would be wrong.'

'You must come, certainly—to confront him, so that

[1] The inn which really bore this sign and legend stood some miles to the north-west of the present scene, wherein the house more immediately referred to is now no longer an inn; and the surroundings are much changed. But another inn, some of whose features are also embodied in this description, the *Red Lion* at Winfrith, still remains as a haven for the wayfarer (1912).

he may make no false representations to me. We shall not be five minutes in the house, and then we'll walk home.'

Entering the open passage she tapped at the door of the private parlour, unfastened it, and looked in.

The back and shoulders of a man came between Mrs. Yeobright's eyes and the fire. Wildeve, whose form it was, immediately turned, arose, and advanced to meet his visitors.

He was quite a young man, and of the two properties, form and motion, the latter first attracted the eye in him. The grace of his movement was singular: it was the pantomimic expression of a lady-killing career. Next came into notice the more material qualities, among which was a profuse crop of hair impending over the top of his face, lending to his forehead the high-cornered outline of an early Gothic shield; and a neck which was smooth and round as a cylinder. The lower half of his figure was of light build. Altogether he was one in whom no man would have seen anything to admire, and in whom no woman would have seen anything to dislike.

He discerned the young girl's form in the passage, and said, 'Thomasin, then, has reached home. How could you leave me in that way, darling?' And turning to Mrs. Yeobright: 'It was useless to argue with her. She would go, and go alone.'

'But what's the meaning of it all?' demanded Mrs. Yeobright haughtily.

'Take a seat,' said Wildeve, placing chairs for the two women. 'Well, it was a very stupid mistake, but such mistakes will happen. The licence was useless at Anglebury. It was made out for Budmouth, but as I didn't read it I wasn't aware of that.'

'But you had been staying at Anglebury?'

'No. I had been at Budmouth—till two days ago—and that was where I had intended to take her; but when I came to fetch her we decided upon Anglebury, forgetting that a new licence would be necessary. There was not time to get to Budmouth afterwards.'

'I think you are very much to blame,' said Mrs. Yeobright.

'It was quite my fault we chose Anglebury,' Thomasin pleaded. 'I proposed it because I was not known there.'

'I know so well that I am to blame that you need not remind me of it,' replied Wildeve shortly.

'Such things don't happen for nothing,' said the aunt. 'It is a great slight to me and my family; and when it gets known there will be a very unpleasant time for us. How can she look her friends in the face to-morrow? It is a very great injury, and one I cannot easily forgive. It may even reflect on her character.'

'Nonsense,' said Wildeve.

Thomasin's large eyes had flown from the face of one to the face of the other during this discussion, and she now said anxiously, 'Will you allow me, aunt, to talk it over alone with Damon for five minutes? Will you, Damon?'

'Certainly, dear,' said Wildeve, 'if your aunt will excuse us.' He led her into an adjoining room, leaving Mrs. Yeobright by the fire.

As soon as they were alone, and the door closed, Thomasin said, turning up her pale, tearful face to him, 'It is killing me, this, Damon! I did not mean to part from you in anger at Anglebury this morning; but I was frightened, and hardly knew what I said. I've not let aunt know how much I have suffered to-day; and it is so hard to command my face and voice, and to smile as if it were a slight thing to me; but I try to do so, that she may not be still more indignant with you. I know you could not help it, dear, whatever aunt may think.'

'She is very unpleasant.'

'Yes,' Thomasin murmured, 'and I suppose I seem so now. . . . Damon, what do you mean to do about me?'

'Do about you?'

'Yes. Those who don't like you whisper things which at moments make me doubt you. We mean to marry, I suppose, don't we?'

'Of course we do. We have only to go to Budmouth on Monday, and we may marry at once.'

'Then do let us go!—O Damon, what you make me say!' She hid her face in her handkerchief. 'Here am I asking you to marry me; when by rights you ought to be on your knees imploring me, your cruel mistress, not to refuse you, and saying it would break your heart if I did. I used to think it would be pretty and sweet like that; but how different!'

'Yes, real life is never at all like that.'

'But I don't care personally if it never takes place,' she added with a little dignity; 'no, I can live without you. It is aunt I think of. She is so proud, and thinks so much of her family respectability, that she will be cut down with mortification if this story should get abroad before—it is done. My cousin Clym, too, will be much wounded.'

'Then he will be very unreasonable. In fact, you are all rather unreasonable.'

Thomasin coloured a little, and not with love. But whatever the momentary feeling which caused that flush in her, it went as it came, and she humbly said, 'I never mean to be, if I can help it. I merely feel that you have my aunt to some extent in your power at last.'

'As a matter of justice it is almost due to me,' said Wildeve. 'Think what I have gone through to win her consent; the insult that it is to any man to have the banns forbidden: the double insult to a man unlucky enough to be cursed with sensitiveness, and blue demons, and Heaven knows what, as I am. I can never forget those banns. A harsher man would rejoice now in the power I have of turning upon your aunt by going no further in the business.'

She looked wistfully at him with her sorrowful eyes as

he said those words, and her aspect showed that more than one person in the room could deplore the possession of sensitiveness. Seeing that she was really suffering he seemed disturbed and added, 'This is merely a reflection, you know. I have not the least intention to refuse to complete the marriage, Tamsie mine—I could not bear it.'

'You could not, I know!' said the fair girl, brightening. 'You, who cannot bear the sight of pain in even an insect, or any disagreeable sound, or unpleasant smell even, will not long cause pain to me and mine.'

'I will not, if I can help it.'

'Your hand upon it, Damon.'

He carelessly gave her his hand.

'Ah, by my crown, what's that?' he said suddenly.

There fell upon their ears the sound of numerous voices singing in front of the house. Among these, two made themselves prominent by their peculiarity: one was a very strong bass, the other a wheezy thin piping. Thomasin recognized them as belonging to Timothy Fairway and Grandfer Cantle respectively.

'What does it mean—it is not skimmity-riding, I hope?' she said, with a frightened gaze at Wildeve.

'Of course not; no, it is that the heath-folk have come to sing to us a welcome. This is intolerable!' He began pacing about, the men outside singing cheerily—

'He told' her that she' was the joy' of his life',
And if' she'd con-sent' he would make her his wife';
She could' not refuse' him; to church' so they went',
Young Will was forgot', and young Sue' was content';
And then' was she kiss'd' and set down' on his knee',
No man' in the world' was so lov' -ing as he'!'

Mrs. Yeobright burst in from the outer room. 'Thomasin, Thomasin!' she said, looking indignantly at Wildeve; 'here's a pretty exposure! Let us escape at once. Come!'

It was, however, too late to get away by the passage.

A rugged knocking had begun upon the door of the front room. Wildeve, who had gone to the window, came back.

'Stop!' he said imperiously, putting his hand upon Mrs. Yeobright's arm. 'We are regularly besieged. There are fifty of them out there if there's one. You stay in this room with Thomasin; I'll go out and face them. You must stay now, for my sake, till they are gone, so that it may seem as if all was right. Come, Tamsie dear, don't go making a scene—we must marry after this; that you can see as well as I. Sit still, that's all—and don't speak much. I'll manage them. Blundering fools!'

He pressed the agitated girl into a seat, returned to the outer room and opened the door. Immediately outside, in the passage, appeared Grandfer Cantle singing in concert with those still standing in front of the house. He came into the room and nodded abstractedly to Wildeve, his lips still parted, and his features excruciatingly strained in the emission of the chorus. This being ended, he said heartily, 'Here's welcome to the new-made couple, and God bless 'em!'

'Thank you,' said Wildeve, with dry resentment, his face as gloomy as a thunderstorm.

At the Grandfer's heels now came the rest of the group, which included Fairway, Christian, Sam the turf-cutter, Humphrey, and a dozen others. All smiled upon Wildeve, and upon his tables and chairs likewise, from a general sense of friendliness towards the articles as well as towards their owner.

'We be not here afore Mrs. Yeobright after all,' said Fairway, recognizing the matron's bonnet through the glass partition which divided the public apartment they had entered from the room where the women sat. 'We struck down across, d'ye see, Mr. Wildeve, and she went round by the path.'

'And I see the young bride's little head!' said Grandfer,

peeping in the same direction, and discerning Thomasin, who was waiting beside her aunt in a miserable and awkward way. 'Not quite settled in yet—well, well, there's plenty of time.'

Wildeve made no reply; and probably feeling that the sooner he treated them the sooner they would go, he produced a stone jar, which threw a warm halo over matters at once.

'That's a drop of the right sort, I can see,' said Grandfer Cantle, with the air of a man too well-mannered to show any hurry to taste it.

'Yes,' said Wildeve, ''tis some old mead. I hope you will like it.'

'O ay!' replied the guests, in the hearty tones natural when the words demanded by politeness coincide with those of deepest feeling. 'There isn't a prettier drink under the sun.'

'I'll take my oath there isn't,' added Grandfer Cantle. 'All that can be said against mead is that 'tis rather heady, and apt to lie about a man a good while. But to-morrow's Sunday, thank God.'

'I feel'd for all the world like some bold soldier after I had had some once,' said Christian.

'You shall feel so again,' said Wildeve, with condescension. 'Cups or glasses, gentlemen?'

'Well, if you don't mind, we'll have the beaker, and pass 'en round; 'tis better than heling it out in dribbles.'

'Jown the slippery glasses,' said Grandfer Cantle. 'What's the good of a thing that you can't put down in the ashes to warm, hey, neighbours; that's what I ask?'

'Right, Grandfer,' said Sam; and the mead then circulated.

'Well,' said Timothy Fairway, feeling demands upon his praise in some form or other, ''tis a worthy thing to be married, Mr. Wildeve; and the woman you've got is a dimant, so says I. Yes,' he continued, to Grandfer Cantle, raising his voice so as to be heard through the partition ; 'her father (inclining his head towards the inner room) was as good a feller as ever lived. He always had his great indignation ready against anything underhand.'

'Is that very dangerous ?' said Christian.

'And there were few in these parts that were upsides with him,' said Sam. 'Whenever a club walked he'd play the clarinet in the band that marched before 'em as if he'd never touched anything but a clarinet all his life. And then, when they got to church-door he'd throw down the clarinet, mount the gallery, snatch up the bass-viol, and rozum away as if he'd never played anything but a bass-viol. Folk would say—folk that knowed what a true stave was—"Surely, surely that's never the same man that I saw handling the clarinet so masterly by now!"'

'I can mind it,' said the furze-cutter. ''Twas a wonderful thing that one body could hold it all and never mix the fingering.'

'There was Kingsbere church likewise,' Fairway recommenced, as one opening a new vein of the same mine of interest.

Wildeve breathed the breath of one intolerably bored, and glanced through the partition at the prisoners.

'He used to walk over there of a Sunday afternoon to visit his old acquaintance Andrew Brown, the first clarinet there ; a good man enough, but rather screechy in his music, if you can mind ?'

''A was.'

'And neighbour Yeobright would take Andrey's place for some part of the service, to let Andrey have a bit of a nap, as any friend would naturally do.'

'As any friend would,' said Grandfer Cantle, the other listeners expressing the same accord by the shorter way of nodding their heads.

'No sooner was Andrey asleep and the first whiff of neighbour Yeobright's wind had got inside Andrey's clarinet than every one in church feeled in a moment there was a great soul among 'em. All heads would turn, and they'd say, "Ah, I thought 'twas he!" One Sunday I can well mind—a bass-viol day that time, and Yeobright had brought his own. 'Twas the Hundred-and-thirty-third to "Lydia"; and when they'd come to "Ran down his beard and o'er his robes its costly moisture shed," neighbour Yeobright, who had just warmed to his work, drove his bow into them strings that glorious grand that he e'en a'most sawed the bass-viol into two pieces. Every winder in church rattled as if 'twere a thunderstorm. Old Pa'son Williams lifted his hands in his great holy surplice as natural as if he'd been in common clothes, and seemed to say to hisself, "O for such a man in our parish!" But not a soul in Kingsbere could hold a candle to Yeobright.'

'Was it quite safe when the winder shook?' Christian inquired.

He received no answer; all for the moment sitting rapt in admiration of the performance described. As with Farinelli's singing before the princesses, Sheridan's renowned Begum Speech, and other such examples, the fortunate condition of its being for ever lost to the world invested the deceased Mr. Yeobright's *tour de force* on that memorable afternoon with a cumulative glory which comparative criticism, had that been possible, might considerably have shorn down.

'He was the last you'd have expected to drop off in the prime of life,' said Humphrey.

'Ah, well: he was looking for the earth some months afore he went. At that time women used to run for smocks and gown-pieces at Greenhill Fair, and my wife that is now, being a long-legged slittering maid, hardly husband-high, went with the rest of the maidens, for 'a was a good runner afore she got so heavy. When she came home I said—we were then just beginning to walk together—"What have ye got, my honey?" "I've won —well, I've won—a gown-piece," says she, her colours coming up in a moment. 'Tis a smock for a crown, I thought; and so it turned out. Ay, when I think what she'll say to me now without a mossel of red in her face, it do seem strange that 'a wouldn't say such a little thing then. . . . However, then she went on, and that's what made me bring up the story, "Well, whatever clothes I've won, white or figured, for eyes to see or for eyes not to see" ('a could do a pretty stroke of modesty in those days), "I'd sooner have lost it than have seen what I have. Poor Mr. Yeobright was took bad directly he reached the fair ground, and was forced to go home again." That was the last time he ever went out of the parish.'

''A faltered on from one day to another, and then we heard he was gone.'

'D'ye think he had great pain when 'a died?' said Christian.

'O no: quite different. Nor any pain of mind. He was lucky enough to be God A'mighty's own man.'

'And other folk—d'ye think 'twill be much pain to 'em, Mister Fairway?'

'That depends on whether they be afeared.'

'I bain't afeared at all, I thank God!' said Christian strenuously. 'I'm glad I bain't, for then 'twon't pain me. . . . I don't think I be afeard—or if I be I can't help it, and I don't deserve to suffer. I wish I was not afeard at all!'

There was a solemn silence, and looking from the window, which was unshuttered and unblinded, Timothy said, 'Well, what a fess little bonfire that one is, out by Cap'n Vye's! 'Tis burning just the same now as ever, upon my life.'

All glances went through the window, and nobody noticed that Wildeve disguised a brief, tell-tale look. Far away up the sombre valley of heath, and to the right of Rainbarrow, could indeed be seen the light, small, but steady and persistent as before.

'It was lighted before ours was,' Fairway continued; 'and yet every one in the country round is out afore 'n.'

'Perhaps there's meaning in it!' murmured Christian.

'How meaning?' said Wildeve sharply.

Christian was too scattered to reply, and Timothy helped him.

'He means, sir, that the lonesome dark-eyed creature up there that some say is a witch—ever I should call a fine young woman such a name—is always up to some odd conceit or other; and so perhaps 'tis she.'

'I'd be very glad to ask her in wedlock, if she'd hae me, and take the risk of her wild dark eyes ill-wishing me,' said Grandfer Cantle staunchly.

'Don't ye say it, father!' implored Christian.

'Well, be dazed if he who do marry the maid won't hae an uncommon picture for his best parlour,' said Fairway in a liquid tone, placing down the cup of mead at the end of a good pull.

'And a partner as deep as the North Star,' said Sam, taking up the cup and finishing the little that remained.

'Well, really, now I think we must be moving,' said Humphrey, observing the emptiness of the vessel.

'But we'll gie 'em another song?' said Grandfer Cantle. 'I'm as full of notes as a bird!'

'Thank you, Grandfer,' said Wildeve. 'But we will not trouble you now. Some other day must do for that—when I have a party.'

'Be jown'd if I don't learn ten new songs for't, or I won't learn a line!' said Grandfer Cantle. 'And you may be sure I won't disappoint ye by biding away, Mr. Wildeve.'

'I quite believe you,' said that gentleman.

All then took their leave, wishing their entertainer long life and happiness as a married man, with recapitulations which occupied some time. Wildeve attended them to the door, beyond which the deep-dyed upward stretch of heath stood awaiting them, an amplitude of darkness reigning from their feet almost to the zenith, where a definite form first became visible in the lowering forehead of Rainbarrow. Diving into the dense obscurity in a line headed by Sam the turf-cutter, they pursued their trackless way home.

When the scratching of the furze against their leggings had fainted upon the ear, Wildeve returned to the room where he had left Thomasin and her aunt. The women were gone.

They could only have left the house in one way, by the back window; and this was open.

Wildeve laughed to himself, remained a moment thinking, and idly returned to the front room. Here his glance fell upon a bottle of wine which stood on the mantelpiece. 'Ah—old Dowden!' he murmured; and going to the kitchen door shouted, 'Is anybody here who can take something to old Dowden?'

There was no reply. The room was empty, the lad who acted as his factotum having gone to bed. Wildeve came back, put on his hat, took the bottle, and left the house, turning the key in the door, for there was no guest at the inn to-night. As soon as he was on the road the little bonfire on Mistover Knap again met his eye.

'Still waiting, are you, my lady?' he murmured.

However, he did not proceed that way just then; but leaving the hill to the left of him, he stumbled over a rutted road that brought him to a cottage which, like all other habitations on the heath at this hour, was only saved from being invisible by a faint shine from its bedroom window. This house was the home of Olly Dowden, the besom-maker, and he entered.

The lower room was in darkness; but by feeling his way he found a table, whereon he placed the bottle, and a minute later emerged again upon the heath. He stood and looked north-east at the undying little fire—high up above him, though not so high as Rainbarrow.

We have been told what happens when a woman deliberates ; and the epigram is not always terminable with woman, provided that one be in the case, and that a fair one. Wildeve stood, and stood longer, and breathed perplexedly, and then said to himself with resignation, 'Yes—by Heaven, I must go to her, I suppose !'

Instead of turning in the direction of home he pressed on rapidly by a path under Rainbarrow towards what was evidently a signal light.

THE FIGURE AGAINST THE SKY

VI

WHEN the whole Egdon concourse had left the site of the bonfire to its accustomed loneliness, a closely wrapped female figure approached the barrow from that quarter of the heath in which the little fire lay. Had the reddleman been watching he might have recognized her as the woman who had first stood there so singularly, and vanished at the approach of strangers. She ascended to her old position at the top, where the red coals of the perishing fire greeted her like living eyes in the corpse of day. There she stood still, around her stretching the vast night atmosphere, whose incomplete darkness in comparison with the total darkness of the heath below it might have represented a venial beside a mortal sin.

That she was tall and straight in build, that she was ladylike in her movements, was all that could be learnt of her just now, her form being wrapped in a shawl folded in the old cornerwise fashion, and her head in a large kerchief, a protection not superfluous at this hour and place. Her back was towards the wind, which blew from the north-west; but whether she had avoided that aspect because of the chilly gusts which played about her exceptional position, or because her interest lay in the south-east, did not at first appear.

Her reason for standing so dead still as the pivot of this circle of heath-country was just as obscure. Her extraordinary fixity, her conspicuous loneliness, her heedlessness of night, betokened among other things an utter absence of fear. A tract of country unaltered from that sinister condition which made Cæsar anxious every year to get clear of its glooms before the autumnal equinox, a kind of landscape and weather which leads travellers from the South to describe our island as Homer's Cimmerian land, was not, on the face of it, friendly to women.

It might reasonably have been supposed that she was listening to the wind, which rose somewhat as the night advanced, and laid hold of the attention. The wind, indeed, seemed made for the scene, as the scene seemed made for the hour. Part of its tone was quite special; what was heard there could be heard nowhere else. Gusts in innumerable series followed each other from the north-west, and when each one of them raced past the sound of its progress resolved into three. Treble, tenor, and bass notes were to be found therein. The general ricochet of the whole over pits and prominences had the gravest pitch of the chime. Next there could be heard the baritone buzz of a holly tree. Below these in force, above them in pitch, a dwindled voice strove hard at a husky tune, which was the peculiar local sound alluded to. Thinner and less immediately traceable than the other two, it was far more impressive than either. In it lay what may be called the linguistic peculiarity of the heath; and being audible nowhere on earth off a heath, it afforded a shadow of reason for the woman's tenseness, which continued as unbroken as ever.

Throughout the blowing of these plaintive November winds that note bore a great resemblance to the ruins of human song which remain to the throat of fourscore and ten. It was a worn whisper, dry and papery, and it brushed so distinctly across the ear that, by the accustomed, the material minutiæ in which it originated could be realized as by touch. It was the united products of infinitesimal vegetable causes, and these were neither stems, leaves, fruit, blades, prickles, lichen, nor moss.

They were the mummied heath-bells of the past summer, originally tender and purple, now washed colourless by Michaelmas rains, and dried to dead skins by October suns. So low was an individual sound from these that a combination of hundreds only just emerged from silence, and the myriads of the whole declivity reached the woman's ear but as a shrivelled and intermittent recitative. Yet scarcely a single accent among the many afloat to-night could have such power to impress a listener with thoughts of its origin. One inwardly saw the infinity of those combined multitudes; and perceived that each of the tiny trumpets was seized on, entered, scoured and emerged from by the wind as thoroughly as if it were as vast as a crater.

'The spirit moved them.' A meaning of the phrase forced itself upon the attention; and an emotional listener's fetichistic mood might have ended in one of more advanced quality. It was not, after all, that the left-hand expanse of old blooms spoke, or the right-hand, or those of the slope in front; but it was the single person of something else speaking through each at once.

Suddenly, on the barrow, there mingled with all this wild rhetoric of night a sound which modulated so naturally into the rest that its beginning and ending were hardly to be distinguished. The bluffs, and the bushes, and the heather-bells had broken silence; at last, so did the woman; and her articulation was but as another phrase of the same discourse as theirs. Thrown out on the winds it became twined in with them, and with them it flew away.

What she uttered was a lengthened sighing, apparently at something in her mind which had led to her presence here. There was a spasmodic abandonment about it as if, in allowing herself to utter the sound, the woman's brain had authorized what it could not regulate. One point was evident in this ; that she had been existing in a suppressed state, and not in one of languor, or stagnation.

Far away down the valley the faint shine from the window of the inn still lasted on ; and a few additional moments proved that the window, or what was within it, had more to do with the woman's sigh than had either her own actions or the scene immediately around. She lifted her left hand, which held a closed telescope. This she rapidly extended, as if she were well accustomed to the operation, and raising it to her eye directed it towards the light beaming from the inn.

The handkerchief which had hooded her head was now a little thrown back, her face being somewhat elevated. A profile was visible against the dull monochrome of cloud around her ; and it was as though side shadows from the features of Sappho and Mrs. Siddons had converged upwards from the tomb to form an image like neither but suggesting both. This, however, was mere superficiality. In respect of character a face may make certain admissions by its outline ; but it fully confesses only in its changes. So much is this the case that what is called the play of the features often helped more in understanding a man or woman than the earnest labours of all the other members together. Thus the night revealed little of her whose form it was embracing, for the mobile parts of her countenance could not be seen.

At last she gave up her spying attitude, closed the telescope, and turned to the decaying embers. From these no appreciable beams now radiated, except when a more than usually smart gust brushed over their faces and raised a fitful glow which came and went like the blush of a girl. She stooped over the silent circle, and selecting from the brands a piece of stick which bore the largest live coal at its end, brought it to where she had been standing before.

She held the brand to the ground, blowing the red

coal with her mouth at the same time; till it faintly illuminated the sod, and revealed a small object, which turned out to be an hour-glass, though she wore a watch. She blew long enough to show that the sand had all slipped through.

'Ah!' she said, as if surprised.

The light raised by her breath had been very fitful, and a momentary irradiation of flesh was all that it had disclosed of her face. That consisted of two matchless lips and a cheek only, her head being still enveloped. She threw away the stick, took the glass in her hand, the telescope under her arm, and moved on.

Along the ridge ran a faint foot-track, which the lady followed. Those who knew it well called it a path; and, while a mere visitor would have passed it unnoticed even by day, the regular haunters of the heath were at no loss for it at midnight. The whole secret of following these incipient paths, when there was not light enough in the atmosphere to show a turnpike-road, lay in the development of the sense of touch in the feet, which comes with years of night-rambling in little-trodden spots. To a walker practised in such places a difference between impact on maiden herbage, and on the crippled stalks of a slight footway, is perceptible through the thickest boot or shoe.

The solitary figure who walked this beat took no notice of the windy tune still played on the dead heath-bells. She did not turn her head to look at a group of dark creatures further on, who fled from her presence as she skirted a ravine where they fed. They were about a score of the small wild ponies known as heath-croppers. They roamed at large on the undulations of Egdon, but in numbers too few to detract much from the solitude.

The pedestrian noticed nothing just now, and a clue to her abstraction was afforded by a trivial incident. A bramble caught hold of her skirt, and checked her progress. Instead of putting it off and hastening along, she yielded herself up to the pull, and stood passively still. When she began to extricate herself it was by turning round and round, and so unwinding the prickly switch. She was in a desponding reverie.

Her course was in the direction of the small undying fire which had drawn the attention of the men on Rain-barrow and of Wildeve in the valley below. A faint illumination from its rays began to glow upon her face, and the fire soon revealed itself to be lit, not on the level ground, but on a salient corner or redan of earth, at the junction of two converging bank fences. Outside was a ditch, dry except immediately under the fire, where there was a large pool, bearded all round by heather and rushes. In the smooth water of the pool the fire appeared upside down.

The banks meeting behind were bare of a hedge, save such as was formed by disconnected tufts of furze, standing upon stems along the top, like impaled heads above a city wall. A white mast, fitted up with spars and other nautical tackle, could be seen rising against the dark clouds whenever the flames played brightly enough to reach it. Altogether the scene had much the appearance of a fortification upon which had been kindled a beacon fire.

Nobody was visible; but ever and anon a whitish something moved above the bank from behind, and vanished again. This was a small human hand, in the act of lifting pieces of fuel into the fire; but for all that could be seen the hand, like that which troubled Belshazzar, was there alone. Occasionally an ember rolled off the bank, and dropped with a hiss into the pool.

At one side of the pool rough steps built of clods enabled any one who wished to do so to mount the bank; which the woman did. Within was a paddock in an uncultivated state, though bearing evidence of having once been tilled; but the heath and fern had insidiously crept in, and were reasserting their old supremacy. Further ahead were dimly visible an irregular dwelling-house, garden, and outbuildings, backed by a clump of firs.

The young lady—for youth had revealed its presence in her buoyant bound up the bank—walked along the top instead of descending inside, and came to the corner where the fire was burning. One reason for the permanence of the blaze was now manifest: the fuel consisted of hard pieces of wood, cleft and sawn—the knotty boles of old thorn trees which grew in twos and threes about the hillsides. A yet unconsumed pile of these lay in the inner angle of the bank; and from this corner the upturned face of a little boy greeted her eyes. He was dilatorily throwing up a piece of wood into the fire every now and then, a business which seemed to have engaged him a considerable part of the evening, for his face was somewhat weary.

'I am glad you have come, Miss Eustacia,' he said, with a sigh of relief. 'I don't like biding by myself.'

'Nonsense. I have only been a little way for a walk. I have been gone only twenty minutes.'

'It seemed long,' murmured the sad boy. 'And you have been so many times.'

'Why, I thought you would be pleased to have a bonfire. Are you not much obliged to me for making you one?'

'Yes; but there's nobody here to play wi' me.'

'I suppose nobody has come while I've been away?'

'Nobody except your grandfather: he looked out of doors once for 'ee. I told him you were walking round upon the hill to look at the other bonfires.'

'A good boy.'

'I think I hear him coming again, miss.'

An old man came into the remoter light of the fire from the direction of the homestead. He was the same who had overtaken the reddleman on the road that afternoon. He looked wistfully to the top of the bank at the woman who stood there, and his teeth, which were quite unimpaired, showed like parian from his parted lips.

'When are you coming indoors, Eustacia?' he asked. ''Tis almost bedtime. I've been home these two hours, and am tired out. Surely 'tis somewhat childish of you to stay out playing at bonfires so long, and wasting such fuel. My precious thorn roots, the rarest of all firing, that I laid by on purpose for Christmas—you have burnt 'em nearly all!'

'I promised Johnny a bonfire, and it pleases him not to let it go out just yet,' said Eustacia, in a way which told at once that she was absolute queen here. 'Grandfather, you go in to bed. I shall follow you soon. You like the fire, don't you, Johnny?'

The boy looked up doubtfully at her and murmured, 'I don't think I want it any longer.'

Her grandfather had turned back again, and did not hear the boy's reply. As soon as the white-haired man had vanished she said in a tone of pique to the child, 'Ungrateful little boy, how can you contradict me? Never shall you have a bonfire again unless you keep it up now. Come, tell me you like to do things for me, and don't deny it.'

The repressed child said, 'Yes, I do, miss,' and continued to stir the fire perfunctorily.

'Stay a little longer and I will give you a crooked sixpence,' said Eustacia, more gently. 'Put in one piece of wood every two or three minutes, but not too much at once. I am going to walk along the ridge a little longer, but I shall keep on coming to you. And if you hear a frog jump into the pond with a flounce like a stone thrown in, be sure you run and tell me, because it is a sign of rain.'

'Yes, Eustacia.'

'Miss Vye, sir.'

'Miss Vy—stacia.'

'That will do. Now put in one stick more.'

The little slave went on feeding the fire as before. He seemed a mere automaton, galvanized into moving and speaking by the wayward Eustacia's will. He might have been the brass statue which Albertus Magnus is said to have animated just so far as to make it chatter, and move, and be his servant.

Before going on her walk again the young girl stood still on the bank for a few instants and listened. It was to the full as lonely a place as Rainbarrow, though at rather a lower level; and it was more sheltered from wind and weather on account of the few firs to the north. The bank which enclosed the homestead, and protected it from the lawless state of the world without, was formed of thick square clods, dug from the ditch on the outside, and built up with a slight batter or incline, which forms no slight defence where hedges will not grow because of the wind and the wilderness, and where wall materials are unattainable. Otherwise the situation was quite open, commanding the whole length of the valley which reached to the river behind Wildeve's house. High above this to the right, and much nearer thitherward than the Quiet Woman Inn, the blurred contour of Rainbarrow obstructed the sky.

After her attentive survey of the wild slopes and hollow ravines a gesture of impatience escaped Eustacia. She vented petulant words every now and then; but there were sighs between her words, and sudden listenings between her sighs. Descending from her perch she again sauntered off towards Rainbarrow, though this time she did not go the whole way.

Twice she reappeared at intervals of a few minutes and each time she said—

'Not any flounce into the pond yet, little man?'

'No, Miss Eustacia,' the child replied.

'Well,' she said at last, 'I shall soon be going in, and then I will give you the crooked sixpence, and let you go home.'

'Thank'ee, Miss Eustacia,' said the tired stoker, breathing more easily. And Eustacia again strolled away from the fire, but this time not towards Rainbarrow. She skirted the bank and went round to the wicket before the house, where she stood motionless, looking at the scene.

Fifty yards off rose the corner of the two converging banks, with the fire upon it: within the bank, lifting up to the fire one stick at a time, just as before, the figure of the little child. She idly watched him as he occasionally climbed up in the nook of the bank and stood beside the brands. The wind blew the smoke, and the child's hair, and the corner of his pinafore, all in the same direction: the breeze died, and the pinafore and hair lay still, and the smoke went up straight.

While Eustacia looked on from this distance the boy's form visibly started: he slid down the bank and ran across towards the white gate.

'Well?' said Eustacia.

'A hop-frog have jumped into the pond. Yes, I heard 'en!'

'Then it is going to rain, and you had better go home. You will not be afraid?' She spoke hurriedly, as if her heart had leapt into her throat at the boy's words.

'No, because I shall hae the crooked sixpence.'

'Yes, here it is. Now run as fast as you can—not that way—through the garden here. No other boy in the heath has had such a bonfire as yours.'

The boy, who clearly had had too much of a good thing, marched away into the shadows with alacrity. When he was gone Eustacia, leaving her telescope and hour-glass by the gate, brushed forward from the wicket towards the angle of the bank, under the fire.

Here, screened by the outwork, she waited. In a few moments a splash was audible from the pond outside. Had the child been there he would have said that a second frog had jumped in; but by most people the sound would have been likened to the fall of a stone into the water. Eustacia stepped upon the bank.

'Yes?' she said, and held her breath.

Thereupon the contour of a man became dimly visible against the low-reaching sky over the valley, beyond the outer margin of the pool. He came round it and leapt upon the bank beside her. A low laugh escaped her—the third utterance which the girl had indulged in to-night. The first, when she stood upon Rainbarrow, had expressed anxiety; the second, on the ridge, had expressed impatience; the present was one of triumphant pleasure. She let her joyous eyes rest upon him without speaking, as upon some wondrous thing she had created out of chaos.

'I have come,' said the man, who was Wildeve. 'You give me no peace. Why do you not leave me alone? I have seen your bonfire all the evening.' The words were not without emotion, and retained their level tone as if by a careful equipoise between imminent extremes.

At this unexpectedly repressing manner in her lover the girl seemed to repress herself also. 'Of course you have seen my fire,' she answered with languid calmness, artificially maintained. 'Why shouldn't I have a bonfire on the Fifth of November, like other denizens of the heath?'

'I knew it was meant for me.'

'How did you know it? I have had no word with you since you—you chose her, and walked about with her, and deserted me entirely, as if I had never been yours life and soul so irretrievably!'

'Eustacia! could I forget that last autumn at this same day of the month and at this same place you lighted exactly such a fire as a signal for me to come and see you? Why should there have been a bonfire again by Captain Vye's house if not for the same purpose?'

'Yes, yes—I own it,' she cried under her breath, with a drowsy fervour of manner and tone which was quite peculiar to her. 'Don't begin speaking to me as you did, Damon; you will drive me to say words I would not wish to say to you. I had given you up, and resolved not to think of you any more; and then I heard the news, and I came out and got the fire ready because I thought that you had been faithful to me.'

'What have you heard to make you think that?' said Wildeve, astonished.

'That you did not marry her!' she murmured exultingly. 'And I knew it was because you loved me best, and couldn't do it. . . . Damon, you have been cruel to me to go away, and I have said I would never forgive you. I do not think I can forgive you entirely, even now —it is too much for a woman of any spirit to quite overlook.'

'If I had known you wished to call me up here only to reproach me, I wouldn't have come.'

'But I don't mind it, and I do forgive you now that you have not married her, and have come back to me!'

'Who told you that I had not married her?'

'My grandfather. He took a long walk to-day, and as he was coming home he overtook some person who told him of a broken-off wedding: he thought it might be yours; and I knew it was.'

'Does anybody else know?'

'I suppose not. Now Damon, do you see why I lit my signal fire? You did not think I would have lit it if I had imagined you to have become the husband of this woman. It is insulting my pride to suppose that.'

Wildeve was silent: it was evident that he had supposed as much.

'Did you indeed think I believed you were married?' she again demanded earnestly. 'Then you wronged me; and upon my life and heart I can hardly bear to recognize that you have such ill thoughts of me! Damon, you are not worthy of me: I see it, and yet I love you. Never mind: let it go—I must bear your mean opinion as best I may. . . . It is true, is it not,' she added with ill-concealed anxiety, on his making no demonstration, 'that you could not bring yourself to give me up, and are still going to love me best of all ?'

'Yes ; or why should I have come ?' he said touchily. 'Not that fidelity will be any great merit in me after your kind speech about my unworthiness, which should have been said by myself if by anybody, and comes with an ill grace from you. However, the curse of inflammability is upon me, and I must live under it, and take any snub from a woman. It has brought me down from engineering to innkeeping : what lower stage it has in store for me I have yet to learn.' He continued to look upon her gloomily.

She seized the moment, and throwing back the shawl so that the firelight shone full upon her face and throat, said with a smile, 'Have you seen anything better than that in your travels ?'

Eustacia was not one to commit herself to such a position without good ground. He said quietly, 'No.'

'Not even on the shoulders of Thomasin ?'

'Thomasin is a pleasing and innocent woman.'

'That's nothing to do with it,' she cried with quick passionateness. 'We will leave her out ; there are only you and me now to think of.' After a long look at him she resumed with the old quiescent warmth : 'Must I go on weakly confessing to you things a woman ought to conceal ; and own that no words can express how gloomy I have been because of that dreadful belief I held till two hours ago—that you had quite deserted me ?'

'I am sorry I caused you that pain.'

'But perhaps it is not wholly because of you that I get gloomy,' she archly added. 'It is in my nature to feel like that. It was born in my blood, I suppose.'

'Hypochondriasis.'

'Or else it was coming into this wild heath. I was happy enough at Budmouth. O the times, O the days at Budmouth! But Egdon will be brighter again now.'

'I hope it will,' said Wildeve moodily. 'Do you know the consequence of this recall to me, my old darling? I shall come to see you again as before, at Rainbarrow.'

'Of course you will.'

'And yet I declare that until I got here to-night I intended, after this one good-bye, never to meet you again.'

'I don't thank you for that,' she said, turning away, while indignation spread through her like subterranean heat. 'You may come again to Rainbarrow if you like, but you won't see me; and you may call, but I shall not listen; and you may tempt me, but I won't give myself to you any more.'

'You have said as much before, sweet; but such natures as yours don't so easily adhere to their words. Neither, for the matter of that, do such natures as mine.'

'This is the pleasure I have won by my trouble,' she whispered bitterly. 'Why did I try to recall you? Damon, a strange warring takes place in my mind occasionally. I think when I become calm after your woundings, "Do I embrace a cloud of common fog after all?" You are a chameleon, and now you are at your worst colour. Go home, or I shall hate you!'

He looked absently towards Rainbarrow while one might have counted twenty, and said, as if he did not much mind all this, 'Yes, I will go home. Do you mean to see me again?'

'If you own to me that the wedding is broken off because you love me best.'

'I don't think it would be good policy,' said Wildeve, smiling. 'You would get to know the extent of your power too clearly.'

'But tell me!'

'You know.'

'Where is she now?'

'I don't know. I prefer not to speak of her to you. I have not yet married her: I have come in obedience to your call. That is enough.'

'I merely lit that fire because I was dull, and thought I would get a little excitement by calling you up and triumphing over you as the Witch of Endor called up Samuel. I determined you should come; and you have come! I have shown my power. A mile and half hither, and a mile and half back again to your home—three miles in the dark for me. Have I not shown my power?'

He shook his head at her. 'I know you too well, my Eustacia; I know you too well. There isn't a note in you which I don't know; and that hot little bosom couldn't play such a cold-blooded trick to save its life. I saw a woman on Rainbarrow at dusk looking down towards my house. I think I drew out you before you drew out me.'

The revived embers of an old passion glowed clearly in Wildeve now; and he leant forward as if about to put his face towards her cheek.

'O no,' she said, intractably moving to the other side of the decayed fire. 'What did you mean by that?'

'Perhaps I may kiss your hand?'

'No, you may not.'

'Then I may shake your hand?'

'No.'

'Then I wish you good-night without caring for either. Good-bye, good-bye.'

She returned no answer, and with the bow of a dancing-master he vanished on the other side of the pool as he had come.

Eustacia sighed: it was no fragile maiden sigh, but a sigh which shook her like a shiver. Whenever a flash of reason darted like an electric light upon her lover—as it sometimes would—and showed his imperfections, she shivered thus. But it was over in a second, and she loved on. She knew that he trifled with her; but she loved on. She scattered the half-burnt brands, went indoors immediately, and up to her bedroom without a light. Amid the rustles which denoted her to be undressing in the darkness other heavy breaths frequently came ; and the same kind of shudder occasionally moved through her when, ten minutes later, she lay on her bed asleep

VII

EUSTACIA VYE was the raw material of a divinity. On Olympus she would have done well with a little preparation. She had the passions and instincts which make a model goddess, that is, those which make not quite a model woman. Had it been possible for the earth and mankind to be entirely in her grasp for a while, had she handled the distaff, the spindle, and the shears at her own free will, few in the world would have noticed the change of government. There would have been the same inequality of lot, the same heaping up of favours here, of contumely there, the same generosity before justice, the same perpetual dilemmas, the same captious alternation of caresses and blows that we endure now.

She was in person full-limbed and somewhat heavy; without ruddiness, as without pallor; and soft to the touch as a cloud. To see her hair was to fancy that a whole winter did not contain darkness enough to form its shadow: it closed over her forehead like nightfall extinguishing the western glow.

Her nerves extended into those tresses, and her temper could always be softened by stroking them down. When her hair was brushed she would instantly sink into stillness and look like the Sphinx. If, in passing under one of the Egdon banks, any of its thick skeins were caught, as they sometimes were, by a prickly tuft of the large

Ulex Europæus—which will act as a sort of hairbrush—she would go back a few steps, and pass against it a second time.

She had Pagan eyes, full of nocturnal mysteries, and their light, as it came and went, and came again, was partially hampered by their oppressive lids and lashes; and of these the under lid was much fuller than it usually is with English women. This enabled her to indulge in reverie without seeming to do so: she might have been believed capable of sleeping without closing them up. Assuming that the souls of men and women were visible essences, you could fancy the colour of Eustacia's soul to be flame-like. The sparks from it that rose into her dark pupils gave the same impression.

The mouth seemed formed less to speak than to quiver, less to quiver than to kiss. Some might have added, less to kiss than to curl. Viewed sideways, the closing-line of her lips formed, with almost geometric precision, the curve so well known in the arts of design as the cima-recta, or ogee. The sight of such a flexible bend as that on grim Egdon was quite an apparition. It was felt at once that that mouth did not come over from Sleswig with a band of Saxon pirates whose lips met like the two halves of a muffin. One had fancied that such lip-curves were mostly lurking underground in the South as fragments of forgotten marbles. So fine were the lines of her lips that, though full, each corner of her mouth was as clearly cut as the point of a spear. This keenness of corner was only blunted when she was given over to sudden fits of gloom, one of the phases of the night-side of sentiment which she knew too well for her years.

Her presence brought memories of such things as Bourbon roses, rubies, and tropical midnights; her moods recalled lotus-eaters and the march in 'Athalie'; her motions, the ebb and flow of the sea; her voice, the viola. In a dim light, and with a slight rearrangement of her hair, her general figure might have stood for that of either of the higher female deities. The new moon behind her head, an old helmet upon it, a diadem of accidental dew-drops round her brow, would have been adjuncts sufficient to strike the note of Artemis, Athena, or Hera respectively, with as close an approximation to the antique as that which passes muster on many respected canvases.

But celestial imperiousness, love, wrath, and fervour had proved to be somewhat thrown away on netherward Egdon. Her power was limited, and the consciousness of this limitation had biassed her development. Egdon was her Hades, and since coming there she had imbibed much of what was dark in its tone, though inwardly and eternally unreconciled thereto. Her appearance accorded well with this smouldering rebelliousness, and the shady splendour of her beauty was the real surface of the sad and stifled warmth within her. A true Tartarean dignity sat upon her brow, and not factitiously or with marks of constraint, for it had grown in her with years.

Across the upper part of her head she wore a thin fillet of black velvet, restraining the luxuriance of her shady hair, in a way which added much to this class of majesty by irregularly clouding her forehead. 'Nothing can embellish a beautiful face more than a narrow band drawn over the brow,' says Richter. Some of the neighbouring girls wore coloured ribbon for the same purpose, and sported metallic ornaments elsewhere; but if any one suggested coloured ribbon and metallic ornaments to Eustacia Vye she laughed and went on.

Why did a woman of this sort live on Egdon Heath? Budmouth was her native place, a fashionable seaside resort at that date. She was the daughter of the bandmaster of a regiment which had been quartered there—a Corfiote by birth, and a fine musician—who met his future wife during her trip thither with her father the captain, a man of good family. The marriage was scarcely in accord with the old man's wishes, for the bandmaster's pockets were as light as his occupation. But the musician did his best; adopted his wife's name, made England permanently his home, took great trouble with his child's education, the expenses of which were defrayed by the grandfather, and throve as the chief local musician till her mother's death, when he left off thriving, drank, and died also. The girl was left to the care of her grandfather, who, since three of his ribs became broken in a shipwreck, had lived in this airy perch on Egdon, a spot which had taken his fancy because the house was to be had for next to nothing, and because a remote blue tinge on the horizon between the hills, visible from the cottage door, was traditionally believed to be the English Channel. She hated the change; she felt like one banished; but here she was forced to abide.

Thus it happened that in Eustacia's brain were juxtaposed the strangest assortment of ideas, from old time and from new. There was no middle distance in her perspective: romantic recollections of sunny afternoons on an esplanade, with military bands, officers, and gallants around, stood like gilded letters upon the dark tablet of surrounding Egdon. Every bizarre effect that could result from the random intertwining of watering-place glitter with the grand solemnity of a heath, was to be found in her. Seeing nothing of human life now, she imagined all the more of what she had seen.

Where did her dignity come from? By a latent vein from Alcinous' line, her father hailing from Phæacia's isle?—or from Fitzalan and De Vere, her maternal grandfather having had a cousin in the peerage? Perhaps it was the gift of Heaven—a happy convergence of natural laws. Among other things opportunity had of late years been denied her of learning to be undignified, for she lived lonely. Isolation on a heath renders vulgarity well-nigh impossible. It would have been as easy for the heath-ponies, bats, and snakes to be vulgar as for her. A narrow life in Budmouth might have completely demeaned her.

The only way to look queenly without realms or hearts to queen it over is to look as if you had lost them; and Eustacia did that to a triumph. In the captain's cottage she could suggest mansions she had never seen. Perhaps that was because she frequented a vaster mansion than any of them, the open hills. Like the summer condition of the place around her, she was an embodiment of the phrase 'a populous solitude'—apparently so listless, void, and quiet, she was really busy and full.

To be loved to madness—such was her great desire. Love was to her the one cordial which could drive away the eating loneliness of her days. And she seemed to long for the abstraction called passionate love more than for any particular lover.

She could show a most reproachful look at times, but it was directed less against human beings than against certain creatures of her mind, the chief of these being Destiny, through whose interference she dimly fancied it arose that love alighted only on gliding youth—that any love she might win would sink simultaneously with the sand in the glass. She thought of it with an ever-growing consciousness of cruelty, which tended to breed actions of reckless unconventionality, framed to snatch a year's, a week's, even an hour's passion from anywhere, while it could be won. Through want of it she had sung without being merry, possessed without enjoying, outshone without triumphing. Her loneliness deepened her desire. On Egdon, coldest and meanest kisses were at famine prices; and where was a mouth matching hers to be found?

Fidelity in love for fidelity's sake had less attraction for her than for most women: fidelity because of love's grip had much. A blaze of love, and extinction, was better than a lantern glimmer of the same which should last long years. On this head she knew by prevision what most women learn only by experience: she had mentally walked round love, told the towers thereof, considered its palaces; and concluded that love was but a doleful joy. Yet she desired it, as one in a desert would be thankful for brackish water.

She often repeated her prayers; not at particular times, but, like the unaffectedly devout, when she desired to pray. Her prayer was always spontaneous, and often ran thus, 'O deliver my heart from this fearful gloom and loneliness: send me great love from somewhere, else I shall die.'

Her high gods were William the Conqueror, Strafford, and Napoleon Buonaparte, as they had appeared in the Lady's History used at the establishment in which she was educated. Had she been a mother she would have christened her boys such names as Saul or Sisera in preference to Jacob or David, neither of whom she admired. At school she had used to side with the Philistines in several battles, and had wondered if Pontius Pilate were as handsome as he was frank and fair.

Thus she was a girl of some forwardness of mind, indeed, weighed in relation to her situation among the very rereward of thinkers, very original. Her instincts towards social nonconformity were at the root of this. In the matter of holidays, her mood was that of horses who, when turned out to grass, enjoy looking upon their kind at work on the highway. She only valued rest to herself when it came in the midst of other people's labour. Hence she hated Sundays when all was at rest, and often said they would be the death of her. To see the heathmen in their Sunday condition, that is, with their hands in their pockets, their boots newly oiled, and not laced up (a particularly Sunday sign), walking leisurely among the turves and furze-faggots they had cut during the week, and kicking them critically as if their use were unknown, was a fearful heaviness to her. To relieve the tedium of this untimely day she would overhaul the cupboards containing her grandfather's old charts and other rubbish, humming Saturday-night ballads of the country people the while. But on Saturday nights she would frequently sing a psalm, and it was always on a week-day that she read the Bible, that she might be unoppressed with a sense of doing her duty.

Such views of life were to some extent the natural begettings of her situation upon her nature. To dwell on a heath without studying its meanings was like wedding a foreigner without learning his tongue. The subtle beauties of the heath were lost to Eustacia; she only caught its vapours. An environment which would have made a contented woman a poet, a suffering woman a devotee, a pious woman a psalmist, even a giddy woman thoughtful, made a rebellious woman saturnine.

Eustacia had got beyond the vision of some marriage of inexpressible glory; yet, though her emotions were in full vigour, she cared for no meaner union. Thus we see her in a strange state of isolation. To have lost the godlike conceit that we may do what we will, and not to have acquired a homely zest for doing what we can, shows a grandeur of temper which cannot be objected to in the abstract, for it denotes a mind that, though disappointed, forswears compromise. But, if congenial to philosophy, it is apt to be dangerous to the commonwealth. In a world where doing means marrying, and the commonwealth is one of hearts and hands, the same peril attends the condition.

And so we see our Eustacia—for at times she was not altogether unlovable—arriving at that stage of enlightenment which feels that nothing is worth while, and filling up the spare hours of her existence by idealizing Wildeve for want of a better object. This was the sole reason of his ascendency: she knew it herself. At moments her pride rebelled against her passion for him, and she even had longed to be free. But there was only one circumstance which could dislodge him, and that was the advent of a greater man.

For the rest, she suffered much from depression of

spirits, and took slow walks to recover them, in which she carried her grandfather's telescope and her grandmother's hour-glass—the latter because of a peculiar pleasure she derived from watching a material representation of time's gradual glide away. She seldom schemed, but when she did scheme, her plans showed rather the comprehensive strategy of a general than the small arts called womanish, though she could utter oracles of Delphian ambiguity when she did not choose to be direct. In heaven she will probably sit between the Héloïses and the Cleopatras.

THOSE WHO ARE FOUND WHERE THERE IS SAID TO BE NOBODY

VIII

AS soon as the sad little boy had withdrawn from the fire he clasped the money tight in the palm of his hand, as if thereby to fortify his courage, and began to run. There was really little danger in allowing a child to go home alone on this part of Egdon Heath. The distance to the boy's house was not more than three-eighths of a mile, his father's cottage, and one other a few yards further on, forming part of the small hamlet of Mistover Knap: the third and only remaining house was that of Captain Vye and Eustacia, which stood quite away from the small cottages, and was the loneliest of lonely houses on these thinly populated slopes.

He ran until he was out of breath, and then, becoming more courageous, walked leisurely along, singing in an old voice a little song about a sailor-boy and a fair one, and bright gold in store. In the middle of this the child stopped: from a pit under the hill ahead of him shone a light, whence proceeded a cloud of floating dust and a smacking noise.

Only unusual sights and sounds frightened the boy. The shrivelled voice of the heath did not alarm him, for that was familiar. The thorn-bushes which arose in his path from time to time were less satisfactory, for they whistled gloomily, and had a ghastly habit after dark of putting on the shapes of jumping madmen, sprawling giants, and hideous cripples. Lights were not uncommon this evening, but the nature of all of them was different from this. Discretion rather than terror prompted the boy to turn back instead of passing the light, with a view of asking Miss Eustacia Vye to let her servant accompany him home.

When the boy had reascended to the top of the valley he found the fire to be still burning on the bank, though lower than before. Beside it, instead of Eustacia's solitary form, he saw two persons, the second being a man. The boy crept along under the bank to ascertain from the nature of the proceedings if it would be prudent to interrupt so splendid a creature as Miss Eustacia on his poor trivial account.

After listening under the bank for some minutes to the talk he turned in a perplexed and doubting manner and began to withdraw as silently as he had come. That he did not, upon the whole, think it advisable to interrupt her conversation with Wildeve, without being prepared to bear the whole weight of her displeasure, was obvious.

Here was a Scyllæo-Charybdean position for a poor boy. Pausing when again safe from discovery he finally decided to face the pit phenomenon as the lesser evil. With a heavy sigh he retraced the slope, and followed the path he had followed before

The light had gone, the rising dust had disappeared—he hoped for ever. He marched resolutely along, and found nothing to alarm him till, coming within a few yards of the sandpit, he heard a slight noise in front, which led him to halt. The halt was but momentary, for the noise resolved itself into the steady bites of two animals grazing.

'Two he'th-croppers down here,' he said aloud. 'I have never known 'em come down so far afore.'

The animals were in the direct line of his path, but that the child thought little of; he had played round the fetlocks of horses from his infancy. On coming nearer, however, the boy was somewhat surprised to find that the little creatures did not run off, and that each wore a clog, to prevent his going astray; this signified that they had been broken in. He could now see the interior of the pit, which, being in the side of the hill, had a level entrance. In the innermost corner the square outline of a van appeared, with its back towards him. A light came from the interior, and threw a moving shadow upon the vertical face of gravel at the further side of the pit into which the vehicle faced.

The child assumed that this was the cart of a gipsy, and his dread of those wanderers reached but to that mild pitch which titillates rather than pains. Only a few inches of mud wall kept him and his family from being gipsies themselves. He skirted the gravel-pit at a respectful distance, ascended the slope, and came forward upon the brow, in order to look into the open door of the van and see the original of the shadow.

The picture alarmed the boy. By a little stove inside the van sat a figure red from head to heels—the man who had been Thomasin's friend. He was darning a stocking, which was red like the rest of him. Moreover, as he darned he smoked a pipe, the stem and bowl of which were red also.

At this moment one of the heath-croppers feeding in the outer shadows was audibly shaking off the clog attached to its foot. Aroused by the sound the reddleman laid down his stocking, lit a lantern which hung beside him, and came out from the van. In sticking up the candle he lifted the lantern to his face, and the light shone into the whites of his eyes and upon his ivory teeth, which, in contrast with the red surrounding, lent him a startling aspect enough to the gaze of a juvenile. The boy knew too well for his peace of mind upon whose lair he had lighted.

Uglier persons than gipsies were known to cross Egdon at times, and a reddleman was one of them.

'How I wish 'twas only a gipsy!' he murmured.

The man was by this time coming back from the horses. In his fear of being seen the boy rendered detection certain by nervous motion. The heather and peat stratum overhung the brow of the pit in mats, hiding the actual verge. The boy had stepped beyond the solid ground; the heather now gave way, and down he rolled over the scarp of grey sand to the very foot of the man.

The red man opened the lantern and turned it upon the figure of the prostrate boy.

'Who be ye?' he said.

'Johnny Nunsuch, master!'

'What were you doing up there?'

'I don't know.'

'Watching me, I suppose?'

'Yes, master.'

'What did you watch me for?'

'Because I was coming home from Miss Vye's bonfire.'

'Beest hurt?'

'No.'

'Why, yes, you be: your hand is bleeding. Come under my tilt and let me tie it up.'

'Please let me look for my sixpence.'

'How did you come by that?'

'Miss Vye gied it to me for keeping up her bonfire.'

The sixpence was found, and the man went to the van, the boy behind, almost holding his breath.

The man took a piece of rag from a satchel containing sewing materials, tore off a strip, which, like everything else, was tinged red, and proceeded to bind up the wound.

'My eyes have got foggy-like—please may I sit down, master?' said the boy.

'To be sure, poor chap. 'Tis enough to make you feel fainty. Sit on that bundle.'

The man finished tying up the gash, and the boy said, 'I think I'll go home now, master.'

'You are rather afraid of me. Do you know what I be?'

The child surveyed his vermilion figure up and down with much misgiving, and finally said, 'Yes.'

'Well, what?'

'The reddleman!' he faltered.

'Yes, that's what I be. Though there's more than one. You little children think there's only one cuckoo, one fox, one giant, one devil, and one reddleman, when there's lots of us all.'

'Is there? You won't carry me off in your bags, will ye, master? 'Tis said that the reddleman will sometimes.'

'Nonsense. All that reddlemen do is sell reddle. You see all these bags at the back of my cart? They are not full of little boys—only full of red stuff.'

'Was you born a reddleman?'

'No, I took to it. I should be as white as you if I were to give up the trade—that is, I should be white in time—perhaps six months: not at first, because 'tis grow'd into my skin and won't wash out. Now, you'll never be afraid of a reddleman again, will ye?'

'No, never. Willy Orchard said he seed a red ghost here t'other day—perhaps that was you?'

'I was here t'other day.'

'Were you making that dusty light I saw by now?'

'O yes: I was beating out some bags. And have you had a good bonfire up there? I saw the light. Why did Miss Vye want a bonfire so bad that she should give you sixpence to keep it up?'

'I don't know. I was tired, but she made me bide and keep up the fire just the same, while she kept going up across Rainbarrow way.'

'And how long did that last?'

'Until a hopfrog jumped into the pond.'

The reddleman suddenly ceased to talk idly. 'A hopfrog ?' he inquired. 'Hopfrogs don't jump into ponds this time of year.'

'They do, for I heard one.'

'Certain-sure ?'

'Yes. She told me afore that I should hear'n ; and so I did. They say she's clever and deep, and perhaps she charmed 'en to come.'

'And what then ?'

'Then I came down here, and I was afeard, and I went back ; but I didn't like to speak to her, because of the gentleman, and I came on here again.'

'A gentleman—ah ! What did she say to him, my man ?'

'Told him she supposed he had not married the other woman because he liked his old sweetheart best ; and things like that.'

'What did the gentleman say to her, my sonny ?'

'He only said he did like her best, and how he was coming to see her again under Rainbarrow o' nights.'

'Ha !' cried the reddleman, slapping his hand against the side of his van so that the whole fabric shook under the blow. 'That's the secret o't !'

The little boy jumped clean from the stool.

'My man, don't you be afraid,' said the dealer in red, suddenly becoming gentle. 'I forgot you were here. That's only a curious way reddlemen have of going mad for a moment ; but they don't hurt anybody. And what did the lady say then ?'

'I can't mind. Please, Master Reddleman, may I go home-along now ?'

'Ay, to be sure you may. I'll go a bit of ways with you.'

He conducted the boy out of the gravel-pit and into the path leading to his mother's cottage. When the little figure had vanished in the darkness the reddleman returned, resumed his seat by the fire, and proceeded to darn again.

LOVE LEADS A SHREWD MAN INTO STRATEGY

IX

REDDLEMEN of the old school are now but seldom seen. Since the introduction of railways Wessex farmers have managed to do without these Mephistophelian visitants, and the bright pigment so largely used by shepherds in preparing sheep for the fair is obtained by other routes. Even those who yet survive are losing the poetry of existence which characterized them when the pursuit of the trade meant periodical journeys to the pit whence the material was dug, a regular camping out from month to month, except in the depth of winter, a peregrination among farms which could be counted by the hundred, and in spite of this Arab existence the preservation of that respectability which is insured by the never-failing production of a well-lined purse.

Reddle spreads its lively hues over everything it lights on, and stamps unmistakably, as with the mark of Cain, any person who has handled it half an hour.

A child's first sight of a reddleman was an epoch in his life. That blood-coloured figure was a sublimation of all the horrid dreams which had afflicted the juvenile spirit since imagination began. 'The reddleman is coming for you!' had been the formulated threat of Wessex mothers for many generations. He was successfully supplanted for a while, at the beginning of the present century, by Buonaparte; but as process of time rendered the latter personage stale and ineffective the older phrase resumed its early prominence. And now the reddleman has in his turn followed Buonaparte to the land of worn-out bogeys, and his place is filled by modern inventions.

The reddleman lived like a gipsy; but gipsies he scorned. He was about as thriving as travelling basket and mat makers; but he had nothing to do with them. He was more decently born and brought up than the cattle-drovers who passed and repassed him in his wanderings; but they merely nodded to him. His stock was more valuable than that of pedlars; but they did not think so, and passed his cart with eyes straight ahead. He was such an unnatural colour to look at that the men of roundabouts and wax-work shows seemed gentlemen beside him; but he considered them low company, and remained aloof. Among all these squatters and folks of the road the reddleman continually found himself; yet he was not of them. His occupation tended to isolate him, and isolated he was mostly seen to be.

It was sometimes suggested that reddlemen were criminals for whose misdeeds other men had wrongfully suffered: that in escaping the law they had not escaped their own consciences, and had taken to the trade as a lifelong penance. Else why should they have chosen it? In the present case such a question would have been particularly apposite. The reddleman who had entered Egdon that afternoon was an instance of the pleasing being wasted to form the ground-work of the singular, when an ugly foundation would have done just as well for that purpose. The one point that was forbidding about this reddleman was his colour. Freed from that he would have been as agreeable a specimen of rustic manhood as one would often see. A keen observer might have been inclined to think—which was, indeed, partly the truth—that he had relinquished his proper station in life for want of interest in it. Moreover, after looking at him one would have hazarded the guess that good-nature, and an acuteness as extreme as it could be without verging on craft, formed the frame-work of his character.

While he darned the stocking his face became rigid with thought. Softer expressions followed this, and then again recurred the tender sadness which had sat upon him during his drive along the highway that afternoon. Presently his needle stopped. He laid down the stocking, arose from his seat, and took a leathern pouch from a hook in the corner of the van. This contained among other articles a brown-paper packet, which, to judge from the hinge-like character of its worn folds, seemed to have been carefully opened and closed a good many times. He sat down on a three-legged milking-stool that formed the only seat in the van, and, examining his packet by the light of a candle, took thence an old letter and spread it open. The writing had originally been traced on white paper, but the letter had now assumed a pale red tinge from the accident of its situation ; and the black strokes of writing thereon looked like the twigs of a winter hedge against a vermilion sunset. The letter bore a date some two years previous to that time, and was signed 'Thomasin Yeobright.' It ran as follows :—

DEAR DIGGORY VENN,—The question you put when you overtook me coming home from Pond-close gave me such a surprise that I am afraid I did not make you exactly understand what I meant. Of course, if my aunt had not met me I could have explained all then at once, but as it was there was no chance. I have been quite uneasy since, as you know I do not wish to pain you, yet I fear I shall be doing so now in contradicting what I seemed to say then. I cannot, Diggory, marry you, or think of letting you call me your sweetheart. I could not, indeed, Diggory. I hope you will not much mind my saying this, and feel in a great pain. It makes me very sad when I think it may, for I like you very much, and I always put you next to my cousin Clym in my mind. There are so many reasons why we cannot be married that I can hardly name them all in a letter. I did not in the least expect that you were going to speak on such a thing when you followed me, because I had never thought of you in the sense of a lover at all. You must not becall me for laughing when you spoke; you mistook when you thought I laughed at you as a foolish man. I laughed because the idea was so odd, and not at you at all. The great reason with my own personal self for not letting you court me is, that I do not feel the things a woman ought to feel who consents to walk with you with the meaning of being your wife. It is not as you think, that I have another in my mind, for I do not encourage anybody, and never have in my life. Another reason is my aunt. She would not, I know, agree to it, even if I wished to have you. She likes you very well, but she will want me to look a little higher than a small dairy-farmer, and marry a professional man. I hope you will not set your heart against me for writing plainly, but I felt you might try to see me again, and it is better that we should not meet. I shall always think of you as a good man, and be anxious for your well-doing. I send this by Jane Orchard's little maid,—And remain Diggory, your faithful friend,

THOMASIN YEOBRIGHT.

To Mr. VENN, Dairy-farmer.

Since the arrival of that letter, on a certain autumn morning long ago, the reddleman and Thomasin had not met till to-day. During the interval he had shifted his position even further from hers than it had originally been, by adopting the reddle trade; though he was really in very good circumstances still. Indeed, seeing that his expenditure was only one-fourth of his income, he might have been called a prosperous man.

Rejected suitors take to roaming as naturally as unhived bees; and the business to which he had cynically devoted himself was in many ways congenial to Venn. But his wanderings, by mere stress of old emotions, had frequently taken an Egdon direction, though he never intruded upon her who attracted him thither. To be in

Thomasin's heath, and near her, yet unseen, was the one ewe-lamb of pleasure left to him.

Then came the incident of that day, and the reddleman, still loving her well, was excited by this accidental service to her at a critical juncture to vow an active devotion to her cause, instead of, as hitherto, sighing and holding aloof. After what had happened it was impossible that he should not doubt the honesty of Wildeve's intentions. But her hope was apparently centred upon him; and dismissing his regrets Venn determined to aid her to be happy in her own chosen way. That this way was, of all others, the most distressing to himself, was awkward enough; but the reddleman's love was generous.

His first active step in watching over Thomasin's interests was taken about seven o'clock the next evening, and was dictated by the news which he had learnt from the sad boy. That Eustacia was somehow the cause of Wildeve's carelessness in relation to the marriage had at once been Venn's conclusion on hearing of the secret meeting between them. It did not occur to his mind that Eustacia's love-signal to Wildeve was the tender effect upon the deserted beauty of the intelligence which her grandfather had brought home. His instinct was to regard her as a conspirator against rather than as an antecedent obstacle to Thomasin's happiness.

During the day he had been exceedingly anxious to learn the condition of Thomasin; but he did not venture to intrude upon a threshold to which he was a stranger, particularly at such an unpleasant moment as this. He had occupied his time in moving with his ponies and load to a new point in the heath, eastward to his previous station; and here he selected a nook with a careful eye to shelter from wind and rain, which seemed to mean that his stay there was to be a comparatively extended one. After this he returned on foot some part of the way that he had come; and, it being now dark, he diverged to the left till he stood behind a holly-bush on the edge of a pit not twenty yards from Rainbarrow.

He watched for a meeting there, but he watched in vain. Nobody except himself came near the spot that night.

But the loss of his labour produced little effect upon the reddleman. He had stood in the shoes of Tantalus, and seemed to look upon a certain mass of disappointment as the natural preface to all realizations, without which preface they would give cause for alarm.

The same hour the next evening found him again at the same place; but Eustacia and Wildeve, the expected trysters, did not appear.

He pursued precisely the same course yet four nights longer, and without success. But on the next, being the day-week of their previous meeting, he saw a female shape floating along the ridge and the outline of a young man ascending from the valley. They met in the little ditch encircling the tumulus—the original excavation from which it had been thrown up by the ancient British people.

The reddleman, stung with suspicion of wrong to Thomasin, was aroused to strategy in a moment. He instantly left the bush and crept forward on his hands and knees. When he had got as close as he might safely venture without discovery he found that, owing to a cross-wind, the conversation of the trysting pair could not be overheard.

Near him, as in divers places about the heath, were areas strewn with large turves, which lay edgeways and upside-down awaiting removal by Timothy Fairway, previous to the winter weather. He took two of these as he lay, and dragged them over him till one covered his head and shoulders, the other his back and legs. The reddleman would now have been quite invisible, even by daylight; the turves, standing upon him with the heather upwards, looked precisely as if they were growing. He crept along again, and the turves upon his back crept with him. Had he approached without any covering the chances are that he would not have been perceived in the dusk; approaching thus, it was as though he burrowed underground. In this manner he came quite close to where the two were standing.

'Wish to consult me on the matter?' reached his ears in the rich, impetuous accents of Eustacia Vye. 'Consult me? It is an indignity to me to talk so: I won't bear it any longer!' She began weeping. 'I have loved you, and have shown you that I loved you, much to my regret; and yet you can come and say in that frigid way that you wish to consult with me whether it would not be better to marry Thomasin. Better—of course it would be. Marry her: she is nearer to your own position in life than I am!'

'Yes, yes; that's very well,' said Wildeve peremptorily. 'But we must look at things as they are. Whatever blame may attach to me for having brought it about, Thomasin's position is at present much worse than yours. I simply tell you that I am in a strait.'

'But you shall not tell me! You must see that it is only harassing me. Damon, you have not acted well; you have sunk in my opinion. You have not valued my courtesy—the courtesy of a lady in loving you—who used to think of far more ambitious things. But it was Thomasin's fault. She won you away from me, and she deserves to suffer for it. Where is she staying now? Not that I care, nor where I am myself. Ah, if I were dead and gone how glad she would be! Where is she, I ask?'

'Thomasin is now staying at her aunt's shut up in a bedroom, and keeping out of everybody's sight,' he said indifferently.

'I don't think you care much about her even now,' said Eustacia with sudden joyousness; 'for if you did you wouldn't talk so coolly about her. Do you talk so coolly to her about me? Ah, I expect you do! Why did you originally go away from me? I don't think I can ever forgive you, except on one condition, that whenever you desert me, you come back again, sorry that you served me so.'

'I never wish to desert you.'

'I do not thank you for that. I should hate it to be all smooth. Indeed, I think I like you to desert me a little once now and then. Love is the dismallest thing where the lover is quite honest. O, it is a shame to say so; but it is true!' She indulged in a little laugh. 'My low spirits begin at the very idea. Don't you offer me tame love, or away you go!'

'I wish Tamsie were not such a confoundedly good little woman,' said Wildeve, 'so that I could be faithful to you without injuring a worthy person. It is I who am the sinner after all; I am not worth the little finger of either of you.'

'But you must not sacrifice yourself to her from any sense of justice,' replied Eustacia quickly. 'If you do not love her it is the most merciful thing in the long run to leave her as she is. That's always the best way. There, now I have been unwomanly, I suppose. When you have left me I am always angry with myself for things that I have said to you.'

Wildeve walked a pace or two among the heather without replying. The pause was filled up by the intonation of a pollard thorn a little way to windward, the breezes filtering through its unyielding twigs as through a strainer. It was as if the night sang dirges with clenched teeth.

She continued, half sorrowfully, 'Since meeting you last, it has occurred to me once or twice that perhaps it was not for love of me you did not marry her. Tell me, Damon: I'll try to bear it. Had I nothing whatever to do with the matter?'

'Do you press me to tell?'

'Yes, I must know. I see I have been too ready to believe in my own power.'

'Well, the immediate reason was that the licence would not do for the place, and before I could get another she ran away. Up to that point you had nothing to do with it. Since then her aunt has spoken to me in a tone which I don't at all like.'

'Yes, yes! I am nothing in it—I am nothing in it. You only trifle with me. Heaven, what can I, Eustacia Vye, be made of to think so much of you!'

'Nonsense; do not be so passionate. . . . Eustacia, how we roved among these bushes last year, when the hot days had got cool, and the shades of the hills kept us almost invisible in the hollows!'

She remained in moody silence till she said, 'Yes; and how I used to laugh at you for daring to look up to me! But you have well made me suffer for that since.'

'Yes, you served me cruelly enough until I thought I had found some one fairer than you. A blessed find for me, Eustacia.'

'Do you still think you found somebody fairer?'

'Sometimes I do, sometimes I don't. The scales are balanced so nicely that a feather would turn them.'

'But don't you really care whether I meet you or whether I don't?' she said slowly.

'I care a little, but not enough to break my rest,' replied the young man languidly. 'No, all that's past. I find there are two flowers where I thought there was only one. Perhaps there are three, or four, or any number as good as the first. . . . Mine is a curious fate. Who would have thought that all this could happen to me?'

She interrupted with a suppressed fire of which either love or anger seemed an equally possible issue, 'Do you love me now?'

'Who can say?'

'Tell me; I will know it!'

'I do, and I do not,' said he mischievously. 'That is, I have my times and my seasons. One moment you are too tall, another moment you are too do-nothing, another too melancholy, another too dark, another I don't know what, except—that you are not the whole world to me that you used to be, my dear. But you are a pleasant lady to know, and nice to meet, and I dare say as sweet as ever—almost.'

Eustacia was silent, and she turned from him, till she said, in a voice of suspended mightiness, 'I am for a walk, and this is my way.'

'Well, I can do worse than follow you.'

'You know you can't do otherwise, for all your moods and changes!' she answered defiantly. 'Say what you will; try as you may; keep away from me all that you can—you will never forget me. You will love me all your life long. You would jump to marry me!'

'So I would!' said Wildeve. 'Such strange thoughts as I've had from time to time, Eustacia; and they come to me this moment. You hate the heath as much as ever; that I know.'

'I do,' she murmured deeply. ''Tis my cross, my shame, and will be my death!'

'I abhor it too,' said he. 'How mournfully the wind blows round us now!'

She did not answer. Its tone was indeed solemn and pervasive. Compound utterances addressed themselves to their senses, and it was possible to view by ear the features of the neighbourhood. Acoustic pictures were returned from the darkened scenery; they could hear where the tracts of heather began and ended; where the furze was growing stalky and tall; where it had been recently cut; in what direction the fir-clump lay, and how near was the pit in which the hollies grew; for these differing features had their voices no less than their shapes and colours.

'God, how lonely it is!' resumed Wildeve. 'What are picturesque ravines and mists to us who see nothing else? Why should we stay here? Will you go with me to America? I have kindred in Wisconsin.'

'That wants consideration.'

'It seems impossible to do well here, unless one were a wild bird or a landscape-painter. Well?'

'Give me time,' she softly said, taking his hand. 'America is so far away. Are you going to walk with me a little way?'

As Eustacia uttered the latter words she retired from the base of the barrow, and Wildeve followed her, so that the reddleman could hear no more.

He lifted the turves and arose. Their black figures sank and disappeared from against the sky. They were as two horns which the sluggish heath had put forth from its crown, like a mollusc, and had now again drawn in.

The reddleman's walk across the vale, and over into the next where his cart lay, was not sprightly for a slim young fellow of twenty-four. His spirit was perturbed to aching. The breezes that blew around his mouth in that walk carried off upon them the accents of a commination.

He entered the van, where there was a fire in a stove. Without lighting his candle he sat down at once on the three-legged stool, and pondered on what he had seen and heard touching that still loved-one of his. He uttered a sound which was neither sigh nor sob, but was even more indicative than either of a troubled mind.

'My Tamsie,' he whispered heavily. 'What can be done? Yes, I will see that Eustacia Vye.'

A DESPERATE ATTEMPT AT PERSUASION

X

THE next morning, at the time when the height of the sun appeared very insignificant from any part of the heath as compared with the altitude of Rainbarrow, and when all the little hills in the lower levels were like an archipelago in a fog-formed Ægean, the reddleman came from the brambled nook which he had adopted as his quarters and ascended the slopes of Mistover Knap.

Though these shaggy hills were apparently so solitary, several keen round eyes were always ready on such a wintry morning as this to converge upon a passer-by. Feathered species sojourned here in hiding which would have created wonder if found elsewhere. A bustard haunted the spot, and not many years before this five and twenty might have been seen in Egdon at one time. Marsh-harriers looked up from the valley by Wildeve's. A cream-coloured courser had used to visit this hill, a bird so rare that not more than a dozen have ever been seen in England; but a barbarian rested neither night nor day till he had shot the African truant, and after that event cream-coloured coursers thought fit to enter Egdon no more.

A traveller who should walk and observe any of these visitants as Venn observed them now could feel himself to be in direct communication with regions unknown to man. Here in front of him was a wild mallard—just arrived from the home of the north wind. The creature brought within him an amplitude of Northern knowledge. Glacial catastrophes, snowstorm episodes, glittering auroral effects, Polaris in the zenith, Franklin underfoot, —the category of his commonplaces was wonderful. But the bird, like many other philosophers, seemed as he looked at the reddleman to think that a present moment of comfortable reality was worth a decade of memories.

Venn passed on through these towards the house of the isolated beauty who lived up among them and despised them. The day was Sunday; but as going to church, except to be married or buried, was exceptional at Egdon, this made little difference. He had determined upon the bold stroke of asking for an interview with Miss Vye—to attack her position as Thomasin's rival either by art or by storm, showing therein, somewhat too conspicuously, the want of gallantry characteristic of a certain astute sort of men, from clowns to kings. The great Frederick making war on the beautiful Archduchess, Napoleon refusing terms to the beautiful Queen of Prussia, were not more dead to difference of sex than the reddleman was, in his peculiar way, in planning the displacement of Eustacia.

To call at the captain's cottage was always more or less an undertaking for the inferior inhabitants. Though occasionally chatty, his moods were erratic, and nobody could be certain how he would behave at any particular moment. Eustacia was reserved, and lived very much to herself. Except the daughter of one of the cotters, who was their servant, and a lad who worked in the garden and stable, scarcely any one but themselves ever entered the house. They were the only genteel people of the district except the Yeobrights, and though far from rich, they did not feel that necessity for preserving a friendly face towards every man, bird, and beast which influenced their poorer neighbours.

When the reddleman entered the garden the old man was looking through his glass at the stain of blue sea in the distant landscape, the little anchors on his buttons twinkling in the sun. He recognized Venn as his companion on the highway, but made no remark on that circumstance, merely saying, 'Ah, reddleman—you here? Have a glass of grog?'

Venn declined, on the plea of it being too early, and stated that his business was with Miss Vye. The captain surveyed him from cap to waistcoat and from waistcoat to leggings for a few moments, and finally asked him to go indoors.

Miss Vye was not to be seen by anybody just then; and the reddleman waited in the window-bench of the kitchen, his hands hanging across his divergent knees, and his cap hanging from his hands.

'I suppose the young lady is not up yet?' he presently said to the servant.

'Not quite yet. Folks never call upon ladies at this time of day.'

'Then I'll step outside,' said Venn. 'If she is willing to see me, will she please send out word, and I'll come in.'

The reddleman left the house and loitered on the hill adjoining. A considerable time elapsed, and no request for his presence was brought. He was beginning to think that his scheme had failed, when he beheld the form of Eustacia herself coming leisurely towards him. A sense of novelty in giving audience to that singular figure had been sufficient to draw her forth.

She seemed to feel, after a bare look at Diggory Venn, that the man had come on a strange errand, and that he was not so mean as she had thought him; for her close approach did not cause him to writhe uneasily, or shift his feet, or show any of those little signs which escape an ingenuous rustic at the advent of the uncommon in womankind. On his inquiring if he might have a conversation with her she replied, ‘ Yes, walk beside me ’; and continued to move on.

Before they had gone far it occurred to the perspicacious reddleman that he would have acted more wisely by appearing less unimpressionable, and he resolved to correct the error as soon as he could find opportunity.

‘ I have made so bold, miss, as to step across and tell you some strange news which has come to my ears about that man.’

‘ Ah ! what man ? ’

He jerked his elbow to south-east—the direction of the Quiet Woman.

Eustacia turned quickly to him. ‘ Do you mean Mr. Wildeve ? ’

‘ Yes, there is trouble in a household on account of him, and I have come to let you know of it, because I believe you might have power to drive it away.’

‘ I ? What is the trouble ? ’

‘ It is quite a secret. It is that he may refuse to marry Thomasin Yeobright after all.’

Eustacia, though set inwardly pulsing by his words, was equal to her part in such a drama as this. She replied coldly, ‘ I do not wish to listen to this, and you must not expect me to interfere.’

‘ But, miss, you will hear one word ? ’

‘ I cannot. I am not interested in the marriage, and even if I were I could not compel Mr. Wildeve to do my bidding.’

‘ As the only lady on the heath I think you might,’ said Venn with subtle indirectness. ‘ This is how the case stands. Mr. Wildeve would marry Thomasin at once, and make all matters smooth, if so be there were not another woman in the case. This other woman is some person he has picked up with, and meets on the heath occasionally, I believe. He will never marry her, and yet through her he may never marry the woman who loves him dearly. Now, if you, miss, who have so much sway over us men-folk, were to insist that he should treat your young neighbour Tamsin with honourable kindness and give up the other woman, he would perhaps do it, and save her a good deal of misery.'

'Ah, my life!' said Eustacia, with a laugh which unclosed her lips so that the sun shone into her mouth as into a tulip, and lent it a similar scarlet fire. 'You think too much of my influence over men-folk indeed, reddleman. If I had such a power as you imagine I would go straight and use it for the good of anybody who has been kind to me—which Thomasin Yeobright has not particularly, to my knowledge.'

'Can it be that you really don't know of it—how much she has always thought of you?'

'I have never heard a word of it. Although we live only two miles apart I have never been inside her aunt's house in my life.'

The superciliousness that lurked in her manner told Venn that thus far he had utterly failed. He inwardly sighed and felt it necessary to unmask his second argument.

'Well, leaving that out of the question, 'tis in your power, I assure you, Miss Vye, to do a great deal of good to another woman.'

She shook her head.

'Your comeliness is law with Mr. Wildeve. It is law with all men who see 'ee. They say, "This well-favoured lady coming—what's her name? How handsome!" Handsomer than Thomasin Yeobright,' the reddleman persisted, saying to himself, 'God forgive a rascal for lying!' And she was handsomer, but the reddleman was far from thinking so. There was a certain obscurity in Eustacia's beauty, and Venn's eye was not trained. In her winter dress, as now, she was like the tiger-beetle, which, when observed in dull situations, seems to be of the quietest neutral colour, but under a full illumination blazes with dazzling splendour.

Eustacia could not help replying, though conscious that she endangered her dignity thereby. 'Many women are lovelier than Thomasin,' she said; 'so not much attaches to that.'

The reddleman suffered the wound and went on: 'He is a man who notices the looks of women, and you could twist him to your will like withywind, if you only had the mind.'

'Surely what she cannot do who has been so much with him I cannot do living up here away from him.'

The reddleman wheeled and looked her in the face. 'Miss Vye!' he said.

'Why do you say that—as if you doubted me?' She spoke faintly, and her breathing was quick. 'The idea of your speaking in that tone to me!' she added, with a forced smile of hauteur. 'What could have been in your mind to lead you to speak like that?'

'Miss Vye, why should you make-believe that you don't know this man?—I know why, certainly. He is beneath you, and you are ashamed.'

'You are mistaken. What do you mean?'

The reddleman had decided to play the card of truth. 'I was at the meeting by Rainbarrow last night and heard every word,' he said. 'The woman that stands between Wildeve and Thomasin is yourself.'

It was a disconcerting lift of the curtain, and the mortification of Candaules' wife glowed in her. The moment had arrived when her lip would tremble in spite of herself, and when the gasp could no longer be kept down.

'I am unwell,' she said hurriedly. 'No—it is not that—I am not in a humour to hear you further. Leave me, please.'

'I must speak, Miss Vye, in spite of paining you. What I would put before you is this. However it may come about—whether she is to blame, or you—her case is without doubt worse than yours. Your giving up

Mr. Wildeve will be a real advantage to you, for how could you marry him? Now she cannot get off so easily—everybody will blame her if she loses him. Then I ask you—not because her right is best, but because her situation is worst—to give him up to her.'

'No—I won't, I won't!' she said impetuously, quite forgetful of her previous manner towards the reddleman as an underling. 'Nobody has ever been served so! It was going on well—I will not be beaten down—by an inferior woman like her. It is very well for you to come and plead for her, but is she not herself the cause of all her own trouble? Am I not to show favour to any person I may choose without asking permission of a parcel of cottagers? She has come between me and my inclination, and now that she finds herself rightly punished she gets you to plead for her!'

'Indeed,' said Venn earnestly, 'she knows nothing whatever about it. It is only I who ask you to give him up. It will be better for her and you both. People will say bad things if they find out that a lady secretly meets a man who has ill-used another woman.'

'I have *not* injured her: he was mine before he was hers! He came back—because—because he liked me best!' she said wildly. 'But I lose all self-respect in talking to you. What am I giving way to!'

'I can keep secrets,' said Venn gently. 'You need not fear. I am the only man who knows of your meetings with him. There is but one thing more to speak of, and then I will be gone. I heard you say to him that you hated living here—that Egdon heath was a jail to you.'

'I did say so. There is a sort of beauty in the scenery, I know; but it is a jail to me. The man you mention does not save me from that feeling, though he lives here. I should have cared nothing for him had there been a better person near.'

The reddleman looked hopeful: after these words from her his third attempt seemed promising. 'As we have now opened our minds a bit, miss,' he said, 'I'll tell you what I have got to propose. Since I have taken to the reddle trade I travel a good deal, as you know.'

She inclined her head, and swept round so that her eyes rested in the misty vale beneath them.

'And in my travels I go near Budmouth. Now Budmouth is a wonderful place—wonderful—a great salt sheening sea bending into the land like a bow—thousands of gentlepeople walking up and down—bands of music playing—officers by sea and officers by land walking among the rest—out of every ten folk you meet nine of 'em in love.'

'I know it,' she said disdainfully. 'I know Budmouth better than you. I was born there. My father came to be a military musician there from abroad. Ah, my soul, Budmouth! I wish I was there now.'

The reddleman was surprised to see how a slow fire could blaze on occasion. 'If you were, miss,' he replied, 'in a week's time you would think no more of Wildeve than of one of those he'th-croppers that we see yond. Now, I could get you there.'

'How?' said Eustacia, with intense curiosity in her heavy eyes.

'My uncle has been for five and twenty years the trusty man of a rich widow-lady who has a beautiful house facing the sea. This lady has become old and lame, and she wants a young company-keeper to read and sing to her, but can't get one to her mind to save her life, though she've advertised in the papers, and tried half a dozen. She would jump to get you, and uncle would make it all easy.'

'I should have to work, perhaps?'

'No, not real work: you'd have a little to do, such as reading and that. You would not be wanted till New Year's Day.'

'I knew it meant work,' she said, drooping to languor again.

'I confess there would be a trifle to do in the way of amusing her; but though idle people might call it work, working people would call it play. Think of the company and the life you'd lead, miss; the gaiety you'd see, and the gentleman you'd marry. My uncle is to inquire for a trustworthy young lady from the country, as she don't like town girls.'

'It is to wear myself out to please her! and I won't go. O, if I could live in a gay town as a lady should, and go my own ways, and do my own doings, I'd give the wrinkled half of my life! Yes, reddleman, that would I.'

'Help me to get Thomasin happy, miss, and the chance shall be yours,' urged her companion.

'Chance!—'tis no chance,' she said proudly. 'What can a poor man like you offer me, indeed?—I am going indoors. I have nothing more to say. Don't your horses want feeding, or your reddlebags want mending, or don't you want to find buyers for your goods, that you stay idling here like this?'

Venn spoke not another word. With his hands behind him he turned away, that she might not see the hopeless disappointment in his face. The mental clearness and power he had found in this lonely girl had indeed filled his manner with misgiving even from the first few minutes of close quarters with her. Her youth and situation had led him to expect a simplicity quite at the beck of his method. But a system of inducement which might have carried weaker country lasses along with it had merely repelled Eustacia. As a rule, the word Budmouth meant fascination on Egdon. That Royal port and watering-place, if truly mirrored in the minds of the heath-folk, must have combined, in a charming and indescribable manner, a Carthaginian bustle of building with Tarentine luxuriousness and Baian health and beauty. Eustacia felt little less extravagantly about the place; but she would not sink her independence to get there.

When Diggory Venn had gone quite away, Eustacia

walked to the bank and looked down the wild and picturesque vale towards the sun, which was also in the direction of Wildeve's. The mist had now so far collapsed that the tips of the trees and bushes around his house could just be discerned, as if boring upwards through a vast white cobweb which cloaked them from the day. There was no doubt that her mind was inclined thitherward; indefinitely, fancifully—twining and untwining about him as the single object within her horizon on which dreams might crystallize. The man who had begun by being merely her amusement, and would never have been more than her hobby but for his skill in deserting her at the right moments, was now again her desire. Cessation in his love-making had revivified her love. Such feeling as Eustacia had idly given to Wildeve was dammed into a flood by Thomasin. She had used to tease Wildeve, but that was before another had favoured him. Often a drop of irony into an indifferent situation renders the whole piquant.

'I will never give him up—never!' she said impetuously.

The reddleman's hint that rumour might show her to disadvantage had no permanent terror for Eustacia. She was as unconcerned at that contingency as a goddess at a lack of linen. This did not originate in inherent shamelessness, but in her living too far from the world to feel the impact of public opinion. Zenobia in the desert could hardly have cared what was said about her at Rome. As far as social ethics were concerned Eustacia approached the savage state, though in emotion she was all the while an epicure. She had advanced to the secret recesses of sensuousness, yet had hardly crossed the threshold of conventionality.

THE DISHONESTY OF AN HONEST WOMAN

XI

THE reddleman had left Eustacia's presence with desponding views on Thomasin's future happiness; but he was awakened to the fact that one other channel remained untried by seeing, as he followed the way to his van, the form of Mrs. Yeobright slowly walking towards the Quiet Woman. He went across to her; and could almost perceive in her anxious face that this journey of hers to Wildeve was undertaken with the same object as his own to Eustacia.

She did not conceal the fact. 'Then,' said the reddleman, 'you may as well leave it alone, Mrs. Yeobright.'

'I half think so myself,' she said. 'But nothing else remains to be done besides pressing the question upon him.'

'I should like to say a word first,' said Venn firmly. 'Mr. Wildeve is not the only man who has asked Thomasin to marry him; and why should not another have a chance? Mrs. Yeobright, I should be glad to marry your niece, and would have done it any time these last two years. There, now it is out, and I have never told anybody before but herself.'

Mrs. Yeobright was not demonstrative, but her eyes

involuntarily glanced towards his singular though shapely figure.

'Looks are not everything,' said the reddleman, noticing the glance. 'There's many a calling that don't bring in so much as mine, if it comes to money; and perhaps I am not so much worse off than Wildeve. There is nobody so poor as these professional fellows who have failed; and if you shouldn't like my redness—well, I am not red by birth, you know; I only took to this business for a freak; and I might turn my hand to something else in good time.'

'I am much obliged to you for your interest in my niece; but I fear there would be objections. More than that, she is devoted to this man.'

'True; or I shouldn't have done what I have this morning.'

'Otherwise there would be no pain in the case, and you would not see me going to his house now. What was Thomasin's answer when you told her of your feelings?'

'She wrote that you would object to me; and other things.'

'She was in a measure right. You must not take this unkindly: I merely state it as a truth. You have been good to her, and we do not forget it. But as she was unwilling on her own account to be your wife, that settles the point without my wishes being concerned.'

'Yes. But there is a difference between then and now, ma'am. She is distressed now, and I have thought that if you were to talk to her about me, and think favourably of me yourself, there might be a chance of winning her round, and getting her quite independent of this Wildeve's backward and forward play, and his not knowing whether he'll have her or no.'

Mrs. Yeobright shook her head. 'Thomasin thinks, and I think with her, that she ought to be Wildeve's wife, if she means to appear before the world without a slur upon her name. If they marry soon, everybody will believe that an accident did really prevent the wedding. If not, it may cast a shade upon her character—at any rate make her ridiculous. In short, if it is anyhow possible they must marry now.'

'I thought that till half an hour ago. But, after all, why should her going off with him to Anglebury for a few hours do her any harm? Anybody who knows how pure she is will feel any such thought to be quite unjust. I have been trying this morning to help on this marriage with Wildeve—yes, I, ma'am—in the belief that I ought to do it, because she was so wrapped up in him. But I much question if I was right, after all. However, nothing came of it. And now I offer myself.'

Mrs. Yeobright appeared disinclined to enter further into the question. 'I fear I must go on,' she said. 'I do not see that anything else can be done.'

And she went on. But though this conversation did not divert Thomasin's aunt from her purposed interview with Wildeve, it made a considerable difference in her mode of conducting that interview. She thanked God for the weapon which the reddleman had put into her hands.

Wildeve was at home when she reached the inn. He showed her silently into the parlour, and closed the door. Mrs. Yeobright began—

'I have thought it my duty to call to-day. A new proposal has been made to me, which has rather astonished me. It will affect Thomasin greatly; and I have decided that it should at least be mentioned to you.'

'Yes? What is it?' he said civilly.

'It is, of course, in reference to her future. You may not be aware that another man has shown himself anxious to marry Thomasin. Now, though I have not encouraged him yet, I cannot conscientiously refuse him a chance any longer. I don't wish to be short with you; but I must be fair to him and to her.'

'Who is the man?' said Wildeve with surprise.

'One who has been in love with her longer than she has

with you. He proposed to her two years ago. At that time she refused him.'

'Well?'

'He has seen her lately, and has asked me for permission to pay his addresses to her. She may not refuse him twice.'

'What is his name?'

Mrs. Yeobright declined to say. 'He is a man Thomasin likes,' she added, 'and one whose constancy she respects at least. It seems to me that what she refused then she would be glad to get now. She is much annoyed at her awkward position.'

'She never once told me of this old lover.'

'The gentlest women are not such fools as to show *every* card.'

'Well, if she wants him I suppose she must have him.'

'It is easy enough to say that; but you don't see the difficulty. He wants her much more than she wants him; and before I can encourage anything of the sort I must have a clear understanding from you that you will not interfere to injure an arrangement which I promote in the belief that it is for the best. Suppose, when they are engaged, and everything is smoothly arranged for their marriage, that you should step between them and renew your suit? You might not win her back, but you might cause much unhappiness.'

'Of course I should do no such thing,' said Wildeve. 'But they are not engaged yet. How do you know that Thomasin would accept him?'

'That's a question I have carefully put to myself; and upon the whole the probabilities are in favour of her accepting him in time. I flatter myself that I have some influence over her. She is pliable, and I can be strong in my recommendations of him.'

'And in your disparagement of me at the same time.'

'Well, you may depend upon my not praising you,' she said drily. 'And if this seems like manœuvring, you must remember that her position is peculiar, and that she has been hardly used. I shall also be helped in making the match by her own desire to escape from the humiliation of her present state ; and a woman's pride in these cases will lead her a very great way. A little managing may be required to bring her round ; but I am equal to that, provided that you agree to the one thing indispensable ; that is, to make a distinct declaration that she is to think no more of you as a possible husband. That will pique her into accepting him.'

'I can hardly say that just now, Mrs. Yeobright. It is so sudden.'

'And so my whole plan is interfered with ! It is very inconvenient that you refuse to help my family even to the small extent of saying distinctly you will have nothing to do with us.'

Wildeve reflected uncomfortably. 'I confess I was not prepared for this,' he said. 'Of course I'll give her up if you wish, if it is necessary. But I thought I might be her husband.'

'We have heard that before.'

'Now, Mrs. Yeobright, don't let us disagree. Give me a fair time. I don't want to stand in the way of any better chance she may have ; only I wish you had let me know earlier. I will write to you or call in a day or two. Will that suffice ? '

'Yes,' she replied, 'provided you promise not to communicate with Thomasin without my knowledge.'

'I promise that,' he said. And the interview then terminated, Mrs. Yeobright returning homeward as she had come.

By far the greatest effect of her simple strategy on that day was, as often happens, in a quarter quite outside her view when arranging it. In the first place, her visit sent Wildeve the same evening after dark to Eustacia's house at Mistover.

At this hour the lonely dwelling was closely blinded

and shuttered from the chill and darkness without. Wildeve's clandestine plan with her was to take a little gravel in his hand and hold it to the crevice at the top of the window-shutter, which was on the outside, so that it should fall with a gentle rustle, resembling that of a mouse, between shutter and glass. This precaution in attracting her attention was to avoid arousing the suspicions of her grandfather.

The soft words, 'I hear; wait for me,' in Eustacia's voice from within told him that she was alone.

He waited in his customary manner by walking round the enclosure and idling by the pool, for Wildeve was never asked into the house by his proud though condescending mistress. She showed no sign of coming out in a hurry. The time wore on, and he began to grow impatient. In the course of twenty minutes she appeared from round the corner, and advanced as if merely taking an airing.

'You would not have kept me so long had you known what I come about,' he said with bitterness. 'Still, you are worth waiting for.'

'What has happened?' said Eustacia. 'I did not know you were in trouble. I too am gloomy enough.'

'I am not in trouble,' said he. 'It is merely that affairs have come to a head, and I must take a clear course.'

'What course is that?' she asked with attentive interest.

'And can you forget so soon what I proposed to you the other night? Why, take you from this place, and carry you away with me abroad.'

'I have not forgotten. But why have you come so unexpectedly to repeat the question, when you only promised to come next Saturday? I thought I was to have plenty of time to consider.'

'Yes, but the situation is different now.'

'Explain to me.'

'I don't want to explain, for I may pain you.'

'But I must know the reason of this hurry.'

'It is simply my ardour, dear Eustacia. Everything is smooth now.'

'Then why are you so ruffled?'

'I am not aware of it. All is as it should be. Mrs. Yeobright—but she is nothing to us.'

'Ah, I knew she had something to do with it! Come, I don't like reserve.'

'No—she has nothing. She only says she wishes me to give up Thomasin because another man is anxious to marry her. The woman, now she no longer needs me, actually shows off!' Wildeve's vexation had escaped him in spite of himself.

Eustacia was silent a long while. 'You are in the awkward position of an official who is no longer wanted,' she said in a changed tone.

'It seems so. But I have not yet seen Thomasin.'

'And that irritates you. Don't deny it, Damon. You are actually nettled by this slight from an unexpected quarter.'

'Well?'

'And you come to get me because you cannot get her. This is certainly a new position altogether. I am to be a stop-gap.'

'Please remember that I proposed the same thing the other day.'

Eustacia again remained in a sort of stupefied silence. What curious feeling was this coming over her? Was it really possible that her interest in Wildeve had been so entirely the result of antagonism that the glory and the dream departed from the man with the first sound that he was no longer coveted by her rival? She was, then, secure of him at last. Thomasin no longer required him. What a humiliating victory! He loved her best, she thought; and yet—dared she to murmur such treacherous criticism ever so softly?—what was the man worth whom a woman inferior to herself did not value? The sentiment which lurks more or less in all animate nature—that of not desiring the undesired of others—was lively as a passion in the supersubtle, epicurean heart of Eustacia. Her social superiority over him, which hitherto had scarcely ever impressed her, became unpleasantly insistent, and for the first time she felt that she had stooped in loving him.

'Well, darling, you agree?' said Wildeve.

'If it could be London, or even Budmouth, instead of America,' she murmured languidly. 'Well, I will think. It is too great a thing for me to decide offhand. I wish I hated the heath less—or loved you more.'

'You can be painfully frank. You loved me a month ago warmly enough to go anywhere with me.'

'And you loved Thomasin.'

'Yes, perhaps that was where the reason lay,' he returned, with almost a sneer. 'I don't hate her now.'

'Exactly. The only thing is that you can no longer get her.'

'Come—no taunts, Eustacia, or we shall quarrel. If you don't agree to go with me, and agree shortly, I shall go by myself.'

'Or try Thomasin again. Damon, how strange it seems that you could have married her or me indifferently, and only have come to me because I am—cheapest! Yes, yes—it is true. There was a time when I should have exclaimed against a man of that sort, and been quite wild; but it is all past now.'

'Will you go, dearest? Come secretly with me to Bristol, marry me, and turn our backs upon this dog-hole of England for ever? Say Yes.'

'I want to get away from here at almost any cost, she said with weariness, 'but I don't like to go with you. Give me more time to decide.'

'I have already,' said Wildeve. 'Well, I give you one more week.'

'A little longer, so that I may tell you decisively. I

have to consider so many things. Fancy Thomasin being anxious to get rid of you! I cannot forget it.'

'Never mind that. Say Monday week. I will be here precisely at this time.'

'Let it be at Rainbarrow,' said she. 'This is too near home; my grandfather may be walking out.'

'Thank you, dear. On Monday week at this time I will be at the Barrow. Till then good-bye.'

'Good-bye. No, no, you must not touch me now. Shaking hands is enough till I have made up my mind.'

Eustacia watched his shadowy form till it had disappeared. She placed her hand to her forehead and breathed heavily; and then her rich, romantic lips parted under that homely impulse—a yawn. She was immediately angry at having betrayed even to herself the possible evanescence of her passion for him. She could not admit at once that she might have over-estimated Wildeve, for to perceive his mediocrity now was to admit her own great folly heretofore. And the discovery that she was the owner of a disposition so purely that of the dog in the manger, had something in it which at first made her ashamed.

The fruit of Mrs. Yeobright's diplomacy was indeed remarkable, though not as yet of the kind she had anticipated. It had appreciably influenced Wildeve, but it was influencing Eustacia far more. Her lover was no longer to her an exciting man whom many women strove for, and herself could only retain by striving with them. He was a superfluity.

She went indoors in that peculiar state of misery which is not exactly grief, and which especially attends the dawnings of reason in the latter days of an ill-judged, transient love. To be conscious that the end of the dream is approaching, and yet has not absolutely come, is one of the most wearisome as well as the most curious stages along the course between the beginning of a passion and its end.

Her grandfather had returned, and was busily engaged in pouring some gallons of newly arrived rum into the square bottles of his square cellaret. Whenever these home supplies were exhausted he would go to the Quiet Woman, and, standing with his back to the fire, grog in hand, tell remarkable stories of how he had lived seven years under the water-line of his ship, and other naval wonders, to the natives, who hoped too earnestly for a treat of ale from the teller to exhibit any doubts of his truth.

He had been there this evening. 'I suppose you have heard the Egdon news, Eustacia?' he said, without looking up from the bottles. 'The men have been talking about it at the Woman as if it were of national importance.'

'I have heard none,' she said.

'Young Clym Yeobright, as they call him, is coming home next week to spend Christmas with his mother. He is a fine fellow by this time, it seems. I suppose you remember him?'

'I never saw him in my life.'

'Ah, true; he left before you came here. I well remember him as a promising boy.'

'Where has he been living all these years?'

'In that rookery of pomp and vanity, Paris, I believe.'

BOOK SECOND

THE ARRIVAL

TIDINGS OF THE COMER

I

ON fine days at this time of the year, and earlier, certain ephemeral operations were apt to disturb, in their trifling way, the majestic calm of Egdon Heath. They were activities which, beside those of a town, a village, or even a farm, would have appeared as the ferment of stagnation merely, a creeping of the flesh of somnolence. But here, away from comparisons, shut in by the stable hills, among which mere walking had the novelty of pageantry, and where any man could imagine himself to be Adam without the least difficulty, they attracted the attention of every bird within eyeshot, every reptile not yet asleep, and set the surrounding rabbits curiously watching from hillocks at a safe distance.

The performance was that of bringing together and building into a stack the furze-faggots which Humphrey had been cutting for the captain's use during the foregoing fine days. The stack was at the end of the dwelling, and the men engaged in building it were Humphrey and Sam, the old man looking on.

It was a fine and quiet afternoon, about three o'clock; but the winter solstice having stealthily come on, the lowness of the sun caused the hour to seem later than it actually was, there being little here to remind an inhabitant that he must unlearn his summer experience of the sky as a dial. In the course of many days and weeks sunrise had advanced its quarters from north-east to south-east, sunset had receded from north-west to south-west; but Egdon had hardly heeded the change.

Eustacia was indoors in the dining-room, which was really more like a kitchen, having a stone floor and a gaping chimney-corner. The air was still, and while she lingered a moment here alone sounds of voices in conversation came to her ears directly down the chimney. She entered the recess, and, listening, looked up the old irregular shaft, with its cavernous hollows, where the smoke blundered about on its way to the square bit of sky at the top, from which the daylight struck down with a pallid glare upon the tatters of soot draping the flue as sea-weed drapes a rocky fissure.

She remembered: the furze-stack was not far from the chimney, and the voices were those of the workers.

Her grandfather joined in the conversation. 'That lad ought never to have left home. His father's occupation would have suited him best, and the boy should have followed on. I don't believe in these new moves in families. My father was a sailor, so was I, and so should my son have been if I had had one.'

'The place he's been living at is Paris,' said Humphrey, 'and they tell me 'tis where the king's head was cut off years ago. My poor mother used to tell me about that business. "Hummy," she used to say, "I was a young maid then, and as I was at home ironing mother's caps one afternoon the parson came in and said, 'They've cut the king's head off, Jane; and what 'twill be next God knows.'"'

'A good many of us knew as well as He before long,' said the captain, chuckling. 'I lived seven years under water on account of it in my boyhood—in that damned surgery of the *Triumph*, seeing men brought down to the cockpit with their legs and arms blown to Jericho. . . . And so the young man has settled in Paris. Manager to a diamond merchant, or some such thing, is he not?'

'Yes, sir, that's it. 'Tis a blazing great business that he belongs to, so I've heard his mother say—like a king's palace, as far as diments go.'

'I can well mind when he left home,' said Sam.

''Tis a good thing for the feller,' said Humphrey. 'A sight of times better to be selling diments than nobbling about here.'

'It must cost a good few shillings to deal at such a place.'

'A good few indeed, my man,' replied the captain. 'Yes, you may make away with a deal of money and be neither drunkard nor glutton.'

'They say, too, that Clym Yeobright is become a real perusing man, with the strangest notions about things. There, that's because he went to school early, such as the school was.'

'Strange notions, has he?' said the old man. 'Ah, there's too much of that sending to school in these days! It only does harm. Every gatepost and barn's door you come to is sure to have some bad word or other chalked upon it by the young rascals: a woman can hardly pass for shame sometimes. If they'd never been taught how to write they wouldn't have been able to scribble such villainy. Their fathers couldn't do it, and the country was all the better for it.'

'Now, I should think, cap'n, that Miss Eustacia had about as much in her head that comes from books as anybody about here?'

'Perhaps if Miss Eustacia, too, had less romantic nonsense in her head it would be better for her,' said the captain shortly; after which he walked away.

'I say, Sam,' observed Humphrey when the old man was gone, 'she and Clym Yeobright would make a very pretty pigeon-pair—hey? If they wouldn't I'll be dazed! Both of one mind about niceties for certain, and learned in print, and always thinking about high doctrine—there couldn't be a better couple if they were made o' purpose. Clym's family is as good as hers. His father was a farmer, that's true ; but his mother was a sort of lady, as we know. Nothing would please me better than to see them two man and wife.'

'They'd look very natty, arm-in-crook together, and their best clothes on, whether or no, if he's at all the well-favoured fellow he used to be.'

'They would, Humphrey. Well, I should like to see the chap terrible much after so many years. If I knew for certain when he was coming I'd stroll out three or four miles to meet him and help carry anything for'n ; though I suppose he's altered from the boy he was. They say he can talk French as fast as a maid can eat blackberries ; and if so, depend upon it we who have stayed at home shall seem no more than scroff in his eyes.'

'Coming across the water to Budmouth by steamer, isn't he ? '

'Yes ; but how he's coming from Budmouth I don't know.'

'That's a bad trouble about his cousin Thomasin. I wonder such a nice-notioned fellow as Clym likes to come home into it. What a nunnywatch we were in, to be sure, when we heard they weren't married at all, after singing to 'em as man and wife that night ! Be dazed if I should like a relation of mine to have been made such a fool of by a man. It makes the family look small.'

'Yes. Poor maid, her heart has ached enough about it. Her health is suffering from it, I hear, for she will bide entirely indoors. We never see her out now, scampering over the furze with a face as red as a rose, as she used to do.'

'I've heard she wouldn't have Wildeve now if he asked her.'

'You have ? 'Tis news to me.'

While the furze-gatherers had desultorily conversed thus Eustacia's face gradually bent to the hearth in a profound reverie, her toe unconsciously tapping the dry turf which lay burning at her feet.

The subject of their discourse had been keenly interesting to her. A young and clever man was coming into that lonely heath from, of all contrasting places in the world, Paris. It was like a man coming from heaven. More singular still, the heathmen had instinctively coupled her and this man together in their minds as a pair born for each other.

That five minutes of overhearing furnished Eustacia with visions enough to fill the whole blank afternoon. Such sudden alternations from mental vacuity do sometimes occur thus quietly. She could never have believed in the morning that her colourless inner world would before night become as animated as water under a microscope, and that without the arrival of a single visitor. The words of Sam and Humphrey on the harmony between the unknown and herself had on her mind the effect of the invading Bard's prelude in the 'Castle of Indolence,' at which myriads of imprisoned shapes arose where had previously appeared the stillness of a void.

Involved in these imaginings she knew nothing of time. When she became conscious of externals it was dusk. The furze-rick was finished; the men had gone home. Eustacia went upstairs, thinking that she would take a walk at this her usual time; and she determined that her walk should be in the direction of Blooms-End, the birthplace of young Yeobright and the present home of his mother. She had no reason for walking elsewhere, and why should she not go that way? The scene of a day-dream is sufficient for a pilgrimage at nineteen. To look at the palings before the Yeobrights' house had the dignity of a necessary performance. Strange that such a piece of idling should have seemed an important errand.

She put on her bonnet, and, leaving the house, descended the hill on the side towards Blooms-End, where she walked slowly along the valley for a distance of a mile and a half. This brought her to a spot in which the green bottom of the dale began to widen, the furze bushes to recede yet further from the path on each side, till they were diminished to an isolated one here and there by the increasing fertility of the soil. Beyond the irregular carpet of grass was a row of white palings, which marked the verge of the heath in this latitude. They showed upon the dusky scene that they bordered as distinctly as white lace on velvet. Behind the white palings was a little garden; behind the garden an old, irregular, thatched house, facing the heath, and commanding a full view of the valley. This was the obscure, removed spot to which was about to return a man whose latter life had been passed in the French capital—the centre and vortex of the fashionable world.

THE PEOPLE AT BLOOMS-END

MAKE READY

II

ALL that afternoon the expected arrival of the subject of Eustacia's ruminations created a bustle of preparation at Blooms-End. Thomasin had been persuaded by her aunt, and by an instinctive impulse of loyalty towards her cousin Clym, to bestir herself on his account with an alacrity unusual in her during these most sorrowful days of her life. At the time that Eustacia was listening to the rick-makers' conversation on Clym's return, Thomasin was climbing into a loft over her aunt's fuel-house, where the store-apples were kept, to search out the best and largest of them for the coming holiday-time.

The loft was lighted by a semicircular hole, through which the pigeons crept to their lodgings in the same high quarters of the premises ; and from this hole the sun shone in a bright yellow patch upon the figure of the maiden as she knelt and plunged her naked arms into the soft brown fern, which, from its abundance, was used on Egdon in packing away stores of all kinds. The pigeons were flying about her head with the greatest unconcern, and the face of her aunt was just visible above the floor of the loft, lit by a few stray motes of light, as she stood half-way up the ladder, looking at a spot into which she was not climber enough to venture.

'Now a few russets, Tamsin. He used to like them almost as well as ribstones.'

Thomasin turned and rolled aside the fern from another nook, where more mellow fruit greeted her with its ripe smell. Before picking them out she stopped a moment.

'Dear Clym, I wonder how your face looks now?' she said, gazing abstractedly at the pigeon-hole, which admitted the sunlight so directly upon her brown hair and transparent tissues that it almost seemed to shine through her.

'If he could have been dear to you in another way,' said Mrs. Yeobright from the ladder, 'this might have been a happy meeting.'

'Is there any use in saying what can do no good, aunt?'

'Yes,' said her aunt, with some warmth. 'To thoroughly fill the air with the past misfortune, so that other girls may take warning and keep clear of it.'

Thomasin lowered her face to the apples again. 'I am a warning to others, just as thieves and drunkards and gamblers are,' she said in a low voice. 'What a class to belong to! Do I really belong to them? 'Tis absurd! Yet why, aunt, does everybody keep on making me think that I do, by the way they behave towards me? Why don't people judge me by my acts? Now, look at me as I kneel here, picking up these apples—do I look like a lost woman? . . . I wish all good women were as good as I!' she added vehemently.

'Strangers don't see you as I do,' said Mrs. Yeobright; 'they judge from false report. Well, it is a silly job, and I am partly to blame.'

'How quickly a rash thing can be done!' replied the girl. Her lips were quivering, and tears so crowded themselves into her eyes that she could hardly distinguish apples from fern as she continued industriously searching to hide her weakness.

'As soon as you have finished getting the apples,' her

aunt said, descending the ladder, 'come down, and we'll go for the holly. There is nobody on the heath this afternoon, and you need not fear being stared at. We must get some berries, or Clym will never believe in our preparations.'

Thomasin came down when the apples were collected, and together they went through the white palings to the heath beyond. The open hills were airy and clear, and the remote atmosphere appeared, as it often appears on a fine winter day, in distinct planes of illumination independently toned, the rays which lit the nearer tracts of landscape streaming visibly across those further off; a stratum of ensaffroned light was imposed on a stratum of deep blue, and behind these lay still remoter scenes wrapped in frigid grey.

They reached the place where the hollies grew, which was in a conical pit, so that the tops of the trees were not much above the general level of the ground. Thomasin stepped up into a fork of one of the bushes, as she had done under happier circumstances on many similar occasions, and with a small chopper that they had brought she began to lop off the heavily-berried boughs.

'Don't scratch your face,' said her aunt, who stood at the edge of the pit, regarding the girl as she held on amid the glistening green and scarlet masses of the tree. 'Will you walk with me to meet him this evening?'

'I should like to. Else it would seem as if I had forgotten him,' said Thomasin, tossing out a bough. 'Not that that would matter much; I belong to one man; nothing can alter that. And that man I must marry, for my pride's sake.'

'I am afraid——' began Mrs. Yeobright.

'Ah, you think, "That weak girl—how is she going to get a man to marry her when she chooses?" But let me tell you one thing, aunt: Mr. Wildeve is not a profligate man, any more than I am an improper woman. He has an unfortunate manner, and doesn't try to make people like him if they don't wish to do it of their own accord.'

'Thomasin,' said Mrs. Yeobright quietly, fixing her eye upon her niece, 'do you think you deceive me in your defence of Mr. Wildeve ?'

'How do you mean ?'

'I have long had a suspicion that your love for him has changed its colour since you have found him not to be the saint you thought him, and that you act a part to me.'

'He wished to marry me, and I wish to marry him.'

'Now, I put it to you : would you at this present moment agree to be his wife if that had not happened to entangle you with him ?'

Thomasin looked into the tree and appeared much disturbed. 'Aunt,' she said presently, 'I have, I think, a right to refuse to answer that question.'

'Yes, you have.'

'You may think what you choose. I have never implied to you by word or deed that I have grown to think otherwise of him, and I never will. And I shall marry him.'

'Well, wait till he repeats his offer. I think he may do it, now that he knows—something I told him. I don't for a moment dispute that it is the most proper thing for you to marry him. Much as I have objected to him in bygone days, I agree with you now, you may be sure. It is the only way out of a false position, and a very galling one.'

'What did you tell him ?'

'That he was standing in the way of another lover of yours.'

'Aunt,' said Thomasin, with round eyes, 'what *do* you mean ?'

'Don't be alarmed ; it was my duty. I can say no more about it now, but when it is over I will tell you exactly what I said, and why I said it.'

Thomasin was perforce content.

'And you will keep the secret of my would-be marriage from Clym for the present?' she next asked.

'I have given my word to. But what is the use of it? He must soon know what has happened. A mere look at your face will show him that something is wrong.'

Thomasin turned and regarded her aunt from the tree. 'Now, hearken to me,' she said, her delicate voice expanding into firmness by a force which was other than physical. 'Tell him nothing. If he finds out that I am not worthy to be his cousin, let him. But, since he loved me once, we will not pain him by telling him my trouble too soon. The air is full of the story, I know; but gossips will not dare to speak of it to him for the first few days. His closeness to me is the very thing that will hinder the tale from reaching him early. If I am not made safe from sneers in a week or two I will tell him myself.'

The earnestness with which Thomasin spoke prevented further objections. Her aunt simply said, 'Very well. He should by rights have been told at the time that the wedding was going to be. He will never forgive you for your secrecy.'

'Yes, he will, when he knows it was because I wished to spare him, and that I did not expect him home so soon. And you must not let me stand in the way of your Christmas party. Putting it off would only make matters worse.'

'Of course I shall not. I do not wish to show myself beaten before all Egdon, and the sport of a man like Wildeve. We have enough berries now, I think, and we had better take them home. By the time we have decked the house with this and hung up the mistletoe, we must think of starting to meet him.'

Thomasin came out of the tree, shook from her hair and dress the loose berries which had fallen thereon, and went down the hill with her aunt, each woman bearing half the gathered boughs. It was now nearly four o'clock, and the sunlight was leaving the vales. When the west grew red the two relatives came again from the house and plunged into the heath in a different direction from the first, towards a point in the distant highway along which the expected man was to return.

HOW A LITTLE SOUND PRODUCED A GREAT DREAM

III

EUSTACIA stood just within the heath, straining her eyes in the direction of Mrs. Yeobright's house and premises. No light, sound, or movement was perceptible there. The evening was chilly; the spot was dark and lonely. She inferred that the guest had not yet come; and after lingering ten or fifteen minutes she turned again towards home.

She had not far retraced her steps when sounds in front of her betokened the approach of persons in conversation along the same path. Soon their heads became visible against the sky. They were walking slowly; and though it was too dark for much discovery of character from aspect, the gait of them showed that they were not workers on the heath. Eustacia stepped a little out of the foot-track to let them pass. They were two women and a man; and the voices of the women were those of Mrs. Yeobright and Thomasin.

They went by her, and at the moment of passing appeared to discern her dusky form. There came to her ears in a masculine voice, 'Good night!'

She murmured a reply, glided by them, and turned round. She could not, for a moment, believe that chance, unrequested, had brought into her presence the soul of the house she had gone to inspect, the man without whom her inspection would not have been thought of.

She strained her eyes to see them, but was unable. Such was her intentness, however, that it seemed as if her ears were performing the functions of seeing as well as hearing. This extension of power can almost be believed in at such moments. The deaf Dr. Kitto was probably under the influence of a parallel fancy when he described his body as having become, by long endeavour, so sensitive to vibrations that he had gained the power of perceiving by it as by ears.

She could follow every word that the ramblers uttered. They were talking no secrets. They were merely indulging in the ordinary vivacious chat of relatives who have long been parted in person though not in soul. But it was not to the words that Eustacia listened; she could not even have recalled, a few minutes later, what the words were. It was to the alternating voice that gave out about one-tenth of them—the voice that had wished her good night. Sometimes this throat uttered Yes, sometimes it uttered No; sometimes it made inquiries about a timeworn denizen of the place. Once it surprised her notions by remarking upon the friendliness and geniality written in the faces of the hills around.

The three voices passed on, and decayed and died out upon her ear. Thus much had been granted her; and all besides withheld. No event could have been more exciting. During the greater part of the afternoon she had been entrancing herself by imagining the fascination which must attend a man come direct from beautiful Paris—laden with its atmosphere, familiar with its charms. And this man had greeted her.

With the departure of the figures the profuse articulations of the women wasted away from her memory; but the accents of the other stayed on. Was there anything in the voice of Mrs. Yeobright's son—for Clym it was—

startling as a sound? No: it was simply comprehensive. All emotional things were possible to the speaker of that 'good night.' Eustacia's imagination supplied the rest—except the solution to one riddle. What *could* the tastes of that man be who saw friendliness and geniality in these shaggy hills?

On such occasions as this a thousand ideas pass through a highly charged woman's head; and they indicate themselves on her face; but the changes, though actual, are minute. Eustacia's features went through a rhythmical succession of them. She glowed; remembering the mendacity of the imagination, she flagged; then she freshened; then she fired; then she cooled again. It was a cycle of aspects, produced by a cycle of visions.

Eustacia entered her own house; she was excited. Her grandfather was enjoying himself over the fire, raking about the ashes and exposing the red-hot surface of the turves, so that their lurid glare irradiated the chimney-corner with the hues of a furnace.

'Why is it that we are never friendly with the Yeobrights?' she said, coming forward and stretching her soft hands over the warmth. 'I wish we were. They seem to be very nice people.'

'Be hanged if I know why,' said the captain. 'I liked the old man well enough, though he was as rough as a hedge. But you would never have cared to go there, even if you might have, I am well sure.'

'Why shouldn't I?'

'Your town tastes would find them far too countrified. They sit in the kitchen, drink mead and elder-wine, and sand the floor to keep it clean. A sensible way of life; but how would you like it?'

'I thought Mrs. Yeobright was a ladylike woman? A curate's daughter, was she not?'

'Yes; but she was obliged to live as her husband did; and I suppose she has taken kindly to it by this time.

Ah, I recollect that I once accidentally offended her, and I have never seen her since.'

That night was an eventful one to Eustacia's brain, and one which she hardly ever forgot. She dreamt a dream; and few human beings, from Nebuchadnezzar to the Swaffham tinker, ever dreamt a more remarkable one. Such an elaborately developed, perplexing, exciting dream was certainly never dreamed by a girl in Eustacia's situation before. It had as many ramifications as the Cretan labyrinth, as many fluctuations as the Northern Lights, as much colour as a parterre in June, and was as crowded with figures as a coronation. To Queen Scheherazade the dream might have seemed not far removed from commonplace; and to a girl just returned from all the courts of Europe it might have seemed not more than interesting. But amid the circumstances of Eustacia's life it was as wonderful as a dream could be.

There was, however, gradually evolved from its transformation scenes a less extravagant episode, in which the heath dimly appeared behind the general brilliancy of the action. She was dancing to wondrous music, and her partner was the man in silver armour who had accompanied her through the previous fantastic changes, the visor of his helmet being closed. The mazes of the dance were ecstatic. Soft whispering came into her ear from under the radiant helmet, and she felt like a woman in Paradise. Suddenly these two wheeled out from the mass of dancers, dived into one of the pools of the heath, and came out somewhere beneath into an iridescent hollow, arched with rainbows. 'It must be here,' said the voice by her side, and blushingly looking up she saw him removing his casque to kiss her. At that moment there was a cracking noise, and his figure fell into fragments like a pack of cards.

She cried aloud, 'O that I had seen his face!'

Eustacia awoke. The cracking had been that of the window-shutter downstairs, which the maid-servant was opening to let in the day, now slowly increasing to Nature's meagre allowance at this sickly time of the year. 'O that I had seen his face!' she said again. ''Twas meant for Mr. Yeobright!'

When she became cooler she perceived that many of the phases of the dream had naturally arisen out of the images and fancies of the day before. But this detracted little from its interest, which lay in the excellent fuel it provided for newly kindled fervour. She was at the modulating point between indifference and love, at the stage called 'having a fancy for.' It occurs once in the history of the most gigantic passions, and it is a period when they are in the hands of the weakest will.

The perfervid woman was by this time half in love with a vision. The fantastic nature of her passion, which lowered her as an intellect, raised her as a soul. If she had had a little more self-control she would have attenuated the emotion to nothing by sheer reasoning, and so have killed it off. If she had had a little less pride she might have gone and circumambulated the Yeobrights' premises at Blooms-End at any maidenly sacrifice until she had seen him. But Eustacia did neither of these things. She acted as the most exemplary might have acted, being so influenced; she took an airing twice or thrice a day upon the Egdon hills, and kept her eyes employed.

The first occasion passed, and he did not come that way.

She promenaded a second time, and was again the sole wanderer there.

The third time there was a dense fog: she looked around, but without much hope. Even if he had been walking within twenty yards of her she could not have seen him.

At the fourth attempt to encounter him it began to rain in torrents, and she turned back.

The fifth sally was in the afternoon: it was fine, and

she remained out long, walking to the very top of the valley in which Blooms-End lay. She saw the white paling about half a mile off; but he did not appear. It was almost with heart-sickness that she came home, and with a sense of shame at her weakness. She resolved to look for the man from Paris no more.

But Providence is nothing if not coquettish; and no sooner had Eustacia formed this resolve than the opportunity came which, while sought, had been entirely withholden.

EUSTACIA IS LED ON TO AN ADVENTURE

IV

IN the evening of this last day of expectation, which was the twenty-third of December, Eustacia was at home alone. She had passed the recent hour in lamenting over a rumour newly come to her ears—that Yeobright's visit to his mother was to be of short duration, and would end some time the next week. 'Naturally,' she said to herself. A man in the full swing of his activities in a gay city could not afford to linger long on Egdon Heath. That she would behold face to face the owner of the awakening voice within the limits of such a holiday was most unlikely, unless she were to haunt the environs of his mother's house like a robin, to do which was difficult and unseemly.

The customary expedient of provincial girls and men in such circumstances is churchgoing. In an ordinary village or country town one can safely calculate that, either on Christmas-day or the Sunday contiguous, any native home for the holidays, who has not through age or *ennui* lost the appetite for seeing and being seen, will turn up in some pew or other, shining with hope, self-consciousness, and new clothes. Thus the congregation on Christmas morning is mostly a Tussaud collection of celebrities who have been born in the neighbourhood. Hither the mistress, left neglected at home all the year, can steal and observe the development of the returned lover who has forgotten her, and think as she watches him over her prayer-book that he may throb with a renewed fidelity when novelties have lost their charm. And hither a comparatively recent settler like Eustacia may betake herself to scrutinize the person of a native son who left home before her advent upon the scene, and consider if the friendship of his parents be worth cultivating during his next absence in order to secure a knowledge of him on his next return.

But these tender schemes were not feasible among the scattered inhabitants of Egdon Heath. In name they were parishioners, but virtually they belonged to no parish at all. People who came to these few isolated houses to keep Christmas with their friends remained in their friends' chimney-corners drinking mead and other comforting liquors till they left again for good and all. Rain, snow, ice, mud everywhere around, they did not care to trudge two or three miles to sit wet-footed and splashed to the nape of their necks among those who, though in some measure neighbours, lived close to the church, and entered it clean and dry. Eustacia knew it was ten to one that Clym Yeobright would go to no church at all during his few days of leave, and that it would be a waste of labour for her to go driving the pony and gig over a bad road in hope to see him there.

It was dusk, and she was sitting by the fire in the dining-room or hall, which they occupied at this time of the year in preference to the parlour, because of its large hearth, constructed for turf-fires, a fuel the captain was partial to in the winter season. The only visible articles in the room were those on the window-sill, which showed their shapes against the low sky : the middle article being the old hour-glass, and the other two a pair of ancient British urns which had been dug from a barrow near, and were used as flower-pots for two razor-leaved cactuses. Somebody knocked at the door. The servant was out; so was her grandfather. The person, after waiting a minute, came in and tapped at the door of the room.

'Who's there?' said Eustacia.

'Please, Cap'n Vye, will you let us——'

Eustacia arose and went to the door. 'I cannot allow you to come in so boldly. You should have waited.'

'The cap'n said I might come in without any fuss,' was answered in a lad's pleasant voice.

'Oh, did he?' said Eustacia more gently. 'What do you want, Charley?'

'Please will your grandfather lend us his fuel-house to try over our parts in, to-night at seven o'clock?'

'What, are you one of the Egdon mummers for this year?'

'Yes, miss. The cap'n used to let the old mummers practise here.'

'I know it. Yes, you may use the fuel-house if you like,' said Eustacia languidly.

The choice of Captain Vye's fuel-house as the scene of rehearsal was dictated by the fact that his dwelling was nearly in the centre of the heath. The fuel-house was as roomy as a barn, and was a most desirable place for such a purpose. The lads who formed the company of players lived at different scattered points around, and by meeting in this spot the distances to be traversed by all the comers would be about equally proportioned.

For mummers and mumming Eustacia had the greatest contempt. The mummers themselves were not afflicted with any such feeling for their art, though at the same time they were not enthusiastic. A traditional pastime is to be distinguished from a mere revival in no more striking feature than in this, that while in the revival all is excitement and fervour, the survival is carried on with a stolidity and absence of stir which sets one wondering why a thing that is done so perfunctorily should be kept up at all.

Like Balaam and other unwilling prophets, the agents seem moved by an inner compulsion to say and do their allotted parts whether they will or no. This unweeting manner of performance is the true ring by which, in this refurbishing age, a fossilized survival may be known from a spurious reproduction.

The piece was the well-known play of 'Saint George,' and all who were behind the scenes assisted in the preparations, including the women of each household. Without the co-operation of sisters and sweethearts the dresses were likely to be a failure; but on the other hand, this class of assistance was not without its drawbacks. The girls could never be brought to respect tradition in designing and decorating the armour; they insisted on attaching loops and bows of silk and velvet in any situation pleasing to their taste. Gorget, gusset, basinet, cuirass, gauntlet, sleeve, all alike in the view of these feminine eyes were practicable spaces whereon to sew scraps of fluttering colour.

It might be that Joe, who fought on the side of Christendom, had a sweetheart, and that Jim, who fought on the side of the Moslem, had one likewise. During the making of the costumes it would come to the knowledge of Joe's sweetheart that Jim's was putting brilliant silk scallops at the bottom of her lover's surcoat, in addition to the ribbons of the visor, the bars of which, being invariably formed of coloured strips about half an inch wide hanging before the face, were mostly of that material. Joe's sweetheart straightway placed brilliant silk on the scallops of the hem in question, and, going a little further, added ribbon tufts to the shoulder pieces. Jim's, not to be outdone, would affix bows and rosettes everywhere.

The result was that in the end the Valiant Soldier, of the Christian army, was distinguished by no peculiarity of accoutrement from the Turkish Knight; and what was worse, on a casual view Saint George himself might be mistaken for his deadly enemy, the Saracen. The guisers themselves, though inwardly regretting this confusion of persons, could not afford to offend those by whose assistance they so largely profited, and the innovations were allowed to stand.

There was, it is true, a limit to this tendency to uniformity. The Leech or Doctor preserved his character intact: his darker habiliments, peculiar hat, and the bottle of physic slung under his arm, could never be mistaken. And the same might be said of the conventional figure of Father Christmas, with his gigantic club, an older man, who accompanied the band as general protector in long night journeys from parish to parish, and was bearer of the purse.

Seven o'clock, the hour of the rehearsal, came round, and in a short time Eustacia could hear voices in the fuel-house. To dissipate in some trifling measure her abiding sense of the murkiness of human life she went to the 'linhay' or lean-to shed, which formed the root-store of their dwelling and abutted on the fuel-house. Here was a small rough hole in the mud wall, originally made for pigeons, through which the interior of the next shed could be viewed. A light came from it now; and Eustacia stepped upon a stool to look in upon the scene.

On a ledge in the fuel-house stood three tall rush-lights, and by the light of them seven or eight lads were marching about, haranguing, and confusing each other, in endeavours to perfect themselves in the play. Humphrey and Sam, the furze and turf cutters, were there looking on, so also was Timothy Fairway, who leant against the wall and prompted the boys from memory, interspersing among the set words remarks and anecdotes of the superior days when he and others were the Egdon mummers-elect that these lads were now.

'Well, ye be as well up to it as ever ye will be,' he said. 'Not that such mumming would have passed in our time. Harry as the Saracen should strut a bit more, and John needn't holler his inside out. Beyond that perhaps you'll do. Have you got all your clothes ready?'

'We shall by Monday.'

'Your first outing will be Monday night, I suppose?'

'Yes. At Mrs. Yeobright's.'

'Oh, Mrs. Yeobright's. What makes her want to see ye? I should think a middle-aged woman was tired of mumming.'

'She's got up a bit of a party, because 'tis the first Christmas that her son Clym has been home for a long time.'

'To be sure, to be sure—her party! I am going myself. I almost forgot it, upon my life.'

Eustacia's face flagged. There was to be a party at the Yeobrights'; she, naturally, had nothing to do with it. She was a stranger to all such local gatherings, and had always held them as scarcely appertaining to her sphere. But had she been going, what an opportunity would have been afforded her of seeing the man whose influence was penetrating her like summer sun! To increase that influence was coveted excitement; to cast it off might be to regain serenity; to leave it as it stood was tantalizing.

The lads and men prepared to leave the premises, and Eustacia returned to her fireside. She was immersed in thought, but not for long. In a few minutes the lad Charley, who had come to ask permission to use the place, returned with the key to the kitchen. Eustacia heard him, and opening the door into the passage, said, 'Charley, come here.'

The lad was surprised. He entered the front room not without blushing; for he, like many, had felt the power of this girl's face and form.

She pointed to a seat by the fire, and entered the other side of the chimney-corner herself. It could be seen in her face that whatever motive she might have had in asking the youth indoors would soon appear.

'Which part do you play, Charley—the Turkish Knight, do you not?' inquired the beauty, looking across the smoke of the fire to him on the other side.

'Yes, miss, the Turkish Knight,' he replied diffidently.

'Is yours a long part?'

'Nine speeches, about.'

'Can you repeat them to me? If so I should like to hear them.'

The lad smiled into the glowing turf and began—

> 'Here come I, a Turkish Knight,
> Who learnt in Turkish land to fight,'

continuing the discourse throughout the scenes to the concluding catastrophe of his fall by the hand of Saint George.

Eustacia had occasionally heard the part recited before. When the lad ended she began, precisely in the same words, and ranted on without hitch or divergence till she too reached the end. It was the same thing, yet how different. Like in form, it had the added softness and finish of a Raffaelle after Perugino, which, while faithfully reproducing the original subject, entirely distances the original art.

Charley's eyes rounded with surprise. 'Well, you be a clever lady!' he said, in admiration. 'I've been three weeks learning mine.'

'I have heard it before,' she quietly observed. 'Now, would you do anything to please me, Charley?'

'I'd do a good deal, miss.'

'Would you let me play your part for one night?'

'O, miss! But your woman's gown—you couldn't.'

'I can get boy's clothes—at least all that would be wanted besides the mumming dress. What should I have to give you to lend me your things, to let me take your place for an hour or two on Monday night, and on no account to say a word about who or what I am? You would, of course, have to excuse yourself from playing that night, and to say that somebody—a cousin of Miss Vye's—would act for you. The other mummers have never spoken to me in their lives, so that it would be safe enough; and if it were not, I should not mind. Now, what must I give you to agree to this? Half a crown?'

The youth shook his head.

'Five shillings?'

He shook his head again. 'Money won't do it,' he said, brushing the iron head of the fire-dog with the hollow of his hand.

'What will then, Charley?' said Eustacia in a disappointed tone.

'You know what you forbade me at the may-poling, miss,' murmured the lad, without looking at her, and still stroking the fire-dog's head.

'Yes,' said Eustacia, with a little more hauteur. 'You wanted to join hands with me in the ring, if I recollect?'

'Half an hour of that, and I'll agree, miss.'

Eustacia regarded the youth steadfastly. He was three years younger than herself, but apparently not backward for his age. 'Half an hour of what?' she said, though she guessed what.

'Holding your hand in mine.'

She was silent. 'Make it a quarter of an hour,' she said.

'Yes, Miss Eustacia—I will, if I may kiss it too. A quarter of an hour. And I'll swear to do the best I can to let you take my place without anybody knowing. Don't you think somebody might know your tongue, miss?'

'It is possible. But I will put a pebble in my mouth to make it less likely. Very well; you shall be allowed to have my hand as soon as you bring the dress and your sword and staff. I don't want you any longer now.'

Charley departed, and Eustacia felt more and more interest in life. Here was something to do: here was some one to see, and a charmingly adventurous way to see him. 'Ah,' she said to herself, 'want of an object to live for—that's all is the matter with me!'

Eustacia's manner was as a rule of a slumberous sort, her passions being of the massive rather than the vivacious kind. But when aroused she would make a dash which, just for the time, was not unlike the move of a naturally lively person.

On the question of recognition she was somewhat indifferent. By the acting lads themselves she was not likely to be known. With the guests who might be assembled she was hardly so secure. Yet detection, after all, would be no such dreadful thing. The fact only could be detected, her true motive never. It would be instantly set down as the passing freak of a girl whose ways were already considered singular. That she was doing for an earnest reason what would most naturally be done in jest was at any rate a safe secret.

The next evening Eustacia stood punctually at the fuel-house door, waiting for the dusk which was to bring Charley with the trappings. Her grandfather was at home to-night, and she would be unable to ask her confederate indoors.

He appeared on the dark ridge of heathland, like a fly on a negro, bearing the articles with him, and came up breathless with his walk.

'Here are the things,' he whispered, placing them upon the threshold. 'And now, Miss Eustacia——'

'The payment. It is quite ready. I am as good as my word.'

She leant against the door-post, and gave him her hand. Charley took it in both his own with a tenderness beyond description, unless it was like that of a child holding a captured sparrow.

'Why, there's a glove on it!' he said in a deprecating way.

'I have been walking,' she observed.

'But, miss!'

'Well—it is hardly fair.' She pulled off the glove, and gave him her bare hand.

They stood together minute after minute, without further speech, each looking at the blackening scene, and each thinking his and her own thoughts.

'I think I won't use it all up to-night,' said Charley devotedly, when six or eight minutes had been passed by him caressing her hand. 'May I have the other few minutes another time?'

'As you like,' said she without the least emotion. 'But it must be over in a week. Now, there is only one thing I want you to do: to wait while I put on the dress, and then to see if I do my part properly. But let me look first indoors.'

She vanished for a minute or two, and went in. Her grandfather was safely asleep in his chair. 'Now, then,' she said, on returning, 'walk down the garden a little way, and when I am ready I'll call you.'

Charley walked and waited, and presently heard a soft whistle. He returned to the fuel-house door.

'Did you whistle, Miss Vye?'

'Yes; come in,' reached him in Eustacia's voice from a back quarter. 'I must not strike a light till the door is shut, or it may be seen shining. Push your hat into the hole through to the wash-house, if you can feel your way across.'

Charley did as commanded, and she struck the light, revealing herself to be changed in sex, brilliant in colours, and armed from top to toe. Perhaps she quailed a little under Charley's vigorous gaze, but whether any shyness at her male attire appeared upon her countenance could not be seen by reason of the strips of ribbon which used to cover the face in mumming costumes, representing the barred visor of the mediæval helmet.

'It fits pretty well,' she said, looking down at the white overalls, 'except that the tunic, or whatever you call it, is long in the sleeve. The bottom of the overalls I can turn up inside. Now pay attention.'

Eustacia then proceeded in her delivery, striking the sword against the staff or lance at the minatory phrases, in the orthodox mumming manner, and strutting up and down. Charley seasoned his admiration with criticism of the gentlest kind, for the touch of Eustacia's hand yet remained with him.

'And now for your excuse to the others,' she said. 'Where do you meet before you go to Mrs. Yeobright's?'

'We thought of meeting here, miss, if you have nothing to say against it. At eight o'clock, so as to get there by nine.'

'Yes. Well, you of course must not appear. I will march in about five minutes late, ready-dressed, and tell them that you can't come. I have decided that the best plan will be for you to be sent somewhere by me, to make a real thing of the excuse. Our two heath-croppers are in the habit of straying into the meads, and to-morrow evening you can go and see if they are gone there. I'll manage the rest. Now you may leave me.'

'Yes, miss. But I think I'll have one minute more of what I am owed, if you don't mind.'

Eustacia gave him her hand as before.

'One minute,' she said, and counted on till she reached seven or eight minutes. Hand and person she then withdrew to a distance of several feet, and recovered some of her old dignity. The contract completed, she raised between them a barrier impenetrable as a wall.

'There, 'tis all gone; and I didn't mean quite all,' he said, with a sigh.

'You had good measure,' said she, turning away.

'Yes, miss. Well, 'tis over, and now I'll get home-along.'

THROUGH THE MOONLIGHT

V

THE next evening the mummers were assembled in the same spot, awaiting the entrance of the Turkish Knight.

'Twenty minutes after eight by the Quiet Woman, and Charley not come.'

'Ten minutes past by Blooms-End.'

'It wants ten minutes to, by Grandfer Cantle's watch.'

'And 'tis five minutes past by the captain's clock.'

On Egdon there was no absolute hour of the day. The time at any moment was a number of varying doctrines professed by the different hamlets, some of them having originally grown up from a common root, and then become divided by secession, some having been alien from the beginning. West Egdon believed in Blooms-End time, East Egdon in the time of the Quiet Woman Inn. Grandfer Cantle's watch had numbered many followers in years gone by, but since he had grown older faiths were shaken. Thus, the mummers having gathered hither from scattered points, each came with his own tenets on early and late; and they waited a little longer as a compromise.

Eustacia had watched the assemblage through the hole; and seeing that now was the proper moment to enter, she went from the 'linhay' and boldly pulled the bobbin of the fuel-house door. Her grandfather was safe at the Quiet Woman.

'Here's Charley at last! How late you be, Charley.'

''Tis not Charley,' said the Turkish Knight from within his visor. ''Tis a cousin of Miss Vye's, come to take Charley's place from curiosity. He was obliged to go and look for the heath-croppers that have got into the meads, and I agreed to take his place, as he knew he couldn't come back here again to-night. I know the part as well as he.'

Her graceful gait, elegant figure, and dignified manner in general won the mummers to the opinion that they had gained by the exchange, if the new-comer were perfect in his part.

'It don't matter—if you be not too young,' said Saint George. Eustacia's voice had sounded somewhat more juvenile and fluty than Charley's.

'I know every word of it, I tell you,' said Eustacia decisively. Dash being all that was required to carry her triumphantly through, she adopted as much as was necessary. 'Go ahead, lads, with the try-over. I'll challenge any of you to find a mistake in me.'

The play was hastily rehearsed, whereupon the other mummers were delighted with the new knight. They extinguished the candles at half-past eight, and set out upon the heath in the direction of Mrs. Yeobright's house at Blooms-End.

There was a slight hoar-frost that night, and the moon, though not more than half full, threw a spirited and enticing brightness upon the fantastic figures of the mumming band, whose plumes and ribbons rustled in their walk like autumn leaves. Their path was not over Rainbarrow now, but down a valley which left that ancient elevation a little to the east. The bottom of the vale was green to a width of ten yards or thereabouts, and the shining facets of frost upon the blades of grass seemed to move on with the shadows of those they surrounded.

The masses of furze and heath to the right and left were dark as ever; a mere half-moon was powerless to silver such sable features as theirs.

Half an hour of walking and talking brought them to the spot in the valley where the grass riband widened and led down to the front of the house. At sight of the place Eustacia, who had felt a few passing doubts during her walk with the youths, again was glad that the adventure had been undertaken. She had come out to see a man who might possibly have the power to deliver her soul from a most deadly oppression. What was Wildeve? Interesting, but inadequate. Perhaps she would see a sufficient hero to-night.

As they drew nearer to the front of the house the mummers became aware that music and dancing were briskly flourishing within. Every now and then a long low note from the serpent, which was the chief wind instrument played at these times, advanced further into the heath than the thin treble part, and reached their ears alone; and next a more than usually loud tread from a dancer would come the same way. With nearer approach these fragmentary sounds became pieced together, and were found to be the salient points of the tune called 'Nancy's Fancy.'

He was there, of course. Who was she that he danced with? Perhaps some unknown woman, far beneath herself in culture, was by that most subtle of lures sealing his fate this very instant. To dance with a man is to concentrate a twelvemonth's regulation fire upon him in the fragment of an hour. To pass to courtship without acquaintance, to pass to marriage without courtship, is a skipping of terms reserved for those alone who tread this royal road. She would see how his heart lay by keen observation of them all.

The enterprising lady followed the mumming company through the gate in the white paling, and stood before the open porch. The house was encrusted with heavy thatchings, which dropped between the upper windows: the front, upon which the moonbeams directly played, had originally been white; but a huge pyracanth now darkened the greater portion.

It became at once evident that the dance was proceeding immediately within the surface of the door, no apartment intervening. The brushing of skirts and elbows, sometimes the bumping of shoulders, could be heard against the very panels. Eustacia, though living within two miles of the place, had never seen the interior of this quaint old habitation. Between Captain Vye and the Yeobrights there had never existed much acquaintance, the former having come as a stranger and purchased the long-empty house at Mistover Knap not long before the death of Mrs. Yeobright's husband; and with that event and the departure of her son such friendship as had grown up became quite broken off.

'Is there no passage inside the door, then?' asked Eustacia as they stood within the porch.

'No,' said the lad who played the Saracen. 'The door opens right upon the front sitting-room, where the spree's going on.'

'So that we cannot open the door without stopping the dance.'

'That's it. Here we must bide till they have done, for they always bolt the back door after dark.'

'They won't be much longer,' said Father Christmas.

This assertion, however, was hardly borne out by the event. Again the instruments ended the tune; again they recommenced with as much fire and pathos as if it were the first strain. The air was now that one without any particular beginning, middle, or end, which perhaps, among all the dances which throng an inspired fiddler's fancy, best conveys the idea of the interminable—the celebrated 'Devil's Dream.' The fury of personal movement that was kindled by the fury of the notes could be approximately imagined by these outsiders under the moon, from the occasional kicks of toes and heels against the door, whenever the whirl round had been of more than customary velocity.

The first five minutes of listening was interesting enough to the mummers. The five minutes extended to ten minutes, and these to a quarter of an hour; but no signs of ceasing were audible in the lively Dream. The bumping against the door, the laughter, the stamping, were all as vigorous as ever, and the pleasure in being outside lessened considerably.

'Why does Mrs. Yeobright give parties of this sort?' Eustacia asked, a little surprised to hear merriment so pronounced.

'It is not one of her bettermost parlour-parties. She's asked the plain neighbours and workpeople without drawing any lines, just to give 'em a good supper and such like. Her son and she wait upon the folks.'

'I see,' said Eustacia.

''Tis the last strain, I think,' said Saint George, with his ear to the panel. 'A young man and woman have just swung into this corner, and he's saying to her, "Ah, the pity; 'tis over for us this time, my own."'

'Thank God,' said the Turkish Knight, stamping, and taking from the wall the conventional lance that each of the mummers carried. Her boots being thinner than those of the young men, the hoar had damped her feet and made them cold.

'Upon my song 'tis another ten minutes for us,' said the Valiant Soldier, looking through the keyhole as the tune modulated into another without stopping. 'Grandfer Cantle is standing in this corner, waiting his turn.'

''Twon't be long; 'tis a six-handed reel,' said the Doctor.

'Why not go in, dancing or no? They sent for us,' said the Saracen.

'Certainly not,' said Eustacia authoritatively, as she paced smartly up and down from door to gate to warm herself. 'We should burst into the middle of them and stop the dance, and that would be unmannerly.'

'He thinks himself somebody because he has had a bit more schooling than we,' said the Doctor.

'You may go to the deuce!' said Eustacia.

There was a whispered conversation between three or four of them, and one turned to her.

'Will you tell us one thing?' he said, not without gentleness. 'Be you Miss Vye? We think you must be.'

'You may think what you like,' said Eustacia slowly. 'But honourable lads will not tell tales upon a lady.'

'We'll say nothing, miss. That's upon our honour.'

'Thank you,' she replied.

At this moment the fiddles finished off with a screech, and the serpent emitted a last note that nearly lifted the roof. When, from the comparative quiet within, the mummers judged that the dancers had taken their seats, Father Christmas advanced, lifted the latch, and put his head inside the door.

'Ah, the mummers, the mummers!' cried several guests at once. 'Clear a space for the mummers.'

Hump-backed Father Christmas then made a complete entry, swinging his huge club, and in a general way clearing the stage for the actors proper, while he informed the company in smart verse that he was come, welcome or welcome not; concluding his speech with

'Make room, make room, my gallant boys,
And give us space to rhyme;
We've come to show Saint George's play,
Upon this Christmas time.'

The guests were now arranging themselves at one end of the room, the fiddler was mending a string, the serpent-player was emptying his mouthpiece, and the play began. First of those outside the Valiant Soldier entered, in the interest of Saint George—

'Here come I, the Valiant Soldier;
Slasher is my name;'

and so on. This speech concluded with a challenge to the infidel, at the end of which it was Eustacia's duty to enter as the Turkish Knight. She, with the rest who were not yet on, had hitherto remained in the moonlight which streamed under the porch. With no apparent effort or backwardness she came in, beginning—

'Here come I, a Turkish Knight,
Who learnt in Turkish land to fight;
I'll fight this man with courage bold:
If his blood's hot I'll make it cold!'

During her declamation Eustacia held her head erect, and spoke as roughly as she could, feeling pretty secure from observation. But the concentration upon her part necessary to prevent discovery, the newness of the scene, the shine of the candles, and the confusing effect upon her vision of the ribboned visor which hid her features, left her absolutely unable to perceive who were present as spectators. On the further side of a table bearing candles she could faintly discern faces, and that was all.

Meanwhile Jim Starks as the Valiant Soldier had come forward, and, with a glare upon the Turk, replied—

'If, then, thou art that Turkish Knight,
Draw out thy sword, and let us fight!'

And fight they did; the issue of the combat being that the Valiant Soldier was slain by a preternaturally inadequate thrust from Eustacia, Jim, in his ardour for genuine histrionic art, coming down like a log upon the stone floor with force enough to dislocate his shoulder. Then after more words from the Turkish Knight, rather too faintly delivered, and statements that he'd fight Saint George and all his crew, Saint George himself magnificently entered with the well-known flourish—

'Here come I, Saint George, the valiant man,
With naked sword and spear in hand,
Who fought the dragon and brought him to the slaughter,
And by this won fair Sabra, the King of Egypt's daughter:
What mortal man would dare to stand
Before me with my sword in hand?'

This was the lad who had first recognised Eustacia; and when she now, as the Turk, replied with suitable defiance, and at once began the combat, the young fellow took especial care to use his sword as gently as possible. Being wounded, the Knight fell upon one knee, according to the direction. The Doctor now entered, restored the Knight by giving him a draught from the bottle which he carried, and the fight was again resumed, the Turk sinking by degrees until quite overcome—dying as hard in this venerable drama as he is said to do at the present day.

This gradual sinking to the earth was, in fact, one reason why Eustacia had thought that the part of the Turkish Knight, though not the shortest, would suit her best. A direct fall from upright to horizontal, which was the end of the other fighting characters, was not an elegant or decorous part for a girl. But it was easy to die like a Turk, by a dogged decline.

Eustacia was now among the number of the slain, though not on the floor, for she had managed to sink into a sloping position against the clock-case, so that her head was well elevated. The play proceeded between Saint George, the Saracen, the Doctor, and Father Christmas; and Eustacia, having no more to do, for the first time found leisure to observe the scene around, and to search for the form that had drawn her hither.

THE TWO STAND FACE TO FACE

VI

THE room had been arranged with a view to the dancing, the large oak table having been moved back till it stood as a breastwork to the fireplace. At each end, behind, and in the chimney-corner were grouped the guests, many of them being warm-faced and panting, among whom Eustacia cursorily recognized some well-to-do persons from beyond the heath. Thomasin, as she had expected, was not visible, and Eustacia recollected that a light had shone from an upper window when they were outside—the window, probably, of Thomasin's room. A nose, chin, hands, knees, and toes projected from the seat within the chimney opening, which members she found to unite in the person of Grandfer Cantle, Mrs. Yeobright's occasional assistant in the garden, and therefore one of the invited. The smoke went up from an Etna of peat in front of him, played round the notches of the chimney-crook, struck against the salt-box, and got lost among the flitches.

Another part of the room soon riveted her gaze. At the other side of the chimney stood the settle, which is the necessary supplement to a fire so open that nothing less than a strong breeze will carry up the smoke. It is, to the hearths of old-fashioned cavernous fireplaces, what the east belt of trees is to the exposed country estate, or the north wall to the garden. Outside the settle candles gutter, locks of hair wave, young women shiver, and old men sneeze. Inside is Paradise. Not a symptom of a draught disturbs the air; the sitters' backs are as warm as their faces, and songs and old tales are drawn from the occupants by the comfortable heat, like fruit from melon-plants in a frame.

It was, however, not with those who sat in the settle that Eustacia was concerned. A face showed itself with marked distinctness against the dark-tanned wood of the upper part. The owner, who was leaning against the settle's outer end, was Clement Yeobright, or Clym, as he was called here; she knew it could be nobody else. The spectacle constituted an area of two feet in Rembrandt's intensest manner. A strange power in the lounger's appearance lay in the fact that, though his whole figure was visible, the observer's eye was only aware of his face.

To one of middle age the countenance was that of a young man, though a youth might hardly have seen any necessity for the term of immaturity. But it was really one of those faces which convey less the idea of so many years as its age than of so much experience as its store. The number of their years may have adequately summed up Jared, Mahalaleel, and the rest of the antediluvians, but the age of a modern man is to be measured by the intensity of his history.

The face was well shaped, even excellently. But the mind within was beginning to use it as a mere waste tablet whereon to trace its idiosyncrasies as they developed themselves. The beauty here visible would in no long time be ruthlessly overrun by its parasite, thought, which might just as well have fed upon a plainer exterior where there was nothing it could harm. Had Heaven preserved Yeobright from a wearing habit of meditation, people would have said, 'A handsome man.' Had his brain unfolded under sharper contours they would have said,

'A thoughtful man.' But an inner strenuousness was preying upon an outer symmetry, and they rated his look as singular.

Hence people who began by beholding him ended by perusing him. His countenance was overlaid with legible meanings. Without being thought-worn he yet had certain marks derived from a perception of his surroundings, such as are not unfrequently found on men at the end of the four or five years of endeavour which follow the close of placid pupilage. He already showed that thought is a disease of flesh, and indirectly bore evidence that ideal physical beauty is incompatible with emotional development and a full recognition of the coil of things. Mental luminousness must be fed with the oil of life, even though there is already a physical need for it; and the pitiful sight of two demands on one supply was just showing itself here.

When standing before certain men the philosopher regrets that thinkers are but perishable tissue, the artist that perishable tissue has to think. Thus to deplore, each from his point of view, the mutually destructive interdependence of spirit and flesh would have been instinctive with these in critically observing Yeobright.

As for his look, it was a natural cheerfulness striving against depression from without, and not quite succeeding. The look suggested isolation, but it revealed something more. As is usual with bright natures, the deity that lies ignominiously chained within an ephemeral human carcase shone out of him like a ray.

The effect upon Eustacia was palpable. The extraordinary pitch of excitement that she had reached beforehand would, indeed, have caused her to be influenced by the most commonplace man. She was troubled at Yeobright's presence.

The remainder of the play ended: the Saracen's head was cut off, and Saint George stood as victor. Nobody commented, any more than they would have commented on the fact of mushrooms coming in autumn or snowdrops in spring. They took the piece as phlegmatically as did the actors themselves. It was a phase of cheerfulness which was, as a matter of course, to be passed through every Christmas; and there was no more to be said.

They sang the plaintive chant which follows the play, during which all the dead men rise to their feet in a silent and awful manner, like the ghosts of Napoleon's soldiers in the Midnight Review. Afterwards the door opened, and Fairway appeared on the threshold, accompanied by Christian and another. They had been waiting outside for the conclusion of the play, as the players had waited for the conclusion of the dance.

'Come in, come in,' said Mrs. Yeobright; and Clym went forward to welcome them. 'How is it you are so late? Grandfer Cantle has been here ever so long, and we thought you'd have come with him, as you live so near one another.'

'Well, I should have come earlier,' Mr. Fairway said, and paused to look along the beam of the ceiling for a nail to hang his hat on; but, finding his accustomed one to be occupied by the mistletoe, and all the nails in the walls to be burdened with bunches of holly, he at last relieved himself of the hat by ticklishly balancing it between the candle-box and the head of the clock-case. 'I should have come earlier, ma'am,' he resumed, with a more composed air, 'but I know what parties be, and how there's none too much room in folks' houses at such times, so I thought I wouldn't come till you'd got settled a bit.'

'And I thought so too, Mrs. Yeobright,' said Christian earnestly; 'but father there was so eager that he had no manners at all, and left home almost afore 'twas dark. I told him 'twas barely decent in a' old man to come so oversoon; but words be wind.'

'Klk! I wasn't going to bide waiting about till half the game was over! I'm as light as a kite when anything's going on!' crowed Grandfer Cantle from the chimney-seat.

Fairway had meanwhile concluded a critical gaze at Yeobright. 'Now, you may not believe it,' he said to the rest of the room, 'but I should never have knowed this gentleman if I had met him anywhere off his own he'th: he's altered so much.'

'You too have altered, and for the better, I think, Timothy,' said Yeobright, surveying the firm figure of Fairway.

'Master Yeobright, look me over too. I have altered for the better, haven't I, hey?' said Grandfer Cantle, rising, and placing himself something above half a foot from Clym's eye, to induce the most searching criticism.

'To be sure we will,' said Fairway, taking the candle and moving it over the surface of the Grandfer's countenance, the subject of his scrutiny irradiating himself with light and pleasant smiles, and giving himself jerks of juvenility.

'You haven't changed much,' said Yeobright.

'If there's any difference, Grandfer is younger,' appended Fairway decisively.

'And yet not my own doing, and I feel no pride in it,' said the pleased ancient. 'But I can't be cured of my vagaries; them I plead guilty to. Yes, Master Cantle always was that, as we know. But I am nothing by the side of you, Mister Clym.'

'Nor any o' us,' said Humphrey, in a low rich tone of admiration, not intended to reach anybody's ears.

'Really, there would have been nobody here who could have stood as decent second to him, or even third, if I hadn't been a soldier in the Bang-up Locals (as we was called for our smartness),' said Grandfer Cantle. 'And even as 'tis we all look a little scammish beside him. But in the year four 'twas said there wasn't a finer figure in the whole South Wessex than I, as I looked when dashing past the shop-winders with the rest of our company on the day we ran out o' Budmouth because it was thoughted that Boney had landed round the point. There was I, straight as a young poplar, wi' my firelock, and my bagnet, and my spatterdashes, and my stock sawing my jaws off, and my accoutrements sheening like the seven stars! Yes, neighbours, I was a pretty sight in my soldiering days. You ought to have seen me in four!'

''Tis his mother's side where Master Clym's figure comes from, bless ye,' said Timothy. 'I know'd her brothers well. Longer coffins were never made in the whole county of South Wessex, and 'tis said that poor George's knees were crumpled up a little e'en as 'twas.'

'Coffins, where?' inquired Christian, drawing nearer. 'Have the ghost of one appeared to anybody, Master Fairway?'

'No, no. Don't let your mind so mislead your ears, Christian; and be a man,' said Timothy reproachfully.

'I will,' said Christian. 'But now I think o't my shadder last night seemed just the shape of a coffin. What is it a sign of when your shade's like a coffin, neighbours? It can't be nothing to be afeard of, I suppose?'

'Afeard, no!' said the Grandfer. 'Faith, I was never afeard of nothing except Boney, or I shouldn't ha' been the soldier I was. Yes, 'tis a thousand pities you didn't see me in four!'

By this time the mummers were preparing to leave; but Mrs. Yeobright stopped them by asking them to sit down and have a little supper. To this invitation Father Christmas, in the name of them all, readily agreed.

Eustacia was happy in the opportunity of staying a little longer. The cold and frosty night without was doubly frigid to her. But the lingering was not without its difficulties. Mrs. Yeobright, for want of room in the larger apartment, placed a bench for the mummers half-way through the pantry-door, which opened from the sitting-room. Here they seated themselves in a row, the door being left open: thus they were still virtually in the same apartment. Mrs. Yeobright now murmured a few words to her son, who crossed the room to the pantry-door, striking his head against the mistletoe as he passed, and brought the mummers beef and bread, cake, pastry, mead, and elder-wine, the waiting being done by him and his mother, that the little maid-servant might sit as guest. The mummers doffed their helmets, and began to eat and drink.

'But you will surely have some?' said Clym to the Turkish Knight, as he stood before that warrior, tray in hand. She had refused, and still sat covered, only the sparkle of her eyes being visible between the ribbons which covered her face.

'None, thank you,' replied Eustacia.

'He's quite a youngster,' said the Saracen apologetically, 'and you must excuse him. He's not one of the old set, but have jined us because t'other couldn't come.'

'But he will take something?' persisted Yeobright. 'Try a glass of mead or elder-wine.'

'Yes, you had better try that,' said the Saracen. 'It will keep the cold out going home-along.'

Though Eustacia could not eat without uncovering her face she could drink easily enough beneath her disguise. The elder-wine was accordingly accepted, and the glass vanished inside the ribbons.

At moments during this performance Eustacia was half in doubt about the security of her position; yet it had a fearful joy. A series of attentions paid to her, and yet not to her but to some imaginary person, by the first man she had ever been inclined to adore, complicated her emotions indescribably. She had loved him partly because he was exceptional in this scene, partly because she had determined to love him, chiefly because she was in desperate need of loving somebody after wearying of Wildeve. Believing that she must love him in spite of herself, she had been influenced after the fashion of the second Lord Lyttleton and other persons, who have dreamed that they were to die on a certain day, and by stress of a morbid imagination have actually brought about that event. Once let a maiden admit the possibility of her being stricken with love for some one at a certain hour and place, and the thing is as good as done.

Did anything at this moment suggest to Yeobright the sex of the creature whom that fantastic guise inclosed, how extended was her scope both in feeling and in making others feel, and how far her compass transcended that of her companions in the band? When the disguised Queen of Love appeared before Æneas a preternatural perfume accompanied her presence and betrayed her quality. If such a mysterious emanation ever was projected by the emotions of an earthly woman upon their object, it must have signified Eustacia's presence to Yeobright now. He looked at her wistfully, then seemed to fall into a reverie, as if he were forgetting what he observed. The momentary situation ended, he passed on, and Eustacia sipped her wine without knowing what she drank. The man for whom she had predetermined to nourish a passion went into the small room, and across it to the further extremity.

The mummers, as has been stated, were seated on a bench, one end of which extended into the small apartment, or pantry, for want of space in the outer room. Eustacia, partly from shyness, had chosen the midmost seat, which thus commanded a view of the interior of the pantry as well as the room containing the guests. When Clym passed down the pantry her eyes followed him in the gloom which prevailed there. At the remote end was a door which, just as he was about to open it for himself, was opened by somebody within; and light streamed forth.

The person was Thomasin, with a candle, looking anxious, pale, and interesting. Yeobright appeared glad to see her, and pressed her hand. 'That's right, Tamsie,' he said heartily, as though recalled to himself by the sight of her: 'you have decided to come down. I am glad of it.'

'Hush—no, no,' she said quickly. 'I only came to speak to you.'

'But why not join us.'

'I cannot. At least I would rather not. I am not well enough, and we shall have plenty of time together now you are going to be home a good long holiday.'

'It isn't nearly so pleasant without you. Are you really ill ?'

'Just a little, my old cousin—here,' she said, playfully sweeping her hand across her heart.

'Ah, mother should have asked somebody else to be present to-night, perhaps ?'

'O no, indeed. I merely stepped down, Clym, to ask you——' Here he followed her through the doorway into the private room beyond, and, the door closing, Eustacia and the mummer who sat next to her, the only other witness of the performance, saw and heard no more.

The heat flew to Eustacia's head and cheeks. She instantly guessed that Clym, having been home only these two or three days, had not as yet been made acquainted with Thomasin's painful situation with regard to Wildeve; and seeing her living there just as she had been living before he left home, he naturally suspected nothing. Eustacia felt a wild jealousy of Thomasin on the instant. Though Thomasin might possibly have tender sentiments towards another man as yet, how long could they be expected to last when she was shut up here with this interesting and travelled cousin of hers ? There was no knowing what affection might not soon break out between the two, so constantly in each other's society, and not a distracting object near. Clym's boyish love for her might have languished, but it might easily be revived again.

Eustacia was nettled by her own contrivances. What a sheer waste of herself to be dressed thus while another was shining to advantage ! Had she known the full effect of the encounter she would have moved heaven and earth to get here in a natural manner. The power of her face all lost, the charm of her emotions all disguised, the fascinations of her coquetry denied existence, nothing but a voice left to her: she had a sense of the doom of Echo. 'Nobody here respects me,' she said. She had overlooked the fact that, in coming as a boy among other boys, she would be treated as a boy. The slight, though of her own causing, and self-explanatory, she was unable to dismiss as unwittingly shown, so sensitive had the situation made her.

Women have done much for themselves in histrionic dress. To look far below those who, like a certain fair personator of Polly Peachum early in the last century, and another of Lydia Languish early in this,[1] have won not only love but ducal coronets into the bargain, whole shoals of them have reached to the initial satisfaction of getting love almost whence they would. But the Turkish Knight was denied even the chance of achieving this by the fluttering ribbons which she dared not brush aside.

Yeobright returned to the room without his cousin. When within two or three feet of Eustacia he stopped, as if again arrested by a thought. He was gazing at her. She looked another way, disconcerted, and wondered how long this purgatory was to last. After lingering a few seconds he passed on again.

To court their own discomfiture by love is a common instinct with certain perfervid women. Conflicting sensations of love, fear, and shame reduced Eustacia to a state of the utmost uneasiness. To escape was her great and immediate desire. The other mummers appeared to be in no hurry to leave; and murmuring to the lad who sat next to her that she preferred waiting for them outside the house, she moved to the door as imperceptibly as possible, opened it, and slipped out.

The calm, lone scene reassured her. She went forward to the palings and leant over them, looking at the moon. She had stood thus but a little time when the door again

[1] Written in 1877.

opened. Expecting to see the remainder of the band Eustacia turned; but no—Clym Yeobright came out as softly as she had done, and closed the door behind him.

He advanced and stood beside her. 'I have an odd opinion,' he said, 'and should like to ask you a question. Are you a woman—or am I wrong?'

'I am a woman.'

His eyes lingered on her with great interest. 'Do girls often play as mummers now? They never used to.'

'They don't now.'

'Why did you?'

'To get excitement and shake off depression,' she said in low tones.

'What depressed you?'

'Life.'

'That's a cause of depression a good many have to put up with.'

'Yes.'

A long silence. 'And do you find excitement?' asked Clym at last.

'At this moment, perhaps.'

'Then you are vexed at being discovered?'

'Yes; though I thought I might be.'

'I would gladly have asked you to our party had I known you wished to come. Have I ever been acquainted with you in my youth?'

'Never.'

'Won't you come in again, and stay as long as you like?'

'No. I wish not to be further recognized.'

'Well, you are safe with me.' After remaining in thought a minute he added gently, 'I will not intrude upon you longer. It is a strange way of meeting, and I will not ask why I find a cultivated woman playing such a part as this.'

She did not volunteer the reason which he seemed to hope for, and he wished her good night, going thence round to the back of the house, where he walked up and down by himself for some time before re-entering.

Eustacia, warmed with an inner fire, could not wait for her companions after this. She flung back the ribbons from her face, opened the gate, and at once struck into the heath. She did not hasten along. Her grandfather was in bed at this hour, for she so frequently walked upon the hills on moonlight nights that he took no notice of her comings and goings, and, enjoying himself in his own way, left her to do likewise. A more important subject than that of getting indoors now engrossed her. Yeobright, if he had the least curiosity, would infallibly discover her name. What then? She first felt a sort of exultation at the way in which the adventure had terminated, even though at moments between her exultations she was abashed and blushful. Then this consideration recurred to chill her: What was the use of her exploit? She was at present a total stranger to the Yeobright family. The unreasonable nimbus of romance with which she had encircled that man might be her misery. How could she allow herself to become so infatuated with a stranger? And to fill the cup of her sorrow there would be Thomasin, living day after day in inflammable proximity to him; for she had just learnt that, contrary to her first belief, he was going to stay at home some considerable time.

She reached the wicket at Mistover Knap, but before opening it she turned and faced the heath once more. The form of Rainbarrow stood above the hills, and the moon stood above Rainbarrow. The air was charged with silence and frost. The scene reminded Eustacia of a circumstance which till that moment she had totally forgotten. She had promised to meet Wildeve by the Barrow this very night at eight, to give a final answer to his pleading for an elopement.

She herself had fixed the evening and the hour. He had probably come to the spot, waited there in the cold, and been greatly disappointed.

'Well, so much the better: it did not hurt him,' she said serenely. Wildeve had at present the rayless outline of the sun through smoked glass, and she could say such things as that with the greatest facility.

She remained deeply pondering; and Thomasin's winning manner towards her cousin arose again upon Eustacia's mind.

'O that she had been married to Damon before this!' she said. 'And she would if it hadn't been for me! If I had only known—if I had only known!'

Eustacia once more lifted her deep stormy eyes to the moonlight, and, sighing that tragic sigh of hers which was so much like a shudder, entered the shadow of the roof. She threw off her trappings in the out-house, rolled them up, and went indoors to her chamber.

A COALITION BETWEEN BEAUTY AND ODDNESS

VII

THE old captain's prevailing indifference to his granddaughter's movements left her free as a bird to follow her own courses; but it so happened that he did take upon himself the next morning to ask her why she had walked out so late.

'Only in search of events, grandfather,' she said, looking out of the window with that drowsy latency of manner which discovered so much force behind it whenever the trigger was pressed.

'Search of events—one would think you were one of the bucks I knew at one-and-twenty.'

'It is so lonely here.'

'So much the better. If I were living in a town my whole time would be taken up in looking after you. I fully expected you would have been home when I returned from the Woman.'

'I won't conceal what I did. I wanted an adventure, and I went with the mummers. I played the part of the Turkish Knight.'

'No, never? Ha, ha! Good gad! I didn't expect it of you, Eustacia.'

'It was my first performance, and it certainly will be

my last. Now I have told you—and remember it is a secret.'

'Of course. But, Eustacia, you never did—ha! ha! Dammy, how 'twould have pleased me forty years ago! But remember, no more of it, my girl. You may walk on the heath night or day, as you choose, so that you don't bother me; but no figuring in breeches again.'

'You need have no fear for me, grandpapa.'

Here the conversation ceased, Eustacia's moral training never exceeding in severity a dialogue of this sort, which, if it ever became profitable to good works, would be a result not dear at the price. But her thoughts soon strayed far from her own personality; and, full of a passionate and indescribable solicitude for one to whom she was not even a name, she went forth into the amplitude of tanned wild around her, restless as Ahasuerus the Jew. She was about half a mile from her residence when she beheld a sinister redness arising from a ravine a little way in advance—dull and lurid like a flame in sunlight, and she guessed it to signify Diggory Venn.

When the farmers who had wished to buy in a new stock of reddle during the last month had inquired where Venn was to be found, people replied, 'On Egdon Heath.' Day after day the answer was the same. Now, since Egdon was populated with heath-croppers and furze-cutters rather than with sheep and shepherds, and the downs where most of the latter were to be found lay some to the north, some to the west of Egdon, his reason for camping about there like Israel in Zin was not apparent. The position was central and occasionally desirable. But the sale of reddle was not Diggory's primary object in remaining on the heath, particularly at so late a period of the year, when most travellers of his class had gone into winter quarters.

Eustacia looked at the lonely man. Wildeve had told her at their last meeting that Venn had been thrust forward by Mrs. Yeobright as one ready and anxious to take his place as Thomasin's betrothed. His figure was perfect, his face young and well outlined, his eye bright, his intelligence keen, and his position one which he could readily better if he chose. But in spite of possibilities it was not likely that Thomasin would accept this Ishmaelitish creature while she had a cousin like Yeobright at her elbow, and Wildeve at the same time not absolutely indifferent. Eustacia was not long in guessing that poor Mrs. Yeobright, in her anxiety for her niece's future, had mentioned this lover to stimulate the zeal of the other. Eustacia was on the side of the Yeobrights now, and entered into the spirit of the aunt's desire.

'Good morning, miss,' said the reddleman, taking off his cap of hareskin, and apparently bearing her no ill-will from recollection of their last meeting.

'Good morning, reddleman,' she said, hardly troubling to lift her heavily shaded eyes to his. 'I did not know you were so near. Is your van here too?'

Venn moved his elbow towards a hollow in which a dense brake of purple-stemmed brambles had grown to such vast dimensions as almost to form a dell. Brambles, though churlish when handled, are kindly shelter in early winter, being the latest of the deciduous bushes to lose their leaves. The roof and chimney of Venn's caravan showed behind the tracery and tangles of the brake.

'You remain near this part?' she asked with more interest.

'Yes, I have business here.'

'Not altogether the selling of reddle?'

'It has nothing to do with that.'

'It has to do with Miss Yeobright?'

Her face seemed to ask for an armed peace, and he therefore said frankly, 'Yes, miss; it is on account of her.'

'On account of your approaching marriage with her?'

Venn flushed through his stain. 'Don't make sport of me, Miss Vye,' he said.

'It isn't true?'

'Certainly not.'

She was thus convinced that the reddleman was a mere *pis aller* in Mrs. Yeobright's mind; one, moreover, who had not even been informed of his promotion to that lowly standing. 'It was a mere notion of mine,' she said quietly; and was about to pass by without further speech, when, looking round to the right, she saw a painfully well-known figure serpentining upwards by one of the little paths which led to the top where she stood. Owing to the necessary windings of his course his back was at present towards them. She glanced quickly round; to escape that man there was only one way. Turning to Venn, she said, 'Would you allow me to rest a few minutes in your van? The banks are damp for sitting on.'

'Certainly, miss; I'll make a place for you.'

She followed him behind the dell of brambles to his wheeled dwelling, into which Venn mounted, placing the three-legged stool just within the door.

'That is the best I can do for you,' he said, stepping down and retiring to the path, where he resumed the smoking of his pipe as he walked up and down.

Eustacia bounded into the vehicle and sat on the stool, ensconced from view on the side towards the track-way. Soon she heard the brushing of other feet than the reddleman's, a not very friendly 'Good day' uttered by two men in passing each other, and then the dwindling of the footfall of one of them in a direction onwards. Eustacia stretched her neck forward till she caught a glimpse of a receding back and shoulders; and she felt a wretched twinge of misery, she knew not why. It was the sickening feeling which, if the changed heart has any generosity at all in its composition, accompanies the sudden sight of a once-loved one who is beloved no more.

When Eustacia descended to proceed on her way the reddleman came near. 'That was Mr. Wildeve who passed, miss,' he said slowly, and expressed by his face that he expected her to feel vexed at having been sitting unseen.

'Yes, I saw him coming up the hill,' replied Eustacia. 'Why should you tell me that?' It was a bold question, considering the reddleman's knowledge of her past love; but her undemonstrative manner had power to repress the opinions of those she treated as remote from her.

'I am glad to hear that you can ask it,' said the reddleman bluntly. 'And, now I think of it, it agrees with what I saw last night.'

'Ah—what was that?' Eustacia wished to leave him, but wished to know.

'Mr. Wildeve stayed at Rainbarrow a long time waiting for a lady who didn't come.'

'You waited too, it seems?'

'Yes, I always do. I was glad to see him disappointed. He will be there again to-night.'

'To be again disappointed. The truth is, reddleman, that that lady, so far from wishing to stand in the way of Thomasin's marriage with Mr. Wildeve, would be very glad to promote it.'

Venn felt much astonishment at this avowal, though he did not show it clearly; that exhibition may greet remarks which are one remove from expectation, but it is usually withheld in complicated cases of two removes and upwards. 'Indeed, miss,' he replied.

'How do you know that Mr. Wildeve will come to Rainbarrow again to-night?' she asked.

'I heard him say to himself that he would. He's in a regular temper.'

Eustacia looked for a moment what she felt, and she murmured, lifting her deep dark eyes anxiously to his, 'I wish I knew what to do. I don't want to be uncivil to him; but I don't wish to see him again; and I have some few little things to return to him.'

'If you choose to send 'em by me, miss, and a note to tell him that you wish to say no more to him, I'll take it for you quite privately. That would be the most straightforward way of letting him know your mind.'

'Very well,' said Eustacia. 'Come towards my house, and I will bring it out to you.'

She went on, and as the path was an infinitely small parting in the shaggy locks of the heath, the reddleman followed exactly in her trail. She saw from a distance that the captain was on the bank sweeping the horizon with his telescope; and bidding Venn to wait where he stood she entered the house alone.

In ten minutes she returned with a parcel and a note, and said, in placing them in his hand, 'Why are you so ready to take these for me?'

'Can you ask that?'

'I suppose you think to serve Thomasin in some way by it. Are you as anxious as ever to help on her marriage?'

Venn was a little moved. 'I would sooner have married her myself,' he said in a low voice. 'But what I feel is that if she cannot be happy without him I will do my duty in helping her to get him, as a man ought.'

Eustacia looked curiously at the singular man who spoke thus. What a strange sort of love, to be entirely free from that quality of selfishness which is frequently the chief constituent of the passion, and sometimes its only one! The reddleman's disinterestedness was so well deserving of respect that it overshot respect by being barely comprehended; and she almost thought it absurd.

'Then we are both of one mind at last,' she said.

'Yes,' replied Venn gloomily. 'But if you would tell me, miss, why you take such an interest in her, I should be easier. It is so sudden and strange.'

Eustacia appeared at a loss. 'I cannot tell you that, reddleman,' she said coldly.

Venn said no more. He pocketed the letter, and, bowing to Eustacia, went away.

Rainbarrow had again become blended with night

when Wildeve ascended the long acclivity at its base. On his reaching the top a shape grew up from the earth immediately behind him. It was that of Eustacia's emissary. He slapped Wildeve on the shoulder. The feverish young innkeeper and ex-engineer started like Satan at the touch of Ithuriel's spear.

'The meeting is always at eight o'clock, at this place,' said Venn, 'and here we are—we three.'

'We three?' said Wildeve, looking quickly round.

'Yes; you, and I, and she. This is she.' He held up the letter and parcel.

Wildeve took them wonderingly. 'I don't quite see what this means,' he said. 'How do you come here? There must be some mistake.'

'It will be cleared from your mind when you have read the letter. Lanterns for one.' The reddleman struck a light, kindled an inch of tallow-candle which he had brought, and sheltered it with his cap.

'Who are you?' said Wildeve, discerning by the candle-light an obscure rubicundity of person in his companion. 'You are the reddleman I saw on the hill this morning—why, you are the man who——'

'Please read the letter.'

'If you had come from the other one I shouldn't have been surprised,' murmured Wildeve as he opened the letter and read. His face grew serious.

To Mr. Wildeve.

After some thought I have decided once and for all that we must hold no further communication. The more I consider the matter the more I am convinced that there must be an end to our acquaintance. Had you been uniformly faithful to me throughout these two years you might now have some ground for accusing me of heartlessness; but if you calmly consider what I bore during the period of your desertion, and how I passively put up with your courtship of another without once interfering, you will, I think, own that I have a right to consult my own feelings when you come back to me again. That these are not what they were towards you may, perhaps, be a fault in me, but it is one which you can scarcely reproach me for when you remember how you left me for Thomasin.

The little articles you gave me in the early part of our friendship are returned by the bearer of this letter. They should rightly have been sent back when I first heard of your engagement to her.

EUSTACIA.

By the time that Wildeve reached her name the blankness with which he had read the first half of the letter intensified to mortification. 'I am made a great fool of, one way and another,' he said pettishly. 'Do you know what is in this letter?'

The reddleman hummed a tune.

'Can't you answer me?' asked Wildeve warmly.

'Ru-um-tum-tum,' sang the reddleman.

Wildeve stood looking on the ground beside Venn's feet, till he allowed his eyes to travel upwards over Diggory's form, as illuminated by the candle, to his head and face. 'Ha-ha! Well, I suppose I deserve it, considering how I have played with them both,' he said at last, as much to himself as to Venn. 'But of all the odd things that ever I knew, the oddest is that you should so run counter to your own interests as to bring this to me.'

'My interests?'

'Certainly. 'Twas your interest not to do anything which would send me courting Thomasin again, now she has accepted you—or something like it. Mrs. Yeobright says you are to marry her. 'Tisn't true, then?'

'Good Lord! I heard of this before, but didn't believe it. When did she say so?'

Wildeve began humming as the reddleman had done.

'I don't believe it now,' cried Venn.

'Ru-um-tum-tum,' sang Wildeve.

'O Lord—how we can imitate!' said Venn contemptuously. 'I'll have this out. I'll go straight to her.'

Diggory withdrew with an emphatic step, Wildeve's eye passing over his form in withering derision, as if he were no more than a heath-cropper. When the reddleman's figure could no longer be seen, Wildeve himself descended and plunged into the rayless hollow of the vale.

To lose the two women—he who had been the well-beloved of both—was too ironical an issue to be endured. He could only decently save himself by Thomasin; and once be became her husband, Eustacia's repentance, he thought, would set in for a long and bitter term. It was no wonder that Wildeve, ignorant of the new man at the back of the scene, should have supposed Eustacia to be playing a part. To believe that the letter was not the result of some momentary pique, to infer that she really gave him up to Thomasin, would have required previous knowledge of her transfiguration by that man's influence. Who was to know that she had grown generous in the greediness of a new passion, that in coveting one cousin she was dealing liberally with another, that in her eagerness to appropriate she gave way?

Full of this resolve to marry in haste, and wring the heart of the proud girl, Wildeve went his way.

Meanwhile Diggory Venn had returned to his van, where he stood looking thoughtfully into the stove. A new vista was opened up to him. But, however promising Mrs. Yeobright's views of him might be as a candidate for her niece's hand, one condition was indispensable to the favour of Thomasin herself, and that was a renunciation of his present wild mode of life. In this he saw little difficulty.

He could not afford to wait till the next day before seeing Thomasin and detailing his plan. He speedily plunged himself into toilet operations, pulled a suit of cloth clothes from a box, and in about twenty minutes stood before the van-lantern as a reddleman in nothing but his face, the vermilion shades of which were not to be removed in a day. Closing the door and fastening it with a padlock Venn set off towards Blooms-End.

He had reached the white palings and laid his hand upon the gate when the door of the house opened, and quickly closed again. A female form had glided in. At the same time a man, who had seemingly been standing with the woman in the porch, came forward from the house till he was face to face with Venn. It was Wildeve again.

'Man alive, you've been quick at it,' said Diggory sarcastically.

'And you slow, as you will find,' said Wildeve. 'And,' lowering his voice, 'you may as well go back again now. I've claimed her, and got her. Good night, reddleman!' Thereupon Wildeve walked away.

Venn's heart sank within him, though it had not risen unduly high. He stood leaning over the palings in an indecisive mood for nearly a quarter of an hour. Then he went up the garden-path, knocked, and asked for Mrs. Yeobright.

Instead of requesting him to enter she came to the porch. A discourse was carried on between them in low measured tones for the space of ten minutes or more. At the end of the time Mrs. Yeobright went in, and Venn sadly retraced his steps into the heath. When he had again regained his van he lit the lantern, and with an apathetic face at once began to pull off his best clothes, till in the course of a few minutes he reappeared as the confirmed and irretrievable reddleman that he had seemed before.

FIRMNESS IS DISCOVERED IN A GENTLE HEART

VIII

ON that evening the interior of Blooms-End, though cosy and comfortable, had been rather silent. Clym Yeobright was not at home. Since the Christmas party he had gone on a few days' visit to a friend about ten miles off.

The shadowy form seen by Venn to part from Wildeve in the porch, and quickly withdraw into the house, was Thomasin's. On entering she threw down a cloak which had been carelessly wrapped round her, and came forward to the light, where Mrs. Yeobright sat at her work-table, drawn up within the settle, so that part of it projected into the chimney-corner.

'I don't like your going out after dark alone, Tamsin,' said her aunt quietly, without looking up from her work.

'I have only been just outside the door.'

'Well?' inquired Mrs. Yeobright, struck by a change in the tone of Thomasin's voice, and observing her. Thomasin's cheek was flushed to a pitch far beyond that which it had reached before her troubles, and her eyes glittered.

'It was *he* who knocked,' she said.

'I thought as much.'

'He wishes the marriage to be at once.'

'Indeed! What—is he anxious?' Mrs. Yeobright directed a searching look upon her niece. 'Why did not Mr. Wildeve come in?'

'He did not wish to. You are not friends with him, he says. He would like the wedding to be the day after to-morrow, quite privately; at the church of his parish—not at ours.'

'Oh! And what did you say?'

'I agreed to it,' Thomasin answered firmly. 'I am a practical woman now. I don't believe in hearts at all. I would marry him under any circumstances since—since Clym's letter.'

A letter was lying on Mrs. Yeobright's work-basket, and at Thomasin's words her aunt reopened it, and silently read for the tenth time that day:

What is the meaning of this silly story that people are circulating about Thomasin and Mr. Wildeve? I should call such a scandal humiliating if there was the least chance of its being true. How could such a gross falsehood have arisen? It is said that one should go abroad to hear news of home, and I appear to have done it. Of course I contradict the tale everywhere; but it is very vexing, and I wonder how it could have originated. It is too ridiculous that such a girl as Thomasin could so mortify us as to get jilted on the wedding-day. What has she done?

'Yes,' Mrs. Yeobright said sadly, putting down the letter. 'If you think you can marry him, do so. And since Mr. Wildeve wishes it to be unceremonious, let it be that too. I can do nothing. It is all in your own hands now. My power over your welfare came to an end when you left this house to go with him to Anglebury.' She continued, half in bitterness, 'I may almost ask, why do you consult me in the matter at all? If you had gone and married him without saying a word to me, I could hardly have been angry—simply because, poor girl, you can't do a better thing.'

'Don't say that and dishearten me.'

'You are right: I will not.'

'I do not plead for him, aunt. Human nature is weak, and I am not a blind woman to insist that he is perfect. I did think so, but I don't now. But I know my course, and you know that I know it. I hope for the best.'

'And so do I, and we will both continue to,' said Mrs. Yeobright, rising and kissing her. 'Then the wedding, if it comes off, will be on the morning of the very day Clym comes home?'

'Yes. I decided that it ought to be over before he came. After that you can look him in the face, and so can I. Our concealments will matter nothing.'

Mrs. Yeobright moved her head in thoughtful assent, and presently said, 'Do you wish me to give you away? I am willing to undertake that, you know, if you wish, as I was last time. After once forbidding the banns I think I can do no less.'

'I don't think I will ask you to come,' said Thomasin reluctantly, but with decision. 'It would be unpleasant, I am almost sure. Better let there be only strangers present, and none of my relations at all. I would rather have it so. I do not wish to do anything which may touch your credit, and I feel that I should be uncomfortable if you were there, after what has passed. I am only your niece, and there is no necessity why you should concern yourself more about me.'

'Well, he has beaten us,' her aunt said. 'It really seems as if he had been playing with you in this way in revenge for my humbling him as I did by standing up against him at first.'

'O no, aunt,' murmured Thomasin.

They said no more on the subject then. Diggory Venn's knock came soon after; and Mrs. Yeobright, on returning from her interview with him in the porch, carelessly observed, 'Another lover has come to ask for you.'

'No?'

'Yes; that queer young man Venn.'

'Asks to pay his addresses to me?'

'Yes; and I told him he was too late.'

Thomasin looked silently into the candle-flame. 'Poor Diggory!' she said, and then aroused herself to other things.

The next day was passed in mere mechanical deeds of preparation, both the women being anxious to immerse themselves in these to escape the emotional aspect of the situation. Some wearing apparel and other articles were collected anew for Thomasin, and remarks on domestic details were frequently made, so as to obscure any inner misgivings about her future as Wildeve's wife.

The appointed morning came. The arrangement with Wildeve was that he should meet her at the church to guard against any unpleasant curiosity which might have affected them had they been seen walking off together in the usual country way.

Aunt and niece stood together in the bedroom where the bride was dressing. The sun, where it could catch it, made a mirror of Thomasin's hair, which she always wore braided. It was braided according to a calendric system: the more important the day the more numerous the strands in the braid. On ordinary working-days she braided it in threes; on ordinary Sundays in fours; at May-polings, gipsyings, and the like, she braided it in fives. Years ago she had said that when she married she would braid it in sevens. She had braided it in sevens to-day.

'I have been thinking that I will wear my blue silk after all,' she said. 'It *is* my wedding day, even though there may be something sad about the time. I mean,' she added, anxious to correct any wrong impression, 'not sad in itself, but in its having had great disappointment and trouble before it.'

Mrs. Yeobright breathed in a way which might have been called a sigh. 'I almost wish Clym had been at home,' she said. 'Of course you chose the time because of his absence.'

'Partly. I have felt that I acted unfairly to him in not telling him all; but, as it was done not to grieve him, I thought I would carry out the plan to its end, and tell the whole story when the sky was clear.'

'You are a practical little woman,' said Mrs. Yeobright smiling. 'I wish you and he—no, I don't wish anything. There, it is nine o'clock,' she interrupted, hearing a whizz and a dinging downstairs.

'I told Damon I would leave at nine,' said Thomasin, hastening out of the room.

Her aunt followed. When Thomasin was going up the little walk from the door to the wicket-gate, Mrs. Yeobright looked reluctantly at her, and said, 'It is a shame to let you go alone.'

'It is necessary,' said Thomasin.

'At any rate,' added her aunt with forced cheerfulness, 'I shall call upon you this afternoon, and bring the cake with me. If Clym has returned by that time he will perhaps come too. I wish to show Mr. Wildeve that I bear him no ill-will. Let the past be forgotten. Well, God bless you! There, I don't believe in old superstitions, but I'll do it.' She threw a slipper at the retreating figure of the girl, who turned, smiled, and went on again.

A few steps further, and she looked back. 'Did you call me, aunt?' she tremulously inquired. 'Good-bye!'

Moved by an uncontrollable feeling as she looked upon Mrs. Yeobright's worn, wet face, she ran back, when her aunt came forward, and they met again. 'O—Tamsie,' said the elder, weeping, 'I don't like to let you go.'

'I—I am——' Thomasin began, giving way likewise. But, quelling her grief, she said 'Good-bye!' again and went on.

Then Mrs. Yeobright saw a little figure wending its way between the scratching furze-bushes, and diminishing far up the valley—a pale-blue spot in a vast field of neutral brown, solitary and undefended except by the power of her own hope.

But the worst feature in the case was one which did not appear in the landscape ; it was the man.

The hour chosen for the ceremony by Thomasin and Wildeve had been so timed as to enable her to escape the awkwardness of meeting her cousin Clym, who was returning the same morning. To own to the partial truth of what he had heard would be distressing as long as the humiliating position resulting from the event was unimproved. It was only after a second and successful journey to the altar that she could lift up her head and prove the failure of the first attempt a pure accident.

She had not been gone from Blooms-End more than half an hour when Yeobright came by the meads from the other direction and entered the house.

'I had an early breakfast,' he said to his mother after greeting her. 'Now I could eat a little more.'

They sat down to the repeated meal, and he went on in a low, anxious voice, apparently imagining that Thomasin had not yet come downstairs. 'What's this I have heard about Thomasin and Mr. Wildeve ?'

'It is true in many points,' said Mrs. Yeobright quietly ; 'but it is all right now, I hope.' She looked at the clock.

'True ?'

'Thomasin is gone to him to-day.'

Clym pushed away his breakfast. 'Then there is a scandal of some sort, and that's what's the matter with Thomasin. Was it this that made her ill ?'

'Yes. Not a scandal : a misfortune. I will tell you all about it, Clym. You must not be angry, but you must listen, and you'll find that what we have done has been done for the best.'

She then told him the circumstances. All that he had known of the affair before he returned from Paris was that there had existed an attachment between Thomasin and Wildeve, which his mother had at first discountenanced, but had since, owing to the arguments of Thomasin, looked upon in a little more favourable light. When she, therefore, proceeded to explain all he was greatly surprised and troubled.

'And she determined that the wedding should be over before you came back,' said Mrs. Yeobright, 'that there might be no chance of her meeting you, and having a very painful time of it. That's why she has gone to him; they have arranged to be married this morning.'

'But I can't understand it,' said Yeobright, rising. ''Tis so unlike her. I can see why you did not write to me after her unfortunate return home. But why didn't you let me know when the wedding was going to be—the first time?'

'Well, I felt vexed with her just then. She seemed to me to be obstinate; and when I found that you were nothing in her mind I vowed that she should be nothing in yours. I felt that she was only my niece after all; I told her she might marry, but that I should take no interest in it, and should not bother you about it either.'

'It wouldn't have been bothering me. Mother, you did wrong.'

'I thought it might disturb you in your business, and that you might throw up your situation, or injure your prospects in some way because of it, so I said nothing. Of course, if they had married at that time in a proper manner, I should have told you at once.'

'Tamsin actually being married while we are sitting here!'

'Yes. Unless some accident happens again, as it did the first time. It may, considering he's the same man.'

'Yes, and I believe it will. Was it right to let her go? Suppose Wildeve is really a bad fellow?'

'Then he won't come, and she'll come home again.'

'You should have looked more into it.'

'It is useless to say that,' his mother answered with an impatient look of sorrow. 'You don't know how bad it has been here with us all these weeks, Clym. You don't know what a mortification anything of that sort is to a woman. You don't know the sleepless nights we've had in this house, and the almost bitter words that have passed between us since that Fifth of November. I hope never to pass seven such weeks again. Tamsin has not gone outside the door, and I have been ashamed to look anybody in the face; and now you blame me for letting her do the only thing that can be done to set that trouble straight.'

'No,' he said slowly. 'Upon the whole I don't blame you. But just consider how sudden it seems to me. Here was I, knowing nothing; and then I am told all at once that Tamsie is gone to be married. Well, I suppose there was nothing better to do. Do you know, mother,' he continued after a moment or two, looking suddenly interested in his own past history, 'I once thought of Tamsin as a sweetheart? Yes, I did. How odd boys are! And when I came home and saw her this time she seemed so much more affectionate than usual, that I was quite reminded of those days, particularly on the night of the party, when she was unwell. We had the party just the same—was not that rather cruel to her?'

'It made no difference. I had arranged to give one, and it was not worth while to make more gloom than necessary. To begin by shutting ourselves up and telling you of Tamsin's misfortunes would have been a poor sort of welcome.'

Clym remained thinking. 'I almost wish you had not had that party,' he said; 'and for other reasons. But I will tell you in a day or two. We must think of Tamsin now.'

They lapsed into silence. 'I'll tell you what,' said Yeobright again, in a tone which showed some slumbering feeling still. 'I don't think it kind to Tamsin to let her be married like this, and neither of us there to keep up her spirits or care a bit about her. She hasn't disgraced herself, or done anything to deserve that. It is bad enough that the wedding should be so hurried and unceremonious, without our keeping away from it in addition. Upon my soul, 'tis almost a shame. I'll go.'

'It is over by this time,' said his mother with a sigh; 'unless they were late, or he——'

'Then I shall be soon enough to see them come out. I don't quite like your keeping me in ignorance, mother, after all. Really, I half hope he has failed to meet her!'

'And ruined her character?'

'Nonsense: that wouldn't ruin Thomasin.'

He took up his hat and hastily left the house. Mrs. Yeobright looked rather unhappy, and sat still, deep in thought. But she was not long left alone. A few minutes later Clym came back again, and in his company came Diggory Venn.

'I find there isn't time for me to get there,' said Clym.

'Is she married?' Mrs. Yeobright inquired, turning to the reddleman a face in which a strange strife of wishes, for and against, was apparent.

Venn bowed. 'She is, ma'am.'

'How strange it sounds,' murmured Clym.

'And he didn't disappoint her this time?' said Mrs. Yeobright.

'He did not. And there is now no slight on her name. I was hastening ath'art to tell you at once, as I saw you were not there.'

'How came you to be there? How did you know it?' she asked.

'I have been in that neighbourhood for some time, and I saw them go in,' said the reddleman. 'Wildeve came up to the door, punctual as the clock. I didn't expect it of him.' He did not add, as he might have added, that how he came to be in that neighbourhood was not by accident; that, since Wildeve's resumption of his right to Thomasin, Venn, with the thoroughness which was part of his character, had determined to see the end of the episode.

'Who was there ?' said Mrs. Yeobright.

'Nobody hardly. I stood right out of the way, and she did not see me.' The reddleman spoke huskily, and looked into the garden.

'Who gave her away ?'

'Miss Vye.'

'How very remarkable ! Miss Vye ! It is to be considered an honour, I suppose ?'

'Who's Miss Vye ?' said Clym.

'Captain Vye's granddaughter, of Mistover Knap.'

'A proud girl from Budmouth,' said Mrs. Yeobright. 'One not much to my liking. People say she's a witch, but of course that's absurd.'

The reddleman kept to himself his acquaintance with that fair personage, and also that Eustacia was there because he went to fetch her, in accordance with a promise he had given as soon as he learnt that the marriage was to take place. He merely said, in continuation of the story—

'I was sitting on the churchyard-wall when they came up, one from one way, the other from the other ; and Miss Vye was walking thereabouts, looking at the head-stones. As soon as they had gone in I went to the door, feeling I should like to see it, as I knew her so well. I pulled off my boots because they were so noisy, and went up into the gallery. I saw then that the parson and clerk were already there.'

'How came Miss Vye to have anything to do with it, if she was only on a walk that way ?'

'Because there was nobody else. She had gone into the church just before me, not into the gallery. The parson looked round before beginning, and as she was the only one near he beckoned to her, and she went up to the rails. After that, when it came to signing the book, she pushed up her veil and signed; and Tamsin seemed to thank her for her kindness.' The reddleman told the tale thoughtfully, for there lingered upon his vision the changing colour of Wildeve, when Eustacia lifted the thick veil which had concealed her from recognition and looked calmly into his face. 'And then,' said Diggory sadly, 'I came away, for her history as Tamsin Yeobright was over.'

'I offered to go,' said Mrs. Yeobright regretfully. 'But she said it was not necessary.'

'Well, it is no matter,' said the reddleman. 'The thing is done at last as it was meant to be at first, and God send her happiness. Now I'll wish you good morning.'

He placed his cap on his head and went out.

From that instant of leaving Mrs. Yeobright's door, the reddleman was seen no more in or about Egdon Heath for a space of many months. He vanished entirely. The nook among the brambles where his van had been standing was as vacant as ever the next morning, and scarcely a sign remained to show that he had been there, excepting a few straws, and a little redness on the turf, which was washed away by the next storm of rain.

The report that Diggory had brought of the wedding, correct as far as it went, was deficient in one significant particular, which had escaped him through his being at some distance back in the church. When Thomasin was tremblingly engaged in signing her name Wildeve had flung towards Eustacia a glance that said plainly, 'I have punished you now.' She had replied in a low tone—and he little thought how truly—'You mistake; it gives me sincerest pleasure to see her your wife to-day.'

BOOK THIRD

THE FASCINATION

'MY MIND TO ME A KINGDOM IS'

I

IN Clym Yeobright's face could be dimly seen the typical countenance of the future. Should there be a classic period to art hereafter, its Pheidias may produce such faces. The view of life as a thing to be put up with, replacing that zest for existence which was so intense in early civilizations, must ultimately enter so thoroughly into the constitution of the advanced races that its facial expression will become accepted as a new artistic departure. People already feel that a man who lives without disturbing a curve of feature, or setting a mark of mental concern anywhere upon himself, is too far removed from modern perceptiveness to be a modern type. Physically beautiful men—the glory of the race when it was young—are almost an anachronism now; and we may wonder whether, at some time or other, physically beautiful women may not be an anachronism likewise.

The truth seems to be that a long line of disillusive centuries has permanently displaced the Hellenic idea of life, or whatever it may be called. What the Greeks only suspected we know well; what their Æschylus imagined our nursery children feel. That old-fashioned revelling in the generai situation grows less and less possible as we uncover the defects of natural laws, and see the quandary that man is in by their operation.

The lineaments which will get embodied in ideals based upon this new recognition will probably be akin to those of Yeobright. The observer's eye was arrested, not by his face as a picture, but by his face as a page; not by what it was, but by what it recorded. His features were attractive in the light of symbols, as sounds intrinsically common become attractive in language, and as shapes intrinsically simple become interesting in writing.

He had been a lad of whom something was expected. Beyond this all had been chaos. That he would be successful in an original way, or that he would go to the dogs in an original way, seemed equally probable. The only absolute certainty about him was that he would not stand still in the circumstances amid which he was born.

Hence, when his name was casually mentioned by neighbouring yeomen, the listener said, 'Ah, Clym Yeobright: what is he doing now?' When the instinctive question about a person is, What is he doing? it is felt that he will not be found to be, like most of us, doing nothing in particular. There is an indefinite sense that he must be invading some region of singularity, good or bad. The devout hope is that he is doing well. The secret faith is that he is making a mess of it. Half a dozen comfortable market-men, who were habitual callers at the Quiet Woman as they passed by in their carts, were partial to the topic. In fact, though they were not Egdon men, they could hardly avoid it while they sucked their long clay tubes and regarded the heath through the window. Clym had been so inwoven with the heath in his boyhood that hardly anybody could look upon it without thinking of him. So the subject recurred: if he were making a fortune and a name, so much the better for him; if he were making a tragical figure in the world, so much the better for a narrative.

The fact was that Yeobright's fame had spread to an

awkward extent before he left home. 'It is bad when your fame outruns your means,' said the Spanish Jesuit Gracian. At the age of six he had asked a Scripture riddle: 'Who was the first man known to wear breeches?' and applause had resounded from the very verge of the heath. At seven he painted the Battle of Waterloo with tiger-lily pollen and black-currant juice, in the absence of water-colours. By the time he reached twelve he had in this manner been heard of as artist and scholar for at least two miles round. An individual whose fame spreads three or four thousand yards in the time taken by the fame of others similarly situated to travel six or eight hundred must of necessity have something in him. Possibly Clym's fame, like Homer's, owed something to the accidents of his situation; nevertheless famous he was.

He grew up and was helped out in life. That waggery of fate which started Clive as a writing clerk, Gay as a linen-draper, Keats as a surgeon, and a thousand others in a thousand other odd ways, banished the wild and ascetic heath lad to a trade whose sole concern was with the especial symbols of self-indulgence and vainglory.

The details of this choice of a business for him it is not necessary to give. At the death of his father a neighbouring gentleman had kindly undertaken to give the boy a start; and this assumed the form of sending him to Budmouth. Yeobright did not wish to go there, but it was the only feasible opening. Thence he went to London; and thence, shortly after, to Paris, where he had remained till now.

Something being expected of him, he had not been at home many days before a great curiosity as to why he stayed on so long began to arise in the heath. The natural term of a holiday had passed, yet he still remained. On the Sunday morning following the week of Thomasin's marriage a discussion on this subject was in progress at a hair-cutting before Fairway's house. Here the local barbering was always done at this hour on this day; to be followed by the great Sunday wash of the inhabitants at noon, which in its turn was followed by the great Sunday dressing an hour later. On Egdon Heath Sunday proper did not begin till dinner-time, and even then it was a somewhat battered specimen of the day.

These Sunday-morning hair-cuttings were performed by Fairway; the victim sitting on a chopping-block in front of the house, without a coat, and the neighbours gossiping around, idly observing the locks of hair as they rose upon the wind after the snip, and flew away out of sight to the four quarters of the heavens. Summer and winter the scene was the same, unless the wind were more than usually blusterous, when the stool was shifted a few feet round the corner. To complain of cold in sitting out of doors, hatless and coatless, while Fairway told true stories between the cuts of the scissors, would have been to pronounce yourself no man at once. To flinch, exclaim, or move a muscle of the face at the small stabs under the ear received from those instruments, or at scarifications of the neck by the comb, would have been thought a gross breach of good manners, considering that Fairway did it all for nothing. A bleeding about the poll on Sunday afternoons was amply accounted for by the explanation, 'I have had my hair cut, you know.'

The conversation on Yeobright had been started by a distant view of the young man rambling leisurely across the heath before them.

'A man who is doing well elsewhere wouldn't bide here two or three weeks for nothing,' said Fairway. 'He's got some project in 's head—depend upon that.'

'Well, 'a can't keep a diment shop here,' said Sam.

'I don't see why he should have had them two heavy boxes home if he had not been going to bide; and what there is for him to do here the Lord in heaven knows.'

Before many more surmises could be indulged in Yeobright had come near; and seeing the hair-cutting group he turned aside to join them. Marching up, and looking critically at their faces for a moment, he said, without introduction, 'Now, folks, let me guess what you have been talking about.'

'Ay, sure, if you will,' said Sam.

'About me.'

'Now, it is a thing I shouldn't have dreamed of doing, otherwise,' said Fairway in a tone of integrity; 'but since you have named it, Master Yeobright, I'll own that we was talking about 'ee. We were wondering what could keep you home here mollyhorning about when you have made such a world-wide name for yourself in the nick-nack trade—now, that's the truth o't.'

'I'll tell you,' said Yeobright, with unexpected earnestness. 'I am not sorry to have the opportunity. I've come home because, all things considered, I can be a trifle less useless here than anywhere else. But I have only lately found this out. When I first got away from home I thought this place was not worth troubling about. I thought our life here was contemptible. To oil your boots instead of blacking them, to dust your coat with a switch instead of a brush: was there ever anything more ridiculous? I said.'

'So 'tis; so 'tis!'

'No, no—you are wrong; it isn't.'

'Beg your pardon, we thought that was your maning.'

'Well, as my views changed my course became very depressing. I found that I was trying to be like people who had hardly anything in common with myself. I was endeavouring to put off one sort of life for another sort of life, which was not better than the life I had known before. It was simply different.'

'True; a sight different,' said Fairway.

'Yes, Paris must be a taking place,' said Humphrey. 'Grand shop-winders, trumpets, and drums; and here be we out of doors in all winds and weathers——'

"But you mistake me,' pleaded Clym. 'All this was very depressing. But not so depressing as something I next perceived—that my business was the idlest, vainest, most effeminate business that ever a man could be put to. That decided me: I would give it up and try to follow some rational occupation among the people I knew best, and to whom I could be of most use. I have come home; and this is how I mean to carry out my plan. I shall keep a school as near to Egdon as possible, so as to be able to walk over here and have a night-school in my mother's house. But I must study a little at first, to get properly qualified. Now, neighbours, I must go.'

And Clym resumed his walk across the heath.

'He'll never carry it out in the world,' said Fairway. 'In a few weeks he'll learn to see things otherwise.'

''Tis good-hearted of the young man,' said another. 'But, for my part, I think he had better mind his business.'

THE NEW COURSE CAUSES DISAPPOINTMENT

II

YEOBRIGHT loved his kind. He had a conviction that the want of most men was knowledge of a sort which brings wisdom rather than affluence. He wished to raise the class at the expense of individuals rather than individuals at the expense of the class. What was more, he was ready at once to be the first unit sacrificed.

In passing from the bucolic to the intellectual life the intermediate stages are usually two at least, frequently many more ; and one of these stages is almost sure to be worldly advance. We can hardly imagine bucolic placidity quickening to intellectual aims without imagining social aims as the transitional phase. Yeobright's local peculiarity was that in striving at high thinking he still cleaved to plain living—nay, wild and meagre living in many respects, and brotherliness with clowns.

He was a John the Baptist who took ennoblement rather than repentance for his text. Mentally he was in a provincial future, that is, he was in many points abreast with the central town thinkers of his date. Much of this development he may have owed to his studious life in Paris, where he had become acquainted with ethical systems popular at the time.

In consequence of this relatively advanced position,

Yeobright might have been called unfortunate. The rural world was not ripe for him. A man should be only partially before his time: to be completely to the vanward in aspirations is fatal to fame. Had Philip's warlike son been intellectually so far ahead as to have attempted civilization without bloodshed, he would have been twice the godlike hero that he seemed, but nobody would have heard of an Alexander.

In the interests of renown the forwardness should lie chiefly in the capacity to handle things. Successful propagandists have succeeded because the doctrine they bring into form is that which their listeners have for some time felt without being able to shape. A man who advocates æsthetic effort and deprecates social effort is only likely to be understood by a class to which social effort has become a stale matter. To argue upon the possibility of culture before luxury to the bucolic world may be to argue truly, but it is an attempt to disturb a sequence to which humanity has been long accustomed. Yeobright preaching to the Egdon eremites that they might rise to a serene comprehensiveness without going through the process of enriching themselves, was not unlike arguing to ancient Chaldeans that in ascending from earth to the pure empyrean it was not necessary to pass first into the intervening heaven of ether.

Was Yeobright's mind well-proportioned? No. A well-proportioned mind is one which shows no particular bias; one of which we may safely say that it will never cause its owner to be confined as a madman, tortured as a heretic, or crucified as a blasphemer. Also, on the other hand, that it will never cause him to be applauded as a prophet, revered as a priest, or exalted as a king. Its usual blessings are happiness and mediocrity. It produces the poetry of Rogers, the paintings of West, the statecraft of North, the spiritual guidance of Tomline; enabling its possessors to find their way to wealth, to wind up well, to step with dignity off the stage, to die comfortably in their beds, and to get the decent monument which, in many cases, they deserve. It never would have allowed Yeobright to do such a ridiculous thing as throw up his business to benefit his fellow-creatures.

He walked along towards home without attending to paths. If any one knew the heath well it was Clym. He was permeated with its scenes, with its substance, and with its odours. He might be said to be its product. His eyes had first opened thereon; with its appearance all the first images of his memory were mingled; his estimate of life had been coloured by it; his toys had been the flint knives and arrow-heads which he found there, wondering why stones should 'grow' to such odd shapes; his flowers, the purple bells and yellow furze; his animal kingdom, the snakes and croppers; his society, its human haunters. Take all the varying hates felt by Eustacia Vye towards the heath, and translate them into loves, and you have the heart of Clym. He gazed upon the wide prospect as he walked, and was glad.

To many persons this Egdon was a place which had slipped out of its century generations ago, to intrude as an uncouth object into this. It was an obsolete thing, and few cared to study it. How could this be otherwise in the days of square fields, plashed hedges, and meadows watered on a plan so rectangular that on a fine day they look like silver gridirons? The farmer, in his ride, who could smile at artificial grasses, look with solicitude at the coming corn, and sigh with sadness at the fly-eaten turnips, bestowed upon the distant upland of heath nothing better than a frown. But as for Yeobright, when he looked from the heights on his way he could not help indulging in a barbarous satisfaction at observing that, in some of the attempts at reclamation from the waste, tillage, after holding on for a year or two, had receded again in despair, the ferns and furze-tufts stubbornly reasserting themselves.

He descended into the valley, and soon reached his

home at Blooms-End. His mother was snipping dead leaves from the window-plants. She looked up at him as if she did not understand the meaning of his long stay with her; her face had worn that look for several days. He could perceive that the curiosity which had been shown by the hair-cutting group amounted in his mother to concern. But she had asked no question with her lips, even when the arrival of his trunks suggested that he was not going to leave her soon. Her silence besought an explanation of him more loudly than words.

'I am not going back to Paris again, mother,' he said. 'At least, in my old capacity. I have given up the business.'

Mrs. Yeobright turned in pained surprise. 'I thought something was amiss, because of the boxes. I wonder you did not tell me sooner.'

'I ought to have done it. But I have been in doubt whether you would be pleased with my plan. I was not quite clear on a few points myself. I am going to take an entirely new course.'

'I am astonished, Clym. How can you want to do better than you've been doing?'

'Very easily. But I shall not do better in the way you mean; I suppose it will be called doing worse. But I hate that business of mine, and I want to do some worthy thing before I die. As a schoolmaster I think to do it—a schoolmaster to the poor and ignorant, to teach them what nobody else will.'

'After all the trouble that has been taken to give you a start, and when there is nothing to do but to keep straight on towards affluence, you say you will be a poor man's schoolmaster. Your fancies will be your ruin, Clym.'

Mrs. Yeobright spoke calmly, but the force of feeling behind the words was but too apparent to one who knew her as well as her son did. He did not answer. There was in his face that hopelessness of being understood which comes when the objector is constitutionally beyond the reach of a logic that, even under favouring conditions, is almost too coarse a vehicle for the subtlety of the argument.

No more was said on the subject till the end of dinner. His mother then began, as if there had been no interval since the morning. 'It disturbs me, Clym, to find that you have come home with such thoughts as those. I hadn't the least idea that you meant to go backward in the world by your own free choice. Of course, I have always supposed you were going to push straight on, as other men do—all who deserve the name—when they have been put in a good way of doing well.'

'I cannot help it,' said Clym, in a troubled tone. 'Mother, I hate the flashy business. Talk about men who deserve the name, can any man deserving the name waste his time in that effeminate way, when he sees half the world going to ruin for want of somebody to buckle to and teach them how to breast the misery they are born to? I get up every morning and see the whole creation groaning and travailing in pain, as St. Paul says, and yet there am I, trafficking in glittering splendours with wealthy women and titled libertines, and pandering to the meanest vanities—I, who have health and strength enough for anything. I have been troubled in my mind about it all the year, and the end is that I cannot do it any more.'

'Why can't you do it as well as others?'

'I don't know, except that there are many things other people care for which I don't; and that's partly why I think I ought to do this. For one thing, my body does not require much of me. I cannot enjoy delicacies; good things are wasted upon me. Well, I ought to turn that defect to advantage, and by being able to do without what other people require I can spend what such things cost upon anybody else.'

Now, Yeobright, having inherited some of these very instincts from the woman before him. could not fail to awaken a reciprocity in her through her feelings, if not by arguments, disguise it as she might for his good. She spoke with less assurance. 'And yet you might have been a wealthy man if you had only persevered. Manager to that large diamond establishment—what better can a man wish for? What a post of trust and respect! I suppose you will be like your father; like him, you are getting weary of doing well.'

'No,' said her son; 'I am not weary of that, though I am weary of what you mean by it. Mother, what is doing well?'

Mrs. Yeobright was far too thoughtful a woman to be content with ready definitions, and, like the 'What is wisdom?' of Plato's Socrates, and the 'What is truth?' of Pontius Pilate, Yeobright's burning question received no answer.

The silence was broken by the clash of the garden gate, a tap at the door, and its opening. Christian Cantle appeared in the room in his Sunday clothes.

It was the custom on Egdon to begin the preface to a story before absolutely entering the house, so as to be well in for the body of the narrative by the time visitor and visited stood face to face. Christian had been saying to them while the door was leaving its latch, 'To think that I, who go from home but once in a while, and hardly then, should have been there this morning!'

''Tis news you have brought us, then, Christian?' said Mrs. Yeobright.

'Ay, sure, about a witch, and ye must overlook my time o' day; for, says I, "I must go and tell 'em though they won't have half done dinner." I assure ye it made me shake like a driven leaf. Do ye think any harm will come o't?'

'Well—what?'

'This morning at church we was all standing up, and the pa'son said, "Let us pray." "Well," thinks I, "one may as well kneel as stand;" so down I went; and, more than that, all the rest were as willing to oblige the man as I. We hadn't been hard at it for more than a minute when a most terrible screech sounded through church, as if somebody had just gied up their heart's blood. All the folk jumped up, and then we found that Susan Nunsuch had pricked Miss Vye with a long stocking-needle, as she had threatened to do as soon as ever she could get the young lady to church, where she don't come very often. She've waited for this chance for weeks, so as to draw her blood and put an end to the bewitching of Susan's children that has been carried on so long. Sue followed her into church, sat next her, and as soon as she could find a chance in went the stocking-needle into my lady's arm.'

'Good heaven, how horrid!' said Mrs. Yeobright.

'Sue pricked her that deep that the maid fainted away; and as I was afeard there might be some tumult among us, I got behind the bass-viol and didn't see no more. But they carried her out into the air, 'tis said; but when they looked round for Sue she was gone. What a scream that girl gied, poor thing! There were the pa'son in his surplice holding up his hand and saying, "Sit down, my good people, sit down!" But the deuce a bit would they sit down. O, and what d'ye think I found out, Mrs. Yeobright? The pa'son wears a suit of clothes under his surplice!—I could see his black sleeve when he held up his arm.'

''Tis a cruel thing,' said Yeobright.

'Yes,' said his mother.

'The nation ought to look into it,' said Christian. 'Here's Humphrey coming, I think.'

In came Humphrey. 'Well, have ye heard the news? But I see you have. 'Tis a very strange thing that whenever one of Egdon folk goes to church some rum job or other is sure to be doing. The last time one of us was there was when neighbour Fairway went in the fall; and that was the day you forbad the banns, Mrs. Yeobright.'

'Has this cruelly treated girl been able to walk home?' said Clym.

'They say she got better, and went home very well. And now I've told it I must be moving homeward myself.'

'And I,' said Humphrey. 'Truly now we shall see if there's anything in what folks say about her.'

When they were gone into the heath again Yeobright said quietly to his mother, 'Do you think I have turned teacher too soon?'

'It is right that there should be schoolmasters, and missionaries, and all such men,' she replied. 'But it is right, too, that I should try to lift you out of this life into something richer, and that you should not come back again, and be as if I had not tried at all.'

Later in the day Sam, the turf-cutter, entered. 'I've come a-borrowing, Mrs. Yeobright. I suppose you have heard what's been happening to the beauty on the hill?'

'Yes, Sam: half a dozen have been telling us.'

'Beauty?' said Clym.

'Yes, tolerably well-favoured,' Sam replied. 'Lord! all the country owns that 'tis one of the strangest things in the world that such a woman should have come to live up there.'

'Dark or fair?'

'Now, though I've seen her twenty times, that's a thing I cannot call to mind.'

'Darker than Tamsin,' murmured Mrs. Yeobright.

'A woman who seems to care for nothing at all, as you may say.'

'She is melancholy, then?' inquired Clym.

'She mopes about by herself, and don't mix in with the people.'

'Is she a young lady inclined for adventures?'

'Not to my knowledge.'

'Doesn't join in with the lads in their games, to get some sort of excitement in this lonely place?'

'No.'

'Mumming, for instance?

'No. Her notions be different. I should rather say her thoughts were far away from here, with lords and ladies she'll never know, and mansions she'll never see again.'

Observing that Clym appeared singularly interested Mrs. Yeobright said rather uneasily to Sam, 'You see more in her than most of us do. Miss Vye is to my mind too idle to be charming. I have never heard that she is of any use to herself or to other people. Good girls don't get treated as witches even on Egdon.'

'Nonsense—that proves nothing either way,' said Yeobright.

'Well, of course I don't understand such niceties,' said Sam, withdrawing from a possibly unpleasant argument; 'and what she is we must wait for time to tell us. The business that I have really called about is this, to borrow the longest and strongest rope you have. The captain's bucket has dropped into the well, and they are in want of water; and as all the chaps are at home to-day we think we can get it out for him. We have three cart-ropes already, but they won't reach to the bottom.'

Mrs. Yeobright told him that he might have whatever ropes he could find in the outhouse, and Sam went out to search. When he passed by the door Clym joined him, and accompanied him to the gate.

'Is this young witch-lady going to stay long at Mistover?' he asked.

'I should say so.'

'What a cruel shame to ill-use her! She must have suffered greatly—more in mind than in body.'

''Twas a graceless trick—such a handsome girl, too. You ought to see her, Mr. Yeobright, being a young man come from far, and with a little more to show for your years than most of us.'

'Do you think she would like to teach children?' said Clym.

Sam shook his head. 'Quite a different sort of body from that, I reckon.'

'O, it was merely something which occurred to me. It would of course be necessary to see her and talk it over—not an easy thing, by the way, for my family and hers are not very friendly.'

'I'll tell you how you mid see her, Mr. Yeobright,' said Sam. 'We are going to grapple for the bucket at six o'clock to-night at her house, and you could lend a hand. There's five or six coming, but the well is deep, and another might be useful, if you don't mind appearing in that shape. She's sure to be walking round.'

'I'll think of it,' said Yeobright; and they parted.

He thought of it a good deal; but nothing more was said about Eustacia inside the house at that time. Whether this romantic martyr to superstition and the melancholy mummer he had conversed with under the full moon were one and the same person remained as yet a problem.

THE FIRST ACT IN A TIMEWORN DRAMA

III

THE afternoon was fine, and Yeobright walked on the heath for an hour with his mother. When they reached the lofty ridge which divided the valley of Blooms-End from the adjoining valley they stood still and looked round. The Quiet Woman Inn was visible on the low margin of the heath in one direction, and afar on the other hand rose Mistover Knap.

'You mean to call on Thomasin ?' he inquired.

'Yes. But you need not come this time,' said his mother.

'In that case I'll branch off here, mother. I am going to Mistover.'

Mrs. Yeobright turned to him inquiringly.

'I am going to help them get the bucket out of the captain's well,' he continued. 'As it is so very deep I may be useful. And I should like to see this Miss Vye—not so much for her good looks as for another reason.'

'Must you go ?' his mother asked.

'I thought to.'

And they parted. 'There is no help for it,' murmured Clym's mother gloomily as he withdrew. 'They are sure to see each other. I wish Sam would carry his news to other houses than mine.'

Clym's retreating figure got smaller and smaller as it rose and fell over the hillocks on his way. 'He is tender-hearted,' said Mrs. Yeobright to herself while she watched him; 'otherwise it would matter little. How he's going on!'

He was, indeed, walking with a will over the furze, as straight as a line, as if his life depended upon it. His mother drew a long breath, and, abandoning the visit to Thomasin, turned back. The evening films began to make nebulous pictures of the valleys, but the high lands still were raked by the declining rays of the winter sun, which glanced on Clym as he walked forward, eyed by every rabbit and fieldfare around, a long shadow advancing in front of him.

On drawing near to the furze-covered bank and ditch which fortified the captain's dwelling he could hear voices within, signifying that operations had been already begun. At the side-entrance gate he stopped and looked over.

Half a dozen able-bodied men were standing in a line from the well-mouth, holding a rope which passed over the well-roller into the depths below. Fairway, with a piece of smaller rope round his body, made fast to one of the standards, to guard against accidents, was leaning over the opening, his right hand clasping the vertical rope that descended into the well.

'Now, silence, folks,' said Fairway.

The talking ceased, and Fairway gave a circular motion to the rope as if he were stirring batter. At the end of a minute a dull splashing reverberated from the bottom of the well; the helical twist he had imparted to the rope had reached the grapnel below.

'Haul!' said Fairway; and the men who held the rope began to gather it over the wheel.

'I think we've got sommat,' said one of the haulers-in.

'Then pull steady,' said Fairway.

They gathered up more and more, till a regular dripping

into the well could be heard below. It grew smarter with the increasing height of the bucket, and presently a hundred and fifty feet of rope had been pulled in.

Fairway then lit a lantern, tied it to another cord, and began lowering it into the well beside the first. Clym came forward and looked down. Strange humid leaves, which knew nothing of the seasons of the year, and quaint-natured mosses were revealed on the well-side as the lantern descended; till its rays fell upon a confused mass of rope and bucket dangling in the dank, dark air.

'We've only got en by the edge of the hoop—steady, for God's sake!' said Fairway.

They pulled with the greatest gentleness, till the wet bucket appeared about two yards below them, like a dead friend come to earth again. Three or four hands were stretched out, then jerk went the rope, whizz went the wheel, the two foremost haulers fell backward, the beating of a falling body was heard, receding down the sides of the well, and a thunderous uproar arose at the bottom. The bucket was gone again.

'Damn the bucket!' said Fairway.

'Lower again,' said Sam.

'I'm as stiff as a ram's horn stooping so long,' said Fairway, standing up and stretching himself till his joints creaked.

'Rest a few minutes, Timothy,' said Yeobright. 'I'll take your place.'

The grapnel was again lowered. Its smart impact upon the distant water reached their ears like a kiss, whereupon Yeobright knelt down, and leaning over the well began dragging the grapnel round and round as Fairway had done.

'Tie a rope round him—it is dangerous!' cried a soft and anxious voice somewhere above them.

Everybody turned. The speaker was a woman, gazing down upon the group from an upper window, whose panes blazed in the ruddy glare from the west. Her lips were parted and she appeared for the moment to forget where she was.

The rope was accordingly tied round his waist, and the work proceeded. At the next haul the weight was not heavy, and it was discovered that they had only secured a coil of the rope detached from the bucket. The tangled mass was thrown into the background. Humphrey took Yeobright's place, and the grapnel was lowered again.

Yeobright retired to the heap of recovered rope in a meditative mood. Of the identity between the lady's voice and that of the melancholy mummer he had not a moment's doubt. 'How thoughtful of her!' he said to himself.

Eustacia, who had reddened when she perceived the effect of her exclamation upon the group below, was no longer to be seen at the window, though Yeobright scanned it wistfully. While he stood there the men at the well succeeded in getting up the bucket without a mishap. One of them then went to inquire for the captain, to learn what orders he wished to give for mending the well-tackle. The captain proved to be away from home; and Eustacia appeared at the door and came out. She had lapsed into an easy and dignified calm, far removed from the intensity of life in her words of solicitude for Clym's safety.

'Will it be possible to draw water here to-night?' she inquired.

'No, miss; the bottom of the bucket is clean knocked out. And as we can do no more now we'll leave off, and come again to-morrow morning.'

'No water,' she murmured, turning away.

'I can send you up some from Blooms-End,' said Clym, coming forward and raising his hat as the men retired.

Yeobright and Eustacia looked at each other for one instant, as if each had in mind those few moments during which a certain moonlight scene was common to both. With the glance the calm fixity of her features sublimed itself to an expression of refinement and warmth: it was like garish noon rising to the dignity of sunset in a couple of seconds.

'Thank you; it will hardly be necessary,' she replied.

'But if you have no water?'

'Well, it is what I call no water,' she said, blushing, and lifting her long-lashed eyelids as if to lift them were a work requiring consideration. 'But my grandfather calls it water enough. I'll show you what I mean.'

She moved away a few yards, and Clym followed. When she reached the corner of the enclosure, where the steps were formed for mounting the boundary bank, she sprang up with a lightness which seemed strange after her listless movement towards the well. It incidentally showed that her apparent languor did not arise from lack of force.

Clym ascended behind her, and noticed a circular burnt patch at the top of the bank. 'Ashes?' he said.

'Yes,' said Eustacia. 'We had a little bonfire here last Fifth of November, and those are the marks of it.'

On that spot had stood the fire she had kindled to attract Wildeve.

'That's the only kind of water we have,' she continued, tossing a stone into the pool, which lay on the outside of the bank like the white of an eye without its pupil. The stone fell with a flounce, but no Wildeve appeared on the other side, as on a previous occasion there. 'My grandfather says he lived for more than twenty years at sea on water twice as bad as that,' she went on, 'and considers it quite good enough for us here on an emergency.'

'Well, as a matter of fact there are no impurities in the water of these pools at this time of the year. It has only just rained into them.'

She shook her head. 'I am managing to exist in a wilderness, but I cannot drink from a pond,' she said.

Clym looked towards the well, which was now deserted, the men having gone home. 'It is a long way to send for spring-water,' he said, after a silence. 'But since you don't like this in the pond, I'll try to get you some myself.' He went back to the well. 'Yes, I think I could do it by tying on this pail.'

'But, since I would not trouble the men to get it, I cannot in conscience let you.'

'I don't mind the trouble at all.'

He made fast the pail to the long coil of rope, put it over the wheel, and allowed it to descend by letting the rope slip through his hands. Before it had gone far, however, he checked it.

'I must make fast the end first, or we may lose the whole,' he said to Eustacia, who had drawn near. 'Could you hold this a moment, while I do it—or shall I call your servant ?'

'I can hold it,' said Eustacia ; and he placed the rope in her hands, going then to search for the end.

'I suppose I may let it slip down ?' she inquired.

'I would advise you not to let it go far,' said Clym. 'It will get much heavier, you will find.'

However, Eustacia had begun to pay out. While he was tying she cried, 'I cannot stop it !'

Clym ran to her side, and found he could only check the rope by twisting the loose part round the upright post, when it stopped with a jerk. 'Has it hurt you ?'

'Yes,' she replied.

'Very much ?'

'No ; I think not.' She opened her hands. One of them was bleeding ; the rope had dragged off the skin. Eustacia wrapped it in her handkerchief.

'You should have let go,' said Yeobright. 'Why didn't you ?'

'You said I was to hold on. . . . This is the second time I have been wounded to-day.'

'Ah, yes ; I have heard of it. I blush for my native Egdon. Was it a serious injury you received in church, Miss Vye ?'

There was such an abundance of sympathy in Clym's tone that Eustacia slowly drew up her sleeve and disclosed her round white arm. A bright red spot appeared on its smooth surface, like a ruby on Parian marble.

'There it is,' she said, putting her finger against the spot.

'It was dastardly of the woman,' said Clym. 'Will not Captain Vye get her punished?'

'He is gone from home on that very business. I did not know that I had such a magic reputation.'

'And you fainted?' said Clym, looking at the scarlet little puncture as if he would like to kiss it and make it well.

'Yes, it frightened me. I had not been to church for a long time. And now I shall not go again for ever so long—perhaps never. I cannot face their eyes after this. Don't you think it dreadfully humiliating? I wished I was dead for hours after, but I don't mind now.'

'I have come to clean away these cobwebs,' said Yeobright. 'Would you like to help me—by high-class teaching? We might benefit them much.'

'I don't feel quite anxious to. I have not much love for my fellow-creatures. Sometimes I quite hate them.'

'Still I think that if you were to hear my scheme you might take an interest in it. There is no use in hating people—if you hate anything, you should hate what produced them.'

'Do you mean Nature? I hate her already. But I shall be glad to hear your scheme at any time.'

The situation had now worked itself out, and the next natural thing was for them to part. Clym knew this well enough, and Eustacia made a move of conclusion; yet he looked at her as if he had one word more to say. Perhaps if he had not lived in Paris it would never have been uttered.

'We have met before,' he said, regarding her with rather more interest than was necessary.

'I do not own it,' said Eustacia, with a repressed, still look.

'But I may think what I like.'

'Yes.'

'You are lonely here.'

'I cannot endure the heath, except in its purple season. The heath is a cruel taskmaster to me.'

'Can you say so?' he asked. 'To my mind it is most exhilarating, and strengthening, and soothing. I would rather live on these hills than anywhere else in the world.'

'It is well enough for artists; but I never would learn to draw.'

'And there is a very curious Druidical stone just out there.' He threw a pebble in the direction signified. 'Do you often go to see it?'

'I was not even aware that there existed any such curious Druidical stone. I am aware that there are Boulevards in Paris.'

Yeobright looked thoughtfully on the ground. 'That means much,' he said.

'It does indeed,' said Eustacia.

'I remember when I had the same longing for town bustle. Five years of a great city would be a perfect cure for that.'

'Heaven send me such a cure! Now, Mr. Yeobright, I will go indoors and plaster my wounded hand.'

They separated, and Eustacia vanished in the increasing shade. She seemed full of many things. Her past was a blank, her life had begun. The effect upon Clym of this meeting he did not fully discover till some time after. During his walk home his most intelligible sensation was that his scheme had somehow become glorified. A beautiful woman had been intertwined with it.

On reaching the house he went up to the room which was to be made his study, and occupied himself during the evening in unpacking his books from the boxes and arranging them on shelves. From another box he drew a lamp and a can of oil. He trimmed the lamp, arranged his table, and said, 'Now, I am ready to begin.'

He rose early the next morning, read two hours before breakfast by the light of his lamp—read all the morning, all the afternoon. Just when the sun was going down his eyes felt weary, and he leant back in his chair.

His room overlooked the front of the premises and the valley of the heath beyond. The lowest beams of the winter sun threw the shadow of the house over the palings, across the grass margin of the heath, and far up the vale, where the chimney outlines and those of the surrounding tree-tops stretched forth in long dark prongs. Having been seated at work all day, he decided to take a turn upon the hills before it got dark; and, going out forthwith, he struck across the heath towards Mistover.

It was an hour and a half later when he again appeared at the garden gate. The shutters of the house were closed, and Christian Cantle, who had been wheeling manure about the garden all day, had gone home. On entering he found that his mother, after waiting a long time for him, had finished her meal.

'Where have you been, Clym?' she immediately said. 'Why didn't you tell me that you were going away at this time?'

'I have been on the heath.'

'You'll meet Eustacia Vye if you go up there.'

Clym paused a minute. 'Yes, I met her this evening,' he said, as though it were spoken under the sheer necessity of preserving honesty.

'I wondered if you had.'

'It was no appointment.'

'No; such meetings never are.'

'But you are not angry, mother?'

'I can hardly say that I am not. Angry? No. But when I consider the usual nature of the drag which causes men of promise to disappoint the world I feel uneasy.'

'You deserve credit for the feeling, mother. But I can assure you that you need not be disturbed by it on my account.'

'When I think of you and your new crotchets,' said Mrs. Yeobright, with some emphasis, 'I naturally don't feel so comfortable as I did a twelvemonth ago. It is incredible to me that a man accustomed to the attractive women of Paris and elsewhere should be so easily worked upon by a girl in a heath. You could just as well have walked another way.'

'I had been studying all day.'

'Well, yes,' she added more hopefully, 'I have been thinking that you might get on as a schoolmaster, and rise that way, since you really are determined to hate the course you were pursuing.'

Yeobright was unwilling to disturb this idea, though his scheme was far enough removed from one wherein the education of youth should be made a mere channel of social ascent. He had no desires of that sort. He had reached the stage in a young man's life when the grimness of the general human situation first becomes clear; and the realization of this causes ambition to halt awhile. In France it is not uncustomary to commit suicide at this stage; in England we do much better, or much worse, as the case may be.

The love between the young man and his mother was strangely invisible now. Of love it may be said, the less earthly the less demonstrative. In its absolutely indestructible form it reaches a profundity in which all exhibition of itself is painful. It was so with these. Had conversations between them been overheard, people would have said, 'How cold they are to each other!'

His theory and his wishes about devoting his future to teaching had made an impression on Mrs. Yeobright. Indeed, how could it be otherwise when he was a part of her—when their discourses were as if carried on between the right and the left hands of the same body? He had despaired of reaching her by argument; and it was almost as a discovery to him that he could reach her by a magnetism which was as superior to words as words are to yells.

Strangely enough he began to feel now that it would not be so hard to persuade her who was his best friend that comparative poverty was essentially the higher course for him, as to reconcile to his feelings the act of persuading her. From every provident point of view his mother was so undoubtedly right, that he was not without a sickness of heart in finding he could shake her.

She had a singular insight into life, considering that she had never mixed with it. There are instances of persons who, without clear ideas of the things they criticize, have yet had clear ideas of the relations of those things. Blacklock, a poet blind from his birth, could describe visual objects with accuracy; Professor Sanderson, who was also blind, gave excellent lectures on colour, and taught others the theory of ideas which they had and he had not. In the social sphere these gifted ones are mostly women; they can watch a world which they never saw, and estimate forces of which they have only heard. We call it intuition.

What was the great world to Mrs. Yeobright? A multitude whose tendencies could be perceived, though not its essences. Communities were seen by her as from a distance; she saw them as we see the throngs which cover the canvases of Sallaert, Van Alsloot, and others of that school—vast masses of beings, jostling, zigzagging, and processioning in definite directions, but whose features are indistinguishable by the very comprehensiveness of the view.

One could see that, as far as it had gone, her life was very complete on its reflective side. The philosophy of her nature, and its limitation by circumstances, was almost written in her movements. They had a majestic foundation, though they were far from being majestic;

and they had a groundwork of assurance, but they were not assured. As her once elastic walk had become deadened by time, so had her natural pride of life been hindered in its blooming by her necessities.

The next slight touch in the shaping of Clym's destiny occurred a few days after. A barrow was opened on the heath, and Yeobright attended the operation, remaining away from his study during several hours. In the afternoon Christian returned from a journey in the same direction, and Mrs. Yeobright questioned him.

'They have dug a hole, and they have found things like flower-pots upside down, Mis'ess Yeobright; and inside these be real charnel bones. They have carried 'em off to men's houses; but I shouldn't like to sleep where they will bide. Dead folks have been known to come and claim their own. Mr. Yeobright had got one pot of the bones, and was going to bring 'em home—real skellington bones—but 'twas ordered otherwise. You'll be relieved to hear that he gave away his, pot and all, on second thoughts; and a blessed thing for ye, Mis'ess Yeobright, considering the wind o' nights.'

'Gave it away?'

'Yes. To Miss Vye. She has a cannibal taste for such churchyard furniture seemingly.'

'Miss Vye was there too?'

'Ay, 'a b'lieve she was.'

When Clym came home, which was shortly after, his mother said, in a curious tone, 'The urn you had meant for me you gave away.'

Yeobright made no reply; the current of her feeling was too pronounced to admit it.

The early weeks of the year passed on. Yeobright certainly studied at home, but he also walked much abroad, and the direction of his walk was always towards some point of a line between Mistover and Rainbarrow.

The month of March arrived, and the heath showed its first faint signs of awakening from winter trance. The awakening was almost feline in its stealthiness. The pool outside the bank by Eustacia's dwelling, which seemed as dead and desolate as ever to an observer who moved and made noises in his observation, would gradually disclose a state of great animation when silently watched awhile. A timid animal world had come to life for the season. Little tadpoles and efts began to bubble up through the water, and to race along beneath it; toads made noises like very young ducks, and advanced to the margin in twos and threes; overhead, bumble-bees flew hither and thither in the thickening light, their drone coming and going like the sound of a gong.

On an evening such as this Yeobright descended into the Blooms-End valley from beside that very pool, where he had been standing with another person quite silently and quite long enough to hear all this puny stir of resurrection in nature; yet he had not heard it. His walk was rapid as he came down, and he went with a springy tread. Before entering upon his mother's premises he stopped and breathed. The light which shone forth on him from the window revealed that his face was flushed and his eye bright. What it did not show was something which lingered upon his lips like a seal set there. The abiding presence of this impress was so real that he hardly dared to enter the house, for it seemed as if his mother might say, 'What red spot is that glowing upon your mouth so vividly?'

But he entered soon after. The tea was ready, and he sat down opposite his mother. She did not speak many words; and as for him, something had been just done and some words had been just said on the hill which prevented him from beginning a desultory chat. His mother's taciturnity was not without ominousness, but he appeared not to care. He knew why she said so little, but he could not remove the cause of her bearing towards him. These half-silent sittings were far from uncommon with them now. At last Yeobright made a beginning of what was intended to strike at the whole root of the matter.

'Five days have we sat like this at meals with scarcely a word. What's the use of it, mother?'

'None,' said she, in a heart-swollen tone. 'But there is only too good a reason.'

'Not when you know all. I have been wanting to speak about this, and I am glad the subject is begun. The reason, of course, is Eustacia Vye. Well, I confess I have seen her lately, and have seen her a good many times.'

'Yes, yes; and I know what that amounts to. It troubles me, Clym. You are wasting your life here; and it is solely on account of her. If it had not been for that woman you would never have entertained this teaching scheme at all.'

Clym looked hard at his mother. 'You know that is not it,' he said.

'Well, I know you had decided to attempt it before you saw her; but that would have ended in intentions. It was very well to talk of, but ridiculous to put in practice. I fully expected that in the course of a month or two you would have seen the folly of such self-sacrifice, and would have been by this time back again to Paris in some business or other. I can understand objections to the diamond trade—I really was thinking that it might be inadequate to the life of a man like you even though it might have made you a millionaire. But now I see how mistaken you are about this girl I doubt if you could be correct about other things.'

'How am I mistaken in her?'

'She is lazy and dissatisfied. But that is not all of it. Supposing her to be as good a woman as any you can find, which she certainly is not, why do you wish to connect yourself with anybody at present?'

'Well, there are practical reasons,' Clym began, and then almost broke off under an overpowering sense of the weight of argument which could be brought against his statement. 'If I take a school an educated woman would be invaluable as a help to me.'

'What! you really mean to marry her?'

'It would be premature to state that plainly. But consider what obvious advantages there would be in doing it. She——'

'Don't suppose she has any money. She hasn't a farthing.'

'She is excellently educated, and would make a good matron in a boarding-school. I candidly own that I have modified my views a little, in deference to you; and it should satisfy you. I no longer adhere to my intention of giving with my own mouth rudimentary education to the lowest class. I can do better. I can establish a good private school for farmers' sons, and without stopping the school I can manage to pass examinations. By this means, and by the assistance of a wife like her——'

'O, Clym!'

'I shall ultimately, I hope, be at the head of one of the best schools in the county.'

Yeobright had enunciated the word 'her' with a fervour which, in conversation with a mother, was absurdly indiscreet. Hardly a maternal heart within the four seas could, in such circumstances, have helped being irritated at that ill-timed betrayal of feeling for a new woman.

'You are blinded, Clym,' she said warmly. 'It was a bad day for you when you first set eyes on her. And your scheme is merely a castle in the air built on purpose to justify this folly which has seized you, and to salve your conscience on the irrational situation you are in.'

'Mother, that's not true,' he firmly answered.

'Can you maintain that I sit and tell untruths, when all I wish to do is to save you from sorrow? For shame, Clym! But it is all through that woman—a hussy!'

Clym reddened like fire and rose. He placed his hand upon his mother's shoulder and said, in a tone which hung strangely between entreaty and command, 'I won't hear it. I may be led to answer you in a way which we shall both regret.'

His mother parted her lips to begin some other vehement truth, but on looking at him she saw that in his face which led her to leave the words unsaid. Yeobright walked once or twice across the room, and then suddenly went out of the house. It was eleven o'clock when he came in, though he had not been further than the precincts of the garden. His mother was gone to bed. A light was left burning on the table, and supper was spread. Without stopping for any food he secured the doors and went upstairs.

AN HOUR OF BLISS AND MANY HOURS OF SADNESS

IV

THE next day was gloomy enough at Blooms-End. Yeobright remained in his study, sitting over the open books; but the work of those hours was miserably scant. Determined that there should be nothing in his conduct towards his mother resembling sullenness, he had occasionally spoken to her on passing matters, and would take no notice of the brevity of her replies. With the same resolve to keep up a show of conversation he said, about seven o'clock in the evening, 'There's an eclipse of the moon to-night. I am going out to see it.' And, putting on his overcoat, he left her.

The low moon was not as yet visible from the front of the house, and Yeobright climbed out of the valley until he stood in the full flood of her light. But even now he walked on, and his steps were in the direction of Rainbarrow.

In half an hour he stood at the top. The sky was clear from verge to verge, and the moon flung her rays over the whole heath, but without sensibly lighting it, except where paths and water-courses had laid bare the white flints and glistening quartz sand, which made streaks upon the general shade. After standing awhile he stooped and felt the heather. It was dry, and he flung himself down upon the barrow, his face towards the moon, which depicted a small image of herself in each of his eyes.

He had often come up here without stating his purpose to his mother; but this was the first time that he had been ostensibly frank as to his purpose while really concealing it. It was a moral situation which, three months earlier, he could hardly have credited of himself. In returning to labour in this sequestered spot he had anticipated an escape from the chafing of social necessities; yet behold they were here also. More than ever he longed to be in some world where personal ambition was not the only recognized form of progress—such, perhaps, as might have been the case at some time or other in the silvery globe then shining upon him. His eye travelled over the length and breadth of that distant country—over the Bay of Rainbows, the sombre Sea of Crises, the Ocean of Storms, the Lake of Dreams, the vast Walled Plains, and the wondrous Ring Mountains—till he almost felt himself to be voyaging bodily through its wild scenes, standing on its hollow hills, traversing its deserts, descending its vales and old sea bottoms, or mounting to the edges of its craters.

While he watched the far-removed landscape a tawny stain grew into being on the lower verge: the eclipse had begun. This marked a preconcerted moment: for the remote celestial phenomenon had been pressed into sublunary service as a lover's signal. Yeobright's mind flew back to earth at the sight; he arose, shook himself, and listened. Minute after minute passed by, perhaps ten minutes passed, and the shadow on the moon perceptibly widened. He heard a rustling on his left hand, a cloaked figure with an upturned face appeared at the base of the Barrow, and Clym descended. In a moment the figure was in his arms and his lips upon hers.

'My Eustacia!'

'Clym, dearest!'

Such a situation had less than three months brought forth.

They remained long without a single utterance, for no language could reach the level of their condition: words were as the rusty implements of a by-gone barbarous epoch, and only to be occasionally tolerated.

'I began to wonder why you did not come,' said Yeobright, when she had withdrawn a little from his embrace.

'You said ten minutes after the first mark of shade on the edge of the moon; and that's what it is now.'

'Well, let us only think that here we are.'

Then, holding each other's hand, they were again silent, and the shadow on the moon's disc grew a little larger.

'Has it seemed long since you last saw me?' she asked.

'It has seemed sad.'

'And not long? That's because you occupy yourself, and so blind yourself to my absence. To me, who can do nothing, it has been like living under stagnant water.'

'I would rather bear tediousness, dear, than have time made short by such means as have shortened mine.'

'In what way is that? You have been thinking you wished you did not love me.'

'How can a man wish that, and yet love on? No, Eustacia.'

'Men can, women cannot.'

'Well, whatever I may have thought, one thing is certain—I do love you—past all compass and description. I love you to oppressiveness—I, who have never before felt more than a pleasant passing fancy for any woman I have ever seen. Let me look right into your moonlit face, and dwell on every line and curve in it! Only a few hairbreadths make the difference between this face and faces I have seen many times before I knew you; yet what a difference—the difference between everything and nothing at all. One touch on that mouth again! there, and there, and there. Your eyes seem heavy, Eustacia.'

'No, it is my general way of looking. I think it arises from my feeling sometimes an agonizing pity for myself that I ever was born.'

'You don't feel it now?'

'No. Yet I know that we shall not love like this always. Nothing can ensure the continuance of love. It will evaporate like a spirit, and so I feel full of fears.'

'You need not.'

'Ah, you don't know. You have seen more than I, and have been into cities and among people that I have only heard of, and have lived more years than I; but yet I am older at this than you. I loved another man once, and now I love you.'

'In God's mercy don't talk so, Eustacia!'

'But I do not think I shall be the one who wearies first. It will, I fear, end in this way: your mother will find out that you meet me, and she will influence you against me!'

'That can never be. She knows of these meetings already.'

'And she speaks against me?'

'I will not say.'

'There, go away! Obey her. I shall ruin you. It is foolish of you to meet me like this. Kiss me, and go away for ever. For ever—do you hear?—for ever!'

'Not I.'

'It is your only chance. Many a man's love has been a curse to him.'

'You are desperate, full of fancies, and wilful; and you misunderstand. I have an additional reason for seeing you to-night besides love of you. For though, unlike you, I feel our affection may be eternal, I feel with you in this, that our present mode of existence cannot last.'

'Oh! 'tis your mother. Yes, that's it! I knew it.'

'Never mind what it is. Believe this, I cannot let

myself lose you. I must have you always with me. This very evening I do not like to let you go. There is only one cure for this anxiety, dearest—you must be my wife.'

She started: then endeavoured to say calmly, 'Cynics say that cures the anxiety by curing the love.'

'But you must answer me. Shall I claim you some day—I don't mean at once?'

'I must think,' Eustacia murmured. 'At present speak of Paris to me. Is there any place like it on earth?'

'It is very beautiful. But will you be mine?'

'I will be nobody else's in the world—does that satisfy you?'

'Yes, for the present.'

'Now tell me of the Tuileries, and the Louvre,' she continued evasively.

'I hate talking of Paris! Well, I remember one sunny room in the Louvre which would make a fitting place for you to live in—the Galerie d'Apollon. Its windows are mainly east; and in the early morning, when the sun is bright, the whole apartment is in a perfect blaze of splendour. The rays bristle and dart from the encrustations of gilding to the magnificent inlaid coffers, from the coffers to the gold and silver plate, from the plate to the jewels and precious stones, from these to the enamels, till there is a perfect network of light which quite dazzles the eye. But now, about our marriage——'

'And Versailles—the King's Gallery is some such gorgeous room, is it not?'

'Yes. But what's the use of talking of gorgeous rooms? By the way, the Little Trianon would suit us beautifully to live in, and you might walk in the gardens in the moonlight and think you were in some English shrubbery; it is laid out in English fashion.'

'I should hate to think that!'

'Then you could keep to the lawn in front of the Grand Palace. All about there you would doubtless feel in a world of historical romance.'

He went on, since it was all new to her, and described Fontainebleau, St. Cloud, the Bois, and many other familiar haunts of the Parisians; till she said——

'When used you to go to these places?'

'On Sundays.'

'Ah, yes. I dislike English Sundays. How I should chime in with their manners over there! Dear Clym, you'll go back again?'

Clym shook his head, and looked at the eclipse.

'If you'll go back again I'll—be something,' she said tenderly, putting her head near his breast. 'If you'll agree I'll give my promise, without making you wait a minute longer.'

'How extraordinary that you and my mother should be of one mind about this!' said Yeobright. 'I have vowed not to go back, Eustacia. It is not the place I dislike; it is the occupation.'

'But you can go in some other capacity.'

'No. Besides, it would interfere with my scheme. Don't press that, Eustacia. Will you marry me?'

'I cannot tell.'

'Now—never mind Paris; it is no better than other spots. Promise, sweet!'

'You will never adhere to your education plan, I am quite sure; and then it will be all right for me; and so I promise to be yours for ever and ever.'

Clym brought her face towards his by a gentle pressure of the hand, and kissed her.

'Ah! but you don't know what you have got in me,' she said. 'Sometimes I think there is not that in Eustacia Vye which will make a good homespun wife. Well, let it go—see how our time is slipping, slipping, slipping!' She pointed towards the half eclipsed moon.

'You are too mournful.'

'No. Only I dread to think of anything beyond the present. What is, we know. We are together now, and it is unknown how long we shall be so: the unknown always fills my mind with terrible possibilities, even when I may reasonably expect it to be cheerful. . . . Clym, the eclipsed moonlight shines upon your face with a strange foreign colour, and shows its shape as if it were cut out in gold. That means that you should be doing better things than this.'

'You are ambitious, Eustacia—no, not exactly ambitious, luxurious. I ought to be of the same vein, to make you happy, I suppose. And yet, far from that, I could live and die in a hermitage here, with proper work to do.'

There was that in his tone which implied distrust of his position as a solicitous lover, a doubt if he were acting fairly towards one whose tastes touched his own only at rare and infrequent points. She saw his meaning, and whispered, in a low, full accent of eager assurance, 'Don't mistake me, Clym: though I should like Paris, I love you for yourself alone. To be your wife and live in Paris would be heaven to me; but I would rather live with you in a hermitage here than not be yours at all. It is gain to me either way, and very great gain. There's my too candid confession.'

'Spoken like a woman. And now I must soon leave you. I'll walk with you towards your house.

'But must you go home yet?' she asked. 'Yes, the sand has nearly slipped away, I see, and the eclipse is creeping on more and more. Don't go yet! Stop till the hour has run itself out; then I will not press you any more. You will go home and sleep well; I keep sighing in my sleep! Do you ever dream of me?'

'I cannot recollect a clear dream of you.'

'I see your face in every scene of my dreams, and hear your voice in every sound. I wish I did not. It is too much what I feel. They say such love never lasts. But it must! And yet once, I remember, I saw an officer of the Hussars ride down the street at Budmouth, and though he was a total stranger and never spoke to me, I loved him till I thought I should really die of love—but

I didn't die, and at last I left off caring for him. How terrible it would be if a time should come when I could not love you, my Clym!'

'Please don't say such reckless things. When we see such a time at hand we will say, "I have outlived my faith and purpose," and die. There, the hour has expired: now let us walk on.'

Hand in hand they went along the path towards Mistover. When they were near the house he said, 'It is too late for me to see your grandfather to-night. Do you think he will object to it?'

'I will speak to him. I am so accustomed to be my own mistress that it did not occur to me that we should have to ask him.'

Then they lingeringly separated, and Clym descended towards Blooms-End.

And as he walked further and further from the charmed atmosphere of his Olympian girl his face grew sad with a new sort of sadness. A perception of the dilemma in which his love had placed him came back in full force. In spite of Eustacia's apparent willingness to wait through the period of an unpromising engagement, till he should be established in his new pursuit, he could not but perceive at moments that she loved him rather as a visitant from a gay world to which she rightly belonged than as a man with a purpose opposed to that recent past of his which so interested her. Often at their meetings a word or a sigh escaped her. It meant that, though she made no conditions as to his return to the French capital, this was what she secretly longed for in the event of marriage; and it robbed him of many an otherwise pleasant hour. Along with that came the widening breach between himself and his mother. Whenever any little occurrence had brought into more prominence than usual the disappointment that he was causing her it had sent him on lone and moody walks; or he was kept awake a great part of the night by the turmoil of spirit which such a recognition created. If Mrs. Yeobright could only have been led to see what a sound and worthy purpose this purpose of his was and how little it was being affected by his devotion to Eustacia, how differently would she regard him!

Thus as his sight grew accustomed to the first blinding halo kindled about him by love and beauty, Yeobright began to perceive what a strait he was in. Sometimes he wished that he had never known Eustacia, immediately to retract the wish as brutal. Three antagonistic growths had to be kept alive: his mother's trust in him, his plan for becoming a teacher, and Eustacia's happiness. His fervid nature could not afford to relinquish one of these, though two of the three were as many as he could hope to preserve. Though his love was as chaste as that of Petrarch for his Laura, it had made fetters of what previously was only a difficulty. A position which was not too simple when he stood whole-hearted had become indescribably complicated by the addition of Eustacia. Just when his mother was beginning to tolerate one scheme he had introduced another still bitterer than the first, and the combination was more than she could bear.

SHARP WORDS ARE SPOKEN AND A CRISIS ENSUES

V

WHEN Yeobright was not with Eustacia he was sitting slavishly over his books; when he was not reading he was meeting her. These meetings were carried on with the greatest secrecy.

One afternoon his mother came home from a morning visit to Thomasin. He could see from a disturbance in the lines of her face that something had happened.

'I have been told an incomprehensible thing,' she said mournfully. 'The captain has let out at the Woman that you and Eustacia Vye are engaged to be married.'

'We are,' said Yeobright. 'But it may not be yet for a very long time.'

'I should hardly think it *would* be yet for a very long time! You will take her to Paris, I suppose?' She spoke with weary hopelessness.

'I am not going back to Paris.'

'What will you do with a wife, then?'

'Keep a school in Budmouth, as I have told you.'

'That's incredible! The place is overrun with schoolmasters. You have no special qualifications. What possible chance is there for such as you?'

'There is no chance of getting rich. But with my

system of education, which is as new as it is true, I shall do a great deal of good to my fellow-creatures.'

'Dreams, dreams! If there had been any system left to be invented they would have found it out at the universities long before this time.'

'Never, mother. They cannot find it out, because their teachers don't come in contact with the class which demands such a system—that is, those who have had no preliminary training. My plan is one for instilling high knowledge into empty minds without first cramming them with what has to be uncrammed again before true study begins.'

'I might have believed you if you had kept yourself free from entanglements; but this woman—if she had been a good girl it would have been bad enough; but being——'

'She is a good girl.'

'So you think. A Corfu bandmaster's daughter! What has her life been? Her surname even is not her true one.'

'She is Captain Vye's granddaughter, and her father merely took her mother's name. And she is a lady by instinct.'

'They call him "captain," but anybody is captain.'

'He was in the Royal Navy!'

'No doubt he has been to sea in some tub or other. Why doesn't he look after her? No lady would rove about the heath at all hours of the day and night as she does. But that's not all of it. There was something queer between her and Thomasin's husband at one time—I am as sure of it as that I stand here.'

'Eustacia has told me. He did pay her a little attention a year ago; but there's no harm in that. I like her all the better.'

'Clym,' said his mother with firmness, 'I have no proofs against her, unfortunately. But if she makes you a good wife, there has never been a bad one.'

'Believe me, you are almost exasperating,' said Yeobright vehemently. 'And this very day I had intended to arrange a meeting between you. But you give me no peace; you try to thwart my wishes in everything.'

'I hate the thought of any son of mine marrying badly! I wish I had never lived to see this; it is too much for me—it is more than I dreamt!' She turned to the window. Her breath was coming quickly, and her lips were pale, parted, and trembling.

'Mother,' said Clym, 'whatever you do, you will always be dear to me—that you know. But one thing I have a right to say, which is, that at my age I am old enough to know what is best for me.'

Mrs. Yeobright remained for some time silent and shaken, as if she could say no more. Then she replied, 'Best? Is it best for you to injure your prospects for such a voluptuous, idle woman as that? Don't you see that by the very fact of your choosing her you prove that you do not know what is best for you? You give up your whole thought—you set your whole soul—to please a woman.'

'I do. And that woman is you.'

'How can you treat me so flippantly!' said his mother, turning again to him with a tearful look. 'You are unnatural, Clym, and I did not expect it.'

'Very likely,' said he cheerlessly. 'You did not know the measure you were going to mete me, and therefore did not know the measure that would be returned to you again.'

'You answer me; you think only of her. You stick to her in all things.'

'That proves her to be worthy. I have never yet supported what is bad. And I do not care only for her. I care for you and for myself, and for anything that is good. When a woman once dislikes another she is merciless!'

'O Clym! please don't go setting down as my fault

what is your obstinate wrong-headedness. If you wished to connect yourself with an unworthy person why did you come home here to do it? Why didn't you do it in Paris?—it is more the fashion there. You have come only to distress me, a lonely woman, and shorten my days! I wish that you would bestow your presence where you bestow your love!'

Clym said huskily, 'You are my mother. I will say no more—beyond this, that I beg your pardon for having thought this my home. I will no longer inflict myself upon you; I'll go.' And he went out with tears in his eyes.

It was a sunny afternoon at the beginning of summer, and the moist hollows of the heath had passed from their brown to their green stage. Yeobright walked to the edge of the basin which extended down from Mistover and Rainbarrow. By this time he was calm, and he looked over the landscape. In the minor valleys, between the hillocks which diversified the contour of the vale, the fresh young ferns were luxuriantly growing up, ultimately to reach a height of five or six feet. He descended a little way, flung himself down in a spot where a path emerged from one of the small hollows, and waited. Hither it was that he had promised Eustacia to bring his mother this afternoon, that they might meet and be friends. His attempt had utterly failed.

He was in a nest of vivid green. The ferny vegetation round him, though so abundant, was quite uniform: it was a grove of machine-made foliage, a world of green triangles with saw-edges, and not a single flower. The air was warm with a vaporous warmth, and the stillness was unbroken. Lizards, grasshoppers, and ants were the only living things to be beheld. The scene seemed to belong to the ancient world of the carboniferous period, when the forms of plants were few, and of the fern kind; when there was neither bud nor blossom, nothing but a monotonous extent of leafage, amid which no bird sang.

When he had reclined for some considerable time,

gloomily pondering, he discerned above the ferns a drawn bonnet of white silk approaching from the left, and Yeobright knew directly that it covered the head of her he loved. His heart awoke from its apathy to a warm excitement, and, jumping to his feet, he said aloud, 'I knew she was sure to come.'

She vanished in a hollow for a few moments, and then her whole form unfolded itself from the brake.

'Only you here?' she exclaimed, with a disappointed air, whose hollowness was proved by her rising redness and her half-guilty low laugh. 'Where is Mrs. Yeobright?'

'She has not come,' he replied in a subdued tone.

'I wish I had known that you would be here alone,' she said seriously, 'and that we were going to have such an idle, pleasant time as this. Pleasure not known beforehand is half wasted; to anticipate it is to double it. I have not thought once to-day of having you all to myself this afternoon, and the actual moment of a thing is so soon gone.'

'It is indeed.'

'Poor Clym!' she continued, looking tenderly into his face. 'You are sad. Something has happened at your home. Never mind what is—let us only look at what seems.'

'But, darling, what shall we do?' said he.

'Still go on as we do now—just live on from meeting to meeting, never minding about another day. You, I know, are always thinking of that—I can see you are. But you must not—will you, dear Clym?'

'You are just like all women. They are ever content to build their lives on any incidental position that offers itself; whilst men would fain make a globe to suit them. Listen to this, Eustacia. There is a subject I have determined to put off no longer. Your sentiment on the wisdom of *Carpe diem* does not impress me to-day. Our present mode of life must shortly be brought to an end.'

'It is your mother!'

'It is. I love you none the less in telling you; it is only right you should know.'

'I have feared my bliss,' she said, with the merest motion of her lips. 'It has been too intense and consuming.'

'There is hope yet. There are forty years of work in me yet, and why should you despair? I am only at an awkward turning. I wish people wouldn't be so ready to think that there is no progress without uniformity.'

'Ah—your mind runs off to the philosophical side of it. Well, these sad and hopeless obstacles are welcome in one sense, for they enable us to look with indifference upon the cruel satires that Fate loves to indulge in. I have heard of people who, upon coming suddenly into happiness, have died from anxiety lest they should not live to enjoy it. I felt myself in that whimsical state of uneasiness lately; but I shall be spared it now. Let us walk on.'

Clym took the hand which was already bared for him—it was a favourite way with them to walk bare hand in bare hand—and led her through the ferns. They formed a very comely picture of love at full flush, as they walked along the valley that late afternoon, the sun sloping down on their right, and throwing their thin spectral shadows, tall as poplar trees, far out across the furze and fern. Eustacia went with her head thrown back fancifully, a certain glad and voluptuous air of triumph pervading her eyes at having won by her own unaided self a man who was her perfect complement in attainments, appearance, and age. On the young man's part, the paleness of face which he had brought with him from Paris, and the incipient marks of time and thought, were less perceptible than when he returned, the healthful and energetic sturdiness which was his by nature having partially recovered its original proportions. They wandered onward till they reached the nether margin of the heath, where it became marshy, and merged in moorland.

'I must part from you here, Clym,' said Eustacia.

They stood still and prepared to bid each other farewell.

Everything before them was on a perfect level. The sun, resting on the horizon line, streamed across the ground from between copper-coloured and lilac clouds, stretched out in flats beneath a sky of pale soft green. All dark objects on the earth that lay towards the sun were overspread by a purple haze, against which groups of wailing gnats shone out, rising upwards and dancing about like sparks of fire.

'O! this leaving you is too hard to bear!' exclaimed Eustacia in a sudden whisper of anguish. 'Your mother will influence you too much; I shall not be judged fairly, it will get afloat that I am not a good girl, and the witch story will be added to make me blacker!'

'They cannot. Nobody dares to speak disrespectfully of you or of me.'

'O how I wish I was sure of never losing you—that you could not be able to desert me anyhow!'

Clym stood silent a moment. His feelings were high, the moment was passionate, and he cut the knot.

'You shall be sure of me, darling,' he said, folding her in his arms. 'We will be married at once.'

'O Clym!'

'Do you agree to it?'

'If—if we can.'

'We certainly can, both being of full age. And I have not followed my occupation all these years without having accumulated money; and if you will agree to live in a tiny cottage somewhere on the heath, until I take a house in Budmouth for the school, we can do it at a very little expense.'

'How long shall we have to live in the tiny cottage, Clym?'

'About six months. At the end of that time I shall have finished my reading—yes, we will do it, and this heart-aching will be over. We shall, of course, live in absolute seclusion, and our married life will only begin to outward view when we take the house in Budmouth, where I have already addressed a letter on the matter. Would your grandfather allow you ?'

'I think he would—on the understanding that it should not last longer than six months.'

'I will guarantee that, if no misfortune happens.'

'If no misfortune happens,' she repeated slowly.

'Which is not likely. Dearest, fix the exact day.'

And then they consulted on the question, and the day was chosen. It was to be a fortnight from that time.

This was the end of their talk, and Eustacia left him. Clym watched her as she retired towards the sun. The luminous rays wrapped her up with her increasing distance, and the rustle of her dress over the sprouting sedge and grass died away. As he watched, the dead flat of the scenery overpowered him, though he was fully alive to the beauty of that untarnished early summer green which was worn for the nonce by the poorest blade. There was something in its oppressive horizontality which too much reminded him of the arena of life ; it gave him a sense of bare equality with, and no superiority to, a single living thing under the sun.

Eustacia was now no longer the goddess but the woman to him, a being to fight for, support, help, be maligned for. Now that he had reached a cooler moment he would have preferred a less hasty marriage ; but the card was laid, and he determined to abide by the game. Whether Eustacia was to add one other to the list of those who love too hotly to love long and well, the forthcoming event was certainly a ready way of proving.

YEOBRIGHT GOES, AND THE BREACH IS COMPLETE

VI

ALL that evening smart sounds denoting an active packing up came from Yeobright's room to the ears of his mother downstairs.

Next morning he departed from the house and again proceeded across the heath. A long day's march was before him, his object being to secure a dwelling to which he might take Eustacia when she became his wife. Such a house, small, secluded, and with its windows boarded up, he had casually observed a month earlier, about two miles beyond the village of East Egdon, and six miles distance altogether; and thither he directed his steps to-day.

The weather was far different from that of the evening before. The yellow and vapoury sunset which had wrapped up Eustacia from his parting gaze had presaged change. It was one of those not infrequent days of an English June which are as wet and boisterous as November. The cold clouds hastened on in a body, as if painted on a moving slide. Vapours from other continents arrived upon the wind, which curled and parted round him as he walked on.

At length Clym reached the margin of a fir and beech

plantation that had been enclosed from heath land in the year of his birth. Here the trees, laden heavily with their new and humid leaves, were now suffering more damage than during the highest winds of winter, when the boughs are specially disencumbered to do battle with the storm. The wet young beeches were undergoing amputations, bruises, cripplings, and harsh lacerations, from which the wasting sap would bleed for many a day to come, and which would leave scars visible till the day of their burning. Each stem was wrenched at the root, where it moved like a bone in its socket, and at every onset of the gale convulsive sounds came from the branches, as if pain were felt. In a neighbouring brake a finch was trying to sing; but the wind blew under his feathers till they stood on end, twisted round his little tail, and made him give up his song.

Yet a few yards to Yeobright's left, on the open heath, how ineffectively gnashed the storm! Those gusts which tore the trees merely waved the furze and heather in a light caress. Egdon was made for such times as these.

Yeobright reached the empty house about mid-day. It was almost as lonely as that of Eustacia's grandfather, but the fact that it stood near a heath was disguised by a belt of firs which almost enclosed the premises. He journeyed on about a mile further to the village in which the owner lived, and, returning with him to the house, arrangements were completed, and the man undertook that one room at least should be ready for occupation the next day. Clym's intention was to live there alone until Eustacia should join him on their wedding-day.

Then he turned to pursue his way homeward through the drizzle that had so greatly transformed the scene. The ferns, among which he had lain in comfort yesterday, were dripping moisture from every frond, wetting his legs through as he brushed past; and the fur of the rabbits leaping before him was clotted into dark locks by the same watery surrounding.

He reached home damp and weary enough after his ten-mile walk. It had hardly been a propitious beginning, but he had chosen his course, and would show no swerving. The evening and the following morning were spent in concluding arrangements for his departure. To stay at home a minute longer than necessary after having once come to his determination would be, he felt, only to give new pain to his mother by some word, look, or deed.

He had hired a conveyance and sent off his goods by two o'clock that day. The next step was to get some furniture, which, after serving for temporary use in the cottage, would be available for the house at Budmouth when increased by goods of a better description. A mart extensive enough for the purpose existed at Anglebury, some miles beyond the spot chosen for his residence, and there he resolved to pass the coming night.

It now only remained to wish his mother good-bye. She was sitting by the window as usual when he came downstairs.

'Mother, I am going to leave you,' he said, holding out his hand.

'I thought you were, by your packing,' replied Mrs. Yeobright in a voice from which every particle of emotion was painfully excluded.

'And you will part friends with me?'

'Certainly, Clym.'

'I am going to be married on the twenty-fifth.'

'I thought you were going to be married.'

'And then—and then you must come and see us. You will understand me better after that, and our situation will not be so wretched as it is now.'

'I do not think it likely I shall come to see you.'

'Then it will not be my fault or Eustacia's, mother. Good-bye!'

He kissed her cheek, and departed in great misery,

which was several hours in lessening itself to a controllable level. The position had been such that nothing more could be said without, in the first place, breaking down a barrier ; and that was not to be done.

No sooner had Yeobright gone from his mother's house than her face changed its rigid aspect for one of blank despair. After a while she wept, and her tears brought some relief. During the rest of the day she did nothing but walk up and down the garden path in a state bordering on stupefaction. Night came, and with it but little rest. The next day, with an instinct to do something which should reduce prostration to mournfulness, she went to her son's room, and with her own hands arranged it in order, for an imaginary time when he should return again. She gave some attention to her flowers, but it was perfunctorily bestowed, for they no longer charmed her.

It was a great relief when, early in the afternoon, Thomasin paid her an unexpected visit. This was not the first meeting between the relatives since Thomasin's marriage ; and past blunders having been in a rough way rectified, they could always greet each other with pleasure and ease.

The oblique band of sunlight which followed her through the door became the young wife well. It illuminated her as her presence illuminated the heath. In her movements, in her gaze, she reminded the beholder of the feathered creatures who lived around her home. All similes and allegories concerning her began and ended with birds. There was as much variety in her motions as in their flight. When she was musing she was a kestrel, which hangs in the air by an invisible motion of its wings. When she was in a high wind her light body was blown against trees and banks like a heron's. When she was frightened she darted noiselessly like a kingfisher. When she was serene she skimmed like a swallow, and that is how she was moving now.

'You are looking very blithe, upon my word, Tamsie,' said Mrs. Yeobright, with a sad smile. 'How is Damon?'

'He is very well.'

'Is he kind to you, Thomasin?' And Mrs. Yeobright observed her narrowly.

'Pretty fairly.'

'Is that honestly said?'

'Yes, aunt. I would tell you if he were unkind.' She added, blushing, and with hesitation, 'He—I don't know if I ought to complain to you about this, but I am not quite sure what to do. I want some money, you know, aunt—some to buy little things for myself—and he doesn't give me any. I don't like to ask him; and yet, perhaps, he doesn't give it me because he doesn't know. Ought I to mention it to him, aunt?'

'Of course you ought. Have you never said a word on the matter?'

'You see, I had some of my own,' said Thomasin evasively; 'and I have not wanted any of his until lately. I did just say something about it last week; but he seems —not to remember.'

'He must be made to remember. You are aware that I have a little box full of spade-guineas, which your uncle put into my hands to divide between yourself and Clym whenever I chose. Perhaps the time has come when it should be done. They can be turned into sovereigns at any moment.'

'I think I should like to have my share—that is, if you don't mind.'

'You shall, if necessary. But it is only proper that you should first tell your husband distinctly that you are without any, and see what he will do.'

'Very well, I will. . . . Aunt, I have heard about Clym. I know you are in trouble about him, and that's why I have come.'

Mrs. Yeobright turned away, and her features worked

in her attempt to conceal her feelings. Then she ceased to make any attempt, and said, weeping, 'O Thomasin, do you think he hates me? How can he bear to grieve me so, when I have lived only for him through all these years?'

'Hate you—no,' said Thomasin soothingly. 'It is only that he loves her too well. Look at it quietly—do. It is not so very bad of him. Do you know, I thought it not the worst match he could have made. Miss Vye's family is a good one on her mother's side; and her father was a romantic wanderer—a sort of Greek Ulysses.'

'It is no use, Thomasin; it is no use. Your intention is good; but I will not trouble you to argue. I have gone through the whole that can be said on either side times, and many times. Clym and I have not parted in anger; we have parted in a worse way. It is not a passionate quarrel that would have broken my heart; it is the steady opposition and persistence in going wrong that he has shown. O Thomasin, he was so good as a little boy—so tender and kind!

'He was, I know.'

'I did not think one whom I called mine would grow up to treat me like this. He spoke to me as if I opposed him to injure him. As though I could wish him ill!'

'There are worse women in the world than Eustacia Vye.'

'There are too many better; that's the agony of it. It was she, Thomasin, and she only, who led your husband to act as he did: I would swear it!'

'No,' said Thomasin eagerly. 'It was before he knew me that he thought of her, and it was nothing but a mere flirtation.'

'Very well; we will let it be so. There is little use in unravelling that now. Sons must be blind if they will. Why is it that a woman can see from a distance what a man cannot see close? Clym must do as he will—he is nothing more to me. And this is maternity—to give one's best years and best love to ensure the fate of being despised!'

'You are too unyielding. Think how many mothers there are whose sons have brought them to public shame by real crimes before you feel so deeply a case like this.

'Thomasin, don't lecture me—I can't have it. It is the excess above what we expect that makes the force of the blow, and that may not be greater in their case than in mine: they may have foreseen the worst. . . . I am wrongly made, Thomasin,' she added, with a mournful smile. 'Some widows can guard against the wounds their children give them by turning their hearts to another husband and beginning life again. But I always was a poor, weak, one-idea'd creature—I had not the compass of heart nor the enterprise for that. Just as forlorn and stupefied as I was when my husband's spirit flew away I have sat ever since—never attempting to mend matters at all. I was comparatively a young woman then, and I might have had another family by this time, and have been comforted by them for the failure of this one son.'

'It is more noble in you that you did not.'

'The more noble, the less wise.'

'Forget it, and be soothed, dear aunt. And I shall not leave you alone for long. I shall come and see you every day.'

And for one week Thomasin literally fulfilled her word. She endeavoured to make light of the wedding; and brought news of the preparations, and that she was invited to be present. The next week she was rather unwell, and did not appear. Nothing had as yet been done about the guineas, for Thomasin feared to address her husband again on the subject, and Mrs. Yeobright had insisted upon this.

One day just before this time Wildeve was standing at the door of the Quiet Woman. In addition to the upward path through the heath to Rainbarrow and Mistover, there was a road which branched from the highway a short distance below the inn, and ascended to Mistover by a circuitous and easy incline. This was the only route on that side for vehicles to the captain's retreat. A light cart from the nearest town descended the road, and the lad who was driving pulled up in front of the inn for something to drink.

'You come from Mistover?' said Wildeve.

'Yes. They are taking in good things up there. Going to be a wedding.' And the driver buried his face in his mug.

Wildeve had not received an inkling of the fact before, and a sudden expression of pain overspread his face. He turned for a moment into the passage to hide it. Then he came back again.

'Do you mean Miss Vye?' he said. 'How is it—that she can be married so soon?'

'By the will of God and a ready young man, I suppose.'

'You don't mean Mr. Yeobright?'

'Yes. He has been creeping about with her all the spring.'

'I suppose—she was immensely taken with him?'

'She is crazy about him, so their general servant of all work tells me. And that lad Charley that looks after the horse is all in a daze about it. The stun-poll has got fond-like of her.'

'Is she lively—is she glad? Going to be married so soon—well!'

'It isn't so very soon.'

'No; not so very soon.'

Wildeve went indoors to the empty room, a curious heart-ache within him. He rested his elbow upon the mantelpiece and his face upon his hand. When Thomasin entered the room he did not tell her of what he had heard. The old longing for Eustacia had reappeared in his soul:

and it was mainly because he had discovered that it was another man's intention to possess her.

To be yearning for the difficult, to be weary of that offered; to care for the remote, to dislike the near; it was Wildeve's nature always. This is the true mark of the man of sentiment. Though Wildeve's fevered feeling had not been elaborated to real poetical compass, it was of the standard sort. He might have been called the Rousseau of Egdon.

THE MORNING AND THE EVENING OF A DAY

VII

THE wedding morning came. Nobody would have imagined from appearances that Blooms-End had any interest in Mistover that day. A solemn stillness prevailed around the house of Clym's mother, and there was no more animation indoors. Mrs. Yeobright, who had declined to attend the ceremony, sat by the breakfast-table in the old room which communicated immediately with the porch, her eyes listlessly directed towards the open door. It was the room in which, six months earlier, the merry Christmas party had met, to which Eustacia came secretly and as a stranger. The only living thing that entered now was a sparrow; and seeing no movements to cause alarm, he hopped boldly round the room, endeavoured to go out by the window, and fluttered among the pot-flowers. This roused the lonely sitter, who got up, released the bird, and went to the door. She was expecting Thomasin, who had written the night before to state that the time had come when she would wish to have the money, and that she would if possible call this day.

Yet Thomasin occupied Mrs. Yeobright's thoughts but slightly as she looked up the valley of the heath, alive with butterflies, and with grasshoppers whose husky noises on every side formed a whispered chorus. A domestic drama, for which the preparations were now being made a mile or two off, was but little less vividly present to her eyes than if enacted before her. She tried to dismiss the vision, and walked about the garden-plot; but her eyes ever and anon sought out the direction of the parish church to which Mistover belonged, and her excited fancy clove the hills which divided the building from her eyes. The morning wore away. Eleven o'clock struck: could it be that the wedding was then in progress? It must be so. She went on imagining the scene at the church, which he had by this time approached with his bride. She pictured the little group of children by the gate as the pony-carriage drove up, in which, as Thomasin had learnt, they were going to perform the short journey. Then she saw them enter and proceed to the chancel and kneel; and the service seemed to go on.

She covered her face with her hands. 'O, it is a mistake!' she groaned. 'And he will rue it some day, and think of me!'

While she remained thus, overcome by her forebodings, the old clock indoors whizzed forth twelve strokes. Soon after, faint sounds floated to her ear from afar over the hills. The breeze came from that quarter, and it had brought with it the notes of distant bells, gaily starting off in a peal: one, two, three, four, five. The ringers at East Egdon were announcing the nuptials of Eustacia and her son.

'Then it is over,' she murmured. 'Well, well! and life too will be over soon. And why should I go on scalding my face like this? Cry about one thing in life, cry about all; one thread runs through the whole piece. And yet we say, "a time to laugh!"'

Towards evening Wildeve came. Since Thomasin's marriage Mrs. Yeobright had shown towards him that grim friendliness which at last arises in all such cases of undesired affinity. The vision of what ought to have been is thrown aside in sheer weariness, and browbeaten human endeavour listlessly makes the best of the fact that is. Wildeve, to do him justice, had behaved very courteously to his wife's aunt; and it was with no surprise that she saw him enter now.

'Thomasin has not been able to come, as she promised to do,' he replied to her inquiry, which had been anxious, for she knew that her niece was badly in want of money. 'The captain came down last night and personally pressed her to join them to-day. So, not to be unpleasant, she determined to go. They fetched her in the pony-chaise, and are going to bring her back.'

'Then it is done,' said Mrs. Yeobright. 'Have they gone to their new home?'

'I don't know. I have had no news from Mistover since Thomasin left to go.'

'You did not go with her?' said she, as if there might be good reasons why.

'I could not,' said Wildeve, reddening slightly. 'We could not both leave the house; it was rather a busy morning, on account of Anglebury Great Market. I believe you have something to give to Thomasin? If you like, I will take it.'

Mrs. Yeobright hesitated, and wondered if Wildeve knew what the something was. 'Did she tell you of this?' she inquired.

'Not particularly. She casually dropped a remark about having arranged to fetch some article or other.'

'It is hardly necessary to send it. She can have it whenever she chooses to come.'

'That won't be yet. In the present state of her health she must not go on walking so much as she has done.' He added, with a faint twang of sarcasm, 'What wonderful thing is it that I cannot be trusted to take?'

'Nothing worth troubling you with.'

'One would think you doubted my honesty,' he said,

with a laugh, though his colour rose in a quick resentfulness frequent with him.

'You need think no such thing,' said she drily. 'It is simply that I, in common with the rest of the world, feel that there are certain things which had better be done by certain people than by others.'

'As you like, as you like,' said Wildeve laconically. 'It is not worth arguing about. Well, I think I must turn homeward again, as the inn must not be left long in charge of the lad and the maid only.'

He went his way, his farewell being scarcely so courteous as his greeting. But Mrs. Yeobright knew him thoroughly by this time, and took little notice of his manner, good or bad.

When Wildeve was gone Mrs. Yeobright stood and considered what would be the best course to adopt with regard to the guineas, which she had not liked to entrust to Wildeve. It was hardly credible that Thomasin had told him to ask for them, when the necessity for them had arisen from the difficulty of obtaining money at his hands. At the same time Thomasin really wanted them, and might be unable to come to Blooms-End for another week at least. To take or send the money to her at the inn would be impolitic, since Wildeve would pretty surely be present, or would discover the transaction; and if, as her aunt suspected, he treated her less kindly than she deserved to be treated, he might then get the whole sum out of her gentle hands. But on this particular evening Thomasin was at Mistover, and anything might be conveyed to her there without the knowledge of her husband. Upon the whole the opportunity was worth taking advantage of.

Her son, too, was there, and was now married. There could be no more proper moment to render him his share of the money than the present. And the chance that would be afforded her, by sending him this gift, of showing how far she was from bearing him ill-will, cheered the sad mother's heart.

She went upstairs and took from a locked drawer a little box, out of which she poured a hoard of broad unworn guineas that had lain there many a year. There were a hundred in all, and she divided them into two heaps, fifty in each. Tying up these in small canvas bags, she went down the garden and called to Christian Cantle, who was loitering about in hope of a supper which was not really owed him. Mrs. Yeobright gave him the money-bags, charged him to go to Mistover, and on no account to deliver them into any one's hands save her son's and Thomasin's. On further thought she deemed it advisable to tell Christian precisely what the two bags contained, that he might be fully impressed with their importance. Christian pocketed the money-bags, promised the greatest carefulness, and set out on his way.

'You need not hurry,' said Mrs. Yeobright. 'It will be better not to get there till after dusk, and then nobody will notice you. Come back here to supper, if it is not too late.'

It was nearly nine o'clock when he began to ascend the vale towards Mistover; but the long days of summer being at their climax, the first obscurity of evening had only just begun to tan the landscape. At this point of his journey Christian heard voices, and found that they proceeded from a company of men and women who were traversing a hollow ahead of him, the tops only of their heads being visible.

He paused and thought of the money he carried. It was almost too early even for Christian seriously to fear robbery; nevertheless he took a precaution which ever since his boyhood he had adopted whenever he carried more than two or three shillings upon his person—a precaution somewhat like that of the owner of the Pitt Diamond when filled with similar misgivings. He took off his boots, untied the guineas, and emptied the contents of one little bag into the right boot, and of the other into the left, spreading them as flatly as possible over the bottom of each, which was really a spacious coffer by no means limited to the size of the foot. Pulling them on again and lacing them to the very top, he proceeded on his way, more easy in his head than under his soles.

His path converged towards that of the noisy company, and on coming nearer he found to his relief that they were several Egdon people whom he knew very well, while with them walked Fairway, of Blooms-End.

'What! Christian going too?' said Fairway as soon as he recognized the new-comer. 'You've got no young woman nor wife to your name to gie a gown-piece to, I'm sure.'

'What d'ye mean?' said Christian.

'Why, the raffle. The one we go to every year. Going to the raffle as well as ourselves?'

'Never knew a word o't. Is it like cudgel-playing or other sportful forms of bloodshed? I don't want to go, thank you, Mister Fairway, and no offence.'

'Christian don't know the fun o't, and 'twould be a fine sight for him,' said a buxom woman. 'There's no danger at all, Christian. Every man puts in a shilling apiece, and one wins a gown-piece for his wife or sweetheart if he's got one.'

'Well, as that's not my fortune there's no meaning in it to me. But I should like to see the fun, if there's nothing of the black art in it, and if a man may look on without cost or getting into any dangerous wrangle?'

'There will be no uproar at all,' said Timothy. 'Sure, Christian, if you'd like to come we'll see there's no harm done.'

'And no ba'dy gaieties, I suppose? You see, neighbours, if so, it would be setting father a bad example, as he is so light moral'd. But a gown-piece for a shilling, and no black art—'tis worth looking in to see, and it wouldn't hinder me half an hour. Yes, I'll come, if you'll step a little way towards Mistover with me afterwards, supposing night should have closed in, and nobody else is going that way?'

One or two promised; and Christian, diverging from his direct path, turned round to the right with his companions towards the Quiet Woman.

When they entered the large common room of the inn they found assembled there about ten men from among the neighbouring population, and the group was increased by the new contingent to double that number. Most of them were sitting round the room in seats divided by wooden elbows like those of crude cathedral stalls, which were carved with the initials of many an illustrious drunkard of former times who had passed his days and his nights between them, and now lay as an alcoholic cinder in the nearest churchyard. Among the cups on the long table before the sitters lay an open parcel of light drapery—the gown-piece, as it was called—which was to be raffled for. Wildeve was standing with his back to the fireplace, smoking a cigar; and the promoter of the raffle, a packman from a distant town, was expatiating upon the value of the fabric as material for a summer dress.

'Now, gentlemen,' he continued, as the new-comers drew up to the table, 'there's five have entered, and we want four more to make up the number. I think, by the faces of those gentlemen who have just come in, that they are shrewd enough to take advantage of this rare opportunity of beautifying their ladies at a very trifling expense.'

Fairway, Sam, and another placed their shillings on the table, and the man turned to Christian.

'No, sir,' said Christian, drawing back, with a quick gaze of misgiving. 'I am only a poor chap come to look on, an it please ye, sir. I don't so much as know how you do it. If so be I was sure of getting it I would put down the shilling; but I couldn't otherwise.'

'I think you might almost be sure,' said the pedlar.

'In fact, now I look into your face, even if I can't say you are sure to win, I can say that I never saw anything look more like winning in my life.'

'You'll anyhow have the same chance as the rest of us,' said Sam.

'And the extra luck of being the last comer,' said another.

'And I was born wi' a caul, and perhaps can be no more ruined than drowned?' Christian added, beginning to give way.

Ultimately Christian laid down his shilling, the raffle began, and the dice went round. When it came to Christian's turn he took the box with a trembling hand, shook it fearfully, and threw a pair-royal. Three of the others had thrown common low pairs, and all the rest mere points.

'The gentleman looked like winning, as I said,' observed the chapman blandly. 'Take it, sir; the article is yours.'

'Haw-haw-haw!' said Fairway. 'I'm damned if this isn't the quarest start that ever I knowed!'

'Mine?' asked Christian, with a vacant stare from his target eyes. 'I—I haven't got neither maid, wife, nor widder belonging to me at all, and I'm afeard it will make me laughed at to ha'e it, Master Traveller. What with being curious to join in I never thought of that! What shall I do wi' a woman's clothes in my bedroom, and not lose my decency!'

'Keep 'em, to be sure,' said Fairway, 'if it is only for luck. Perhaps 'twill tempt some woman that thy poor carcase had no power over when standing empty-handed.'

'Keep it, certainly,' said Wildeve, who had idly watched the scene from a distance.

The table was then cleared of the articles, and the men began to drink.

'Well, to be sure!' said Christian, half to himself. 'To think I should have been born so lucky as this, and not have found it out until now! What curious creatures these dice be—powerful rulers of us all, and yet at my command! I am sure I never need be afeard of anything after this.' He handled the dice fondly one by one. 'Why, sir,' he said in a confidential whisper to Wildeve, who was near his left hand, 'if I could only use this power that's in me of multiplying money I might do some good to a near relation of yours, seeing what I've got about me of hers—eh?' He tapped one of his money-laden boots upon the floor.

'What do you mean?' said Wildeve.

'That's a secret. Well, I must be going now.' He looked anxiously towards Fairway.

'Where are you going?' Wildeve asked.

'To Mistover Knap. I have to see Mrs. Thomasin there—that's all.'

'I am going there, too, to fetch Mrs. Wildeve. We can walk together.'

Wildeve became lost in thought, and a look of inward illumination came into his eyes. It was money for his wife that Mrs. Yeobright could not trust him with. 'Yet she could trust this fellow,' he said to himself. 'Why doesn't that which belongs to the wife belong to the husband too?'

He called to the pot-boy to bring him his hat, and said, 'Now, Christian, I am ready.'

'Mr. Wildeve,' said Christian timidly, as he turned to leave the room, 'would you mind lending me them wonderful little things that carry my luck inside 'em, that I might practise a bit by myself, you know?' He looked wistfully at the dice and box lying on the mantelpiece.

'Certainly,' said Wildeve carelessly. 'They were only cut out by some lad with his knife, and are worth nothing.' And Christian went back and privately pocketed them.

Wildeve opened the door and looked out. The night was warm and cloudy. 'By Gad! 'tis dark,' he continued. 'But I suppose we shall find our way.'

'If we should lose the path it might be awkward,' said Christian. 'A lantern is the only shield that will make it safe for us.'

'Let's have a lantern by all means.' The stable-lantern was fetched and lighted. Christian took up his gown-piece, and the two set out to ascend the hill.

Within the room the men fell into chat till their attention was for a moment drawn to the chimney-corner. This was large, and, in addition to its proper recess, contained within its jambs, like many on Egdon, a receding seat, so that a person might sit there absolutely unobserved, provided there was no fire to light him up, as was the case now and throughout the summer. From the niche a single object protruded into the light from the candles on the table. It was a clay pipe, and its colour was reddish. The men had been attracted to this object by a voice behind the pipe asking for a light.

'Upon my life, it fairly startled me when the man spoke!' said Fairway, handing a candle. 'Oh—'tis the reddleman! You've kept a quiet tongue, young man.'

'Yes, I had nothing to say,' observed Venn. In a few minutes he arose and wished the company good night.

Meanwhile Wildeve and Christian had plunged into the heath.

It was a stagnant, warm, and misty night, full of all the heavy perfumes of new vegetation not yet dried by hot sun, and among these particularly the scent of the fern. The lantern, dangling from Christian's hand, brushed the feathery fronds in passing by, disturbing moths and other winged insects, which flew out and alighted upon its horny panes.

'So you have money to carry to Mrs. Wildeve?' said Christian's companion, after a silence. 'Don't you think it very odd that it shouldn't be given to me?'

'As man and wife be one flesh, 'twould have been all the same, I should think,' said Christian. 'But my strict documents was, to give the money into Mrs. Wildeve's hand : and 'tis well to do things right.'

'No doubt,' said Wildeve. Any person who had known the circumstances might have perceived that Wildeve was mortified by the discovery that the matter in transit was money, and not, as he had supposed when at Blooms-End, some fancy nick-nack which only interested the two women themselves. Mrs. Yeobright's refusal implied that his honour was not considered to be of sufficiently good quality to make him a safe bearer of his wife's property.

'How very warm it is to-night, Christian!' he said, panting, when they were nearly under Rainbarrow. 'Let us sit down for a few minutes, for Heaven's sake.'

Wildeve flung himself down on the soft ferns; and Christian, placing the lantern and parcel on the ground, perched himself in a cramped position hard by, his knees almost touching his chin. He presently thrust one hand into his coat-pocket and began shaking it about.

'What are you rattling in there?' said Wildeve.

'Only the dice, sir,' said Christian, quickly withdrawing his hand. 'What magical machines these little things be, Mr. Wildeve! 'Tis a game I should never get tired of. Would you mind my taking 'em out and looking at 'em for a minute, to see how they are made? I didn't like to look close before the other men, for fear they should think it bad manners in me.' Christian took them out and examined them in the hollow of his hand by the lantern light. 'That these little things should carry such luck, and such charm, and such a spell, and such power in 'em, passes all I ever heard or zeed,' he went on, with a fascinated gaze at the dice, which, as is frequently the case in country places, were made of wood, the points being burnt upon each face with the end of a wire.

'They are a great deal in a small compass, you think?'

'Yes. Do ye suppose they really be the devil's playthings, Mr. Wildeve? If so, 'tis no good sign that I be such a lucky man.'

'You ought to win some money, now that you've got them. Any woman would marry you then. Now is your time, Christian, and I would recommend you not to let it slip. Some men are born to luck, some are not. I belong to the latter class.'

'Did you ever know anybody who was born to it besides myself?'

'O yes. I once heard of an Italian, who sat down at a gaming-table with only a louis (that's a foreign sovereign) in his pocket. He played on for twenty-four hours, and won ten thousand pounds, stripping the bank he had played against. Then there was another man who had lost a thousand pounds, and went to the broker's next day to sell stock, that he might pay the debt. The man to whom he owed the money went with him in a hackney-coach; and to pass the time they tossed who should pay the fare. The ruined man won, and the other was tempted to continue the game, and they played all the way. When the coachman stopped he was told to drive home again: the whole thousand pounds had been won back by the man who was going to sell.'

'Ha—ha—splendid!' exclaimed Christian. 'Go on—go on!'

'Then there was a man of London, who was only a waiter at White's club-house. He began playing first half-crown stakes, and then higher and higher, till he became very rich, got an appointment in India, and rose to be Governor of Madras. His daughter married a member of parliament, and the Bishop of Carlisle stood godfather to one of the children.'

'Wonderful! wonderful!'

'And once there was a young man in America who gambled till he had lost his last dollar. He staked his watch and chain; and lost as before: staked his umbrella; lost again: staked his hat; lost again: staked his coat and stood in his shirt-sleeves ; lost again. Began taking off his breeches, and then a looker-on gave him a trifle for his pluck. With this he won. Won back his coat, won back his hat, won back his umbrella, his watch, his money, and went out of the door a rich man.'

'O, 'tis too good—it takes away my breath ! Mr. Wildeve, I think I will try another shilling with you, as I am one of that sort ; no danger can come o't, and you can afford to lose.'

'Very well,' said Wildeve, rising. Searching about with the lantern, he found a large flat stone, which he placed between himself and Christian, and sat down again. The lantern was opened to give more light, and its rays directed upon the stone. Christian put down a shilling, Wildeve another, and each threw. Christian won. They played for two. Christian won again.

'Let us try four,' said Wildeve. They played for four. This time the stakes were won by Wildeve.

'Ah, those little accidents will, of course, sometimes happen to the luckiest man,' he observed.

'And now I have no more money !' exclaimed Christian excitedly. 'And yet, if I could go on, I should get it back again, and more. I wish this was mine.' He struck his boot upon the ground, so that the guineas chinked within.

'What! you have not put Mrs. Wildeve's money there ?'

'Yes. 'Tis for safety. Is it any harm to raffle with a married lady's money when, if I win, I shall only keep my winnings, and give her her own all the same ; and if t'other man wins, her money will go to the lawful owner ?'

'None at all.'

Wildeve had been brooding ever since they started on the mean estimation in which he was held by his wife's friends ; and it cut his heart severely. As the minutes passed he had gradually drifted into a revengeful intention without knowing the precise moment of forming it. This was to teach Mrs. Yeobright a lesson, as he considered it to be ; in other words, to show her if he could, that her niece's husband was the proper guardian of her niece's money.

'Well, here goes!' said Christian, beginning to unlace one boot. 'I shall dream of it nights and nights, I suppose; but I shall always swear my flesh don't crawl when I think o't!'

He thrust his hand into the boot and withdrew one of poor Thomasin's precious guineas, piping hot. Wildeve had already placed a sovereign on the stone. The game was then resumed. Wildeve won first, and Christian ventured another, winning himself this time. The game fluctuated, but the average was in Wildeve's favour. Both men became so absorbed in the game that they took no heed of anything but the pigmy objects immediately beneath their eyes; the flat stone, the open lantern, the dice, and the few illuminated fern-leaves which lay under the light, were the whole world to them.

At length Christian lost rapidly; and presently, to his horror, the whole fifty guineas belonging to Thomasin had been handed over to his adversary.

'I don't care—I don't care!' he moaned, and desperately set about untying his left boot to get at the other fifty. 'The devil will toss me into the flames on his three-pronged fork for this night's work, I know! But perhaps I shall win yet, and then I'll get a wife to sit up with me o' nights, and I won't be afeared, I won't! Here's another for'ee, my man!' He slapped another guinea down upon the stone, and the dice-box was rattled again.

Time passed on. Wildeve began to be as excited as Christian himself. When commencing the game his intention had been nothing further than a bitter practical joke on Mrs. Yeobright. To win the money, fairly or otherwise, and to hand it contemptuously to Thomasin in her aunt's presence, had been the dim outline of his purpose. But men are drawn from their intentions even in the course of carrying them out, and it was extremely doubtful, by the time the twentieth guinea had been reached, whether Wildeve was conscious of any other intention than that of winning for his own personal benefit. Moreover, he was now no longer gambling for his wife's money, but for Yeobright's ; though of this fact Christian, in his apprehensiveness, did not inform him till afterwards.

It was nearly eleven o'clock, when, with almost a shriek, Christian placed Yeobright's last gleaming guinea upon the stone. In thirty seconds it had gone the way of its companions.

Christian turned and flung himself on the ferns in a convulsion of remorse. 'O, what shall I do with my wretched self ?' he groaned. 'What shall I do ? Will any good Heaven hae mercy upon my wicked soul ?'

'Do ? Live on just the same.'

'I won't live on just the same ! I'll die ! I say you are a—a——'

'A man sharper than my neighbour.'

'Yes, a man sharper than my neighbour ; a regular sharper !'

'Poor chips-in-porridge, you are very unmannerly.'

'I don't know about that ! And I say you be unmannerly ! You've got money that isn't your own. Half the guineas are poor Mr. Clym's.'

'How's that ?'

'Because I had to gie fifty of 'em to him. Mrs. Yeobright said so.'

'Oh ? . . . Well, 'twould have been more graceful of her to have given them to his wife Eustacia. But they are in my hands now.'

Christian pulled on his boots, and with heavy breathings, which could be heard to some distance, dragged his limbs together, arose, and tottered away out of sight. Wildeve set about shutting the lantern to return to the house, for he deemed it too late to go to Mistover to meet his wife, who was to be driven home in the captain's four-wheel. While he was closing the little horn door a figure rose from behind a neighbouring bush and came forward into the lantern light. It was the reddleman approaching.

A NEW FORCE DISTURBS THE CURRENT

VIII

WILDEVE stared. Venn looked coolly towards Wildeve, and, without a word being spoken, he deliberately sat himself down where Christian had been seated, thrust his hand into his pocket, drew out a sovereign, and laid it on the stone.

'You have been watching us from behind that bush?' said Wildeve.

The reddleman nodded. 'Down with your stake,' he said. 'Or haven't you pluck enough to go on?'

Now, gambling is a species of amusement which is much more easily begun with full pockets than left off with the same; and though Wildeve in a cooler temper might have prudently declined this invitation, the excitement of his recent success carried him completely away. He placed one of the guineas on the slab beside the reddleman's sovereign. 'Mine is a guinea,' he said.

'A guinea that's not your own,' said Venn sarcastically.

'It is my own,' answered Wildeve haughtily. 'It is my wife's, and what is hers is mine.'

'Very well; let's make a beginning.' He shook the box, and threw eight, ten, and nine; the three casts amounted to twenty-seven.

This encouraged Wildeve. He took the box; and his three casts amounted to forty-five.

Down went another of the reddleman's sovereigns against his first one which Wildeve laid. This time Wildeve threw fifty-one points, but no pair. The reddleman looked grim, threw a raffle of aces, and pocketed the stakes.

'Here you are again,' said Wildeve contemptuously. 'Double the stakes.' He laid two of Thomasin's guineas, and the reddleman his two pounds. Venn won again. New stakes were laid on the stone, and the gamblers proceeded as before.

Wildeve was a nervous and excitable man; and the game was beginning to tell upon his temper. He writhed, fumed, shifted his seat; and the beating of his heart was almost audible. Venn sat with lips impassively closed and eyes reduced to a pair of unimportant twinkles; he scarcely appeared to breathe. He might have been an Arab, or an automaton; he would have been like a red-sandstone statue but for the motion of his arm with the dice-box.

The game fluctuated, now in favour of one, now in favour of the other, without any great advantage on the side of either. Nearly twenty minutes were passed thus. The light of the candle had by this time attracted heath-flies, moths, and other winged creatures of night, which floated round the lantern, flew into the flame, or beat about the faces of the two players.

But neither of the men paid much attention to these things, their eyes being concentrated upon the little flat stone, which to them was an arena vast and important as a battle-field. By this time a change had come over the game; the reddleman won continually. At length sixty guineas—Thomasin's fifty, and ten of Clym's—had passed into his hands. Wildeve was reckless, frantic, exasperated.

'"Won back his coat,"' said Venn slily.

Another throw, and the money went the same way.

'"Won back his hat,"' continued Venn.

'Oh, oh!' said Wildeve.

'"Won back his watch, won back his money, and went out of the door a rich man,"' added Venn sentence by sentence, as stake after stake passed over to him.

'Five more!' shouted Wildeve, dashing down the money. 'And three casts be hanged—one shall decide.'

The red automaton opposite lapsed into silence, nodded, and followed his example. Wildeve rattled the box, and threw a pair of sixes and five points. He clapped his hands; 'I have done it this time—hurrah!'

'There are two playing, and only one has thrown,' said the reddleman, quietly bringing down the box. The eyes of each were then so intently converged upon the stone that one could fancy their beams were visible, like rays in a fog.

Venn lifted the box, and behold a triplet of sixes was disclosed.

Wildeve was full of fury. While the reddleman was grasping the stakes Wildeve seized the dice and hurled them, box and all, into the darkness, uttering a fearful imprecation. Then he arose and began stamping up and down like a madman.

'It is all over, then?' said Venn.

'No, no!' cried Wildeve. 'I mean to have another chance yet. I must!'

'But, my good man, what have you done with the dice?'

'I threw them away—it was a momentary irritation. What a fool I am! Here—come and help me to look for them—we must find them again.'

Wildeve snatched up the lantern and began anxiously prowling among the furze and fern.

'You are not likely to find them there,' said Venn, following. 'What did you do such a crazy thing as that for? Here's the box. The dice can't be far off.'

Wildeve turned the light eagerly upon the spot where Venn had found the box, and mauled the herbage right and left. In the course of a few minutes one of the dice was found. They searched on for some time, but no other was to be seen.

'Never mind,' said Wildeve; 'let's play with one.'

'Agreed,' said Venn.

Down they sat again, and recommenced with single guinea stakes; and the play went on smartly. But Fortune had unmistakably fallen in love with the reddleman to-night. He won steadily, till he was the owner of fourteen more of the gold pieces. Seventy-nine of the hundred guineas were his, Wildeve possessing only twenty-one. The aspect of the two opponents was now singular. Apart from motions, a complete diorama of the fluctuations of the game went on in their eyes. A diminutive candle-flame was mirrored in each pupil, and it would have been possible to distinguish therein between the moods of hope and the moods of abandonment, even as regards the reddleman, though his facial muscles betrayed nothing at all. Wildeve played on with the recklessness of despair.

'What's that?' he suddenly exclaimed, hearing a rustle; and they both looked up.

They were surrounded by dusky forms between four and five feet high, standing a few paces beyond the rays of the lantern. A moment's inspection revealed that the encircling figures were heath-croppers, their heads being all towards the players, at whom they gazed intently.

'Hoosh!' said Wildeve; and the whole forty or fifty animals at once turned and galloped away. Play was again resumed.

Ten minutes passed away. Then a large death's head moth advanced from the obscure outer air, wheeled twice round the lantern, flew straight at the candle, and extinguished it by the force of the blow. Wildeve had just thrown, but had not lifted the box to see what he had cast; and now it was impossible.

'What the infernal!' he shrieked. 'Now, what shall

we do? Perhaps I have thrown six—have you any matches?'

'None,' said Venn.

'Christian had some—I wonder where he is. Christian!'

But there was no reply to Wildeve's shout, save a mournful whining from the herons which were nesting lower down the vale. Both men looked blankly round without rising. As their eyes grew accustomed to the darkness they perceived faint greenish points of light among the grass and fern. These lights dotted the hillside like stars of a low magnitude.

'Ah—glowworms,' said Wildeve. 'Wait a minute. We can continue the game.'

Venn sat still, and his companion went hither and thither till he had gathered thirteen glowworms—as many as he could find in a space of four or five minutes—upon a foxglove leaf which he pulled for the purpose. The reddleman vented a low humorous laugh when he saw his adversary return with these. 'Determined to go on, then?' he said drily.

'I always am!' said Wildeve angrily. And shaking the glowworms from the leaf he ranged them with a trembling hand in a circle on the stone, leaving a space in the middle for the descent of the dice-box, over which the thirteen tiny lamps threw a pale phosphoric shine. The game was again renewed. It happened to be that season of the year at which glowworms put forth their greatest brilliancy, and the light they yielded was more than ample for the purpose, since it is possible on such nights to read the handwriting of a letter by the light of two or three.

The incongruity between the men's deeds and their environment was great. Amid the soft juicy vegetation of the hollow in which they sat, the motionless and the uninhabited solitude, intruded the chink of guineas, the rattle of dice, the exclamations of the reckless players.

Wildeve had lifted the box as soon as the lights were obtained, and the solitary die proclaimed that the game was still against him.

'I won't play any more: you've been tampering with the dice,' he shouted.

'How—when they were your own?' said the reddleman.

'We'll change the game: the lowest point shall win the stake—it may cut off my ill luck. Do you refuse?'

'No—go on,' said Venn.

'O, there they are again—damn them!' cried Wildeve, looking up. The heath-croppers had returned noiselessly, and were looking on with erect heads just as before, their timid eyes fixed upon the scene, as if they were wondering what mankind and candle-light could have to do in these haunts at this untoward hour.

'What a plague those creatures are—staring at me so!' he said, and flung a stone, which scattered them; when the game was continued as before.

Wildeve had now ten guineas left; and each laid five. Wildeve threw three points; Venn two, and raked in the coins. The other seized the die, and clenched his teeth upon it in sheer rage, as if he would bite it in pieces. 'Never give in—here are my last five!' he cried, throwing them down. 'Hang the glowworms—they are going out. Why don't you burn, you little fools? Stir them up with a thorn.'

He probed the glowworms with a bit of stick, and rolled them over, till the bright side of their tails was upwards.

'There's light enough. Throw on,' said Venn.

Wildeve brought down the box within the shining circle and looked eagerly. He had thrown ace. 'Well done!—I said it would turn, and it has turned.' Venn said nothing; but his hand shook slightly.

He threw ace also.

'O!' said Wildeve. 'Curse me!'

The die smacked the stone a second time. It was ace again. Venn looked gloomy, threw: the die was seen to be lying in two pieces, the cleft sides uppermost.

'I've thrown nothing at all,' he said.

'Serves me right—I split the die with my teeth. Here—take your money. Blank is less than one.'

'I don't wish it.'

'Take it, I say—you've won it!' And Wildeve threw the stakes against the reddleman's chest. Venn gathered them up, arose, and withdrew from the hollow, Wildeve sitting stupefied.

When he had come to himself he also arose, and, with the extinguished lantern in his hand, went towards the high-road. On reaching it he stood still. The silence of night pervaded the whole heath except in one direction; and that was towards Mistover. There he could hear the noise of light wheels, and presently saw two carriage-lamps descending the hill. Wildeve screened himself under a bush and waited.

The vehicle came on and passed before him. It was a hired carriage, and behind the coachman were two persons whom he knew well. There sat Eustacia and Yeobright, the arm of the latter being round her waist. They turned the sharp corner at the bottom towards the temporary home which Clym had hired and furnished, about five miles to the eastward.

Wildeve forgot the loss of the money at the sight of his lost love, whose preciousness in his eyes was increasing in geometrical progression with each new incident that reminded him of their hopeless division. Brimming with the subtilized misery that he was capable of feeling, he followed the opposite way towards the inn.

About the same moment that Wildeve stepped into the highway Venn also had reached it at a point a hundred yards further on; and he, hearing the same wheels, likewise waited till the carriage should come up. When he saw who sat therein he seemed to be disappointed.

Reflecting a minute or two, during which interval the carriage rolled on, he crossed the road, and took a short cut through the furze and heath to a point where the turnpike-road bent round in ascending a hill. He was now again in front of the carriage, which presently came up at a walking pace. Venn stepped forward and showed himself.

Eustacia started when the lamp shone upon him, and Clym's arm was involuntarily withdrawn from her waist. He said, 'What, Diggory? You are having a lonely walk.'

'Yes—I beg your pardon for stopping you,' said Venn. 'But I am waiting about for Mrs. Wildeve: I have something to give her from Mrs. Yeobright. Can you tell me if she's gone home from the party yet?'

'No. But she will be leaving soon. You may possibly meet her at the corner.'

Venn made a farewell obeisance, and walked back to his former position, where the by-road from Mistover joined the highway. Here he remained fixed for nearly half an hour; and then another pair of lights came down the hill. It was the old-fashioned wheel nondescript belonging to the captain, and Thomasin sat in it alone, driven by Charley.

The reddleman came up as they slowly turned the corner. 'I beg pardon for stopping you, Mrs. Wildeve,' he said. 'But I have something to give you privately from Mrs. Yeobright.' He handed a small parcel; it consisted of the hundred guineas he had just won, roughly twisted up in a piece of paper.

Thomasin recovered from her surprise, and took the packet. 'That's all, ma'am—I wish you good-night,' he said, and vanished from her view.

Thus Venn, in his anxiety to rectify matters, had placed in Thomasin's hands not only the fifty guineas which rightly belonged to her, but also the fifty intended for her cousin Clym. His mistake had been based upon Wildeve's words at the opening of the game, when he indignantly denied that the guinea was not his own. It had not been comprehended by the reddleman that at half-way through the performance the game was continued with the money of another person; and it was an error which afterwards helped to cause more misfortune than treble the loss in money value could have done.

The night was now somewhat advanced; and Venn plunged deeper into the heath, till he came to a ravine where his van was standing—a spot not more than two hundred yards from the site of the gambling bout. He entered this movable home of his, lit his lantern, and, before closing his door for the night, stood reflecting on the circumstances of the preceding hours. While he stood the dawn grew visible in the north-east quarter of the heavens, which, the clouds having cleared off, was bright with a soft sheen at this midsummer time, though it was only between one and two o'clock. Venn, thoroughly weary, then shut his door and flung himself down to sleep.

BOOK FOURTH

THE CLOSED DOOR

THE RENCOUNTER BY THE POOL

I

THE July sun shone over Egdon and fired its crimson heather to scarlet. It was the one season of the year, and the one weather of the season, in which the heath was gorgeous. This flowering period represented the second or noontide division in the cycle of those superficial changes which alone were possible here; it followed the green or young-fern period, representing the morn, and preceded the brown period, when the heath-bells and ferns would wear the russet tinges of evening; to be in turn displaced by the dark hue of the winter period, representing night.

Clym and Eustacia, in their little house at Alderworth, beyond East Egdon, were living on with a monotony which was delightful to them. The heath and changes of weather were quite blotted out from their eyes for the present. They were enclosed in a sort of luminous mist, which hid from them surroundings of any inharmonious colour, and gave to all things the character of light. When it rained they were charmed, because they could remain indoors together all day with such a show of reason; when it was fine they were charmed, because they could sit together on the hills. They were like those double stars which revolve round each other, and from a distance appear to be one. The absolute solitude in which they lived intensified their reciprocal thoughts ; yet some might have said that it had the disadvantage of consuming their mutual affections at a fearfully prodigal rate. Yeobright did not fear for his own part ; but recollection of Eustacia's old speech about the evanescence of love, now apparently forgotten by her, sometimes caused him to ask himself a question ; and he recoiled at the thought that the quality of finiteness was not foreign to Eden.

When three or four weeks had been passed thus, Yeobright resumed his reading in earnest. To make up for lost time he studied indefatigably, for he wished to enter his new profession with the least possible delay.

Now, Eustacia's dream had always been that, once married to Clym, she would have the power of inducing him to return to Paris. He had carefully withheld all promise to do so ; but would he be proof against her coaxing and argument ? She had calculated to such a degree on the probability of success that she had represented Paris, and not Budmouth, to her grandfather as in all likelihood their future home. Her hopes were bound up in this dream. In the quiet days since their marriage, when Yeobright had been poring over her lips, her eyes, and the lines of her face, she had mused and mused on the subject, even while in the act of returning his gaze ; and now the sight of the books, indicating a future which was antagonistic to her dream, struck her with a positively painful jar. She was hoping for the time when, as the mistress of some pretty establishment, however small, near a Parisian Boulevard, she would be passing her days on the skirts at least of the gay world, and catching stray wafts from those town pleasures she was so well fitted to enjoy. Yet Yeobright was as firm in the contrary intention as if the tendency of marriage were rather to develop the fantasies of young philanthropy than to sweep them away.

Her anxiety reached a high pitch ; but there was

something in Clym's undeviating manner which made her hesitate before sounding him on the subject. At this point in their experience, however, an incident helped her. It occurred one evening about six weeks after their union, and arose entirely out of the unconscious misapplication by Venn of the fifty guineas intended for Yeobright.

A day or two after the receipt of the money Thomasin had sent a note to her aunt to thank her. She had been surprised at the largeness of the amount; but as no sum had ever been mentioned she set that down to her late uncle's generosity. She had been strictly charged by her aunt to say nothing to her husband of this gift; and Wildeve, as was natural enough, had not brought himself to mention to his wife a single particular of the midnight scene in the heath. Christian's terror, in like manner, had tied his tongue on the share he took in that proceeding; and hoping that by some means or other the money had gone to its proper destination, he simply asserted as much, without giving details.

Therefore, when a week or two had passed away, Mrs. Yeobright began to wonder why she never heard from her son of the receipt of the present; and to add gloom to her perplexity came the possibility that resentment might be the cause of his silence. She could hardly believe as much, but why did he not write? She questioned Christian, and the confusion in his answers would at once have led her to believe that something was wrong, had not one-half of his story been corroborated by Thomasin's note.

Mrs. Yeobright was in this state of uncertainty when she was informed one morning that her son's wife was visiting her grandfather at Mistover. She determined to walk up the hill, see Eustacia, and ascertain from her daughter-in-law's lips whether the family guineas, which were to Mrs. Yeobright what family jewels are to wealthier dowagers, had miscarried or not.

When Christian learnt where she was going his concern reached its height. At the moment of her departure he could prevaricate no longer, and, confessing to the gambling, told her the truth as far as he knew it—that the guineas had been won by Wildeve.

'What, is he going to keep them?' Mrs. Yeobright cried.

'I hope and trust not!' moaned Christian. 'He's a good man, and perhaps will do right things. He said you ought to have gied Mr. Clym's share to Eustacia, and that's perhaps what he'll do himself.'

To Mrs. Yeobright, as soon as she could calmly reflect, there was much likelihood in this, for she could hardly believe that Wildeve would really appropriate money belonging to her son. The intermediate course of giving it to Eustacia was the sort of thing to please Wildeve's fancy. But it filled the mother with anger none the less. That Wildeve should have got command of the guineas after all, and should rearrange the disposal of them, placing Clym's share in Clym's wife's hands, because she had been his own sweetheart, and might be so still, was as irritating a pain as any that Mrs. Yeobright had ever borne.

She instantly dismissed the wretched Christian from her employ for his conduct in the affair; but, feeling quite helpless and unable to do without him, told him afterwards that he might stay a little longer if he chose. Then she hastened off to Eustacia, moved by a much less promising emotion towards her daughter-in-law than she had felt half an hour earlier, when planning her journey. At that time it was to inquire in a friendly spirit if there had been any accidental loss; now it was to ask plainly if Wildeve had privately given her money which had been intended as a sacred gift to Clym.

She started at two o'clock, and her meeting with Eustacia was hastened by the appearance of the young lady beside the pool and bank which bordered her grandfather's premises, where she stood surveying the scene, and perhaps thinking of the romantic enactments it had witnessed in past days. When Mrs. Yeobright approached, Eustacia surveyed her with the calm stare of a stranger.

The mother-in-law was the first to speak. 'I was coming to see you,' she said.

'Indeed!' said Eustacia with surprise, for Mrs. Yeobright, much to the girl's mortification, had refused to be present at the wedding. 'I did not at all expect you.'

'I was coming on business only,' said the visitor, more coldly than at first. 'Will you excuse my asking this—Have you received a gift from Thomasin's husband?'

'A gift?'

'I mean money!'

'What—I myself?'

'Well, I meant yourself, privately—though I was not going to put it in that way.'

'Money from Mr. Wildeve? No—never! Madam, what do you mean by that?' Eustacia fired up all too quickly, for her own consciousness of the old attachment between herself and Wildeve led her to jump to the conclusion that Mrs. Yeobright also knew of it, and might have come to accuse her of receiving dishonourable presents from him now.

'I simply ask the question,' said Mrs. Yeobright. 'I have been——'

'You ought to have better opinions of me—I feared you were against me from the first!' exclaimed Eustacia.

'No. I was simply for Clym,' replied Mrs. Yeobright, with too much emphasis in her earnestness. 'It is the instinct of every one to look after their own.'

'How can you imply that he required guarding against me?' cried Eustacia, passionate tears in her eyes. 'I have not injured him by marrying him! What sin have I done that you should think so ill of me? You had no right to speak against me to him when I have never wronged you.'

'I only did what was fair under the circumstances,' said Mrs. Yeobright more softly. 'I would rather not have gone into this question at present, but you compel me. I am not ashamed to tell you the honest truth. I was firmly convinced that he ought not to marry you —therefore I tried to dissuade him by all the means in my power. But it is done now, and I have no idea of complaining any more. I am ready to welcome you.'

'Ah, yes, it is very well to see things in that business point of view,' murmured Eustacia with a smothered fire of feeling. 'But why should you think there is anything between me and Mr. Wildeve? I have a spirit as well as you. I am indignant; and so would any woman be. It was a condescension in me to be Clym's wife, and not a manœuvre, let me remind you; and therefore I will not be treated as a schemer whom it becomes necessary to bear with because she has crept into the family.'

'Oh!' said Mrs. Yeobright, vainly endeavouring to control her anger. 'I have never heard anything to show that my son's lineage is not as good as the Vyes'— perhaps better. It is amusing to hear you talk of condescension.'

'It was condescension, nevertheless,' said Eustacia vehemently. 'And if I had known then what I know now, that I should be living in this wild heath a month after my marriage, I—I should have thought twice before agreeing.'

'It would be better not to say that; it might not sound truthful. I am not aware that any deception was used on his part—I know there was not—whatever might have been the case on the other side.'

'This is too exasperating!' answered the younger woman huskily, her face crimsoning, and her eyes darting light. 'How can you dare to speak to me like that? I insist upon repeating to you that had I known that my life would from my marriage up to this time have been as it is, I should have said *No*. I don't complain. I have never uttered a sound of such a thing to him; but it is true. I hope therefore that in the future you will be silent on my eagerness. If you injure me now you injure yourself.'

'Injure you? Do you think I am an evil-disposed person?'

'You injured me before my marriage, and you have now suspected me of secretly favouring another man for money!'

'I could not help what I thought. But I have never spoken of you outside my house.'

'You spoke of me within it, to Clym, and you could not do worse.'

'I did my duty.'

'And I'll do mine.'

'A part of which will possibly be to set him against his mother. It is always so. But why should I not bear it as others have borne it before me!'

'I understand you,' said Eustacia, breathless with emotion. 'You think me capable of every bad thing. Who can be worse than a wife who encourages a lover, and poisons her husband's mind against his relative? Yet that is now the character given to me. Will you not come and drag him out of my hands?'

Mrs. Yeobright gave back heat for heat.

'Don't rage at me, madam! It ill becomes your beauty, and I am not worth the injury you may do it on my account, I assure you. I am only a poor old woman who has lost a son.'

'If you had treated me honourably you would have had him still,' Eustacia said, while scalding tears trickled from her eyes. 'You have brought yourself to folly; you have caused a division which can never be healed!'

'I have done nothing. This audacity from a young woman is more than I can bear.'

'It was asked for: you have suspected me, and you have made me speak of my husband in a way I would not have done. You will let him know that I have spoken thus, and it will cause misery between us. Will you go away from me ? You are no friend ! '

' I will go when I have spoken a word. If any one says I have come here to question you without good grounds for it, that person speaks untruly. If any one says that I attempted to stop your marriage by any but honest means, that person, too, does not speak the truth. I have fallen on an evil time ; God has been unjust to me in letting you insult me ! Probably my son's happiness does not lie on this side of the grave, for he is a foolish man who neglects the advice of his parent. You, Eustacia, stand on the edge of a precipice without knowing it. Only show my son one-half the temper you have shown me to-day—and you may before long—and you will find that though he is as gentle as a child with you now, he can be as hard as steel ! '

The excited mother then withdrew, and Eustacia, panting, stood looking into the pool.

HE IS SET UPON BY ADVERSITIES BUT HE SINGS A SONG

II

THE result of that unpropitious interview was that Eustacia, instead of passing the afternoon with her grandfather, hastily returned home to Clym, where she arrived three hours earlier than she had been expected.

She came indoors with her face flushed, and her eyes still showing traces of her recent excitement. Yeobright looked up astonished; he had never seen her in any way approaching to that state before. She passed him by, and would have gone upstairs unnoticed, but Clym was so concerned that he immediately followed her.

'What is the matter, Eustacia?' he said. She was standing on the hearthrug in the bedroom, looking upon the floor, her hands clasped in front of her, her bonnet yet unremoved. For a moment she did not answer; and then she replied in a low voice—

'I have seen your mother; and I will never see her again!'

A weight fell like a stone upon Clym. That same morning, when Eustacia had arranged to go and see her grandfather, Clym had expressed a wish that she would drive down to Blooms-End and inquire for her mother-in-law, or adopt any other means she might think fit to bring about a reconciliation. She had set out gaily; and he had hoped for much.

'Why is this?' he asked.

'I cannot tell—I cannot remember. I met your mother. And I will never meet her again.'

'Why?'

'What do I know about Mr. Wildeve now? I won't have wicked opinions passed on me by anybody. O! it was too humiliating to be asked if I had received any money from him, or encouraged him, or something of the sort—I don't exactly know what!'

'How could she have asked you that?'

'She did.'

'Then there must have been some meaning in it. What did my mother say besides?'

'I don't know what she said, except in so far as this, that we both said words which can never be forgiven!'

'O, there must be some misapprehension. Whose fault was it that her meaning was not made clear?'

'I would rather not say. It may have been the fault of the circumstances, which were awkward at the very least. O Clym—I cannot help expressing it—this is an unpleasant position that you have placed me in. But you must improve it—yes, say you will—for I hate it all now! Yes, take me to Paris, and go on with your old occupation, Clym! I don't mind how humbly we live there at first, if it can only be Paris, and not Egdon Heath.'

'But I have quite given up that idea,' said Yeobright, with surprise. 'Surely I never led you to expect such a thing?'

'I own it. Yet there are thoughts which cannot be kept out of mind, and that one was mine. Must I not have a voice in the matter, now I am your wife and the sharer of your doom?'

'Well, there are things which are placed beyond the

pale of discussion ; and I thought this was specially so, and by mutual agreement.'

'Clym, I am unhappy at what I hear,' she said in a low voice ; and her eyes drooped, and she turned away.

This indication of an unexpected mine of hope in Eustacia's bosom disconcerted her husband. It was the first time that he had confronted the fact of the indirectness of a woman's movement towards her desire. But his intention was unshaken, though he loved Eustacia well. All the effect that her remark had upon him was a resolve to chain himself more closely than ever to his books, so as to be the sooner enabled to appeal to substantial results from another course in arguing against her whim.

Next day the mystery of the guineas was explained. Thomasin paid them a hurried visit, and Clym's share was delivered up to him by her own hands. Eustacia was not present at the time.

'Then this is what my mother meant,' exclaimed Clym. 'Thomasin, do you know that they have had a bitter quarrel ?'

There was a little more reticence now than formerly in Thomasin's manner towards her cousin. It is the effect of marriage to engender in several directions some of the reserve it annihilates in one. 'Your mother told me,' she said quietly. 'She came back to my house after seeing Eustacia.'

'The worst thing I dreaded has come to pass. Was mother much disturbed when she came to you, Thomasin?'

'Yes.'

'Very much indeed ?'

'Yes.'

Clym leant his elbow upon the post of the garden gate, and covered his eyes with his hand.

'Don't trouble about it, Clym. They may get to be friends.'

He shook his head. 'Not two people with inflammable natures like theirs. Well, what must be will be.'

'One thing is cheerful in it—the guineas are not lost.'

'I would rather have lost them twice over than have had this happen.'

Amid these jarring events Yeobright felt one thing to be indispensable—that he should speedily make some show of progress in his scholastic plans. With this view he read far into the small hours during many nights.

One morning, after a severer strain than usual, he woke with a strange sensation in his eyes. The sun was shining directly upon the window-blind, and at first glance thitherward a sharp pain obliged him to close his eyelids quickly. At every new attempt to look about him the same morbid sensibility to light was manifested, and excoriating tears ran down his cheeks. He was obliged to tie a bandage over his brow while dressing; and during the day it could not be abandoned. Eustacia was thoroughly alarmed. On finding that the case was no better the next morning they decided to send to Anglebury for a surgeon.

Towards evening he arrived, and pronounced the disease to be acute inflammation induced by Clym's night studies, continued in spite of a cold previously caught, which had weakened his eyes for the time.

Fretting with impatience at this interruption to a task he was so anxious to hasten, Clym was transformed into an invalid. He was shut up in a room from which all light was excluded, and his condition would have been one of absolute misery had not Eustacia read to him by the glimmer of a shaded lamp. He hoped that the worst would soon be over; but at the surgeon's third visit he learnt to his dismay that although he might venture out of doors with shaded eyes in the course of a month, all thought of pursuing his work, or of reading print of any description, would have to be given up for a long time to come.

One week and another week wore on, and nothing seemed to lighten the gloom of the young couple. Dreadful imaginings occurred to Eustacia, but she carefully refrained from uttering them to her husband. Suppose he should become blind, or, at all events, never recover sufficient strength of sight to engage in an occupation which would be congenial to her feelings, and conduce to her removal from this lonely dwelling among the hills? That dream of beautiful Paris was not likely to cohere into substance in the presence of this misfortune. As day after day passed by, and he got no better, her mind ran more and more in this mournful groove, and she would go away from him into the garden and weep despairing tears.

Yeobright thought he would send for his mother; and then he thought he would not. Knowledge of his state could only make her the more unhappy; and the seclusion of their life was such that she would hardly be likely to learn the news except through a special messenger. Endeavouring to take the trouble as philosophically as possible, he waited on till the third week had arrived, when he went into the open air for the first time since the attack. The surgeon visited him again at this stage, and Clym urged him to express a distinct opinion. The young man learnt with added surprise that the date at which he might expect to resume his labours was as uncertain as ever, his eyes being in that peculiar state which, though affording him sight enough for walking about, would not admit of their being strained upon any definite object without incurring the risk of reproducing ophthalmia in its acute form.

Clym was very grave at the intelligence, but not despairing. A quiet firmness, and even cheerfulness, took possession of him. He was not to be blind; that was enough. To be doomed to behold the world through smoked glass for an indefinite period was bad enough, and fatal to any kind of advance; but Yeobright was an absolute stoic in the face of mishaps which only affected his social standing; and, apart from Eustacia, the humblest walk of life would satisfy him if it could be made to work in with some form of his culture scheme. To keep a cottage night-school was one such form; and his affliction did not master his spirit as it might otherwise have done.

He walked through the warm sun westward into those tracts of Egdon with which he was best acquainted, being those lying nearer to his old home. He saw before him in one of the valleys the gleaming of whetted iron, and advancing, dimly perceived that the shine came from the tool of a man who was cutting furze. The worker recognized Clym, and Yeobright learnt from the voice that the speaker was Humphrey.

Humphrey expressed his sorrow at Clym's condition; and added, 'Now, if yours was low-class work like mine, you could go on with it just the same.'

'Yes; I could,' said Yeobright musingly. 'How much do you get for cutting these faggots?'

'Half-a-crown a hundred, and in these long days I can live very well on the wages.'

During the whole of Yeobright's walk home to Alderworth he was lost in reflections which were not of an unpleasant kind. On his coming up to the house Eustacia spoke to him from the open window, and he went across to her.

'Darling,' he said, 'I am much happier. And if my mother were reconciled to me and to you I should, I think, be happy quite.'

'I fear that will never be,' she said, looking afar with her beautiful stormy eyes. 'How *can* you say "I am happier," and nothing changed?'

'It arises from my having at last discovered something I can do, and get a living at, in this time of misfortune.'

'Yes?'

'I am going to be a furze and turf cutter.'

'No, Clym!' she said, the slight hopefulness previously apparent in her face going off again, and leaving her worse than before.

'Surely I shall. Is it not very unwise in us to go on spending the little money we've got when I can keep down expenditure by an honest occupation? The outdoor exercise will do me good, and who knows but that in a few months I shall be able to go on with my reading again?'

'But my grandfather offers to assist us, if we require assistance.'

'We don't require it. If I go furze-cutting we shall be fairly well off.'

'In comparison with slaves, and the Israelites in Egypt, and such people!' A bitter tear rolled down Eustacia's face, which he did not see. There had been *nonchalance* in his tone, showing her that he felt no absolute grief at a consummation which to her was a positive horror.

The very next day Yeobright went to Humphrey's cottage, and borrowed of him leggings, gloves, a whetstone, and a hook, to use till he should be able to purchase some for himself. Then he sallied forth with his new fellow-labourer and old acquaintance, and selecting a spot where the furze grew thickest he struck the first blow in his adopted calling. His sight, like the wings in 'Rasselas,' though useless to him for his grand purpose, sufficed for this strait, and he found that when a little practice should have hardened his palms against blistering he would be able to work with ease.

Day after day he rose with the sun, buckled on his leggings, and went off to the rendezvous with Humphrey. His custom was to work from four o'clock in the morning till noon; then, when the heat of the day was at its highest, to go home and sleep for an hour or two; afterwards coming out again and working till dusk at nine.

This man from Paris was now so disguised by his leather accoutrements, and by the goggles he was obliged to wear over his eyes, that his closest friend might have passed by without recognizing him. He was a brown spot in the midst of an expanse of olive-green gorse, and nothing more. Though frequently depressed in spirit when not actually at work, owing to thoughts of Eustacia's position and his mother's estrangement, when in the full swing of labour he was cheerfully disposed and calm.

His daily life was of a curious microscopic sort, his whole world being limited to a circuit of a few feet from his person. His familiars were creeping and winged things, and they seemed to enroll him in their band. Bees hummed around his ears with an intimate air, and tugged at the heath and furze-flowers at his side in such numbers as to weigh them down to the sod. The strange amber-coloured butterflies which Egdon produced, and which were never seen elsewhere, quivered in the breath of his lips, alighted upon his bowed back, and sported with the glittering point of his hook as he flourished it up and down. Tribes of emerald-green grasshoppers leaped over his feet, falling awkwardly on their backs, heads, or hips, like unskilful acrobats, as chance might rule ; or engaged themselves in noisy flirtations under the fern-fronds with silent ones of homely hue. Huge flies, ignorant of larders and wire-netting, and quite in a savage state, buzzed about him without knowing that he was a man. In and out of the fern-dells snakes glided in their most brilliant blue and yellow guise, it being the season immediately following the shedding of their old skins, when their colours are brightest. Litters of young rabbits came out from their forms to sun themselves upon hillocks, the hot beams blazing through the delicate tissue of each thin-fleshed ear, and firing it to a blood-red transparency in which the veins could be seen. None of them feared him.

The monotony of his occupation soothed him, and was in itself a pleasure. A forced limitation of effort offered a justification of homely courses to an unambitious man, whose conscience would hardly have allowed him to remain in such obscurity while his powers were unimpeded.

Hence Yeobright sometimes sang to himself, and when obliged to accompany Humphrey in search of brambles for faggot-bonds he would amuse his companion with sketches of Parisian life and character, and so while away the time.

On one of these warm afternoons Eustacia walked out alone in the direction of Yeobright's place of work. He was busily chopping away at the furze, a long row of faggots which stretched downward from his position representing the labour of the day. He did not observe her approach, and she stood close to him, and heard his undercurrent of song. It shocked her. To see him there, a poor afflicted man, earning money by the sweat of his brow, had at first moved her to tears; but to hear him sing and not at all rebel against an occupation which, however satisfactory to himself, was degrading to her, as an educated lady-wife, wounded her through. Unconscious of her presence, he still went on singing:—

" Le point du jour
A nos bosquets rend toute leur parure;
Flore est plus belle à son retour;
L'oiseau reprend doux chant d'amour;
Tout célébre dans la nature
Le point du jour.

" Le point du jour
Cause parfois, cause douleur extrême;
Que l'espace des nuits est court
Pour le berger brûlant d'amour,
Forcé de quitter ce qu'il aime
Au point du jour!"

It was bitterly plain to Eustacia that he did not care much about social failure; and the proud fair woman bowed her head and wept in sick despair at thought of the blasting effect upon her own life of that mood and condition in him. Then she came forward.

'I would starve rather than do it!' she exclaimed vehemently. 'And you can sing! I will go and live with my grandfather again!'

'Eustacia! I did not see you, though I noticed something moving,' he said gently. He came forward, pulled off his huge leather glove, and took her hand. 'Why do you speak in such a strange way? It is only a little old song which struck my fancy when I was in Paris, and now just applies to my life with you. Has your love for me all died, then, because my appearance is no longer that of a fine gentleman?'

'Dearest, you must not question me unpleasantly, or it may make me not love you.'

'Do you believe it possible that I would run the risk of doing that?'

'Well, you follow out your own ideas, and won't give in to mine when I wish you to leave off this shameful labour. Is there anything you dislike in me that you act so contrarily to my wishes? I am your wife, and why will you not listen? Yes, I am your wife indeed!'

'I know what that tone means.'

'What tone?'

'The tone in which you said, "Your wife indeed." It meant, "Your wife, worse luck."'

'It is hard in you to probe me with that remark. A woman may have reason, though she is not without heart, and if I felt "worse luck," it was no ignoble feeling—it was only too natural. There, you see that at any rate I do not attempt untruths. Do you remember how, before we were married, I warned you that I had not good wifely qualities?'

'You mock me to say that now. On that point at least the only noble course would be to hold your tongue, for you are still queen of me, Eustacia, though I may no longer be king of you.'

'You are my husband. Does not that content you?'

'Not unless you are my wife without regret.'

'I cannot answer you. I remember saying that I should be a serious matter on your hands.'

'Yes, I saw that.'

'Then you were too quick to see! No true lover would have seen any such thing; you are too severe upon me, Clym—I don't like your speaking so at all.'

'Well, I married you in spite of it, and don't regret doing so. How cold you seem this afternoon! and yet I used to think there never was a warmer heart than yours.'

'Yes, I fear we are cooling—I see it as well as you,' she sighed mournfully. 'And how madly we loved two months ago! You were never tired of contemplating me, nor I of contemplating you. Who could have thought then that by this time my eyes would not seem so very bright to yours, nor your lips so very sweet to mine? Two months—is it possible? Yes, 'tis too true!'

'You sigh, dear, as if you were sorry for it; and that's a hopeful sign.'

'No. I don't sigh for that. There are other things for me to sigh for, or any other woman in my place.'

'That your chances in life are ruined by marrying in haste an unfortunate man?'

'Why will you force me, Clym, to say bitter things? I deserve pity as much as you. As much?—I think I deserve it more. For you can sing! It would be a strange hour which should catch me singing under such a cloud as this! Believe me, sweet, I could weep to a degree that would astonish and confound such an elastic mind as yours. Even had you felt careless about your own affliction, you might have refrained from singing out of sheer pity for mine. God! if I were a man in such a position I would curse rather than sing.'

Yeobright placed his hand upon her arm. 'Now, don't you suppose, my inexperienced girl, that I cannot rebel, in high Promethean fashion, against the gods and fate as well as you. I have felt more steam and smoke of that sort than you have ever heard of. But the more I see of life the more do I perceive that there is nothing particularly great in its greatest walks, and therefore nothing particularly small in mine of furze-cutting. If I feel that the greatest blessings vouchsafed to us are not very valuable, how can I feel it to be any great hardship when they are taken away? So I sing to pass the time. Have you indeed lost all tenderness for me, that you begrudge me a few cheerful moments?'

'I have still some tenderness left for you.'

'Your words have no longer their old flavour. And so love dies with good fortune!'

'I cannot listen to this, Clym—it will end bitterly,' she said in a broken voice. 'I will go home.'

SHE GOES OUT TO BATTLE AGAINST DEPRESSION

III

A FEW days later, before the month of August had expired, Eustacia and Yeobright sat together at their early dinner.

Eustacia's manner had become of late almost apathetic. There was a forlorn look about her beautiful eyes which, whether she deserved it or not, would have excited pity in the breast of any one who had known her during the full flush of her love for Clym. The feelings of husband and wife varied, in some measure, inversely with their positions. Clym, the afflicted man, was cheerful; and he even tried to comfort her, who had never felt a moment of physical suffering in her whole life.

'Come, brighten up, dearest; we shall be all right again. Some day perhaps I shall see as well as ever. And I solemnly promise that I'll leave off cutting furze as soon as I have the power to do anything better. You cannot seriously wish me to stay idling at home all day?'

'But it is so dreadful—a furze-cutter! and you a man who have lived about the world, and speak French, and German, and who are fit for what is so much better than this.'

'I suppose when you first saw me and heard about me I was wrapped in a sort of golden halo to your eyes—a man who knew glorious things, and had mixed in brilliant scenes—in short, an adorable, delightful, distracting hero?'

'Yes,' she said, sobbing.

'And now I am a poor fellow in brown leather.'

'Don't taunt me. But enough of this. I will not be depressed any more. I am going from home this afternoon, unless you greatly object. There is to be a village picnic—a gipsying, they call it—at East Egdon, and I shall go.'

'To dance?'

'Why not? You can sing.'

'Well, well, as you will. Must I come to fetch you?'

'If you return soon enough from your work. But do not inconvenience yourself about it. I know the way home, and the heath has no terror for me.'

'And can you cling to gaiety so eagerly as to walk all the way to a village festival in search of it?'

'Now, you don't like my going alone! Clym, you are not jealous?'

'No. But I would come with you if it could give you any pleasure; though, as things stand, perhaps you have too much of me already. Still, I somehow wish that you did not want to go. Yes, perhaps I am jealous; and who could be jealous with more reason than I, a half-blind man, over such a woman as you?'

'Don't think like it. Let me go, and don't take all my spirits away!'

'I would rather lose all my own, my sweet wife. Go and do whatever you like. Who can forbid your indulgence in any whim? You have all my heart yet, I believe; and because you bear with me, who am in truth a drag upon you, I owe you thanks. Yes, go alone and shine. As for me, I will stick to my doom. At that kind of meeting people would shun me. My hook and gloves are like the St. Lazarus rattle of the leper, warning the world to get out of the way of a sight that would sadden them.' He kissed her, put on his leggings, and went out.

When he was gone she rested her head upon her hands and said to herself, 'Two wasted lives—his and mine. And I am come to this! Will it drive me out of my mind?'

She cast about for any possible course which offered the least improvement on the existing state of things, and could find none. She imagined how all those Budmouth ones who should learn what had become of her would say, 'Look at the girl for whom nobody was good enough!' To Eustacia the situation seemed such a mockery of her hopes that death appeared the only door of relief if the satire of Heaven should go much further.

Suddenly she aroused herself and exclaimed, 'But I'll shake it off. Yes, I *will* shake it off! No one shall know my suffering. I'll be bitterly merry, and ironically gay, and I'll laugh in derision! And I'll begin by going to this dance on the green.'

She ascended to her bedroom and dressed herself with scrupulous care. To an onlooker her beauty would have made her feelings almost seem reasonable. The gloomy corner into which accident as much as indiscretion had brought this woman might have led even a moderate partisan to feel that she had cogent reasons for asking the Supreme Power by what right a being of such exquisite finish had been placed in circumstances calculated to make of her charms a curse rather than a blessing.

It was five in the afternoon when she came out from the house ready for her walk. There was material enough in the picture for twenty new conquests. The rebellious sadness that was rather too apparent when she sat indoors without a bonnet was cloaked and softened by her outdoor attire, which always had a sort of nebulousness about it, devoid of harsh edges anywhere; so that her face looked from its environment as from a cloud, with no noticeable lines of demarcation between flesh and clothes. The heat of the day had scarcely declined as yet, and she went along the sunny hills at a leisurely pace, there being ample time for her idle expedition. Tall ferns buried her in their leafage whenever her path lay through them, which now formed miniature forests, though not one stem of them would remain to bud the next year.

The site chosen for the village festivity was one of the lawn-like oases which were occasionally, yet not often, met with on the plateaux of the heath district. The brakes of furze and fern terminated abruptly round the margin, and the grass was unbroken. A green cattle-track skirted the spot, without, however, emerging from the screen of fern, and this path Eustacia followed, in order to reconnoitre the group before joining it. The lusty notes of the East Egdon band had directed her unerringly, and she now beheld the musicians themselves, sitting in a blue waggon with red wheels scrubbed as bright as new, and arched with sticks, to which boughs and flowers were tied. In front of this was the grand central dance of fifteen or twenty couples, flanked by minor dances of inferior individuals whose gyrations were not always in strict keeping with the tune.

The young men wore blue and white rosettes, and with a flush on their faces footed it to the girls, who, with the excitement and the exercise, blushed deeper than the pink of their numerous ribbons. Fair ones with long curls, fair ones with short curls, fair ones with love-locks, fair ones with braids, flew round and round; and a beholder might well have wondered how such a prepossessing set of young women of like size, age, and disposition, could have been collected together where there were only one or two villages to choose from. In the background was one happy man dancing by himself, with closed eyes, totally oblivious of all the rest. A fire was burning under a pollard thorn a few paces off, over which three kettles hung in a row. Hard by was a table where elderly dames prepared tea, but Eustacia looked among them in vain for the cattle-dealer's wife who had suggested that she should come, and had promised to obtain a courteous welcome for her.

This unexpected absence of the only local resident whom Eustacia knew considerably damaged her scheme for an afternoon of reckless gaiety. Joining in became a matter of difficulty, notwithstanding that, were she to advance, cheerful dames would come forward with cups of tea and make much of her as a stranger of superior grace and knowledge to themselves. Having watched the company through the figures of two dances, she decided to walk a little further, to a cottage where she might get some refreshment, and then return homeward in the shady time of evening.

This she did; and by the time that she retraced her steps towards the scene of the gipsying, which it was necessary to repass on her way to Alderworth, the sun was going down. The air was now so still that she could hear the band afar off, and it seemed to be playing with more spirit, if that were possible, than when she had come away. On reaching the hill the sun had quite disappeared; but this made little difference either to Eustacia or to the revellers, for a round yellow moon was rising before her, though its rays had not yet outmastered those from the west. The dance was going on just the same, but strangers had arrived and formed a ring around the figure, so that Eustacia could stand among these without a chance of being recognized.

A whole village-full of sensuous emotion, scattered abroad all the year long, surged here in a focus for an hour. The forty hearts of those waving couples were beating as they had not done since, twelve months before, they had come together in similar jollity. For the time Paganism was revived in their hearts, the pride of life was all in all, and they adored none other than themselves.

How many of those impassioned but temporary embraces were destined to become perpetual was possibly the wonder of some of those who indulged in them, as well as of Eustacia who looked on. She began to envy those pirouetters, to hunger for the hope and happiness which the fascination of the dance seemed to engender within them. Desperately fond of dancing herself, one of Eustacia's expectations of Paris had been the opportunity it might afford her of indulgence in this favourite pastime. Unhappily, that expectation was now extinct within her for ever.

Whilst she abstractedly watched them spinning and fluctuating in the increasing moonlight she suddenly heard her name whispered by a voice over her shoulder. Turning in surprise, she beheld at her elbow one whose presence instantly caused her to flush to the temples.

It was Wildeve. Till this moment he had not met her eye since the morning of his marriage, when she had been loitering in the church, and had startled him by lifting her veil and coming forward to sign the register as witness. Yet why the sight of him should have instigated that sudden rush of blood she could not tell.

Before she could speak he whispered, 'Do you like dancing as much as ever?'

'I think I do,' she replied in a low voice.

'Will you dance with me?'

'It would be a great change for me; but will it not seem strange?'

'What strangeness can there be in relations dancing together?'

'Ah—yes, relations. Perhaps none.'

'Still, if you don't like to be seen, pull down your veil; though there is not much risk of being known by this light. Lots of strangers are here.'

She did as he suggested; and the act was a tacit acknowledgment that she accepted his offer.

Wildeve gave her his arm and took her down on the outside of the ring to the bottom of the dance, which they entered. In two minutes more they were involved in the figure and began working their way upwards to the top. Till they had advanced half-way thither Eustacia wished more than once that she had not yielded to his request ; from the middle to the top she felt that, since she had come out to seek pleasure, she was only doing a natural thing to obtain it. Fairly launched into the ceaseless glides and whirls which their new position as top couple opened up to them, Eustacia's pulses began to move too quickly for longer rumination of any kind.

Through the length of five-and-twenty couples they threaded their giddy way, and a new vitality entered her form. The pale ray of evening lent a fascination to the experience. There is a certain degree and tone of light which tends to disturb the equilibrium of the senses, and to promote dangerously the tenderer moods ; added to movement, it drives the emotions to rankness, the reason becoming sleepy and unperceiving in inverse proportion ; and this light fell now upon these two from the disc of the moon. All the dancing girls felt the symptoms, but Eustacia most of all. The grass under their feet became trodden away, and the hard, beaten surface of the sod, when viewed aslant towards the moonlight, shone like a polished table. The air became quite still ; the flag above the waggon which held the musicians clung to the pole, and the players appeared only in outline against the sky ; except when the circular mouths of the trombone, ophicleide, and French horn gleamed out like huge eyes from the shade of their figures. The pretty dresses of the maids lost their subtler day colours and showed more or less of a misty white. Eustacia floated round and round on Wildeve's arm, her face rapt and statuesque ; her soul had passed away from and forgotten her features, which were left empty and quiescent, as they always are when feeling goes beyond their register.

How near she was to Wildeve ! it was terrible to think of. She could feel his breathing, and he, of course, could feel hers. How badly she had treated him ! yet, here they were treading one measure. The enchantment of the dance surprised her. A clear line of difference divided like a tangible fence her experience within this maze of motion from her experience without it. Her beginning to dance had been like a change of atmosphere; outside, she had been steeped in arctic frigidity by comparison with the tropical sensations here. She had entered the dance from the troubled hours of her late life as one might enter a brilliant chamber after a night walk in a wood. Wildeve by himself would have been merely an agitation; Wildeve added to the dance, and the moonlight, and the secrecy, began to be a delight. Whether his personality supplied the greater part of this sweetly compounded feeling, or whether the dance and the scene weighed the more therein, was a nice point upon which Eustacia herself was entirely in a cloud.

People began to say 'Who are they?' but no invidious inquiries were made. Had Eustacia mingled with the other girls in their ordinary daily walks the case would have been different: here she was not inconvenienced by excessive inspection, for all were wrought to their brightest grace by the occasion. Like the planet Mercury surrounded by the lustre of sunset, her permanent brilliancy passed without much notice in the temporary glory of the situation.

As for Wildeve, his feelings are easy to guess. Obstacles were a ripening sun to his love, and he was at this moment in a delirium of exquisite misery. To clasp as his for five minutes what was another man's through all the rest of the year was a kind of thing he of all men could appreciate. He had long since begun to sigh again for Eustacia; indeed, it may be asserted that signing the marriage register with Thomasin was the natural signal to his heart to return to its first quarters, and that the extra complication of Eustacia's marriage was the one addition required to make that return compulsory.

Thus, for different reasons, what was to the rest an exhilarating movement was to these two a riding upon the whirlwind. The dance had come like an irresistible attack upon whatever sense of social order there was in their minds, to drive them back into old paths which were now doubly irregular. Through three dances in succession they spun their way ; and then, fatigued with the incessant motion, Eustacia turned to quit the circle in which she had already remained too long. Wildeve led her to a grassy mound a few yards distant, where she sat down, her partner standing beside her. From the time that he addressed her at the beginning of the dance till now they had not exchanged a word.

'The dance and the walking have tired you ?' he said tenderly.

'No; not greatly.'

'It is strange that we should have met here of all places, after missing each other so long.'

'We have missed because we tried to miss, I suppose.'

'Yes. But you began that proceeding—by breaking a promise.'

'It is scarcely worth while to talk of that now. We have formed other ties since then—you no less than I.'

'I am sorry to hear that your husband is ill.'

'He is not ill—only incapacitated.'

'Yes : that is what I mean. I sincerely sympathize with you in your trouble. Fate has treated you cruelly.'

She was silent awhile. 'Have you heard that he has chosen to work as a furze-cutter ?' she said in a low, mournful voice.

'It has been mentioned to me,' answered Wildeve hesitatingly. 'But I hardly believed it.'

'It is true. What do you think of me as a furze-cutter's wife ?'

'I think the same as ever of you, Eustacia. Nothing of that sort can degrade you : you ennoble the occupation of your husband.'

'I wish I could feel it.'

'Is there any chance of Mr. Yeobright getting better ?'

'He thinks so. I doubt it.'

'I was quite surprised to hear that he had taken a cottage. I thought, in common with other people, that he would have taken you off to a home in Paris immediately after you had married him. "What a gay, bright future she has before her!" I thought. He will, I suppose, return there with you, if his sight gets strong again?'

Observing that she did not reply he regarded her more closely. She was almost weeping. Images of a future never to be enjoyed, the revived sense of her bitter disappointment, the picture of the neighbours' suspended ridicule which was raised by Wildeve's words, had been too much for proud Eustacia's equanimity.

Wildeve could hardly control his own too forward feelings when he saw her silent perturbation. But he affected not to notice this, and she soon recovered her calmness.

'You did not intend to walk home by yourself?' he asked.

'O yes,' said Eustacia. 'What could hurt me on this heath, who have nothing?'

'By diverging a little I can make my way home the same as yours. I shall be glad to keep you company as far as Throope Corner.' Seeing that Eustacia sat on in hesitation he added, 'Perhaps you think it unwise to be seen in the same road with me after the events of last summer?'

'Indeed I think no such thing,' she said haughtily. 'I shall accept whose company I choose, for all that may be said by the miserable inhabitants of Egdon.'

'Then let us walk on—if you are ready. Our nearest way is towards that holly-bush with the dark shadow that you see down there.'

Eustacia arose, and walked beside him in the direction signified, brushing her way over the damping heath and fern, and followed by the strains of the merrymakers, who still kept up the dance. The moon had now waxed bright and silvery, but the heath was proof against such illumination, and there was to be observed the striking scene of a dark, rayless tract of country under an atmosphere charged from its zenith to its extremities with whitest light. To an eye above them their two faces would have appeared amid the expanse like two pearls on a table of ebony.

On this account the irregularities of the path were not visible, and Wildeve occasionally stumbled; whilst Eustacia found it necessary to perform some graceful feats of balancing whenever a small tuft of heather or root of furze protruded itself through the grass of the narrow track and entangled her feet. At these junctures in her progress a hand was invariably stretched forward to steady her, holding her firmly until smooth ground was again reached, when the hand was again withdrawn to a respectful distance.

They performed the journey for the most part in silence, and drew near to Throope Corner, a few hundred yards from which a short path branched away to Eustacia's house. By degrees they discerned coming towards them a pair of human figures, apparently of the male sex.

When they came a little nearer Eustacia broke the silence by saying, 'One of those men is my husband. He promised to come to meet me.'

'And the other is my greatest enemy,' said Wildeve.

'It looks like Diggory Venn.'

'That is the man.'

'It is an awkward meeting,' said she; 'but such is my fortune. He knows too much about me, unless he could know more, and so prove to himself that what he now knows counts for nothing. Well, let it be: you must deliver me up to them.'

'You will think twice before you direct me to do that. Here is a man who has not forgotten an item in our meetings at Rainbarrow: he is in company with your husband. Which of them, seeing us together here, will believe that our meeting and dancing at the gipsy-party was by chance?'

'Very well,' she whispered gloomily. 'Leave me before they come up.'

Wildeve bade her a tender farewell, and plunged across the fern and furze, Eustacia slowly walking on. In two or three minutes she met her husband and his companion.

'My journey ends here for to-night, reddleman,' said Yeobright as soon as he perceived her. 'I turn back with this lady. Good night.'

'Good night, Mr. Yeobright,' said Venn. 'I hope to see you better soon.'

The moonlight shone directly upon Venn's face as he spoke, and revealed all its lines to Eustacia. He was looking suspiciously at her. That Venn's keen eye had discerned what Yeobright's feeble vision had not—a man in the act of withdrawing from Eustacia's side—was within the limits of the probable.

If Eustacia had been able to follow the reddleman she would soon have found striking confirmation of her thought. No sooner had Clym given her his arm and led her off the scene than the reddleman turned back from the beaten track towards East Egdon, whither he had been strolling merely to accompany Clym in his walk, Diggory's van being again in the neighbourhood. Stretching out his long legs he crossed the pathless portion of the heath somewhat in the direction which Wildeve had taken. Only a man accustomed to nocturnal rambles could at this hour have descended those shaggy slopes with Venn's velocity without falling headlong into a pit, or snapping off his leg by jamming his foot into some rabbit-burrow. But Venn went on without much inconvenience to himself, and the course of his scamper was towards the Quiet Woman Inn. This place he reached in about half an hour, and he was well aware that no person who had been near Throope Corner when he started could have got down here before him.

The lonely inn was not yet closed, though scarcely an individual was there, the business done being chiefly with travellers who passed the inn on long journeys, and these had now gone on their way. Venn went to the public room, called for a mug of ale, and inquired of the maid in an indifferent tone if Mr. Wildeve was at home.

Thomasin sat in an inner room and heard Venn's voice. When customers were present she seldom showed herself, owing to her inherent dislike for the business; but perceiving that no one else was there to-night she came out.

'He is not at home yet, Diggory,' she said pleasantly. 'But I expected him sooner. He has been to East Egdon to buy a horse.'

'Did he wear a light wideawake?'

'Yes.'

'Then I saw him at Throope Corner, leading one home,' said Venn drily. 'A beauty, with a white face and a mane as black as night. He will soon be here, no doubt.' Rising and looking for a moment at the pure, sweet face of Thomasin, over which a shadow of sadness had passed since the time when he had last seen her, he ventured to add, 'Mr. Wildeve seems to be often away at this time.'

'O yes,' cried Thomasin in what was intended to be a tone of gaiety. 'Husbands will play the truant, you know. I wish you could tell me of some secret plan that would help me to keep him home at my will in the evenings.'

'I will consider if I know of one,' replied Venn in that same light tone which meant no lightness. And then he bowed in a manner of his own invention and moved to go. Thomasin offered him her hand; and without a sigh, though with food for many, the reddleman went out.

When Wildeve returned, a quarter of an hour later,

Thomasin said simply, and in the abashed manner usual with her now, ‘ Where is the horse, Damon ? ’

‘ O, I have not bought it, after all. The man asks too much.’

‘ But somebody saw you at Throope Corner leading it home—a beauty, with a white face and a mane as black as night.’

‘ Ah ! ’ said Wildeve, fixing his eyes upon her ; ‘ who told you that ? ’

‘ Venn the reddleman.’

The expression of Wildeve’s face became curiously condensed. ‘ That is a mistake—it must have been some one else,’ he said slowly and testily, for he perceived that Venn’s counter-moves had begun again.

ROUGH COERCION IS EMPLOYED

IV

THOSE words of Thomasin, which seemed so little, but meant so much, remained in the ears of Diggory Venn: 'Help me to keep him home in the evenings.'

On this occasion Venn had arrived on Egdon Heath only to cross to the other side: he had no further connection with the interests of the Yeobright family, and he had a business of his own to attend to. Yet he suddenly began to feel himself drifting into the old track of manœuvring on Thomasin's account.

He sat in his van and considered. From Thomasin's words and manner he had plainly gathered that Wildeve neglected her. For whom could he neglect her if not for Eustacia? Yet it was scarcely credible that things had come to such a head as to indicate that Eustacia systematically encouraged him. Venn resolved to reconnoitre somewhat carefully the lonely road which led along the vale from Wildeve's dwelling to Clym's house at Alderworth.

At this time, as has been seen, Wildeve was quite innocent of any predetermined act of intrigue, and except at the dance on the green he had not once met Eustacia since her marriage. But that the spirit of intrigue was in him had been shown by a recent romantic habit of his: a habit of going out after dark and strolling towards Alderworth, there looking at the moon and stars, looking at Eustacia's house, and walking back at leisure.

Accordingly, when watching on the night after the festival, the reddleman saw him ascend by the little path, lean over the front gate of Clym's garden, sigh, and turn to go back again. It was plain that Wildeve's intrigue was rather ideal than real. Venn retreated before him down the hill to a place where the path was merely a deep groove between the heather; here he mysteriously bent over the ground for a few minutes, and retired. When Wildeve came on to that spot his ankle was caught by something, and he fell headlong.

As soon as he had recovered the power of respiration he sat up and listened. There was not a sound in the gloom beyond the spiritless stir of the summer wind. Feeling about for the obstacle which had flung him down, he discovered that two tufts of heath had been tied together across the path, forming a loop, which to a traveller was certain overthrow. Wildeve pulled off the string that bound them, and went on with tolerable quickness. On reaching home he found the cord to be of a reddish colour. It was just what he had expected.

Although his weaknesses were not specially those akin to physical fear, this species of *coup-de-Jarnac* from one he knew too well troubled the mind of Wildeve. But his movements were unaltered thereby. A night or two later he again went along the vale to Alderworth, taking the precaution of keeping out of any path. The sense that he was watched, that craft was employed to circumvent his errant tastes, added piquancy to a journey so entirely sentimental, so long as the danger was of no fearful sort. He imagined that Venn and Mrs. Yeobright were in league, and felt that there was a certain legitimacy in combating such a coalition.

The heath to-night appeared to be totally deserted ; and Wildeve, after looking over Eustacia's garden gate for some little time, with a cigar in his mouth, was tempted by the fascination that emotional smuggling had for his nature to advance towards the window, which was not quite closed, the blind being only partly drawn down. He could see into the room, and Eustacia was sitting there alone. Wildeve contemplated her for a minute, and then retreating into the heath beat the ferns lightly, whereupon moths flew out alarmed. Securing one, he returned to the window, and, holding the moth to the chink, opened his hand. The moth made towards the candle upon Eustacia'a table, hovered round it two or three times, and flew into the flame.

Eustacia started up. This had been a well-known signal in old times when Wildeve had used to come secretly wooing to Mistover. She at once knew that Wildeve was outside, but before she could consider what to do her husband came in from upstairs. Eustacia's face burnt crimson at the unexpected collision of incidents, and filled with an animation that it too frequently lacked.

'You have a very high colour, dearest,' said Yeobright, when he came close enough to see it. 'Your appearance would be no worse if it were always so.'

'I am warm,' said Eustacia. 'I think I will go into the air for a few minutes.'

'Shall I go with you ?'

'O no. I am only going to the gate.'

She arose, but before she had time to get out of the room a loud rapping began upon the front door.

'I'll go—I'll go,' said Eustacia in an unusually quick tone for her ; and she glanced eagerly towards the window whence the moth had flown ; but nothing appeared there.

'You had better not at this time of the evening,' he said. Clym stepped before her into the passage, and Eustacia waited, her somnolent manner covering her inner heat and agitation.

She listened, and Clym opened the door. No words were uttered outside, and presently he closed it and came back, saying, 'Nobody was there. I wonder what that could have meant?'

He was left to wonder during the rest of the evening, for no explanation offered itself, and Eustacia said nothing, the additional fact that she knew of only adding more mystery to the performance.

Meanwhile a little drama had been acted outside which saved Eustacia from all possibility of compromising herself that evening at least. Whilst Wildeve had been preparing his moth-signal another person had come behind him up to the gate. This man, who carried a gun in his hand, looked on for a moment at the other's operation by the window, walked up to the house, knocked at the door, and then vanished round the corner and over the hedge.

'Damn him!' said Wildeve. 'He has been watching me again.'

As his signal had been rendered futile by this uproarious rapping Wildeve withdrew, passed out at the gate, and walked quickly down the path without thinking of anything except getting away unnoticed. Half-way down the hill the path ran near a knot of stunted hollies, which in the general darkness of the scene stood as the pupil in a black eye. When Wildeve reached this point a report startled his ear, and a few spent gunshots fell among the leaves around him.

There was no doubt that he himself was the cause of that gun's discharge; and he rushed into the clump of hollies, beating the bushes furiously with his stick; but nobody was there. This attack was a more serious matter than the last, and it was some time before Wildeve recovered his equanimity. A new and most unpleasant system of menace had begun, and the intent appeared to be to do him grievous bodily harm. Wildeve had looked upon Venn's first attempt as a species of horse-play, which the reddleman had indulged in for want of knowing better; but now the boundary-line was passed which divides the annoying from the perilous.

Had Wildeve known how thoroughly in earnest Venn had become he might have been still more alarmed. The reddleman had been almost exasperated by the sight of Wildeve outside Clym's house, and he was prepared to go to any lengths short of absolutely shooting him, to terrify the young innkeeper out of his recalcitrant impulses. The doubtful legitimacy of such rough coercion did not disturb the mind of Venn. It troubles few such minds in such cases, and sometimes this is not to be regretted. From the impeachment of Strafford to Farmer Lynch's short way with the scamps of Virginia there have been many triumphs of justice which are mockeries of law.

About half a mile below Clym's secluded dwelling lay a hamlet where lived one of the two constables who preserved the peace in the parish of Alderworth, and Wildeve went straight to the constable's cottage. Almost the first thing that he saw on opening the door was the constable's truncheon hanging to a nail, as if to assure him that here were the means to his purpose. On inquiry, however, of the constable's wife he learnt that the constable was not at home. Wildeve said he would wait.

The minutes ticked on, and the constable did not arrive. Wildeve cooled down from his state of high indignation to a restless dissatisfaction with himself, the scene, the constable's wife, and the whole set of circumstances. He arose and left the house. Altogether, the experience of that evening had had a cooling, not to say a chilling, effect on misdirected tenderness, and Wildeve was in no mood to ramble again to Alderworth after nightfall in hope of a stray glance from Eustacia.

Thus far the reddleman had been tolerably successful in his rude contrivances for keeping down Wildeve's inclination to rove in the evening. He had nipped in the bud the possible meeting between Eustacia and her old lover this very night. But he had not anticipated that the tendency of his action would be to divert Wildeve's movement rather than to stop it. The gambling with the guineas had not conduced to make him a welcome guest to Clym; but to call upon his wife's relative was natural, and he was determined to see Eustacia. It was necessary to choose some less untoward hour than ten o'clock at night. 'Since it is unsafe to go in the evening,' he said, 'I'll go by day.'

Meanwhile Venn had left the heath and gone to call upon Mrs. Yeobright, with whom he had been on friendly terms since she had learnt what a providential countermove he had made towards the restitution of the family guineas. She wondered at the lateness of his call, but had no objection to see him.

He gave her a full account of Clym's affliction, and of the state in which he was living; then, referring to Thomasin, touched gently upon the apparent sadness of her days. 'Now, ma'am, depend upon it,' he said, 'you couldn't do a better thing for either of 'em than to make yourself at home in their houses, even if there should be a little rebuff at first.'

'Both she and my son disobeyed me in marrying; therefore I have no interest in their households. Their troubles are of their own making.' Mrs. Yeobright tried to speak severely; but the account of her son's state had moved her more than she cared to show.

'Your visits would make Wildeve walk straighter than he is inclined to do, and might prevent unhappiness down the heath.'

'What do you mean?'

'I saw something to-night out there which I didn't like at all. I wish your son's house and Mr. Wildeve's were a hundred miles apart instead of four or five.'

'Then there *was* an understanding between him and Clym's wife when he made a fool of Thomasin!'

'We'll hope there's no understanding now.'

'And our hope will probably be very vain. O Clym! O Thomasin!'

'There's no harm done yet. In fact, I've persuaded Wildeve to mind his own business.'

'How?'

'O, not by talking—by a plan of mine called the silent system.'

'I hope you'll succeed.'

'I shall if you help me by calling and making friends with your son. You'll have a chance then of using your eyes.'

'Well, since it has come to this,' said Mrs. Yeobright sadly, 'I will own to you, reddleman, that I thought of going. I should be much happier if we were reconciled. The marriage is unalterable, my life may be cut short, and I should wish to die in peace. He is my only son; and since sons are made of such stuff I am not sorry I have no other. As for Thomasin, I never expected much from her; and she has not disappointed me. But I forgave her long ago; and I forgive him now. I'll go.'

At this very time of the reddleman's conversation with Mrs. Yeobright at Blooms-End another conversation on the same subject was languidly proceeding at Alderworth.

All the day Clym had borne himself as if his mind were too full of its own matter to allow him to care about outward things, and his words now showed what had occupied his thoughts. It was just after the mysterious knocking that he began the theme. 'Since I have been away to-day, Eustacia, I have considered that something must be done to heal up this ghastly breach between my dear mother and myself. It troubles me.'

'What do you propose to do?' said Eustacia abstractedly, for she could not clear away from her the excitement caused by Wildeve's recent manœuvre for an interview.

'You seem to take a very mild interest in what I propose, little or much,' said Clym, with tolerable warmth.

'You mistake me,' she answered, reviving at his reproach. 'I am only thinking.'

'What of ?'

'Partly of that moth whose skeleton is getting burnt up in the wick of the candle,' she said slowly. 'But you know I always take an interest in what you say.'

'Very well, dear. Then I think I must go and call upon her.' . . . He went on with tender feeling : 'It is a thing I am not at all too proud to do, and only a fear that I might irritate her has kept me away so long. But I must do something. It is wrong in me to allow this sort of thing to go on.'

'What have you to blame yourself about ?'

'She is getting old, and her life is lonely, and I am her only son.'

'She has Thomasin.'

'Thomasin is not her daughter ; and if she were that would not excuse me. But this is beside the point. I have made up my mind to go to her, and all I wish to ask you is whether you will do your best to help me—that is, forget the past ; and if she shows her willingness to be reconciled, meet her half-way by welcoming her to our house, or by accepting a welcome to hers ?'

At first Eustacia closed her lips as if she would rather do anything on the whole globe than what he suggested. But the lines of her mouth softened with thought, though not so far as they might have softened ; and she said, 'I will put nothing in your way ; but after what has passed it is asking too much that I go and make advances.'

'You never distinctly told me what did pass between you.'

'I could not do it then, nor can I now. Sometimes more bitterness is sown in five minutes than can be got rid of in a whole life ; and that may be the case here.' She paused a few moments, and added, 'If you had never returned to your native place, Clym, what a blessing it would have been for you! . . . It has altered the destinies of——'

'Three people.'

'Five,' Eustacia thought; but she kept that in.

THE JOURNEY ACROSS THE HEATH

V

THURSDAY, the thirty-first of August, was one of a series of days during which snug houses were stifling, and when cool draughts were treats; when cracks appeared in clayey gardens, and were called 'earthquakes' by apprehensive children; when loose spokes were discovered in the wheels of carts and carriages; and when stinging insects haunted the air, the earth, and every drop of water that was to be found.

In Mrs. Yeobright's garden large-leaved plants of a tender kind flagged by ten o'clock in the morning; rhubarb bent downward at eleven; and even stiff cabbages were limp by noon.

It was about eleven o'clock on this day that Mrs. Yeobright started across the heath towards her son's house, to do her best in getting reconciled with him and Eustacia, in conformity with her words to the reddleman. She had hoped to be well advanced in her walk before the heat of the day was at its highest, but after setting out she found that this was not to be done. The sun had branded the whole heath with his mark, even the purple heath-flowers having put on a brownness under the dry blazes of the few preceding days. Every valley was filled with air like that of a kiln, and the clean quartz sand of the winter water-courses, which formed summer paths, had undergone a species of incineration since the drought had set in.

In cool, fresh weather Mrs. Yeobright would have found no inconvenience in walking to Alderworth, but the present torrid attack made the journey a heavy undertaking for a woman past middle age; and at the end of the third mile she wished that she had hired Fairway to drive her a portion at least of the distance. But from the point at which she had arrived it was as easy to reach Clym's house as to get home again. So she went on, the air around her pulsating silently, and oppressing the earth with lassitude. She looked at the sky overhead, and saw that the sapphirine hue of the zenith in spring and early summer had been replaced by a metallic violet.

Occasionally she came to a spot where independent worlds of ephemerons were passing their time in mad carousal, some in the air, some on the hot ground and vegetation, some in the tepid and stringy water of a nearly dried pool. All the shallower ponds had decreased to a vaporous mud amid which the maggoty shapes of innumerable obscure creatures could be indistinctly seen, heaving and wallowing with enjoyment. Being a woman not disinclined to philosophize she sometimes sat down under her umbrella to rest and to watch their happiness, for a certain hopefulness as to the result of her visit gave ease to her mind, and between important thoughts left it free to dwell on any infinitesimal matter which caught her eyes.

Mrs. Yeobright had never before been to her son's house, and its exact position was unknown to her. She tried one ascending path and another, and found that they led her astray. Retracing her steps she came again to an open level, where she perceived at a distance a man at work. She went towards him and inquired the way.

The labourer pointed out the direction, and added, 'Do you see that furze-cutter, ma'am, going up that footpath yond ?'

Mrs. Yeobright strained her eyes, and at last said that she did perceive him.

'Well, if you follow him you can make no mistake. He's going to the same place, ma'am.'

She followed the figure indicated. He appeared of a russet hue, not more distinguishable from the scene around him than the green caterpillar from the leaf it feeds on. His progress when actually walking was more rapid than Mrs. Yeobright's ; but she was enabled to keep at an equable distance from him by his habit of stopping whenever he came to a brake of brambles, where he paused awhile. On coming in her turn to each of these spots she found half a dozen long limp brambles which he had cut from the bush during his halt and laid out straight beside the path. They were evidently intended for furze-faggot bonds which he meant to collect on his return.

The silent being who thus occupied himself seemed to be of no more account in life than an insect. He appeared as a mere parasite of the heath, fretting its surface in his daily labour as a moth frets a garment, entirely engrossed with its products, having no knowledge of anything in the world but fern, furze, heath, lichens, and moss.

The furze-cutter was so absorbed in the business of his journey that he never turned his head ; and his leather-legged and gauntleted form at length became to her as nothing more than a moving handpost to show her the way. Suddenly she was attracted to his individuality by observing peculiarities in his walk. It was a gait she had seen somewhere before ; and the gait revealed the man to her, as the gait of Ahimaaz in the distant plain made him known to the watchman of the king. 'His walk is exactly as my husband's used to be,' she said; and then the thought burst upon her that the furze-cutter was her son.

She was scarcely able to familiarize herself with this strange reality. She had been told that Clym was in the habit of cutting furze, but she had supposed that he occupied himself with the labour only at odd times, by way of useful pastime; yet she now beheld him as a furze-cutter and nothing more—wearing the regulation dress of the craft, and thinking the regulation thoughts, to judge by his motions. Planning a dozen hasty schemes for at once preserving him and Eustacia from this mode of life she throbbingly followed the way, and saw him enter his own door.

At one side of Clym's house was a knoll, and on the top of the knoll a clump of fir trees so highly thrust up into the sky that their foliage from a distance appeared as a black spot in the air above the crown of the hill. On reaching this place Mrs. Yeobright felt distressingly agitated, weary, and unwell. She ascended, and sat down under their shade to recover herself, and to consider how best to break the ground with Eustacia, so as not to irritate a woman underneath whose apparent indolence lurked passions even stronger and more active than her own.

The trees beneath which she sat were singularly battered, rude, and wild, and for a few minutes Mrs. Yeobright dismissed thoughts of her own storm-broken and exhausted state to contemplate theirs. Not a bough in the nine trees which composed the group but was splintered, lopped, and distorted by the fierce weather that there held them at its mercy whenever it prevailed. Some were blasted and split as if by lightning, black stains as from fire marking their sides, while the ground at their feet was strewn with dead fir-needles and heaps of cones blown down in the gales of past years. The place was called the Devil's Bellows, and it was only necessary to come there on a March or November night to discover the forcible reasons for that name. On the present heated afternoon, when no perceptible wind was blowing, the trees kept up a perpetual moan which one could hardly believe to be caused by the air.

Here she sat for twenty minutes or more ere she could summon resolution to go down to the door, her courage being lowered to zero by her physical lassitude. To any other person than a mother it might have seemed a little humiliating that she, the elder of the two women, should be the first to make advances. But Mrs. Yeobright had well considered all that, and she only thought how best to make her visit appear to Eustacia not abject but wise.

From her elevated position the exhausted woman could perceive the roof of the house below, and the garden and the whole enclosure of the little domicile. And now, at the moment of rising, she saw a second man approaching the gate. His manner was peculiar, hesitating, and not that of a person come on business or by invitation. He surveyed the house with interest, and then walked round and scanned the outer boundary of the garden, as one might have done had it been the birthplace of Shakespeare, the prison of Mary Stuart, or the Château of Hougomont. After passing round and again reaching the gate he went in. Mrs. Yeobright was vexed at this, having reckoned on finding her son and his wife by themselves; but a moment's thought showed her that the presence of an acquaintance would take off the awkwardness of her first appearance in the house, by confining the talk to general matters until she had begun to feel comfortable with them. She came down the hill to the gate, and looked into the hot garden.

There lay the cat asleep on the bare gravel of the path, as if beds, rugs, and carpets were unendurable. The leaves of the hollyhocks hung like half-closed umbrellas, the sap almost simmered in the stems, and foliage with a smooth surface glared like metallic mirrors.

A small apple tree, of the sort called Ratheripe, grew just inside the gate, the only one which throve in the garden, by reason of the lightness of the soil; and among the fallen apples on the ground beneath were wasps rolling drunk with the juice, or creeping about the little caves in each fruit which they had eaten out before stupefied by its sweetness. By the door lay Clym's furze-hook and the last handful of faggot-bonds she had seen him gather; they had plainly been thrown down there as he entered the house.

A CONJUNCTURE, AND ITS RESULT UPON THE PEDESTRIAN

VI

WILDEVE, as has been stated, was determined to visit Eustacia boldly, by day, and on the easy terms of a relation, since the reddleman had spied out and spoilt his walks to her by night. The spell that she had thrown over him in the moonlight dance made it impossible for a man having no strong puritanic force within him to keep away altogether. He merely calculated on meeting her and her husband in an ordinary manner, chatting a little while, and leaving again. Every outward sign was to be conventional; but the one great fact would be there to satisfy him: he would see her. He did not even desire Clym's absence, since it was just possible that Eustacia might resent any situation which could compromise her dignity as a wife, whatever the state of her heart towards him. Women were often so.

He went accordingly; and it happened that the time of his arrival coincided with that of Mrs. Yeobright's pause on the hill near the house. When he had looked round the premises in the manner she had noticed he went and knocked at the door. There was a few minutes' interval, and then the key turned in the lock, the door opened, and Eustacia herself confronted him.

Nobody could have imagined from her bearing now that here stood the woman who had joined with him in the impassioned dance of the week before, unless indeed he could have penetrated below the surface and gauged the real depth of that still stream.

'I hope you reached home safely?' said Wildeve.

'O yes,' she carelessly returned.

'And were you not tired the next day? I feared you might be.'

'I was rather. You need not speak low—nobody will overhear us. My small servant is gone on an errand to the village.'

'Then Clym is not at home?'

'Yes, he is.'

'O! I thought that perhaps you had locked the door because you were alone and were afraid of tramps.'

'No—here is my husband.'

They had been standing in the entry. Closing the front door and turning the key, as before, she threw open the door of the adjoining room and asked him to walk in. Wildeve entered, the room appearing to be empty; but as soon as he had advanced a few steps he started. On the hearthrug lay Clym asleep. Beside him were the leggings, thick boots, leather gloves, and sleeve-waistcoat in which he worked.

'You may go in; you will not disturb him,' she said, following behind. 'My reason for fastening the door is that he may not be intruded upon by any chance comer while lying here, if I should be in the garden or upstairs.'

'Why is he sleeping there?' said Wildeve in low tones.

'He is very weary. He went out at half-past four this morning, and has been working ever since. He cuts furze because it is the only thing he can do that does not put any strain upon his poor eyes.' The contrast between the sleeper's appearance and Wildeve's at this moment was painfully apparent to Eustacia, Wildeve being elegantly dressed in a new summer suit and light hat; and she continued: 'Ah! you don't know how differently he appeared when I first met him, though it is such a little while ago. His hands were as white and soft as mine; and look at them now, how rough and brown they are! His complexion is by nature fair, and that rusty look he has now, all of a colour with his leather clothes, is caused by the burning of the sun.'

'Why does he go out at all?' Wildeve whispered.

'Because he hates to be idle; though what he earns doesn't add much to our exchequer. However, he says that when people are living upon their capital they must keep down current expenses by turning a penny where they can.'

'The fates have not been kind to you, Eustacia Yeobright.'

'I have nothing to thank them for.'

'Nor has he—except for their one great gift to him.'

'What's that?'

Wildeve looked her in the eyes.

Eustacia blushed for the first time that day. 'Well, I am a questionable gift,' she said quietly. 'I thought you meant the gift of content—which he has, and I have not.'

'I can understand content in such a case—though how the outward situation can attract him puzzles me.'

'That's because you don't know him. He's an enthusiast about ideas, and careless about outward things. He often reminds me of the Apostle Paul.'

'I am glad to hear that he's so grand in character as that.'

'Yes; but the worst of it is that though Paul was excellent as a man in the Bible he would hardly have done in real life.'

Their voices had instinctively dropped lower, though at first they had taken no particular care to avoid awakening Clym. 'Well, if that means that your marriage is a misfortune to you, you know who is to blame,' said Wildeve.

'The marriage is no misfortune in itself,' she retorted with some little petulance. 'It is simply the accident which has happened since that has been the cause of my ruin. I have certainly got thistles for figs in a worldly sense, but how could I tell what time would bring forth?'

'Sometimes, Eustacia, I think it is a judgment upon you. You rightly belonged to me, you know; and I had no idea of losing you.'

'No, it was not my fault! Two could not belong to you; and remember that, before I was aware, you turned aside to another woman. It was cruel levity in you to do that. I never dreamt of playing such a game on my side till you began it on yours.'

'I meant nothing by it,' replied Wildeve. 'It was a mere interlude. Men are given to the trick of having a passing fancy for somebody else in the midst of a permanent love, which reasserts itself afterwards just as before. On account of your rebellious manner to me I was tempted to go further than I should have done; and when you still would keep playing the same tantalizing part I went further still, and married her.' Turning and looking again at the unconscious form of Clym he murmured, 'I am afraid that you don't value your prize, Clym. . . . He ought to be happier than I in one thing at least. He may know what it is to come down in the world, and to be afflicted with a great personal calamity; but he probably doesn't know what it is to lose the woman he loved.'

'He is not ungrateful for winning her,' whispered Eustacia, 'and in that respect he is a good man. Many women would go far for such a husband. But do I desire unreasonably much in wanting what is called life—music, poetry, passion, war, and all the beating and pulsing that is going on in the great arteries of the world?

That was the shape of my youthful dream; but I did not get it. Yet I thought I saw the way to it in my Clym.'

'And you only married him on that account?'

'There you mistake me. I married him because I loved him, but I won't say that I didn't love him partly because I thought I saw a promise of that life in him.'

'You have dropped into your old mournful key.'

'But I am not going to be depressed,' she cried perversely. 'I began a new system by going to that dance, and I mean to stick to it. Clym can sing merrily; why should not I?'

Wildeve looked thoughtfully at her. 'It is easier to say you will sing than to do it; though if I could I would encourage you in your attempt. But as life means nothing to me, without one thing which is now impossible, you will forgive me for not being able to encourage you.'

'Damon, what is the matter with you, that you speak like that?' she asked, raising her deep shady eyes to his.

'That's a thing I shall never tell plainly; and perhaps if I try to tell you in riddles you will not care to guess them.'

Eustacia remained silent for a minute, and she said, 'We are in a strange relationship to-day. You mince matters to an uncommon nicety. You mean, Damon, that you still love me. Well, that gives me sorrow, for I am not made so entirely happy by my marriage that I am willing to spurn you for the information, as I ought to do. But we have said too much about this. Do you mean to wait until my husband is awake?'

'I thought to speak to him; but it is unnecessary, Eustacia, if I offend you by not forgetting you, you are right to mention it; but do not talk of spurning.'

She did not reply, and they stood looking musingly at Clym as he slept on in that profound sleep which is the result of physical labour carried on in circumstances that wake no nervous fear.

'God, how I envy him that sweet sleep!' said Wildeve. 'I have not slept like that since I was a boy—years and years ago.'

While they thus watched him a click at the gate was audible, and a knock came to the door. Eustacia went to a window and looked out.

Her countenance changed. First she became crimson, and then the red subsided till it even partially left her lips.

'Shall I go away?' said Wildeve, standing up.

'I hardly know.'

'Who is it?'

'Mrs. Yeobright. O, what she said to me that day! I cannot understand this visit—what does she mean? And she suspects that past time of ours.'

'I am in your hands. If you think she had better not see me here I'll go into the next room.'

'Well, yes: go.'

Wildeve at once withdrew; but before he had been half a minute in the adjoining apartment Eustacia came after him.

'No,' she said, 'we won't have any of this. If she comes in she must see you—and think if she likes there's something wrong! But how can I open the door to her, when she dislikes me—wishes to see not me, but her son? I won't open the door!'

Mrs. Yeobright knocked again more loudly.

'Her knocking will, in all likelihood, awaken him,' continued Eustacia; 'and then he will let her in himself Ah—listen.'

They could hear Clym moving in the other room, as if disturbed by the knocking, and he uttered the word 'Mother.'

'Yes—he is awake—he will go to the door,' she said, with a breath of relief. 'Come this way. I have a bad name with her, and you must not be seen. Thus I am obliged to act by stealth, not because I do ill, but because others are pleased to say so.'

By this time she had taken him to the back door, which was open, disclosing a path leading down the garden. 'Now, one word, Damon,' she remarked as he stepped forth. 'This is your first visit here; let it be your last. We have been hot lovers in our time, but it won't do now. Good-bye.'

'Good-bye,' said Wildeve. 'I have had all I came for, and I am satisfied.'

'What was it?'

'A sight of you. Upon my eternal honour I came for no more.'

Wildeve kissed his hand to the beautiful girl he addressed, and passed into the garden, where she watched him down the path, over the stile at the end, and into the ferns outside, which brushed his hips as he went along till he became lost in their thickets. When he had quite gone she slowly turned, and directed her attention to the interior of the house.

But it was possible that her presence might not be desired by Clym and his mother at this moment of their first meeting, or that it would be superfluous. At all events, she was in no hurry to meet Mrs. Yeobright. She resolved to wait till Clym came to look for her, and glided back into the garden. Here she idly occupied herself for a few minutes, till finding no notice was taken of her she retraced her steps through the house to the front, where she listened for voices in the parlour. But hearing none she opened the door and went in. To her astonishment Clym lay precisely as Wildeve and herself had left him, his sleep apparently unbroken. He had been disturbed and made to dream and murmur by the knocking, but he had not awakened. Eustacia hastened to the door, and in spite of her reluctance to open it to a woman who had spoken of her so bitterly, she unfastened it and looked out. Nobody was to be seen. There, by the scraper, lay Clym's hook and the handful of faggot-bonds he had brought home; in front of her were the empty path, the garden gate standing slightly ajar; and, beyond, the great valley of purple heath thrilling silently in the sun. Mrs. Yeobright was gone.

Clym's mother was at this time following a path which lay hidden from Eustacia by a shoulder of the hill. Her walk thither from the garden gate had been hasty and determined, as of a woman who was now no less anxious to escape from the scene than she had previously been to enter it. Her eyes were fixed on the ground; within her two sights were graven—that of Clym's hook and brambles at the door, and that of a woman's face at a window. Her lips trembled, becoming unnaturally thin as she murmured, ''Tis too much—Clym, how can he bear to do it! He is at home; and yet he lets her shut the door against me!'

In her anxiety to get out of the direct view of the house she had diverged from the straightest path homeward, and while looking about to regain it she came upon a little boy gathering whortle-berries in a hollow. The boy was Johnny Nunsuch, who had been Eustacia's stoker at the bonfire, and, with the tendency of a minute body to gravitate towards a greater, he began hovering round Mrs. Yeobright as soon as she appeared, and trotted on beside her without perceptible consciousness of his act.

Mrs. Yeobright spoke to him as one in a mesmeric sleep. ''Tis a long way home, my child, and we shall not get there till evening.'

'I shall,' said her small companion. 'I am going to play marnels afore supper, and we go to supper at six o'clock, because father comes home. Does your father come home at six too?'

'No: he never comes; nor my son either, nor anybody.'

'What have made you so down? Have you seen a ooser?'

'I have seen what's worse—a woman's face looking at me through a window-pane.

'Is that a bad sight?'

'Yes. It is always a bad sight to see a woman looking out at a weary wayfarer and not letting her in.'

'Once when I went to Throope Great Pond to catch effets I seed myself looking up at myself, and I was frightened and jumped back like anything.'

. . . 'If they had only shown signs of meeting my advances half-way how well it might have been done! But there is no chance. Shut out! She must have set him against me. Can there be beautiful bodies without hearts inside? I think so. I would not have done it against a neighbour's cat on such a fiery day as this!'

'What is it you say?'

'Never again—never! Not even if they send for me!'

'You must be a very curious woman to talk like that.'

'O no, not at all,' she said, returning to the boy's prattle. 'Most people who grow up and have children talk as I do. When you grow up your mother will talk as I do too.'

'I hope she won't; because 'tis very bad to talk nonsense.'

'Yes, child; it is nonsense, I suppose. Are you not nearly spent with the heat?'

'Yes. But not so much as you be.'

'How do you know?'

'Your face is white and wet, and your head is hanging-down-like.'

'Ah, I am exhausted from inside.'

'Why do you, every time you take a step, go like this?' The child in speaking gave to his motion the jerk and limp of an invalid.

'Because I have a burden which is more than I can bear.'

The little boy remained silently pondering, and they tottered on side by side until more than a quarter of an hour had elapsed, when Mrs. Yeobright, whose weakness plainly increased, said to him, 'I must sit down here to rest.'

When she had seated herself he looked long in her face and said, 'How funny you draw your breath—like a lamb when you drive him till he's nearly done for. Do you always draw your breath like that ?'

'Not always.' Her voice was now so low as to be scarcely above a whisper.

'You will go to sleep there, I suppose, won't you ? You have shut your eyes already.'

'No. I shall not sleep much till—another day, and then I hope to have a long, long one—very long. Now can you tell me if Rimsmoor Pond is dry this summer ?'

'Rimsmoor Pond is, but Oker's Pool isn't, because he is deep, and is never dry—'tis just over there.'

'Is the water clear ?'

'Yes, middling—except where the heath-croppers walk into it.'

'Then, take this, and go as fast as you can, and dip me up the clearest you can find. I am very faint.'

She drew from the small willow reticule that she carried in her hand an old-fashioned china teacup without a handle ; it was one of half a dozen of the same sort lying in the reticule, which she had preserved ever since her childhood, and had brought with her to-day as a small present for Clym and Eustacia.

The boy started on his errand, and soon came back with the water, such as it was. Mrs. Yeobright attempted to drink, but it was so warm as to give her nausea, and she threw it away. Afterwards she still remained sitting, with her eyes closed.

The boy waited, played near her, caught several of the little brown butterflies which abounded, and then said as he waited again, 'I like going on better than biding still. Will you soon start again ?'

'I don't know.'

'I wish I might go on by myself,' he resumed, fearing,

apparently, that he was to be pressed into some unpleasant service. 'Do you want me any more, please?'

Mrs. Yeobright made no reply.

'What shall I tell mother?' the boy continued.

'Tell her you have seen a broken-hearted woman cast off by her son.'

Before quite leaving her he threw upon her face a wistful glance, as if he had misgivings on the generosity of forsaking her thus. He gazed into her face in a vague, wondering manner, like that of one examining some strange old manuscript the key to whose characters is undiscoverable. He was not so young as to be absolutely without a sense that sympathy was demanded, he was not old enough to be free from the terror felt in childhood at beholding misery in adult quarters hitherto deemed impregnable; and whether she were in a position to cause trouble or to suffer from it, whether she and her affliction were something to pity or something to fear, it was beyond him to decide. He lowered his eyes and went on without another word. Before he had gone half a mile he had forgotten all about her, except that she was a woman who had sat down to rest.

Mrs. Yeobright's exertions, physical and emotional, had well-nigh prostrated her; but she continued to creep along in short stages with long breaks between. The sun had now got far to the west of south and stood directly in her face, like some merciless incendiary, brand in hand, waiting to consume her. With the departure of the boy all visible animation disappeared from the landscape, though the intermittent husky notes of the male grasshoppers from every tuft of furze were enough to show that amid the prostration of the larger animal species an unseen insect world was busy in all the fulness of life.

In two hours she reached a slope about three-fourths the whole distance from Alderworth to her own home, where a little patch of shepherd's-thyme intruded upon the path; and she sat down upon the perfumed mat it formed there.

In front of her a colony of ants had established a thoroughfare across the way, where they toiled a never-ending and heavy-laden throng. To look down upon them was like observing a city street from the top of a tower. She remembered that this bustle of ants had been in progress for years at the same spot—doubtless those of the old times were the ancestors of these which walked there now. She leant back to obtain more thorough rest, and the soft eastern portion of the sky was as great a relief to her eyes as the thyme was to her head. While she looked a heron arose on that side of the sky and flew on with his face towards the sun. He had come dripping wet from some pool in the valleys, and as he flew the edges and lining of his wings, his thighs, and his breast were so caught by the bright sunbeams that he appeared as if formed of burnished silver. Up in the zenith where he was seemed a free and happy place, away from all contact with the earthly ball to which she was pinioned; and she wished that she could arise uncrushed from its surface and fly as he flew then.

But, being a mother, it was inevitable that she should soon cease to ruminate upon her own condition. Had the track of her next thought been marked by a streak in the air, like the path of a meteor, it would have shown a direction contrary to the heron's, and have descended to the eastward upon the roof of Clym's house.

THE TRAGIC MEETING OF
TWO OLD FRIENDS

VII

HE in the meantime had aroused himself from sleep, sat up, and looked around. Eustacia was sitting in a chair hard by him, and though she held a book in her hand she had not looked into it for some time.

'Well, indeed!' said Clym, brushing his eyes with his hands. 'How soundly I have slept! I have had such a tremendous dream, too: one I shall never forget.'

'I thought you had been dreaming,' said she.

'Yes. It was about my mother. I dreamt that I took you to her house to make up differences, and when we got there we couldn't get in, though she kept on crying to us for help. However, dreams are dreams. What o'clock is it, Eustacia?'

'Half-past two.'

'So late, is it? I didn't mean to stay so long. By the time I have had something to eat it will be after three.'

'Ann is not come back from the village, and I thought I would let you sleep on till she returned.'

Clym went to the window and looked out. Presently he said, musingly, 'Week after week passes, and yet mother does not come. I thought I should have heard something from her long before this.'

Misgiving, regret, fear, resolution, ran their swift

course of expression in Eustacia's dark eyes. She was face to face with a monstrous difficulty, and she resolved to get free of it by postponement.

'I must certainly go to Blooms-End soon,' he continued, 'and I think I had better go alone.' He picked up his leggings and gloves, threw them down again, and added, 'As dinner will be so late to-day I will not go back to the heath, but work in the garden till the evening, and then, when it will be cooler, I will walk to Blooms-End. I am quite sure that if I make a little advance mother will be willing to forget all. It will be rather late before I can get home, as I shall not be able to do the distance either way in less than an hour and a half. But you will not mind for one evening, dear? What are you thinking of to make you look so abstracted?'

'I cannot tell you,' she said heavily. 'I wish we didn't live here, Clym. The world seems all wrong in this place.'

'Well—if we make it so. I wonder if Thomasin has been to Blooms-End lately. I hope so. But probably not, as she is, I believe, expecting to be confined in a month or so. I wish I had thought of that before. Poor mother must indeed be very lonely.'

'I don't like you going to-night.'

'Why not to-night?'

'Something may be said which will terribly injure me.'

'My mother is not vindictive,' said Clym, his colour faintly rising.

'But I wish you would not go,' Eustacia repeated in a low tone. 'If you agree not to go to-night I promise to go by myself to her house to-morrow, and make it up with her, and wait till you fetch me.'

'Why do you want to do that at this particular time, when at every previous time that I have proposed it you have refused?'

'I cannot explain further than that I should like to see her alone before you go,' she answered, with an impatient move of her head, and looking at him with an anxiety more frequently seen upon those of a sanguine temperament than upon such as herself.

'Well, it is very odd that just when I had decided to go myself you should want to do what I proposed long ago. If I wait for you to go to-morrow another day will be lost; and I know I shall be unable to rest another night without having been. I want to get this settled, and will. You must visit her afterwards: it will be all the same.'

'I could even go with you now?'

'You could scarcely walk there and back without a longer rest than I shall take. No, not to-night, Eustacia.'

'Let it be as you say, then,' she replied in the quiet way of one who, though willing to ward off evil consequences by a mild effort, would let events fall out as they might sooner than wrestle hard to direct them.

Clym then went into the garden; and a thoughtful languor stole over Eustacia for the remainder of the afternoon, which her husband attributed to the heat of the weather.

In the evening he set out on the journey. Although the heat of summer was yet intense the days had considerably shortened, and before he had advanced a mile on his way all the heath purples, browns, and greens had merged in a uniform dress without airiness or gradation, and broken only by touches of white where the little heaps of clean quartz sand showed the entrance to a rabbit-burrow, or where the white flints of a footpath lay like a thread over the slopes. In almost every one of the isolated and stunted thorns which grew here and there a night-hawk revealed his presence by whirring like the clack of a mill as long as he could hold his breath, then stopping, flapping his wings, wheeling round the bush, alighting, and after a silent interval of listening beginning to whirr again. At each brushing of Clym's feet white miller-moths flew into the air just high enough to catch upon their dusty wings the mellowed light from the west, which now shone across the depressions and levels of the ground without falling thereon to light them up.

Yeobright walked on amid this quiet scene with a hope that all would soon be well. Three miles on he came to a spot where a soft perfume was wafted across his path, and he stood still for a moment to inhale the familiar scent. It was the place at which, four hours earlier, his mother had sat down exhausted on the knoll covered with shepherd's-thyme. While he stood a sound between a breathing and a moan suddenly reached his ears.

He looked to where the sound came from ; but nothing appeared there save the verge of the hillock stretching against the sky in an unbroken line. He moved a few steps in that direction, and now he perceived a recumbent figure almost close at his feet.

Among the different possibilities as to the person's individuality there did not for a moment occur to Yeobright that it might be one of his own family. Sometimes furze-cutters had been known to sleep out of doors at these times, to save a long journey homeward and back again; but Clym remembered the moan and looked closer, and saw that the form was feminine ; and a distress came over him like cold air from a cave. But he was not absolutely certain that the woman was his mother till he stooped and beheld her face, pallid, and with closed eyes.

His breath went, as it were, out of his body and the cry of anguish which would have escaped him died upon his lips. During the momentary interval that elapsed before he became conscious that something must be done all sense of time and place left him, and it seemed as if he and his mother were as when he was a child with her many years ago on this heath at hours similar to the present. Then he awoke to activity ; and bending yet lower he found that she still breathed, and that her breath though feeble was regular, except when disturbed by an occasional gasp.

'O, what is it! Mother, are you very ill—you are not dying?' he cried, pressing his lips to her face. 'I am your Clym. How did you come here? What does it all mean?'

At that moment the chasm in their lives which his love for Eustacia had caused was not remembered by Yeobright, and to him the present joined continuously with that friendly past that had been their experience before the division.

She moved her lips, appeared to know him, but could not speak; and then Clym strove to consider how best to move her, as it would be necessary to get her away from the spot before the dews were intense. He was able-bodied, and his mother was thin. He clasped his arms round her, lifted her a little, and said, 'Does that hurt you?'

She shook her head, and he lifted her up; then, at a slow pace, went onward with his load. The air was now completely cool; but whenever he passed over a sandy patch of ground uncarpeted with vegetation there was reflected from its surface into his face the heat which it had imbibed during the day. At the beginning of his undertaking he had thought but little of the distance which yet would have to be traversed before Blooms-End could be reached; but though he had slept that afternoon he soon began to feel the weight of his burden. Thus he proceeded, like Æneas with his father; the bats circling round his head, nightjars flapping their wings within a yard of his face, and not a human being within call.

While he was yet nearly a mile from the house his mother exhibited signs of restlessness under the constraint of being borne along, as if his arms were irksome to her. He lowered her upon his knees and looked around. The point they had now reached, though far from any road, was not more than a mile from the Blooms-End cottages occupied by Fairway, Sam, Humphrey, and the Cantles. Moreover, fifty yards off stood a hut, built of clods and covered with thin turves, but now entirely disused. The simple outline of the lonely shed was visible, and thither he determined to direct his steps. As soon as he arrived he laid her down carefully by the entrance, and then ran and cut with his pocket-knife an armful of the dryest fern. Spreading this within the shed, which was entirely open on one side, he placed his mother thereon: then he ran with all his might towards the dwelling of Fairway.

Nearly a quarter of an hour had passed, disturbed only by the broken breathing of the sufferer, when moving figures began to animate the line between heath and sky. In a few moments Clym arrived with Fairway, Humphrey, and Susan Nunsuch; Olly Dowden, who had chanced to be at Fairway's, Christian and Grandfer Cantle following helter-skelter behind. They had brought a lantern and matches, water, a pillow, and a few other articles which had occurred to their minds in the hurry of the moment. Sam had been despatched back again for brandy, and a boy brought Fairway's pony, upon which he rode off to the nearest medical man, with directions to call at Wildeve's on his way, and inform Thomasin that her aunt was unwell.

Sam and the brandy soon arrived, and it was administered by the light of the lantern; after which she became sufficiently conscious to signify by signs that something was wrong with her foot. Olly Dowden at length understood her meaning, and examined the foot indicated. It was swollen and red. Even as they watched the red began to assume a more livid colour, in the midst of which appeared a scarlet speck, smaller than a pea, and it was found to consist of a drop of blood, which rose above the smooth flesh of her ankle in a hemisphere.

'I know what it is,' cried Sam. 'She has been stung by an adder!'

'Yes,' said Clym instantly. 'I remember when I was a child seeing just such a bite. O, my poor mother!'

'It was my father who was bit,' said Sam. 'And there's only one way to cure it. You must rub the place with the fat of other adders, and the only way to get that is by frying them. That's what they did for him.'

''Tis an old remedy,' said Clym distrustfully, 'and I have doubts about it. But we can do nothing else till the doctor comes,'

''Tis a sure cure,' said Olly Dowden, with emphasis. 'I've used it when I used to go out nursing.'

'Then we must pray for daylight, to catch them,' said Clym gloomily.

'I will see what I can do,' said Sam.

He took a green hazel which he had used as a walking-stick, split it at the end, inserted a small pebble, and with the lantern in his hand went out into the heath. Clym had by this time lit a small fire, and despatched Susan Nunsuch for a frying-pan. Before she had returned Sam came in with three adders, one briskly coiling and uncoiling in the cleft of the stick, and the other two hanging dead across it.

'I have only been able to get one alive and fresh as he ought to be,' said Sam. 'These limp ones are two I killed to-day at work; but as they don't die till the sun goes down they can't be very stale meat.'

The live adder regarded the assembled group with a sinister look in its small black eye, and the beautiful brown and jet pattern on its back seemed to intensify with indignation. Mrs. Yeobright saw the creature, and the creature saw her: she quivered throughout, and averted her eyes.

'Look at that,' murmured Christian Cantle. 'Neighbours, how do we know but that something of the old serpent in God's garden, that gied the apple to the young woman with no clothes, lives on in adders and snakes still? Look at his eye—for all the world like a villainous sort of black current. 'Tis to be hoped he can't ill-wish us! There's folks in heath who've been overlooked already. I will never kill another adder as long as I live.'

'Well, 'tis right to be afeard of things, if folks can't

help it,' said Grandfer Cantle. ''Twould have saved me many a brave danger in my time.'

'I fancy I heard something outside the shed,' said Christian. 'I wish troubles would come in the daytime, for then a man could show his courage, and hardly beg for mercy of the most broomstick old woman he should see, if he was a brave man, and able to run out of her sight!'

'Even such an ignorant fellow as I should know better than do that,' said Sam.

'Well, there's calamities where we least expect it, whether or no. Neighbours, if Mrs. Yeobright were to die, d'ye think we should be took up and tried for the manslaughter of a woman?'

'No, they couldn't bring it in as that,' said Sam, 'unless they could prove we had been poachers at some time of our lives. But she'll fetch round.'

'Now, if I had been stung by ten adders I should hardly have lost a day's work for't,' said Grandfer Cantle. 'Such is my spirit when I am on my mettle. But perhaps 'tis natural in a man trained for war. Yes, I've gone through a good deal; but nothing ever came amiss to me after I joined the Locals in four.' He shook his head and smiled at a mental picture of himself in uniform. 'I was always first in the most galliantest scrapes in my younger days!'

'I suppose that was because they always used to put the biggest fool afore,' said Fairway from the fire, beside which he knelt, blowing it with his breath.

'D'ye think so, Timothy?' said Grandfer Cantle, coming forward to Fairway's side with sudden depression in his face. 'Then a man may feel for years that he is good solid company, and be wrong about himself after all?'

'Never mind that question, Grandfer. Stir your stumps and get some more sticks. 'Tis very nonsense of an old man to prattle so when life and death's in mangling.'

'Yes, yes,' said Grandfer Cantle, with melancholy conviction. 'Well, this is a bad night altogether for them that have done well in their time; and if I were ever such a dab at the hautboy or tenor-viol, I shouldn't have the heart to play tunes upon 'em now.'

Susan now arrived with the frying-pan, when the live adder was killed and the heads of the three taken off. The remainders, being cut into lengths and split open, were tossed into the pan, which began hissing and crackling over the fire. Soon a rill of clear oil trickled from the carcases, whereupon Clym dipped the corner of his handkerchief into the liquid and anointed the wound.

EUSTACIA HEARS OF GOOD FORTUNE AND BEHOLDS EVIL

VIII

IN the meantime Eustacia, left alone in her cottage at Alderworth, had become considerably depressed by the posture of affairs. The consequences which might result from Clym's discovery that his mother had been turned from his door that day were likely to be disagreeable, and this was a quality in events which she hated as much as the dreadful.

To be left to pass the evening by herself was irksome to her at any time, and this evening it was more irksome than usual by reason of the excitements of the past hours. The two visits had stirred her into restlessness. She was not wrought to any great pitch of uneasiness by the probability of appearing in an ill light in the discussion between Clym and his mother, but she was wrought to vexation; and her slumbering activities were quickened to the extent of wishing that she had opened the door. She had certainly believed that Clym was awake, and the excuse would be an honest one as far as it went; but nothing could save her from censure in refusing to answer at the first knock. Yet, instead of blaming herself for the issue she laid the fault upon the shoulders of some indistinct, colossal Prince of the World, who had framed her situation and ruled her lot.

At this time of the year it was pleasanter to walk by night than by day, and when Clym had been absent about an hour she suddenly resolved to go out in the direction of Blooms-End, on the chance of meeting him on his return. When she reached the garden gate she heard wheels approaching, and looking round beheld her grandfather coming up in his car.

'I can't stay a minute, thank ye,' he answered to her greeting. 'I am driving to East Egdon; but I came round here just to tell you the news. Perhaps you have heard—about Mr. Wildeve's fortune?'

'No,' said Eustacia blankly.

'Well, he has come into a fortune of eleven thousand pounds—uncle died in Canada, just after hearing that all his family, whom he was sending home, had gone to the bottom in the *Cassiopeia*; so Wildeve has come into everything, without in the least expecting it.'

Eustacia stood motionless awhile. 'How long has he known of this?' she asked.

'Well, it was known to him this morning early, for I knew it at ten o'clock, when Charley came back. Now, he is what I call a lucky man. What a fool you were, Eustacia!'

'In what way?' she said, lifting her eyes in apparent calmness.

'Why, in not sticking to him when you had him.'

'Had him, indeed!'

'I did not know there had ever been anything between you till lately; and, faith, I should have been hot and strong against it if I had known; but since it seems that there was some sniffing between ye, why the deuce didn't you stick to him?'

Eustacia made no reply, but she looked as if she could say as much upon that subject as he if she chose.

'And how is your poor purblind husband?' continued

the old man. ‘ Not a bad fellow either, as far as he goes.’

‘ He is quite well.’

‘ It is a good thing for his cousin what-d’ye-call-her ? By George, you ought to have been in that galley, my girl ! Now I must drive on. Do you want any assistance ? What’s mine is yours, you know.’

‘ Thank you, grandfather, we are not in want at present,’ she said coldly. ‘ Clym cuts furze, but he does it mostly as a useful pastime, because he can do nothing else.’

‘ He is paid for his pastime, isn’t he ? Three shillings a hundred, I heard.’

‘Clym has money,’ she said, colouring ; ‘ but he likes to earn a little.’

‘ Very well ; good night.’ And the captain drove on.

When her grandfather was gone Eustacia went on her way mechanically ; but her thoughts were no longer concerning her mother-in-law and Clym. Wildeve, notwithstanding his complaints against his fate, had been seized upon by destiny and placed in the sunshine once more. Eleven thousand pounds ! From every Egdon point of view he was a rich man. In Eustacia’s eyes, too, it was an ample sum—one sufficient to supply those wants of hers which had been stigmatized by Clym in his more austere moods as vain and luxurious. Though she was no lover of money she loved what money could bring ; and the new accessories she imagined around him clothed Wildeve with a great deal of interest. She recollected now how quietly well-dressed he had been that morning : he had probably put on his newest suit, regardless of damage by briars and thorns. And then she thought of his manner towards herself.

‘ O I see it, I see it,’ she said. ‘ How much he wishes he had me now, that he might give me all I desire ! ’

In recalling the details of his glances and words—at the time scarcely regarded—it became plain to her how greatly they had been dictated by his knowledge of this new event. 'Had he been a man to bear a jilt ill-will he would have told me of his good fortune in crowing tones; instead of doing that he mentioned not a word, in deference to my misfortunes, and merely implied that he loved me still, as one superior to him.'

Wildeve's silence that day on what had happened to him was just the kind of behaviour calculated to make an impression on such a woman. Those delicate touches of good taste were, in fact, one of the strong points in his demeanour towards the other sex. The peculiarity of Wildeve was that, while at one time passionate, upbraiding, and resentful towards a woman, at another he would treat her with such unparalleled grace as to make previous neglect appear as no discourtesy, injury as no insult, interference as a delicate attention, and the ruin of her honour as excess of chivalry. This man, whose admiration to-day Eustacia had disregarded, whose good wishes she had scarcely taken the trouble to accept, whom she had shown out of the house by the back door, was the possessor of eleven thousand pounds—a man of fair professional education, and one who had served his articles with a civil engineer.

So intent was Eustacia upon Wildeve's fortunes that she forgot how much closer to her own course were those of Clym; and instead of walking on to meet him at once she sat down upon a stone. She was disturbed in her reverie by a voice behind, and turning her head beheld the old lover and fortunate inheritor of wealth immediately beside her.

She remained sitting, though the fluctuation in her look might have told any man who knew her so well as Wildeve that she was thinking of him.

'How did you come here?' she said in her clear low tone. 'I thought you were at home.'

'I went on to the village after leaving your garden; and now I have come back again: that's all. Which way are you walking, may I ask?'

She waved her hand in the direction of Blooms-End. 'I am going to meet my husband. I think I may possibly have got into trouble whilst you were with me to-day.'

'How could that be?'

'By not letting in Mrs. Yeobright.'

'I hope that visit of mine did you no harm.'

'None. It was not your fault,' she said quietly.

By this time she had risen; and they involuntarily sauntered on together, without speaking, for two or three minutes; when Eustacia broke silence by saying, 'I assume I must congratulate you.'

'On what? O yes; on my eleven thousand pounds, you mean. Well, since I didn't get something else, I must be content with getting that.'

'You seem very indifferent about it. Why didn't you tell me to-day when you came?' she said in the tone of a neglected person. 'I heard of it quite by accident.'

'I did mean to tell you,' said Wildeve. 'But I—well, I will speak frankly—I did not like to mention it when I saw, Eustacia, that your star was not high. The sight of a man lying wearied out with hard work, as your husband lay, made me feel that to brag of my own fortune to you would be greatly out of place. Yet, as you stood there beside him, I could not help feeling too that in many respects he was a richer man than I.'

At this Eustacia said, with slumbering mischievousness, 'What, would you exchange with him—your fortune for me?'

'I certainly would,' said Wildeve.

'As we are imagining what is impossible and absurd, suppose we change the subject?'

'Very well; and I will tell you of my plans for the future, if you care to hear them. I shall permanently invest nine thousand pounds, keep one thousand as ready money, and with the remaining thousand travel for a year or so.'

'Travel? What a bright idea! Where will you go to?'

'From here to Paris, where I shall pass the winter and spring. Then I shall go to Italy, Greece, Egypt, and Palestine, before the hot weather comes on. In the summer I shall go to America; and then, by a plan not yet settled, I shall go to Australia and round to India. By that time I shall have begun to have had enough of it. Then I shall probably come back to Paris again, and there I shall stay as long as I can afford to.'

'Back to Paris again,' she murmured in a voice that was nearly a sigh. She had never once told Wildeve of the Parisian desires which Clym's description had sown in her; yet here was he involuntarily in a position to gratify them. 'You think a good deal of Paris?' she added.

'Yes. In my opinion it is the central beauty-spot of the world.'

'And in mine! And Thomasin will go with you?'

'Yes, if she cares to. She may prefer to stay at home.'

'So you will be going about, and I shall be staying here!'

'I suppose you will. But we know whose fault that is.'

'I am not blaming you,' she said quickly.

'Oh, I thought you were. If ever you *should* be inclined to blame me, think of a certain evening by Rainbarrow, when you promised to meet me and did not. You sent me a letter; and my heart ached to read that as I hope yours never will. That was one point of divergence. I then did something in haste. . . . But she is a good woman, and I will say no more.'

'I know that the blame was on my side that time,' said Eustacia. 'But it had not always been so. However, it is my misfortune to be too sudden in feeling. O Damon, don't reproach me any more—I can't bear that.'

They went on silently for a distance of two or three miles, when Eustacia said suddenly, 'Haven't you come out of your way, Mr. Wildeve?'

'My way is anywhere to-night. I will go with you as far as the hill on which we can see Blooms-End, as it is getting late for you to be alone.'

'Don't trouble. I am not obliged to be out at all. I think I would rather you did not accompany me further. This sort of thing would have an odd look if known.'

'Very well, I will leave you.' He took her hand unexpectedly, and kissed it—for the first time since her marriage. 'What light is that on the hill ?' he added, as it were to hide the caress.

She looked, and saw a flickering firelight proceeding from the open side of a hovel a little way before them. The hovel, which she had hitherto always found empty, seemed to be inhabited now.

'Since you have come so far,' said Eustacia, 'will you see me safely past that hut ? I thought I should have met Clym somewhere about here, but as he doesn't appear I will hasten on and get to Blooms-End before he leaves.'

They advanced to the turf-shed, and when they got near it the firelight and the lantern inside showed distinctly enough the form of a woman reclining on a bed of fern, a group of heath men and women standing around her. Eustacia did not recognize Mrs. Yeobright in the reclining figure, nor Clym as one of the standers-by till she came close. Then she quickly pressed her hand upon Wildeve's arm and signified to him to come back from the open side of the shed into the shadow.

'It is my husband and his mother,' she whispered in an agitated voice. 'What can it mean ? Will you step forward and tell me ?'

Wildeve left her side and went to the back wall of the hut. Presently Eustacia perceived that he was beckoning to her, and she advanced and joined him.

'It is a serious case,' said Wildeve.

From their position they could hear what was proceeding inside.

'I cannot think where she could have been going,'

said Clym to some one. 'She had evidently walked a long way, but even when she was able to speak just now she would not tell me where. What do you really think of her?'

'There is a great deal to fear,' was gravely answered, in a voice which Eustacia recognized as that of the only surgeon in the district. 'She has suffered somewhat from the bite of the adder; but it is exhaustion which has overpowered her. My impression is that her walk must have been exceptionally long.'

'I used to tell her not to overwalk herself this weather,' said Clym, with distress. 'Do you think we did well in using the adder's fat?'

'Well, it is a very ancient remedy—the old remedy of the viper-catchers, I believe,' replied the doctor. 'It is mentioned as an infallible ointment by Hoffmann, Mead, and I think the Abbé Fontana. Undoubtedly it was as good a thing as you could do; though I question if some other oils would not have been equally efficacious.'

'Come here, come here!' was then rapidly said in anxious female tones; and Clym and the doctor could be heard rushing forward from the back part of the shed to where Mrs. Yeobright lay.

'O, what is it?' whispered Eustacia.

''Twas Thomasin who spoke,' said Wildeve. 'Then they have fetched her. I wonder if I had better go in—yet it might do harm.'

For a long time there was utter silence among the group within; and it was broken at last by Clym saying, in an agonized voice, 'O doctor, what does it mean?'

The doctor did not reply at once; ultimately he said, 'She is sinking fast. Her heart was previously affected, and physical exhaustion has dealt the finishing blow.'

Then there was a weeping of women, then waiting, then hushed exclamations, then a strange gasping sound, then a painful stillness.

'It is all over,' said the doctor.

Further back in the hut the cotters whispered, 'Mrs. Yeobright is dead.'

Almost at the same moment the two watchers observed the form of a small old-fashioned child entering at the open side of the shed. Susan Nunsuch, whose boy it was, went forward to the opening and silently beckoned to him to go back.

'I've got something to tell 'ee, mother,' he cried in a shrill tone. 'That woman asleep there walked along with me to-day; and she said I was to say that I had seed her, and she was a broken-hearted woman and cast off by her son, and then I came on home.'

A confused sob as from a man was heard within, upon which Eustacia gasped faintly, 'That's Clym—I must go to him—yet dare I do it? No: come away!'

When they had withdrawn from the neighbourhood of the shed she said huskily, 'I am to blame for this. There is evil in store for me.'

'Was she not admitted to your house after all?' Wildeve inquired.

'No; and that's where it all lies! O, what shall I do! I shall not intrude upon them: I shall go straight home. Damon, good-bye! I cannot speak to you any more now.'

They parted company; and when Eustacia had reached the next hill she looked back. A melancholy procession was wending its way by the light of the lantern from the hut towards Blooms-End. Wildeve was nowhere to be seen.

BOOK FIFTH

THE DISCOVERY

‘*WHEREFORE IS LIGHT GIVEN*

TO HIM THAT IS IN MISERY?’

I

ONE evening, about three weeks after the funeral of Mrs. Yeobright, when the silver face of the moon sent a bundle of beams directly upon the floor of Clym's house at Alderworth, a woman came forth from within. She reclined over the garden gate as if to refresh herself awhile. The pale lunar touches which make beauties of hags lent divinity to this face, already beautiful.

She had not long been there when a man came up the road and with some hesitation said to her, ‘How is he to-night, ma'am, if you please?’

‘He is better, though still very unwell, Humphrey,’ replied Eustacia.

‘Is he light-headed, ma'am?’

‘No. He is quite sensible now.’

‘Do he rave about his mother just the same, poor fellow?’ continued Humphrey.

‘Just as much, though not quite so wildly,’ she said in a low voice.

‘It was very unfortunate, ma'am, that the boy Johnny should ever ha' told him his mother's dying words, about her being broken-hearted and cast off by her son. 'Twas enough to upset any man alive.’

Eustacia made no reply beyond that of a slight catch

in her breath, as of one who fain would speak but could not; and Humphrey, declining her invitation to come in, went away.

Eustacia turned, entered the house, and ascended to the front bedroom, where a shaded light was burning. In the bed lay Clym, pale, haggard, wide awake, tossing to one side and to the other, his eyes lit by a hot light, as if the fire in their pupils were burning up their substance.

'Is it you, Eustacia?' he said as she sat down.

'Yes, Clym. I have been down to the gate. The moon is shining beautifully, and there is not a leaf stirring.'

'Shining, is it? What's the moon to a man like me? Let it shine—let anything be, so that I never see another day! . . . Eustacia, I don't know where to look: my thoughts go through me like swords. O, if any man wants to make himself immortal by painting a picture of wretchedness, let him come here!'

'Why do you say so?'

'I cannot help feeling that I did my best to kill her.'

'No, Clym.'

'Yes, it was so; it is useless to excuse me! My conduct to her was too hideous—I made no advances; and she could not bring herself to forgive me. Now she is dead! If I had only shown myself willing to make it up with her sooner, and we had been friends, and then she had died, it wouldn't be so hard to bear. But I never went near her house, so she never came near mine, and didn't know how welcome she would have been—that's what troubles me. She did not know I was going to her house that very night, for she was too insensible to understand me. If she had only come to see me! I longed that she would. But it was not to be.'

There escaped from Eustacia one of those shivering sighs which used to shake her like a pestilent blast. She had not yet told.

But Yeobright was too deeply absorbed in the ramblings incidental to his remorseful state to notice her. During his illness he had been continually talking thus. Despair had been added to his original grief by the unfortunate disclosure of the boy who had received the last words of Mrs. Yeobright—words too bitterly uttered in an hour of misapprehension. Then his distress had overwhelmed him, and he longed for death as a field labourer longs for the shade. It was the pitiful sight of a man standing in the very focus of sorrow. He continually bewailed his tardy journey to his mother's house, because it was an error which could never be rectified, and insisted that he must have been horribly perverted by some fiend not to have thought before that it was his duty to go to her, since she did not come to him. He would ask Eustacia to agree with him in his self-condemnation; and when she, seared inwardly by a secret she dared not tell, declared that she could not give an opinion, he would say, 'That's because you didn't know my mother's nature. She was always ready to forgive if asked to do so; but I seemed to her to be as an obstinate child, and that made her unyielding. Yet not unyielding: she was proud and reserved, no more. . . . Yes, I can understand why she held out against me so long. She was waiting for me. I dare say she said a hundred times in her sorrow, "What a return he makes for all the sacrifices I have made for him!" I never went to her! When I set out to visit her it was too late. To think of that is nearly intolerable!'

Sometimes his condition had been one of utter remorse, unsoftened by a single tear of pure sorrow: and then he writhed as he lay, fevered far more by thought than by physical ills. 'If I could only get one assurance that she did not die in a belief that I was resentful,' he said one day when in this mood, 'it would be better to think of than a hope of heaven. But that I cannot do.'

'You give yourself up too much to this wearying despair,' said Eustacia. 'Other men's mothers have died.'

'That doesn't make the loss of mine less. Yet it is less the loss than the circumstances of the loss. I sinned against her, and on that account there is no light for me.'

'She sinned against you, I think.'

'No: she did not. I committed the guilt; and may the whole burden be upon my head!'

'I think you might consider twice before you say that,' Eustacia replied. 'Single men have, no doubt, a right to curse themselves as much as they please; but men with wives involve two in the doom they pray down.'

'I am in too sorry a state to understand what you are refining on,' said the wretched man. 'Day and night shout at me, "You have helped to kill her." But in loathing myself I may, I own, be unjust to you, my poor wife. Forgive me for it, Eustacia, for I scarcely know what I do.'

Eustacia was always anxious to avoid the sight of her husband in such a state as this, which had become as dreadful to her as the trial scene was to Judas Iscariot. It brought before her eyes the spectre of a worn-out woman knocking at a door which she would not open; and she shrank from contemplating it. Yet it was better for Yeobright himself when he spoke openly of his sharp regret, for in silence he endured infinitely more, and would sometimes remain so long in a tense, brooding mood, consuming himself by the gnawing of his thought, that it was imperatively necessary to make him talk aloud, that his grief might in some degree expend itself in the effort.

Eustacia had not been long indoors after her look at the moonlight when a soft footstep came up to the house, and Thomasin was announced by the woman downstairs.

'Ah, Thomasin! Thank you for coming to-night,' said Clym when she entered the room. 'Here am I, you see. Such a wretched spectacle am I, that I shrink from being seen by a single friend, and almost from you.'

'You must not shrink from me, dear Clym,' said Thomasin earnestly, in that sweet voice of hers which came to a sufferer like fresh air into a Black Hole.

'Nothing in you can ever shock me or drive me away. I have been here before, but you don't remember it.'

'Yes, I do; I am not delirious, Thomasin, nor have I been so at all. Don't you believe that if they say so. I am only in great misery at what I have done: and that, with the weakness, makes me seem mad. But it has not upset my reason. Do you think I should remember all about my mother's death if I were out of my mind? No such good luck. Two months and a half, Thomasin, the last of her life, did my poor mother live alone, distracted and mourning because of me; yet she was unvisited by me, though I was living only six miles off. Two months and a half—seventy-five days did the sun rise and set upon her in that deserted state which a dog didn't deserve! Poor people who had nothing in common with her would have cared for her, and visited her had they known her sickness and loneliness; but I, who should have been all to her, stayed away like a cur. If there is any justice in God let Him kill me now. He has nearly blinded me, but that is not enough. If He would only strike me with more pain I would believe in Him for ever!'

'Hush, hush! O, pray, Clym, don't, don't say it!' implored Thomasin, affrighted into sobs and tears; while Eustacia, at the other side of the room, though her pale face remained calm, writhed in her chair. Clym went on without heeding his cousin.

'But I am not worth receiving further proof even of Heaven's reprobation. Do you think, Thomasin, that she knew me—that she did not die in that horrid mistaken notion about my not forgiving her, which I can't tell you how she acquired? If you could only assure me of that! Do you think so, Eustacia? Do speak to me.'

'I think I can assure you that she knew better at last,' said Thomasin. The pallid Eustacia said nothing.

'Why didn't she come to my house? I would have

taken her in and showed her how I loved her in spite of all. But she never came ; and I didn't go to her, and she died on the heath like an animal kicked out, nobody to help her till it was too late. If you could have seen her, Thomasin, as I saw her—a poor dying woman, lying in the dark upon the bare ground, moaning, nobody near, believing she was utterly deserted by all the world, it would have moved you to anguish, it would have moved a brute. And this poor woman my mother ! No wonder she said to the child, " You have seen a broken-hearted woman." What a state she must have been brought to, to say that ! and who can have done it but I ? It is too dreadful to think of, and I wish I could be punished more heavily than I am. How long was I what they called out of my senses ? '

' A week, I think.'

' And then I became calm.'

' Yes, for four days.'

' And now I have left off being calm.'

' But try to be quiet : please do, and you will soon be strong. If you could remove that impression from your mind—— '

' Yes, yes,' he said impatiently. ' But I don't want to get strong. What's the use of my getting well ? It would be better for me if I die, and it would certainly be better for Eustacia. Is Eustacia there ? '

' Yes.'

' It would be better for you, Eustacia, if I were to die ? '

' Don't press such a question, dear Clym.'

' Well, it really is but a shadowy supposition ; for unfortunately I am going to live. I feel myself getting better. Thomasin, how long are you going to stay at the inn, now that all this money has come to your husband ? '

' Another month or two, probably ; until my illness is over. We cannot get off till then. I think it will be a month or more.'

'Yes, yes. Of course. Ah, Cousin Tamsie, you will get over your trouble—one little month will take you through it, and bring something to console you; but I shall never get over mine, and no consolation will come!'

'Clym, you are unjust to yourself. Depend upon it, aunt thought kindly of you. I know that, if she had lived, you would have been reconciled with her.'

'But she didn't come to see me, though I asked her, before I married, if she would come. Had she come, or had I gone there, she would never have died saying, "I am a broken-hearted woman, cast off by my son." My door has always been open to her—a welcome here has always awaited her. But that she never came to see.'

'You had better not talk any more now, Clym,' said Eustacia faintly from the other part of the room, for the scene was growing intolerable to her.

'Let me talk to you instead for the little time I shall be here,' Thomasin said soothingly. 'Consider what a one-sided way you have of looking at the matter, Clym. When she said that to the little boy you had not found her and taken her into your arms; and it might have been uttered in a moment of bitterness. It was rather like aunt to say things in haste. She sometimes used to speak so to me. Though she did not come I am convinced that she thought of coming to see you. Do you suppose a man's mother could live two or three months without one forgiving thought? She forgave me; and why should she not have forgiven you?'

'You laboured to win her round; I did nothing. I, who was going to teach people the higher secrets of happiness, did not know how to keep out of that gross misery which the most untaught are wise enough to avoid.'

'How did you get here to-night, Thomasin?' said Eustacia.

'Damon set me down at the end of the lane. He

has driven into East Egdon on business, and he will come and pick me up by-and-by.'

Accordingly they soon after heard the noise of wheels. Wildeve had come, and was waiting outside with his horse and gig.

'Send out and tell him I will be down in two minutes,' said Thomasin.

'I will run down myself,' said Eustacia.

She went down. Wildeve had alighted, and was standing before the horse's head when Eustacia opened the door. He did not turn for a moment, thinking the comer Thomasin. Then he looked, started ever so little, and said one word: 'Well?'

'I have not yet told him,' she replied in a whisper.

'Then don't do so till he is well—it will be fatal. You are ill yourself.'

'I am wretched. . . . O Damon,' she said, bursting into tears, 'I—I can't tell you how unhappy I am! I can hardly bear this. I can tell nobody of my trouble—nobody knows of it but you.'

'Poor girl!' said Wildeve, visibly affected at her distress, and at last led on so far as to take her hand. 'It is hard, when you have done nothing to deserve it, that you should have got involved in such a web as this. You were not made for these sad scenes. I am to blame most. If I could only have saved you from it all!'

'But, Damon, please pray tell me what I must do? To sit by him hour after hour, and hear him reproach himself as being the cause of her death, and to know that I am the sinner if any human being is at all, drives me into cold despair. I don't know what to do. Should I tell him or should I not tell him? I always am asking myself that. O, I want to tell him; and yet I am afraid. If he finds it out he must surely kill me, for nothing else will be in proportion to his feelings now. "Beware the fury of a patient man" sounds day by day in my ears as I watch him.'

'Well, wait till he is better, and trust to chance. And when you tell, you must only tell part—for his own sake.'

'Which part should I keep back?'

Wildeve paused. 'That I was in the house at the time,' he said in a low tone.

'Yes; it must be concealed, seeing what has been whispered. How much easier are hasty actions than speeches that will excuse them!'

'If he were only to die——' Wildeve murmured.

'Do not think of it! I would not buy hope of immunity by so cowardly a desire even if I hated him. Now I am going up to him again. Thomasin bade me tell you she would be down in a few minutes. Good-bye.'

She returned, and Thomasin soon appeared. When she was seated in the gig with her husband, and the horse was turning to go off, Wildeve lifted his eyes to the bedroom windows. Looking from one of them he could discern a pale, tragic face watching him drive away. It was Eustacia's.

A LURID LIGHT BREAKS IN UPON
A DARKENED UNDERSTANDING

II

CLYM'S grief became mitigated by wearing itself out. His strength returned, and a month after the visit of Thomasin he might have been seen walking about the garden. Endurance and despair, equanimity and gloom, the tints of health and the pallor of death, mingled weirdly in his face. He was now unnaturally silent upon all of the past that related to his mother; and though Eustacia knew that he was thinking of it none the less, she was only too glad to escape the topic ever to bring it up anew. When his mind had been weaker his heart had led him to speak out; but reason having now somewhat recovered itself he sank into taciturnity.

One evening when he was thus standing in the garden, abstractedly spudding up a weed with his stick, a bony figure turned the corner of the house and came up to him.

'Christian, isn't it?' said Clym. 'I am glad you have found me out. I shall soon want you to go to Blooms-End and assist me in putting the house in order. I suppose it is all locked up as I left it?'

'Yes, Mister Clym.'

'Have you dug up the potatoes and other roots?'

'Yes, without a drop o' rain, thank God. But I was coming to tell 'ee of something else which is quite different from what we have lately had in the family. I am sent by the rich gentleman at the Woman, that we used to call the landlord, to tell 'ee that Mrs. Wildeve is doing well of a girl, which was born punctually at one o'clock at noon, or a few minutes more or less; and 'tis said that expecting of this increase is what have kept 'em there since they came into their money.'

'And she is getting on well, you say?'

'Yes, sir. Only Mr. Wildeve is twanky because 'tisn't a boy—that's what they say in the kitchen, but I was not supposed to notice that.'

'Christian, now listen to me.'

'Yes, sure, Mr. Yeobright.'

'Did you see my mother the day before she died?'

'No, I did not.'

Yeobright's face expressed disappointment.

'But I zeed her the morning of the same day she died.'

Clym's look lighted up. 'That's nearer still to my meaning,' he said.

'Yes, I know 'twas the same day; for she said, "I be going to see him, Christian; so I shall not want any vegetables brought in for dinner."'

'See whom?'

'See you. She was going to your house, you understand.'

Yeobright regarded Christian with intense surprise. 'Why did you never mention this?' he said. 'Are you sure it was my house she was coming to?'

'O yes. I didn't mention it because I've never zeed you lately. And as she didn't get there it was all nought, and nothing to tell.'

'And I have been wondering why she should have walked in the heath on that hot day! Well, did she say what she was coming for? It is a thing, Christian, I am very anxious to know.'

'Yes, Mister Clym. She didn't say it to me, though I think she did to one here and there.'

'Do you know one person to whom she spoke of it?'

'There is one man, please, sir, but I hope you won't mention my name to him, as I have seen him in strange places, particular in dreams. One night last summer he glared at me like Famine and Sword, and it made me feel so low that I didn't comb out my few hairs for two days. He was standing, as it might be, Mister Yeobright, in the middle of the path to Mistover, and your mother came up, looking as pale——'

'Yes, when was that?'

'Last summer, in my dream.'

'Pooh! Who's the man?'

'Diggory, the reddleman. He called upon her and sat with her the evening before she set out to see you. I hadn't gone home from work when he came up to the gate.'

'I must see Venn—I wish I had known it before,' said Clym anxiously. 'I wonder why he has not come to tell me?'

'He went out of Egdon Heath the next day, so would not be likely to know you wanted him.'

'Christian,' said Clym, 'you must go and find Venn. I am otherwise engaged, or I would go myself. Find him at once, and tell him I want to speak to him.'

'I am a good hand at hunting up folk by day,' said Christian, looking dubiously round at the declining light; 'but as to night-time, never is such a bad hand as I, Mister Yeobright.'

'Search the heath when you will, so that you bring him soon. Bring him to-morrow, if you can.'

Christian then departed. The morrow came, but no Venn. In the evening Christian arrived, looking very weary. He had been searching all day, and had heard nothing of the reddleman.

'Inquire as much as you can to-morrow without neglecting your work,' said Yeobright. 'Don't come again till you have found him.'

The next day Yeobright set out for the old house at Blooms-End, which, with the garden, was now his own. His severe illness had hindered all preparations for his removal thither; but it had become necessary that he should go and overlook its contents, as administrator to his mother's little property; for which purpose he decided to pass the next night on the premises.

He journeyed onward, not quickly or decisively, but in the slow walk of one who has been awakened from a stupefying sleep. It was early afternoon when he reached the valley. The expression of the place, the tone of the hour, were precisely those of many such occasions in days gone by; and these antecedent similarities fostered the illusion that she, who was there no longer, would come out to welcome him. The garden gate was locked and the shutters were closed, just as he himself had left them on the evening after the funeral. He unlocked the gate, and found that a spider had already constructed a large web, tying the door to the lintel, on the supposition that it was never to be opened again. When he had entered the house and flung back the shutters he set about his task of overhauling the cupboards and closets, burning papers, and considering how best to arrange the place for Eustacia's reception, until such time as he might be in a position to carry out his long-delayed scheme, should that time ever arrive.

As he surveyed the rooms he felt strongly disinclined for the alterations which would have to be made in the time-honoured furnishing of his parents and grandparents, to suit Eustacia's modern ideas. The gaunt oak-cased clock, with the picture of the Ascension on the door-panel and the Miraculous Draught of Fishes on the base; his grandmother's corner cupboard with the glass door, through which the spotted china was visible; the dumb-waiter; the wooden tea-trays; the hanging fountain with the brass tap—whither would these venerable articles have to be banished?

He noticed that the flowers in the window had died for want of water, and he placed them out upon the ledge, that they might be taken away. While thus engaged he heard footsteps on the gravel without, and somebody knocked at the door.

Yeobright opened it, and Venn was standing before him.

'Good morning,' said the reddleman. 'Is Mrs. Yeobright at home?'

Yeobright looked upon the ground. 'Then you have not seen Christian or any of the Egdon folks?' he said.

'No. I have only just returned after a long stay away. I called here the day before I left.'

'And you have heard nothing?'

'Nothing.'

'My mother is—dead.'

'Dead!' said Venn mechanically.

'Her home now is where I shouldn't mind having mine.'

Venn regarded him, and then said, 'If I didn't see your face I could never believe your words. Have you been ill?'

'I had an illness.'

'Well, the change! When I parted from her a month ago everything seemed to say that she was going to begin a new life.'

'And what seemed came true.'

'You say right, no doubt. Trouble has taught you a deeper vein of talk than mine. All I meant was regarding her life here. She has died too soon.'

'Perhaps through my living too long. I have had a bitter experience on that score this last month, Diggory. But come in; I have been wanting to see you.'

He conducted the reddleman into the large room where the dancing had taken place the previous Christmas; and they sat down in the settle together. 'There's the cold fireplace, you see,' said Clym. 'When that half-burnt log and those cinders were alight she was alive! Little has been changed here yet. I can do nothing. My life creeps like a snail.'

'How came she to die?' said Venn.

Yeobright gave him some particulars of her illness and death, and continued: 'After this no kind of pain will ever seem more than an indisposition to me.—I began saying that I wanted to ask you something, but I stray from subjects like a drunken man. I am anxious to know what my mother said to you when she last saw you. You talked with her a long time, I think?'

'I talked with her more than half an hour.'

'About me?'

'Yes. And it must have been on account of what we said that she was on the heath. Without question she was coming to see you.'

'But why should she come to see me if she felt so bitterly against me? There's the mystery.'

'Yet I know she quite forgave 'ee.'

'But, Diggory—would a woman, who had quite forgiven her son, say, when she felt herself ill on the way to his house, that she was broken-hearted because of his ill-usage? Never!'

'What I know is that she didn't blame you at all. She blamed herself for what had happened, and only herself. I had it from her own lips.'

'You had it from her lips that I had *not* ill-treated her; and at the same time another had it from her lips that I *had* ill-treated her? My mother was no impulsive woman who changed her opinion every hour without reason. How can it be, Venn, that she should have told such different stories in close succession?'

'I cannot say. It is certainly odd, when she had forgiven you, and had forgiven your wife, and was going to see ye on purpose to make friends.'

'If there was one thing wanting to bewilder me it was this incomprehensible thing! . . . Diggory, if we, who remain alive, were only allowed to hold conversation with the dead—just once, a bare minute, even through a screen of iron bars, as with persons in prison—what we might learn! How many who now ride smiling would hide their heads! And this mystery—I should then be at the bottom of it at once. But the grave has for ever shut her in; and how shall it be found out now?'

No reply was returned by his companion, since none could be given; and when Venn left, a few minutes later, Clym had passed from the dulness of sorrow to the fluctuation of carking incertitude.

He continued in the same state all the afternoon. A bed was made up for him in the same house by a neighbour, that he might not have to return again the next day; and when he retired to rest in the deserted place it was only to remain awake hour after hour thinking the same thoughts. How to discover a solution to this riddle of death seemed a query of more importance than highest problems of the living. There was housed in his memory a vivid picture of the face of a little boy as he entered the hovel where Clym's mother lay. The round eyes, eager gaze, the piping voice which enunciated the words, had operated like stilettos on his brain.

A visit to the boy suggested itself as a means of gleaning new particulars; though it might be quite unproductive. To probe a child's mind after the lapse of six weeks, not for facts which the child had seen and understood, but to get at those which were in their nature beyond him, did not promise much; yet when every obvious channel is blocked we grope towards the small and obscure. There was nothing else left to do; after that he would allow the enigma to drop into the abyss of undiscoverable things.

It was about daybreak when he had reached this decision, and he at once arose. He locked up the house and went out into the green patch which merged in heather further on. In front of the white garden-palings the path branched into three like a broad-arrow. The road to the right led to the Quiet Woman and its neighbourhood; the middle track led to Mistover Knap; the left-hand track led over the hill to another part of Mistover, where the child lived. On inclining into the latter path Yeobright felt a creeping chilliness, familiar enough to most people, and probably caused by the unsunned morning air. In after days he thought of it as a thing of singular significance.

When Yeobright reached the cottage of Susan Nunsuch, the mother of the boy he sought, he found that the inmates were not yet astir. But in upland hamlets the transition from a-bed to abroad is surprisingly swift and easy. There no dense partition of yawns and toilets divides humanity by night from humanity by day. Yeobright tapped at the upper window-sill, which he could reach with his walking-stick; and in three or four minutes the woman came down.

It was not till this moment that Clym recollected her to be the person who had behaved so barbarously to Eustacia. It partly explained the insuavity with which the woman greeted him. Moreover, the boy had been ailing again; and Susan now, as ever since the night when he had been pressed into Eustacia's service at the bonfire, attributed his indispositions to Eustacia's influence as a witch. It was one of those sentiments which lurk like moles underneath the visible surface of manners, and may have been kept alive by Eustacia's entreaty to the captain, at the time that he had intended to prosecute Susan for the pricking in church, to let the matter drop; which he accordingly had done.

Yeobright overcame his repugnance, for Susan had at least borne his mother no ill-will. He asked kindly for the boy; but her manner did not improve.

'I wish to see him,' continued Yeobright, with some hesitation; 'to ask him if he remembers anything more of his walk with my mother than what he has previously told.'

She regarded him in a peculiar and criticizing manner. To anybody but a half-blind man it would have said, 'You want another of the knocks which have already laid you so low.'

She called the boy downstairs, asked Clym to sit down on a stool, and continued, 'Now, Johnny, tell Mr. Yeobright anything you can call to mind.'

'You have not forgotten how you walked with the poor lady on that hot day?' said Clym.

'No,' said the boy.

'And what she said to you?'

The boy repeated the exact words he had used on entering the hut. Yeobright rested his elbow on the table and shaded his face with his hand; and the mother looked as if she wondered how a man could want more of what had stung him so deeply.

'She was going to Alderworth when you first met her?'

'No; she was coming away.'

'That can't be.'

'Yes; she walked along with me. I was coming away too.'

'Then where did you first see her?'

'At your house.'

'Attend, and speak the truth!' said Clym sternly.

'Yes, sir; at your house was where I seed her first.'

Clym started up, and Susan smiled in an expectant way which did not embellish her face; it seemed to mean, 'Something sinister is coming!'

'What did she do at my house?'

'She went and sat under the trees at the Devil's Bellows.'

'Good God! this is all news to me!'

'You never told me this before?' said Susan.

'No, mother; because I didn't like to tell 'ee I had been so far. I was picking black-hearts, and went further than I meant.'

'What did she do then?' said Yeobright.

'Looked at a man who came up and went into your house.'

'That was myself—a furze-cutter, with brambles in his hand.'

'No; 'twas not you. 'Twas a gentleman. You had gone in afore.'

'Who was he?'

'I don't know.'

'Now tell me what happened next.'

'The poor lady went and knocked at your door, and the lady with black hair looked out of the side-window at her.'

The boy's mother turned to Clym and said, 'This is something you didn't expect?'

Yeobright took no more notice of her than if he had been of stone. 'Go on, go on,' he said hoarsely to the boy.

'And when she saw the young lady look out of the window the old lady knocked again; and when nobody came she took up the furze-hook and looked at it, and put it down again, and then she looked at the faggot-bonds; and then she went away, and walked across to me, and blowed her breath very hard like this. We walked on together, she and I, and I talked to her and she talked to me a bit, but not much, because she couldn't blow her breath.'

'O!' murmured Clym, in a low tone, and bowed his head. 'Let's have more,' he said.

'She couldn't talk much, and she couldn't walk; and her face was, O so queer!'

'How was her face?'

'Like yours is now.'

The woman looked at Yeobright, and beheld him colourless, in a cold sweat. 'Isn't there meaning in it?' she said stealthily. 'What do you think of her now?'

'Silence!' said Clym fiercely. And, turning to the boy, 'And then you left her to die?'

'No,' said the woman, quickly and angrily. 'He did not leave her to die! She sent him away. Whoever says he forsook her says what's not true.'

'Trouble no more about that,' answered Clym, with a quivering mouth. 'What he did is a trifle in comparison with what he saw. Door kept shut, did you say? Kept shut, she looking out of window? Good heart of God!—what does it mean?'

The child shrank away from the gaze of his questioner.

'He said so,' answered the mother, 'and Johnny's a God-fearing boy and tells no lies.'

'"Cast off by my son!" No, by my best life, dear mother, it is not so! But by your son's, your son's—— May all murderesses get the torment they deserve!'

With these words Yeobright went forth from the little dwelling. The pupils of his eyes, fixed steadfastly on blankness, were vaguely lit with an icy shine; his mouth had passed into the phase more or less imaginatively rendered in studies of Oedipus. The strangest deeds were possible to his mood. But they were not possible to his situation. Instead of there being before him the pale face of Eustacia, and a masculine shape unknown, there was only the imperturbable countenance of the heath, which, having defied the cataclysmal onsets of centuries, reduced to insignificance by its seamed and antique features the wildest turmoil of a single man.

EUSTACIA DRESSES HERSELF
ON A BLACK MORNING

III

A CONSCIOUSNESS of a vast impassivity in all which lay around him took possession even of Yeobright in his wild walk towards Alderworth. He had once before felt in his own person this overpowering of the fervid by the inanimate; but then it had tended to enervate a passion far sweeter than that which at present pervaded him. It was once when he stood parting from Eustacia in the moist still levels beyond the hills.

But dismissing all this he went onward home, and came to the front of his house. The blinds of Eustacia's bedroom were still closely drawn, for she was no early riser. All the life visible was in the shape of a solitary thrush cracking a small snail upon the door-stone for his breakfast, and his tapping seemed a loud noise in the general silence which prevailed; but on going to the door Clym found it unfastened, the young girl who attended upon Eustacia being astir in the back part of the premises. Yeobright entered and went straight to his wife's room.

The noise of his arrival must have aroused her, for when he opened the door she was standing before the looking-glass in her night-dress, the ends of her hair gathered into one hand, with which she was coiling the whole mass round her head, previous to beginning toilette operations. She was not a woman given to speaking first at a meeting, and she allowed Clym to walk across in silence, without turning her head. He came behind her, and she saw his face in the glass. It was ashy, haggard, and terrible. Instead of starting towards him in sorrowful surprise, as even Eustacia, undemonstrative wife as she was, would have done in days before she burdened herself with a secret, she remained motionless, looking at him in the glass. And while she looked the carmine flush with which warmth and sound sleep had suffused her cheeks and neck, dissolved from view, and the death-like pallor in his face flew across into hers. He was close enough to see this, and the sight instigated his tongue.

'You know what is the matter,' he said huskily. 'I see it in your face.'

Her hand relinquished the rope of hair and dropped to her side, and the pile of tresses, no longer supported, fell from the crown of her head about her shoulders and over the white night-gown. She made no reply.

'Speak to me,' said Yeobright peremptorily.

The blanching process did not cease in her, and her lips now became as white as her face. She turned to him and said, 'Yes, Clym, I'll speak to you. Why do you return so early? Can I do anything for you?'

'Yes, you can listen to me. It seems that my wife is not very well?'

'Why?'

'Your face, my dear; your face. Or perhaps it is the pale morning light which takes your colour away? Now I am going to reveal a secret to you. Ha-ha!'

'O, that is ghastly!'

'What?'

'Your laugh.'

'There's reason for ghastliness. Eustacia; you have held my happiness in the hollow of your hand, and like a devil you have dashed it down!'

She started back from the dressing-table, retreated

a few steps from him, and looked him in the face. 'Ah! you think to frighten me,' she said, with a slight laugh. 'Is it worth while? I am undefended, and alone.'

'How extraordinary!'

'What do you mean?'

'As there is ample time I will tell you, though you know well enough. I mean that it is extraordinary that you should be alone in my absence. Tell me, now, where is he who was with you on the afternoon of the thirty-first of August? Under the bed? Up the chimney?'

A shudder overcame her and shook the light fabric of her night-dress throughout. 'I do not remember dates so exactly,' she said. 'I cannot recollect that anybody was with me besides yourself.'

'The day I mean,' said Yeobright, his voice growing louder and harsher, 'was the day you shut the door against my mother and killed her. O, it is too much—too bad!' He leant over the footpiece of the bedstead for a few moments, with his back towards her; then rising again: 'Tell me, tell me! tell me—do you hear?' he cried, rushing up to her and seizing her by the loose folds of her sleeve.

The superstratum of timidity which often overlies those who are daring and defiant at heart had been passed through, and the mettlesome substance of the woman was reached. The red blood inundated her face, previously so pale.

'What are you going to do?' she said in a low voice, regarding him with a proud smile. 'You will not alarm me by holding on so; but it would be a pity to tear my sleeve.'

Instead of letting go he drew her closer to him. 'Tell me the particulars of—my mother's death,' he said in a hard, panting whisper; 'or—I'll—I'll——'

'Clym,' she answered slowly, 'do you think you dare do anything to me that I dare not bear? But before you strike me listen. You will get nothing from me by a blow, even though it should kill me, as it probably will. But perhaps you do not wish me to speak—killing may be all you mean ?'

'Kill you ! Do you expect it ?'

'I do.'

'Why ?'

'No less degree of rage against me will match your previous grief for her.'

'Phew—I shall not kill you,' he said contemptuously, as if under a sudden change of purpose. 'I did think of it ; but—I shall not. That would be making a martyr of you, and sending you to where she is ; and I would keep you away from her till the universe come to an end, if I could.'

'I almost wish you would kill me,' said she with gloomy bitterness. 'It is with no strong desire, I assure you, that I play the part I have lately played on earth. You are no blessing, my husband.'

'You shut the door—you looked out of the window upon her—you had a man in the house with you—you sent her away to die. The inhumanity—the treachery—I will not touch you—stand away from me—and confess every word !'

'Never ! I'll hold my tongue like the very death that I don't mind meeting, even though I can clear myself of half you believe by speaking. Yes. I will ! Who of any dignity would take the trouble to clear cobwebs from a wild man's mind after such language as this ? No ; let him go on, and think his narrow thoughts, and run his head into the mire. I have other cares.'

''Tis too much—but I must spare you.'

'Poor charity.'

'By my wretched soul you sting me, Eustacia ! I can keep it up, and hotly too. Now, then, madam, tell me his name !'

'Never, I am resolved.'

'How often does he write to you ? Where does he put

his letters—when does he meet you ? Ah, his letters ! Do you tell me his name ? '

' I do not.'

' Then I'll find it myself.' His eye had fallen upon a small desk that stood near, on which she was accustomed to write her letters. He went to it. It was locked.

' Unlock this ! '

' You have no right to say it. That's mine.'

Without another word he seized the desk and dashed it to the floor. The hinge burst open, and a number of letters tumbled out.

' Stay ! ' said Eustacia, stepping before him with more excitement than she had hitherto shown.

' Come, come ! stand away ! I must see them.'

She looked at the letters as they lay, checked her feeling, and moved indifferently aside ; when he gathered them up, and examined them.

By no stretch of meaning could any but a harmless construction be placed upon a single one of the letters themselves. The solitary exception was an empty envelope directed to her, and the handwriting was Wildeve's. Yeobright held it up. Eustacia was doggedly silent.

' Can you read, madam ? Look at this envelope. Doubtless we shall find more soon, and what was inside them. I shall no doubt be gratified by learning in good time what a well-finished and full-blown adept in a certain trade my lady is.'

' Do you say it to me—do you ? ' she gasped.

He searched further, but found nothing more. ' What was in this letter ? ' he said.

' Ask the writer. Am I your hound that you should talk to me in this way ? '

' Do you brave me ? do you stand me out, mistress ? Answer. Don't look at me with those eyes as if you would bewitch me again ! Sooner than that I die. You refuse to answer ? '

'I wouldn't tell you after this, if I were as innocent as the sweetest babe in heaven!'

'Which you are not.'

'Certainly I am not absolutely,' she replied. 'I have not done what you suppose; but if to have done no harm at all is the only innocence recognized, I am beyond forgiveness. But I require no help from your conscience.'

'You can resist, and resist again! Instead of hating you I could, I think, mourn for and pity you, if you were contrite, and would confess all. Forgive you I never can. I don't speak of your lover—I will give you the benefit of the doubt in that matter, for it only affects me personally. But the other: had you half-killed *me*, had it been that you wilfully took the sight away from these feeble eyes of mine, I could have forgiven you. But *that's* too much for nature!'

'Say no more. I will do without your pity. But I would have saved you from uttering what you will regret.'

'I am going away now. I shall leave you.'

'You need not go, as I am going myself. You will keep just as far away from me by staying here.'

'Call her to mind—think of her—what goodness there was in her: it showed in every line of her face! Most women, even when but slightly annoyed, show a flicker of evil in some curl of the mouth or some corner of the cheek; but as for her, never in her angriest moments was there anything malicious in her look. She was angered quickly, but she forgave just as readily, and underneath her pride there was the meekness of a child. What came of it?—what cared you? You hated her just as she was learning to love you. O! couldn't you see what was best for you, but must bring a curse upon me, and agony and death upon her, by doing that cruel deed! What was the fellow's name who was keeping you company and causing you to add cruelty to her to your wrong to me? Was it Wildeve? Was it poor Thomasin's husband? Heaven, what wickedness! Lost your voice, have you? It is natural after detection of that most noble trick. . . . Eustacia, didn't any tender thought of your own mother lead you to think of being gentle to mine at such a time of weariness? Did not one grain of pity enter your heart as she turned away? Think what a vast opportunity was then lost of beginning a forgiving and honest course. Why did not you kick him out, and let her in, and say, I'll be an honest wife and a noble woman from this hour? Had I told you to go and quench eternally our last flickering chance of happiness here you could have done no worse. Well, she's asleep now; and have you a hundred gallants, neither they nor you can insult her any more.'

'You exaggerate fearfully,' she said in a faint, weary voice; 'but I cannot enter into my defence—it is not worth doing. You are nothing to me in future, and the past side of the story may as well remain untold. I have lost all through you, but I have not complained. Your blunders and misfortunes may have been a sorrow to you, but they have been a wrong to me. All persons of refinement have been scared away from me since I sank into the mire of marriage. Is this your cherishing—to put me into a hut like this, and keep me like the wife of a hind? You deceived me—not by words, but by appearances, which are less seen through than words. But the place will serve as well as any other—as somewhere to pass from—into my grave.' Her words were smothered in her throat, and her head drooped down.

'I don't know what you mean by that. Am I the cause of your sin?' (Eustacia made a trembling motion towards him.) 'What, you can begin to shed tears and offer me your hand? Good God! can you? No, not I. I'll not commit the fault of taking that.' (The hand she had offered dropped nervelessly, but the tears continued flowing.) 'Well, yes, I'll take it, if only for the sake of my own foolish kisses that were wasted there before I knew what I cherished. How bewitched I was! How could there be any good in a woman that everybody spoke ill of ?'

'O, O, O !' she cried, breaking down at last ; and, shaking with sobs which choked her, she sank upon her knees. 'O, will you have done ! O, you are too relentless—there's a limit to the cruelty of savages ! I have held out long—but you crush me down. I beg for mercy—I cannot bear this any longer—it is inhuman to go further with this ! If I had—killed your—mother with my own hand—I should not deserve such a scourging to the bone as this. O, O ! God have mercy upon a miserable woman! . . . You have beaten me in this game—I beg you to stay your hand in pity ! . . . I confess that I—wilfully did not undo the door the first time she knocked—but—I—should have unfastened it the second—if I had not thought you had gone to do it yourself. When I found you had not I opened it, but she was gone. That's the extent of my crime—towards *her*. Best natures commit bad faults sometimes, don't they ?—I think they do. Now I will leave you—for ever and ever !'

'Tell all, and I *will* pity you. Was the man in the house with you Wildeve ?'

'I cannot tell,' she said desperately through her sobbing. 'Don't insist further—I cannot tell. I am going from this house. We cannot both stay here.'

'You need not go : I will go. You can stay here.'

'No, I will dress, and then I will go.'

'Where ?'

'Where I came from, or *else*where.'

She hastily dressed herself, Yeobright moodily walking up and down the room the whole of the time. At last all her things were on. Her little hands quivered so violently as she held them to her chin to fasten her bonnet that she could not tie the strings, and after a few moments she relinquished the attempt. Seeing this he moved forward and said, 'Let me tie them.'

She assented in silence, and lifted her chin. For once

at least in her life she was totally oblivious of the charm of her attitude. But he was not, and he turned his eyes aside, that he might not be tempted to softness.

The strings were tied; she turned from him. 'Do you still prefer going away yourself to my leaving you?' he inquired again.

'I do.'

'Very well—let it be. And when you will confess to the man I may pity you.'

She flung her shawl about her and went downstairs, leaving him standing in the room.

Eustacia had not long been gone when there came a knock at the door of the bedroom; and Yeobright said, 'Well?'

It was the servant; and she replied, 'Somebody from Mrs. Wildeve's have called to tell 'ee that the mis'ess and the baby are getting on wonderful well, and the baby's name is to be Eustacia Clementine.' And the girl retired.

'What a mockery!' said Clym. 'This unhappy marriage of mine to be perpetuated in that child's name!'

THE MINISTRATIONS OF A HALF-FORGOTTEN ONE

IV

EUSTACIA'S journey was at first as vague in direction as that of thistledown on the wind. She did not know what to do. She wished it had been night instead of morning, that she might at least have borne her misery without the possibility of being seen. Tracing mile after mile along between the dying ferns and the wet white spiders' webs, she at length turned her steps towards her grandfather's house. She found the front door closed and locked. Mechanically she went round to the end where the stable was, and on looking in at the stable-door she saw Charley standing within.

'Captain Vye is not at home?' she said.

'No, ma'am,' said the lad in a flutter of feeling; 'he's gone to Weatherbury, and won't be home till night. And the servant is gone home for a holiday. So the house is locked up.'

Eustacia's face was not visible to Charley as she stood at the doorway, her back being to the sky, and the stable but indifferently lighted; but the wildness of her manner arrested his attention. She turned and walked away across the enclosure to the gate, and was hidden by the bank.

When she had disappeared Charley, with misgiving in

his eyes, slowly came from the stable-door, and going to another point in the bank he looked over. Eustacia was leaning against it on the outside, her face covered with her hands, and her head pressing the dewy heather which bearded the bank's outer side. She appeared to be utterly indifferent to the circumstance that her bonnet, hair, and garments were becoming wet and disarranged by the moisture of her cold, harsh pillow. Clearly something was wrong.

Charley had always regarded Eustacia as Eustacia had regarded Clym when she first beheld him—as a romantic and sweet vision, scarcely incarnate. He had been so shut off from her by the dignity of her look and the pride of her speech, except at that one blissful interval when he was allowed to hold her hand, that he had hardly deemed her a woman, wingless and earthly, subject to household conditions and domestic jars. The inner details of her life he had only conjectured. She had been a lovely wonder, predestined to an orbit in which the whole of his own was but a point; and this sight of her leaning like a helpless, despairing creature against a wild wet bank, filled him with an amazed horror. He could no longer remain where he was. Leaping over, he came up, touched her with his finger, and said tenderly, 'You are poorly, ma'am. What can I do?'

Eustacia started up, and said, 'Ah, Charley—you have followed me. You did not think when I left home in the summer that I should come back like this!'

'I did not, dear ma'am. Can I help you now?'

'I am afraid not. I wish I could get into the house. I feel giddy—that's all.'

'Lean on my arm, ma'am, till we get to the porch; and I will try to open the door.'

He supported her to the porch, and there depositing her on a seat hastened to the back, climbed to a window by the help of a ladder, and descending inside opened the door. Next he assisted her into the room, where there was an old-fashioned horsehair settee as large as a donkey-waggon. She lay down here, and Charley covered her with a cloak he found in the hall.

'Shall I get you something to eat and drink?' he said.

'If you please, Charley. But I suppose there is no fire?'

'I can light it, ma'am.'

He vanished, and she heard a splitting of wood and a blowing of bellows; and presently he returned, saying, 'I have lighted a fire in the kitchen, and now I'll light one here.'

He lit the fire, Eustacia dreamily observing him from her couch. When it was blazing up he said, 'Shall I wheel you round in front of it, ma'am, as the morning is chilly?'

'Yes, if you like.'

'Shall I go and bring the victuals now?'

'Yes, do,' she murmured languidly.

When he had gone, and the dull sounds occasionally reached her ears of his movements in the kitchen, she forgot where she was, and had for a moment to consider by an effort what the sounds meant. After an interval which seemed short to her whose thoughts were elsewhere, he came in with a tray on which steamed tea and toast, though it was nearly lunch-time.

'Place it on the table,' she said. 'I shall be ready soon.'

He did so, and retired to the door: when, however, he perceived that she did not move he came back a few steps.

'Let me hold it to you, if you don't wish to get up,' said Charley. He brought the tray to the front of the couch, where he knelt down, adding, 'I will hold it for you.'

Eustacia sat up and poured out a cup of tea. 'You are very kind to me, Charley,' she murmured as she sipped.

'Well, I ought to be,' said he diffidently, taking great trouble not to rest his eyes upon her, though this was their only natural position, Eustacia being immediately before him. 'You have been kind to me.'

'How have I?' said Eustacia.

'You let me hold your hand when you were a maiden at home.'

'Ah, so I did. Why did I do that? My mind is lost—it had to do with the mumming, had it not?'

'Yes, you wanted to go in my place.'

'I remember. I do indeed remember—too well!'

She again became utterly downcast; and Charley, seeing that she was not going to eat or drink any more, took away the tray.

Afterwards he occasionally came in to see if the fire was burning, to ask her if she wanted anything, to tell her that the wind had shifted from south to west, to ask her if she would like him to gather her some blackberries; to all which inquiries she replied in the negative or with indifference.

She remained on the settee some time longer, when she aroused herself and went upstairs. The room in which she had formerly slept still remained much as she had left it, and the recollection that this forced upon her of her own greatly changed and infinitely worsened situation again set on her face the undetermined and formless misery which it had worn on her first arrival. She peeped into her grandfather's room, through which the fresh autumn air was blowing from the open window. Her eye was arrested by what was a familiar sight enough, though it broke upon her now with a new significance.

It was a brace of pistols, hanging near the head of her grandfather's bed, which he always kept there loaded, as a precaution against possible burglars, the house being very lonely. Eustacia regarded them long, as if they were the page of a book in which she read a new and a strange matter. Quickly, like one afraid of herself, she returned downstairs and stood in deep thought.

'If I could only do it!' she said. 'It would be doing much good to myself and all connected with me, and no harm to a single one.'

The idea seemed to gather force within her, and she remained in a fixed attitude nearly ten minutes, when a certain finality was expressed in her gaze, and no longer the blankness of indecision.

She turned and went up the second time—softly and stealthily now—and entered her grandfather's room, her eyes at once seeking the head of the bed. The pistols were gone.

The instant quashing of her purpose by their absence affected her brain as a sudden vacuum affects the body: she nearly fainted. Who had done this? There was only one person on the premises besides herself. Eustacia involuntarily turned to the open window which overlooked the garden as far as the bank that bounded it. On the summit of the latter stood Charley, sufficiently elevated by its height to see into the room. His gaze was directed eagerly and solicitously upon her.

She went downstairs to the door and beckoned to him.

'You have taken them away?'

'Yes, ma'am.'

'Why did you do it?'

'I saw you looking at them too long.'

'What has that to do with it?'

'You have been heart-broken all the morning, as if you did not want to live.'

'Well?'

'And I could not bear to leave them in your way. There was meaning in your look at them.'

'Where are they now?'

'Locked up.'

'Where?'

'In the stable.'

'Give them to me.'

'No, ma'am.'

'You refuse?'

'I do. I care too much for you to give 'em up.'

She turned aside, her face for the first time softening

from the stony immobility of the earlier day, and the corners of her mouth resuming something of that delicacy of cut which was always lost in her moments of despair. At last she confronted him again.

'Why should I not die if I wish?' she said tremulously. 'I have made a bad bargain with life, and I am weary of it—weary. And now you have hindered my escape. O, why did you, Charley! What makes death painful except the thought of others' grief?—and that is absent in my case, for not a sigh would follow me!'

'Ah, it is trouble that has done this! I wish in my very soul that he who brought it about might die and rot, even if 'tis transportation to say it!'

'Charley, no more of that. What do you mean to do about this you have seen?'

'Keep it close as night, if you promise not to think of it again.'

'You need not fear. The moment has passed. I promise.' She then went away, entered the house, and lay down.

Later in the afternoon her grandfather returned. He was about to question her categorically; but on looking at her he withheld his words.

'Yes, it is too bad to talk of,' she slowly returned in answer to his glance. 'Can my old room be got ready for me to-night, grandfather? I shall want to occupy it again.'

He did not ask what it all meant, or why she had left her husband, but ordered the room to be prepared.

AN OLD MOVE
INADVERTENTLY REPEATED

V

CHARLEY'S attentions to his former mistress were unbounded. The only solace to his own trouble lay in his attempts to relieve hers. Hour after hour he considered her wants: he thought of her presence there with a sort of gratitude, and, while uttering imprecations on the cause of her unhappiness, in some measure blessed the result. Perhaps she would always remain there, he thought, and then he would be as happy as he had been before. His dread was lest she should think fit to return to Alderworth, and in that dread his eyes, with all the inquisitiveness of affection, frequently sought her face when she was not observing him, as he would have watched the head of a stockdove to learn if it contemplated flight. Having once really succoured her, and possibly preserved her from the rashest of acts, he mentally assumed in addition a guardian's responsibility for her welfare.

For this reason he busily endeavoured to provide her with pleasant distractions, bringing home curious objects which he found in the heath, such as white trumpet-shaped mosses, red-headed lichens, stone arrow-heads used by the old tribes on Egdon, and faceted crystals from the hollows of flints. These he deposited on the premises in such positions that she should see them as if by accident.

A week passed, Eustacia never going out of the house. Then she walked into the enclosed plot and looked through her grandfather's spy-glass, as she had been in the habit of doing before her marriage. One day she saw, at a place where the high-road crossed the distant valley, a heavily laden waggon passing along. It was piled with household furniture. She looked again and again, and recognized it to be her own. In the evening her grandfather came indoors with a rumour that Yeobright had removed that day from Alderworth to the old house at Blooms-End.

On another occasion when reconnoitring thus she beheld two female figures walking in the vale. The day was fine and clear; and the persons not being more than half a mile off she could see their every detail with the telescope. The woman walking in front carried a white bundle in her arms, from one end of which hung a long appendage of drapery; and when the walkers turned, so that the sun fell more directly upon them, Eustacia could see that the object was a baby. She called Charley, and asked him if he knew who they were, though she well guessed.

'Mrs. Wildeve and the nurse-girl,' said Charley.

'The nurse is carrying the baby?' said Eustacia.

'No, 'tis Mrs. Wildeve carrying that,' he answered, 'and the nurse walks behind carrying nothing.'

The lad was in good spirits that day, for the fifth of November had again come round, and he was planning yet another scheme to divert her from her too absorbing thoughts. For two successive years his mistress had seemed to take pleasure in lighting a bonfire on the bank overlooking the valley; but this year she had apparently quite forgotten the day and the customary deed. He was careful not to remind her, and went on with his secret preparations for a cheerful surprise, the more zealously that he had been absent last time and unable to assist. At every vacant minute he hastened to gather furze-stumps, thorn-tree roots, and other solid materials from the adjacent slopes, hiding them from cursory view.

The evening came, and Eustacia was still seemingly unconscious of the anniversary. She had gone indoors after her survey through the glass, and had not been visible since. As soon as it was quite dark Charley began to build the bonfire, choosing precisely that spot on the bank which Eustacia had chosen at previous times.

When all the surrounding bonfires had burst into existence Charley kindled his, and arranged its fuel so that it should not require tending for some time. He then went back to the house, and lingered round the door and windows till she should by some means or other learn of his achievement and come out to witness it. But the shutters were closed, the door remained shut, and no heed whatever seemed to be taken of his performance. Not liking to call her he went back and replenished the fire, continuing to do this for more than half an hour. It was not till his stock of fuel had greatly diminished that he went to the back door and sent in to beg that Mrs. Yeobright would open the window-shutters and see the sight outside.

Eustacia, who had been sitting listlessly in the parlour, started up at the intelligence and flung open the shutters. Facing her on the bank blazed the fire, which at once sent a ruddy glare into the room where she was, and overpowered the candles.

'Well done, Charley!' said Captain Vye from the chimney-corner. 'But I hope it is not my wood that he's burning. . . . Ah, it was this time last year that I met with that man Venn, bringing home Thomasin Yeobright—to be sure it was! Well, who would have thought that girl's troubles would have ended so well? What a snipe you were in that matter, Eustacia! Has your husband written to you yet?'

'No,' said Eustacia, looking vaguely through the window at the fire, which just then so much engaged her mind that she did not resent her grandfather's blunt opinion. She could see Charley's form on the bank, shovelling and stirring the fire; and there flashed upon her imagination some other form which that fire might call up.

She left the room, put on her garden-bonnet and cloak, and went out. Reaching the bank she looked over with a wild curiosity and misgiving, when Charley said to her, with a pleased sense of himself, 'I made it o' purpose for you, ma'am.'

'Thank you,' she said hastily. 'But I wish you to put it out now.'

'It will soon burn down,' said Charley, rather disappointed. 'Is it not a pity to knock it out?'

'I don't know,' she musingly answered.

They stood in silence, broken only by the crackling of the flames, till Charley, perceiving that she did not want to talk to him, moved reluctantly away.

Eustacia remained within the bank looking at the fire, intending to go indoors, yet lingering still. Had she not by her situation been inclined to hold in indifference all things honoured of the gods and of men she would probably have come away. But her state was so hopeless that she could play with it. To have lost is less disturbing than to wonder if we may possibly have won: and Eustacia could now, like other people at such a stage, take a standing-point outside herself, observe herself as a disinterested spectator, and think what a sport for Heaven this woman Eustacia was.

While she stood she heard a sound. It was the splash of a stone in the pond.

Had Eustacia received the stone full in the bosom her heart could not have given a more decided thump. She had thought of the possibility of such a signal in answer to that which had been unwittingly given by Charley; but she had not expected it yet. How prompt Wildeve was! Yet how could he think her capable of deliberately wishing to renew their assignations now? An impulse to leave the spot, a desire to stay, struggled within her; and the desire held its own. More than that it did not do, for she refrained even from ascending the bank and looking over. She remained motionless, not disturbing a muscle of her face or raising her eyes; for were she to turn up her face the fire on the bank would shine upon it, and Wildeve might be looking down.

There was a second splash into the pond.

Why did he stay so long without advancing and looking over? Curiosity had its way: she ascended one or two of the earth-steps in the bank and glanced out.

Wildeve was before her. He had come forward after throwing the last pebble, and the fire now shone into each of their faces from the bank stretching breast-high between them.

'I did not light it!' cried Eustacia quickly. 'It was lit without my knowledge. Don't, don't come over to me!'

'Why have you been living here all these days without telling me? You have left your home. I fear I am something to blame in this?'

'I did not let in his mother; that's how it is!'

'You do not deserve what you have got, Eustacia; you are in great misery; I see it in your eyes, your mouth, and all over you. My poor, poor girl!' He stepped over the bank. 'You are beyond everything unhappy!'

'No, no; not exactly——'

'It has been pushed too far—it is killing you: I do think it!'

Her usually quiet breathing had grown quicker with his words. 'I—I——' she began, and then burst into quivering sobs, shaken to the very heart by the unexpected voice of pity—a sentiment whose existence in relation to herself she had almost forgotten.

This outbreak of weeping took Eustacia herself so much by surprise that she could not leave off, and she turned aside from him in some shame, though turning hid nothing from him. She sobbed on desperately; then the outpour lessened, and she became quieter. Wildeve had resisted the impulse to clasp her, and stood without speaking.

'Are you not ashamed of me, who used never to be a crying animal?' she asked in a weak whisper as she wiped her eyes. 'Why didn't you go away? I wish you had not seen quite all that; it reveals too much by half.'

'You might have wished it, because it makes me as sad as you,' he said with emotion and deference. 'As for revealing—the word is impossible between us two.'

'I did not send for you—don't forget it, Damon; I am in pain, but I did not send for you! As a wife, at least, I've been straight.'

'Never mind—I came. O, Eustacia, forgive me for the harm I have done you in these two past years! I see more and more that I have been your ruin.'

'Not you. This place I live in.'

'Ah, your generosity may naturally make you say that. But I am the culprit. I should either have done more or nothing at all.'

'In what way?'

'I ought never to have hunted you out; or, having done it, I ought to have persisted in retaining you. But of course I have no right to talk of that now. I will only ask this: can I do anything for you? Is there anything on the face of the earth that a man can do to make you happier than you are at present? If there is, I will do it. You may command me, Eustacia, to the limit of my influence; and don't forget that I am richer now. Surely something can be done to save you from this! Such a rare plant in such a wild place it grieves me to see. Do you want anything bought? Do you want to go anywhere? Do you want to escape the place altogether? Only say it, and I'll do anything to put an end to those tears, which but for me would never have been at all.'

'We are each married to another person,' she said

faintly; 'and assistance from you would have an evil sound—after—after——'

'Well, there's no preventing slanderers from having their fill at any time; but you need not be afraid. Whatever I may feel I promise you on my word of honour never to speak to you about—or act upon—until you say I may. I know my duty to Thomasin quite as well as I know my duty to you as a woman unfairly treated. What shall I assist you in?'

'In getting away from here.'

'Where do you wish to go to?'

'I have a place in my mind. If you could help me as far as Budmouth I can do all the rest. Steamers sail from there across the Channel, and so I can get to Paris, where I want to be. Yes,' she pleaded earnestly, 'help me to get to Budmouth harbour without my grandfather's or my husband's knowledge, and I can do all the rest.'

'Will it be safe to leave you there alone?'

'Yes, yes. I know Budmouth well.'

'Shall I go with you? I am rich now.'

She was silent.

'Say yes, sweet!'

She was silent still.

'Well, let me know when you wish to go. We shall be at our present house till December; after that we remove to Casterbridge. Command me in anything till that time.'

'I will think of this,' she said hurriedly. 'Whether I can honestly make use of you as a friend, or must close with you as a lover—that is what I must ask myself. If I wish to go and decide to accept your company I will signal to you some evening at eight o'clock punctually, and this will mean that you are to be ready with a horse and trap at twelve o'clock the same night to drive me to Budmouth harbour in time for the morning boat.'

'I will look out every night at eight, and no signal shall escape me.'

'Now please go away. If I decide on this escape I can

only meet you once more unless—I cannot go without you. Go—I cannot bear it longer. Go—go!'

Wildeve slowly went up the steps and descended into the darkness on the other side; and as he walked he glanced back, till the bank blotted out her form from his further view.

THOMASIN ARGUES WITH

HER COUSIN, AND HE

WRITES A LETTER

VI

YEOBRIGHT was at this time at Blooms-End, hoping that Eustacia would return to him. The removal of furniture had been accomplished only that day, though Clym had lived in the old house for more than a week. He had spent the time in working about the premises, sweeping leaves from the garden-paths, cutting dead stalks from the flower-beds, and nailing up creepers which had been displaced by the autumn winds. He took no particular pleasure in these deeds, but they formed a screen between himself and despair. Moreover, it had become a religion with him to preserve in good condition all that had lapsed from his mother's hands to his own.

During these operations he was constantly on the watch for Eustacia. That there should be no mistake about her knowing where to find him he had ordered a notice-board to be affixed to the garden gate at Alderworth, signifying in white letters whither he had removed. When a leaf floated to the earth he turned his head, thinking it might be her footfall. A bird searching for worms in the mould of the flower-beds sounded like her hand on the latch of the gate ; and at dusk, when soft, strange ventriloquisms came from holes in the ground, hollow stalks, curled dead leaves, and other crannies wherein breezes, worms, and insects can work their will, he fancied that they were Eustacia, standing without and breathing wishes of reconciliation.

Up to this hour he had persevered in his resolve not to invite her back. At the same time the severity with which he had treated her lulled the sharpness of his regret for his mother, and awoke some of his old solicitude for his mother's supplanter. Harsh feelings produce harsh usage, and this by reaction quenches the sentiments that gave it birth. The more he reflected the more he softened. But to look upon his wife as innocence in distress was impossible, though he could ask himself whether he had given her quite time enough—if he had not come a little too suddenly upon her on that sombre morning.

Now that the first flush of his anger had paled he was disinclined to ascribe to her more than an indiscreet friendship with Wildeve, for there had not appeared in her manner the signs of dishonour. And this once admitted, an absolutely dark interpretation of her act towards his mother was no longer forced upon him.

On the evening of the fifth November his thoughts of Eustacia were intense. Echoes from those past times when they had exchanged tender words all the day long came like the diffused murmur of a seashore left miles behind. 'Surely,' he said, 'she might have brought herself to communicate with me before now, and confess honestly what Wildeve was to her.'

Instead of remaining at home that night he determined to go and see Thomasin and her husband. If he found opportunity he would allude to the cause of the separation between Eustacia and himself, keeping silence, however, on the fact that there was a third person in his house when his mother was turned away. If it proved that Wildeve was innocently there he would doubtless openly mention it. If he were there with unjust intentions Wildeve, being a man of quick feeling, might possibly say something to reveal the extent to which Eustacia was compromised.

But on reaching his cousin's house he found that only Thomasin was at home, Wildeve being at that time on his way towards the bonfire innocently lit by Charley at Mistover. Thomasin then, as always, was glad to see Clym, and took him in to inspect the sleeping baby, carefully screening the candlelight from the infant's eyes with her hand.

'Tamsin, have you heard that Eustacia is not with me now?' he said when they had sat down again.

'No,' said Thomasin, alarmed.

'And not that I have left Alderworth?'

'No. I never hear tidings from Alderworth unless you bring them. What is the matter?'

Clym in a disturbed voice related to her his visit to Susan Nunsuch's boy, the revelation he had made, and what had resulted from his charging Eustacia with having wilfully and heartlessly done the deed. He suppressed all mention of Wildeve's presence with her.

'All this, and I not knowing it!' murmured Thomasin in an awestruck tone. 'Terrible! What could have made her—— O, Eustacia! And when you found it out you went in hot haste to her? Were you too cruel?—or is she really so wicked as she seems?'

'Can a man be too cruel to his mother's enemy?'

'I can fancy so.'

'Very well, then—I'll admit that he can. But now what is to be done?'

'Make it up again—if a quarrel so deadly can ever be made up. I almost wish you had not told me. But do try to be reconciled. There are ways, after all, if you both wish to.'

'I don't know that we do both wish to make it up,' said Clym. 'If she had wished it, would she not have sent to me by this time?'

'You seem to wish to, and yet you have not sent to her.'

'True; but I have been tossed to and fro in doubt if I ought, after such strong provocation. To see me now, Thomasin, gives you no idea of what I have been; of what depths I have descended to in these few last days. O, it was a bitter shame to shut out my mother like that! Can I ever forget it, or even agree to see her again?'

'She might not have known that anything serious would come of it, and perhaps she did not mean to keep aunt out altogether.'

'She says herself that she did not. But the fact remains that keep her out she did.'

'Believe her sorry, and send for her.'

'How if she will not come?'

'It will prove her guilty, by showing that it is her habit to nourish enmity But I do not think that for a moment.'

'I will do this. I will wait for a day or two longer—not longer than two days certainly; and if she does not send to me in that time I will indeed send to her. I thought to have seen Wildeve here to-night. Is he from home?'

Thomasin blushed a little. 'No,' she said. 'He is merely gone out for a walk.'

'Why didn't he take you with him? The evening is fine. You want fresh air as well as he.'

'O, I don't care for going anywhere; besides, there is baby.'

'Yes, yes. Well, I have been thinking whether I should not consult your husband about this as well as you,' said Clym steadily.

'I fancy I would not,' she quickly answered. 'It can do no good.'

Her cousin looked her in the face. No doubt Thomasin was ignorant that her husband had any share in the events of that tragic afternoon; but her countenance seemed to signify that she concealed some suspicion or thought of the reputed tender relations between Wildeve and Eustacia in days gone by.

Clym, however, could make nothing of it, and he rose to depart, more in doubt than when he came.

'You will write to her in a day or two?' said the young woman earnestly. 'I do so hope the wretched separation may come to an end.'

'I will,' said Clym; 'I don't rejoice in my present state at all.'

And he left her and climbed over the hill to Blooms-End. Before going to bed he sat down and wrote the following letter:—

'MY DEAR EUSTACIA,—I must obey my heart without consulting my reason too closely. Will you come back to me? Do so, and the past shall never be mentioned. I was too severe; but O, Eustacia, the provocation! You don't know, you never will know, what those words of anger cost me which you drew down upon yourself. All that an honest man can promise you I promise now, which is that from me you shall never suffer anything on this score again. After all the vows we have made, Eustacia, I think we had better pass the remainder of our lives in trying to keep them. Come to me, then, even if you reproach me. I have thought of your sufferings that morning on which I parted from you; I know they were genuine, and they are as much as you ought to bear. Our love must still continue. Such hearts as ours would never have been given us but to be concerned with each other. I could not ask you back at first, Eustacia, for I was unable to persuade myself that he who was with you was not there as a lover. But if you will come and explain distracting appearances I do not question that you can show your honesty to me. Why have you not come before? Do you think I will not listen to you? Surely not, when you remember the kisses and vows we exchanged under the summer moon. Return then, and you shall be warmly welcomed. I can no longer think of you to your prejudice—I am but too much absorbed in justifying you.—Your husband as ever, CLYM.'

'There,' he said, as he laid it in his desk, 'that's a good thing done. If she does not come before to-morrow night I will send it to her.'

Meanwhile, at the house he had just left Thomasin sat sighing uneasily. Fidelity to her husband had that evening induced her to conceal all suspicion that Wildeve's interest in Eustacia had not ended with his marriage. But she knew nothing positive ; and though Clym was her well-beloved cousin there was one nearer to her still.

When, a little later, Wildeve returned from his walk to Mistover, Thomasin said, 'Damon, where have you been ? I was getting quite frightened, and thought you had fallen into the river. I dislike being in the house by myself.'

'Frightened ?' he said, touching her cheek as if she were some domestic animal. 'Why, I thought nothing could frighten you. It is that you are getting proud, I am sure, and don't like living here since we have risen above our business. Well, it is a tedious matter, this getting a new house ; but I couldn't have set about it sooner, unless our ten thousand pounds had been a hundred thousand, when we could have afforded to despise caution.'

'No—I don't mind waiting—I would rather stay here twelve months longer than run any risk with baby. But I don't like your vanishing so in the evenings. There's something on your mind—I know there is, Damon. You go about so gloomily, and look at the heath as if it were somebody's gaol instead of a nice wild place to walk in.'

He looked towards her with pitying surprise. 'What, do you like Egdon Heath ?' he said.

'I like what I was born near to ; I admire its grim old face.'

'Pooh, my dear. You don't know what you like.'

'I am sure I do. There's only one thing unpleasant about Egdon.'

'What's that ?'

'You never take me with you when you walk there. Why do you wander so much in it yourself if you so dislike it ?'

The inquiry, though a simple one, was plainly disconcerting, and he sat down before replying. 'I don't think you often see me there. Give an instance.'

'I will,' she answered triumphantly. 'When you went out this evening I thought that as baby was asleep I would see where you were going to so mysteriously without telling me. So I ran out and followed behind you. You stopped at the place where the road forks, looked round at the bonfires, and then said, "Damn it, I'll go!" And you went quickly up the left-hand road. Then I stood and watched you.'

Wildeve frowned, afterwards saying, with a forced smile, 'Well, what wonderful discovery did you make?'

'There—now you are angry, and we won't talk of this any more.' She went across to him, sat on a footstool, and looked up in his face.

'Nonsense!' he said; 'that's how you always back out. We will go on with it now we have begun. What did you next see? I particularly want to know.'

'Don't be like that, Damon!' she murmured. 'I didn't see anything. You vanished out of sight, and then I looked round at the bonfires and came in.'

'Perhaps this is not the only time you have dogged my steps. Are you trying to find out something bad about me?'

'Not at all! I have never done such a thing before, and I shouldn't have done it now if words had not sometimes been dropped about you.'

'What *do* you mean?' he impatiently asked.

'They say—they say you used to go to Alderworth in the evenings, and it puts into my mind what I have heard about——'

Wildeve turned angrily and stood up in front of her. 'Now,' he said, flourishing his hand in the air, 'just out with it, madam! I demand to know what remarks you have heard.'

'Well, I heard that you used to be very fond of Eustacia

—nothing more than that, though dropped in a bit-by-bit way. You ought not to be angry !'

He observed that her eyes were brimming with tears. 'Well,' he said, 'there is nothing new in that, and of course I don't mean to be rough towards you, so you need not cry. Now, don't let us speak of the subject any more.'

And no more was said, Thomasin being glad enough of a reason for not mentioning Clym's visit to her that evening, and his story.

THE NIGHT OF THE SIXTH OF NOVEMBER

VII

HAVING resolved on flight Eustacia at times seemed anxious that something should happen to thwart her own intention. The only event that could really change her position was the appearance of Clym. The glory which had encircled him as her lover was departed now; yet some good simple quality of his would occasionally return to her memory and stir a momentary throb of hope that he would again present himself before her. But calmly considered it was not likely that such a severance as now existed would ever close up: she would have to live on as a painful object, isolated, and out of place. She had used to think of the heath alone as an uncongenial spot to be in; she felt it now of the whole world.

Towards evening on the sixth her determination to go away again revived. About four o'clock she packed up anew the few small articles she had brought in her flight from Alderworth, and also some belonging to her which had been left here: the whole formed a bundle not too large to be carried in her hand for a distance of a mile or two. The scene without grew darker; mud-coloured clouds bellied downwards from the sky like vast hammocks slung across it, and with the increase of night a stormy wind arose; but as yet there was no rain.

Eustacia could not rest indoors, having nothing more to do, and she wandered to and fro on the hill, not far from the house she was soon to leave. In these desultory ramblings she passed the cottage of Susan Nunsuch, a little lower down than her grandfather's. The door was ajar, and a riband of bright firelight fell over the ground without. As Eustacia crossed the firebeams she appeared for an instant as distinct as a figure in a phantasmagoria—a creature of light surrounded by an area of darkness: the moment passed, and she was absorbed in night again.

A woman who was sitting inside the cottage had seen and recognized her in that momentary irradiation. This was Susan herself, occupied in preparing a posset for her little boy, who, often ailing, was now seriously unwell. Susan dropped the spoon, shook her fist at the vanished figure, and then proceeded with her work in a musing, absent way.

At eight o'clock, the hour at which Eustacia had promised to signal to Wildeve if ever she signalled at all, she looked around the premises to learn if the coast was clear, went to the furze-rick, and pulled thence a long-stemmed bough of that fuel. This she carried to the corner of the bank, and, glancing behind to see if the shutters were all closed, she struck a light, and kindled the furze. When it was thoroughly ablaze Eustacia took it by the stem and waved it in the air above her head till it had burned itself out.

She was gratified, if gratification were possible to such a mood, by seeing a similar light in the vicinity of Wildeve's residence a minute or two later. Having agreed to keep watch at this hour every night, in case she should require assistance, this promptness proved how strictly he had held to his word. Four hours after the present time, that is, at midnight, he was to be ready to drive her to Budmouth, as prearranged.

Eustacia returned to the house. Supper having been got over she retired early, and sat in her bedroom waiting for the time to go by. The night being dark and threatening Captain Vye had not strolled out to gossip in any cottage or to call at the inn, as was sometimes his custom on these long autumn nights; and he sat sipping grog alone downstairs. About ten o'clock there was a knock at the door. When the servant opened it the rays of the candle fell upon the form of Fairway.

'I was a-forced to go to Lower Mistover to-night,' he said; 'and Mr. Yeobright asked me to leave this here on my way; but, faith, I put it in the lining of my hat, and thought no more about it till I got back and was hasping my gate before going to bed. So I have run back with it at once.'

He handed in a letter and went his way. The girl brought it to the captain, who found that it was directed to Eustacia. He turned it over and over, and fancied that the writing was her husband's, though he could not be sure. However, he decided to let her have it at once if possible, and took it upstairs for that purpose; but on reaching the door of her room and looking in at the keyhole he found there was no light within, the fact being that Eustacia, without undressing, had flung herself upon the bed, to rest and gather a little strength for her coming journey. Her grandfather concluded from what he saw that he ought not to disturb her; and descending again to the parlour he placed the letter on the mantelpiece to give it to her in the morning.

At eleven o'clock he went to bed himself, smoked for some time in his bedroom, put out his light at half-past eleven, and then, as was his invariable custom, pulled up the blind before getting into bed, that he might see which way the wind blew on opening his eyes in the morning, his bedroom window commanding a view of the flagstaff and vane. Just as he had lain down he was surprised to observe the white pole of the staff flash into existence like a streak of phosphorus drawn downwards across the shade of night without. Only one explanation met this—a light had been suddenly thrown upon the pole from the direction of the house. As everybody had retired to rest the old man felt it necessary to get out of bed, open the window softly, and look to the right and left. Eustacia's bedroom was lighted up, and it was the shine from her window which had lighted the pole. Wondering what had aroused her he remained undecided at the window, and was thinking of fetching the letter to slip it under her door, when he heard a slight brushing of garments on the partition dividing his room from the passage.

The captain concluded that Eustacia, feeling wakeful, had gone for a book, and would have dismissed the matter as unimportant if he had not also heard her distinctly weeping as she passed.

'She is thinking of that husband of hers,' he said to himself. 'Ah, the silly goose! she had no business to marry him. I wonder if that letter is really his?'

He arose, threw his boat-cloak round him, opened the door, and said, 'Eustacia!' There was no answer. 'Eustacia!' he repeated louder, 'there is a letter on the mantelpiece for you.'

But no response was made to this statement save an imaginary one from the wind, which seemed to gnaw at the corners of the house, and the stroke of a few drops of rain upon the windows.

He went on to the landing, and stood waiting nearly five minutes. Still she did not return. He went back for a light, and prepared to follow her; but first he looked into her bedroom. There, on the outside of the quilt, was the impression of her form, showing that the bed had not been opened; and, what was more significant, she had not taken her candlestick downstairs. He was now thoroughly alarmed; and hastily putting on his clothes he descended to the front door, which he himself had bolted and locked. It was now unfastened. There was no longer any doubt that Eustacia had left the house at this midnight hour; and whither could she have gone? To follow her was almost impossible. Had the dwelling stood in an ordinary road, two persons setting out, one in each direction, might have made sure of overtaking her; but it was a hopeless task to seek for anybody on a heath in the dark, the practicable directions for flight across it from any point being as numerous as the meridians radiating from the pole. Perplexed what to do he looked into the parlour, and was vexed to find that the letter still lay there untouched.

At half-past eleven, finding that the house was silent, Eustacia had lighted her candle, put on some warm outer wrappings, taken her bag in her hand, and, extinguishing the light again, descended the staircase. When she got into the outer air she found that it had begun to rain, and as she stood pausing at the door it increased, threatening to come on heavily. But having committed herself to this line of action there was no retreating for bad weather. Even the receipt of Clym's letter would not have stopped her now. The gloom of the night was funereal; all nature seemed clothed in crape. The spiky points of the fir trees behind the house rose into the sky like the turrets and pinnacles of an abbey. Nothing below the horizon was visible save a light which was still burning in the cottage of Susan Nunsuch.

Eustacia opened her umbrella and went out from the enclosure by the steps over the bank, after which she was beyond all danger of being perceived. Skirting the pool she followed the path towards Rainbarrow, occasionally stumbling over twisted furze-roots, tufts of rushes, or oozing lumps of fleshy fungi, which at this season lay scattered about the heath like the rotten liver and lungs of some colossal animal. The moon and stars were closed up by cloud and rain to the degree of extinction. It was a night which led the traveller's thoughts instinctively to dwell on nocturnal scenes of disaster in the chronicles of the world, on all that is terrible and dark in history and legend—the last plague of Egypt, the destruction of Sennacherib's host, the agony in Gethsemane.

Eustacia at length reached Rainbarrow, and stood still there to think. Never was harmony more perfect than that between the chaos of her mind and the chaos of the world without. A sudden recollection had flashed on her this moment: she had not money enough for undertaking a long journey. Amid the fluctuating sentiments of the day her unpractical mind had not dwelt on the necessity of being well-provided, and now that she thoroughly realized the conditions she sighed bitterly and ceased to stand erect, gradually crouching down under the umbrella as if she were drawn into the Barrow by a hand from beneath. Could it be that she was to remain a captive still? Money: she had never felt its value before. Even to efface herself from the country means were required. To ask Wildeve for pecuniary aid without allowing him to accompany her was impossible to a woman with a shadow of pride left in her: to fly as his mistress—and she knew that he loved her—was of the nature of humiliation.

Any one who had stood by now would have pitied her, not so much on account of her exposure to weather, and isolation from all of humanity except the mouldered remains inside the tumulus; but for that other form of misery which was denoted by the slightly rocking movement that her feelings imparted to her person. Extreme unhappiness weighed visibly upon her. Between the drippings of the rain from her umbrella to her mantle, from her mantle to the heather, from the heather to the earth, very similar sounds could be heard coming from her lips; and the tearfulness of the outer scene was repeated upon her face. The wings of her soul were broken by the cruel obstructiveness of all about her; and even had she seen herself in a promising way of getting to Budmouth, entering a steamer, and sailing to some opposite port, she would have been but little more buoyant, so fearfully malignant were other things. She uttered words aloud. When a woman in such a situation, neither old, deaf, crazed, nor whimsical, takes upon herself to sob and soliloquize aloud there is something grievous the matter.

'Can I go, can I go?' she moaned. 'He's not *great* enough for me to give myself to—he does not suffice for my desire! . . . If he had been a Saul or a Bonaparte—ah! But to break my marriage vow for him—it is too poor a luxury! . . . And I have no money to go alone! And if I could, what comfort to me? I must drag on next year, as I have dragged on this year, and the year after that as before. How I have tried and tried to be a splendid woman, and how destiny has been against me! . . . I do not deserve my lot!' she cried in a frenzy of bitter revolt. 'O, the cruelty of putting me into this ill-conceived world! I was capable of much; but I have been injured and blighted and crushed by things beyond my control! O, how hard it is of Heaven to devise such tortures for me, who have done no harm to Heaven at all!'

The distant light which Eustacia had cursorily observed in leaving the house came, as she had divined, from the cottage-window of Susan Nunsuch. What Eustacia did not divine was the occupation of the woman within at that moment. Susan's sight of her passing figure earlier in the evening, not five minutes after the sick boy's exclamation, 'Mother, I do feel so bad!' persuaded the matron that an evil influence was certainly exercised by Eustacia's propinquity.

On this account Susan did not go to bed as soon as the evening's work was over, as she would have done at ordinary times. To counteract the malign spell which she imagined poor Eustacia to be working, the boy's mother busied herself with a ghastly invention of superstition, calculated to bring powerlessness, atrophy, and annihilation on any human being against whom it was directed. It was a practice well known on Egdon at that date, and one that is not quite extinct at the present day.

She passed with her candle into an inner room, where, among other utensils, were two large brown pans, containing together perhaps a hundredweight of liquid honey, the produce of the bees during the foregoing summer. On a shelf over the pans was a smooth and solid yellow mass of a hemispherical form, consisting of beeswax from the same take of honey. Susan took down the lump, and, cutting off several thin slices, heaped them in an iron ladle, with which she returned to the living-room, and placed the vessel in the hot ashes of the fireplace. As soon as the wax had softened to the plasticity of dough she kneaded the pieces together. And now her face became more intent. She began moulding the wax; and it was evident from her manner of manipulation that she was endeavouring to give it some preconceived form. The form was human.

By warming and kneading, cutting and twisting, dismembering and re-joining the incipient image she had in about a quarter of an hour produced a shape which tolerably well resembled a woman, and was about six inches high. She laid it on the table to get cold and hard. Meanwhile she took the candle and went upstairs to where the little boy was lying.

'Did you notice, my dear, what Mrs. Eustacia wore this afternoon besides the dark dress?'

'A red ribbon round her neck.'

'Anything else?'

'No—except sandal-shoes.'

'A red ribbon and sandal-shoes,' she said to herself.

Mrs. Nunsuch went and searched till she found a fragment of the narrowest red ribbon, which she took downstairs and tied round the neck of the image. Then fetching ink and a quill from the rickety bureau by the window, she blackened the feet of the image to the extent presumably covered by shoes; and on the instep of each foot marked cross-lines in the shape taken by the sandal-strings of those days. Finally she tied a bit of black thread round the upper part of the head, in faint resemblance to a snood worn for confining the hair.

Susan held the object at arm's length and contemplated it with a satisfaction in which there was no smile. To anybody acquainted with the inhabitants of Egdon Heath the image would have suggested Eustacia Yeobright.

From her work-basket in the window-seat the woman took a paper of pins, of the old long and yellow sort, whose heads were disposed to come off at their first usage. These she began to thrust into the image in all directions, with apparently excruciating energy. Probably as many as fifty were thus inserted, some into the head of the wax model, some into the shoulders, some into the trunk, some upwards through the soles of the feet, till the figure was completely permeated with pins.

She turned to the fire. It had been of turf; and though the high heap of ashes which turf fires produce was somewhat dark and dead on the outside, upon raking it abroad with the shovel the inside of the mass showed a glow of red heat. She took a few pieces of fresh turf from the chimney-corner and built them together over the glow, upon which the fire brightened. Seizing with the tongs the image that she had made of Eustacia, she held it in the heat, and watched it as it began to waste slowly away. And while she stood thus engaged there came from between her lips a murmur of words.

It was a strange jargon—the Lord's Prayer repeated backwards—the incantation usual in proceedings for obtaining unhallowed assistance against an enemy. Susan uttered the lugubrious discourse three times slowly, and when it was completed the image had considerably diminished. As the wax dropped into the fire a long flame arose from the spot, and curling its tongue round the figure eat still further into its substance. A pin occasionally dropped with the wax, and the embers heated it red as it lay.

RAIN, DARKNESS, AND ANXIOUS WANDERERS

VIII

WHILE the effigy of Eustacia was melting to nothing, and the fair woman herself was standing on Rainbarrow, her soul in an abyss of desolation seldom plumbed by one so young, Yeobright sat lonely at Blooms-End. He had fulfilled his word to Thomasin by sending off Fairway with the letter to his wife, and now waited with increased impatience for some sound or signal of her return. Were Eustacia still at Mistover the very least he expected was that she would send him back a reply to-night by the same hand ; though, to leave all to her inclination, he had cautioned Fairway not to ask for an answer. If one were handed to him he was to bring it immediately ; if not, he was to go straight home without troubling to come round to Blooms-End again that night.

But secretly Clym had a more pleasing hope. Eustacia might possibly decline to use her pen—it was rather her way to work silently—and surprise him by appearing at his door. How fully her mind was made up to do otherwise he did not know.

To Clym's regret it began to rain and blow hard as the evening advanced. The wind rasped and scraped at the corners of the house, and filliped the eavesdroppings like peas against the panes. He walked restlessly about the untenanted rooms, stopping strange noises in windows and doors by jamming splinters of wood into the casements and crevices, and pressing together the lead-work of the quarries where it had become loosened from the glass. It was one of those nights when cracks in the walls of old churches widen, when ancient stains on the ceilings of decayed manor-houses are renewed and enlarged from the size of a man's hand to an area of many feet. The little gate in the palings before his dwelling continually opened and clicked together again, but when he looked out eagerly nobody was there; it was as if invisible shapes of the dead were passing in on their way to visit him.

Between ten and eleven o'clock, finding that neither Fairway nor anybody else came to him, he retired to rest, and despite his anxieties soon fell asleep. His sleep, however, was not very sound, by reason of the expectancy he had given way to, and he was easily awakened by a knocking which began at the door about an hour after. Clym arose and looked out of the window. Rain was still falling heavily, the whole expanse of heath before him emitting a subdued hiss under the downpour. It was too dark to see anything at all.

'Who's there?' he cried.

Light footsteps shifted their position in the porch, and he could just distinguish in a plaintive female voice the words, 'O Clym, come down and let me in!'

He flushed hot with agitation. 'Surely it is Eustacia!' he murmured. If so, she had indeed come to him unawares.

He hastily got a light, dressed himself, and went down. On his flinging open the door the rays of the candle fell upon a woman closely wrapped up, who at once came forward.

'Thomasin!' he exclaimed in an indescribable tone of disappointment. 'It is Thomasin, and on such a night as this! O, where is Eustacia?'

Thomasin it was, wet, frightened, and panting.

'Eustacia? I don't know, Clym; but I can think,' she said with much perturbation. 'Let me come in and rest—I will explain this. There is a great trouble brewing—my husband and Eustacia!'

'What, what?'

'I think my husband is going to leave me or do something dreadful—I don't know what—Clym, will you go and see? I have nobody to help me but you! Eustacia has not yet come home?'

'No.'

She went on breathlessly: 'Then they are going to run off together! He came indoors to-night about eight o'clock and said in an off-hand way, "Tamsie, I have just found that I must go a journey." "When?" I said. "To-night," he said. "Where?" I asked him. "I cannot tell you at present," he said; "I shall be back again to-morrow." He then went and busied himself in looking up his things, and took no notice of me at all. I expected to see him start, but he did not, and then it came to be ten o'clock, when he said, "You had better go to bed." I didn't know what to do, and I went to bed. I believe he thought I fell asleep, for half an hour after that he came up and unlocked the oak chest we keep money in when we have much in the house and took out a roll of something which I believe was bank-notes, though I was not aware that he had 'em there. These he must have got from the bank when he went there the other day. What does he want bank-notes for, if he is only going off for a day? When he had gone down I thought of Eustacia, and how he had met her the night before—I know he did meet her, Clym, for I followed him part of the way; but I did not like to tell you when you called, and so make you think ill of him, as I did not think it was so serious. Then I could not stay in bed: I got up and dressed myself, and when I heard him out in the stable I thought I would come and tell you. So I came downstairs without any noise and slipped out.'

'Then he was not absolutely gone when you left?'

'No. Will you, dear Cousin Clym, go and try to persuade him not to go? He takes no notice of what I say, and puts me off with the story of his going on a journey, and will be home to-morrow, and all that; but I don't believe it. I think you could influence him.'

'I'll go,' said Clym. 'O, Eustacia!'

Thomasin carried in her arms a large bundle; and having by this time seated herself she began to unroll it, when a baby appeared as the kernel to the husks—dry, warm, and unconscious of travel or rough weather. Thomasin briefly kissed the baby, and then found time to begin crying as she said, 'I brought baby, for I was afraid what might happen to her. I suppose it will be her death, but I couldn't leave her with Rachel!'

Clym hastily put together the logs on the hearth, raked abroad the embers, which were scarcely yet extinct, and blew up a flame with the bellows.

'Dry yourself,' he said. 'I'll go and get some more wood.'

'No, no—don't stay for that. I'll make up the fire. Will you go at once—please will you?'

Yeobright ran upstairs to finish dressing himself. While he was gone another rapping came to the door. This time there was no delusion that it might be Eustacia's: the footsteps just preceding it had been heavy and slow. Yeobright, thinking it might possibly be Fairway with a note in answer, descended again and opened the door.

'Captain Vye?' he said to a dripping figure.

'Is my grand-daughter here?' said the captain.

'No.'

'Then where is she?'

'I don't know.'

'But you ought to know—you are her husband.'

'Only in name apparently,' said Clym with rising

excitement. 'I believe she means to elope to-night with Wildeve. I am just going to look to it.'

'Well, she has left my house; she left about half an hour ago. Who's sitting there?'

'My cousin Thomasin.'

The captain bowed in a preoccupied way to her. 'I only hope it is no worse than an elopement,' he said.

'Worse? What's worse than the worst a wife can do?'

'Well, I have been told a strange tale. Before starting in search of her I called up Charley, my stable-lad. I missed my pistols the other day.'

'Pistols?'

'He said at the time that he took them down to clean. He has now owned that he took them because he saw Eustacia looking curiously at them; and she afterwards owned to him that she was thinking of taking her life, but bound him to secrecy, and promised never to think of such a thing again. I hardly suppose she will ever have bravado enough to use one of them; but it shows what has been lurking in her mind; and people who think of that sort of thing once think of it again.'

'Where are the pistols?'

'Safely locked up. O no, she won't touch them again. But there are more ways of letting out life than through a bullet-hole. What did you quarrel about so bitterly with her to drive her to all this? You must have treated her badly indeed. Well, I was always against the marriage, and I was right.'

'Are you going with me?' said Yeobright, paying no attention to the captain's latter remark. 'If so I can tell you what we quarrelled about as we walk along.'

'Where to?'

'To Wildeve's — that was her destination, depend upon it.'

Thomasin here broke in, still weeping: 'He said he was only going on a sudden short journey; but if so why did he want so much money? O, Clym, what do you think will happen? I am afraid that you, my poor baby, will soon have no father left to you!'

'I am off now,' said Yeobright, stepping into the porch.

'I would fain go with 'ee,' said the old man doubtfully. 'But I begin to be afraid that my legs will hardly carry me there such a night as this. I am not so young as I was. If they are interrupted in their flight she will be sure to come back to me, and I ought to be at the house to receive her. But be it as 'twill I can't walk to the Quiet Woman, and that's an end on't. I'll go straight home.'

'It will perhaps be best,' said Clym. 'Thomasin, dry yourself, and be as comfortable as you can.'

With this he closed the door upon her, and left the house in company with Captain Vye, who parted from him outside the gate, taking the middle path, which led to Mistover. Clym crossed by the right-hand track towards the inn.

Thomasin, being left alone, took off some of her wet garments, carried the baby upstairs to Clym's bed, and then came down to the sitting-room again, where she made a larger fire, and began drying herself. The fire soon flared up the chimney, giving the room an appearance of comfort that was doubled by contrast with the drumming of the storm without, which snapped at the window-panes and breathed into the chimney strange low utterances that seemed to be the prologue to some tragedy.

But the least part of Thomasin was in the house, for her heart being at ease about the little girl upstairs she was mentally following Clym on his journey. Having indulged in this imaginary peregrination for some considerable interval, she became impressed with a sense of the intolerable slowness of time. But she sat on. The moment then came when she could scarcely sit longer;

and it was like a satire on her patience to remember that Clym could hardly have reached the inn as yet. At last she went to the baby's bedside. The child was sleeping soundly; but her imagination of possibly disastrous events at her home, the predominance within her of the unseen over the seen, agitated her beyond endurance. She could not refrain from going down and opening the door. The rain still continued, the candlelight falling upon the nearest drops and making glistening darts of them as they descended across the throng of invisible ones behind. To plunge into that medium was to plunge into water slightly diluted with air. But the difficulty of returning to her house at this moment made her all the more desirous of doing so: anything was better than suspense. 'I have come here well enough,' she said, 'and why shouldn't I go back again? It is a mistake for me to be away.'

She hastily fetched the infant, wrapped it up, cloaked herself as before, and shovelling the ashes over the fire, to prevent accidents, went into the open air. Pausing first to put the door-key in its old place behind the shutter, she resolutely turned her face to the confronting pile of firmamental darkness beyond the palings, and stepped into its midst. But Thomasin's imagination being so actively engaged elsewhere, the night and the weather had for her no terror beyond that of their actual discomfort and difficulty.

She was soon ascending Blooms-End valley and traversing the undulations on the side of the hill. The noise of the wind over the heath was shrill, and as if it whistled for joy at finding a night so congenial as this. Sometimes the path led her to hollows between thickets of tall and dripping bracken, dead, though not yet prostrate, which enclosed her like a pool. When they were more than usually tall she lifted the baby to the top of her head, that it might be out of the reach of their drenching fronds. On higher ground, where the wind was brisk and sustained, the rain flew in a level flight without sensible descent, so that it was beyond all power to imagine the remoteness of the point at which it left the bosoms of the clouds. Here self-defence was impossible, and individual drops stuck into her like the arrows into Saint Sebastian. She was enabled to avoid puddles by the nebulous paleness which signified their presence, though beside anything less dark than the heath they themselves would have appeared as blackness.

Yet in spite of all this Thomasin was not sorry that she had started. To her there were not, as to Eustacia, demons in the air, and malice in every bush and bough. The drops which lashed her face were not scorpions, but prosy rain; Egdon in the mass was no monster whatever, but impersonal open ground. Her fears of the place were rational, her dislikes of its worst moods reasonable. At this time it was in her view a windy, wet place, in which a person might experience much discomfort, lose the path without care, and possibly catch cold.

If the path is well known the difficulty at such times of keeping therein is not altogether great, from its familiar feel to the feet; but once lost it is irrecoverable. Owing to her baby, who somewhat impeded Thomasin's view forward and distracted her mind, she did at last lose the track. This mishap occurred when she was descending an open slope about two-thirds home. Instead of attempting, by wandering hither and thither, the hopeless task of finding such a mere thread, she went straight on, trusting for guidance to her general knowledge of the contours, which was scarcely surpassed by Clym's or by that of the heath-croppers themselves.

At length Thomasin reached a hollow and began to discern through the rain a faint blotted radiance, which presently assumed the oblong form of an open door. She knew that no house stood hereabouts, and was soon aware of the nature of the door by its height above the ground.

'Why, it is Diggory Venn's van, surely!' she said.

A certain secluded spot near Rainbarrow was, she knew, often Venn's chosen centre when staying in this neighbourhood; and she guessed at once that she had stumbled upon this mysterious retreat. The question arose in her mind whether or not she should ask him to guide her into the path. In her anxiety to reach home she decided that she would appeal to him, notwithstanding the strangeness of appearing before his eyes at this place and season. But when, in pursuance of this resolve, Thomasin reached the van and looked in she found it to be untenanted; though there was no doubt that it was the reddleman's. The fire was burning in the stove, the lantern hung from the nail. Round the doorway the floor was merely sprinkled with rain, and not saturated, which told her that the door had not long been opened.

While she stood uncertainly looking in Thomasin heard a footstep advancing from the darkness behind her; and turning, beheld the well-known form in corduroy, lurid from head to foot, the lantern beams falling upon him through an intervening gauze of raindrops.

'I thought you went down the slope,' he said, without noticing her face. 'How do you come back here again?'

'Diggory?' said Thomasin faintly.

'Who are you?' said Venn, still unperceiving. 'And why were you crying so just now?'

'O, Diggory! don't you know me?' said she. 'But of course you don't, wrapped up like this. What do you mean? I have not been crying here, and I have not been here before.'

Venn then came nearer till he could see the illuminated side of her form.

'Mrs. Wildeve!' he exclaimed, starting. 'What a time for us to meet! And the baby too! What dreadful thing can have brought you out on such a night as this?'

She could not immediately answer ; and without asking her permission he hopped into his van, took her by the arm, and drew her up after him.

'What is it ?' he continued when they stood within.

'I have lost my way coming from Blooms-End, and I am in a great hurry to get home. Please show me as quickly as you can ! It is so silly of me not to know Egdon better, and I cannot think how I came to lose the path. Show me quickly, Diggory, please.'

'Yes, of course. I will go with 'ee. But you came to me before this, Mrs. Wildeve ?'

'I only came this minute.'

'That's strange. I was lying down here asleep about five minutes ago, with the door shut to keep out the weather, when the brushing of a woman's clothes over the heath-bushes just outside woke me up (for I don't sleep heavy), and at the same time I heard a sobbing or crying from the same woman. I opened my door and held out my lantern, and just as far as the light would reach I saw a woman : she turned her head when the light sheened on her, and then hurried on downhill. I hung up the lantern, and was curious enough to pull on my things and dog her a few steps, but I could see nothing of her any more. That was where I had been when you came up ; and when I saw you I thought you were the same one.'

'Perhaps it was one of the heath-folk going home ?'

'No, it couldn't be. 'Tis too late. The noise of her gown over the he'th was of a whistling sort that nothing but silk will make.'

'It wasn't I, then. My dress is not silk, you see. . . . Are we anywhere in a line between Mistover and the inn ?'

'Well, yes ; not far out.'

'Ah, I wonder if it was she ! Diggory, I must go at once !'

She jumped down from the van before he was aware, when Venn unhooked the lantern and leaped down after her. 'I'll take the baby, ma'am,' he said. 'You must be tired out by the weight.'

Thomasin hesitated a moment, and then delivered the baby into Venn's hands. 'Don't squeeze her, Diggory,' she said, 'or hurt her little arm ; and keep the cloak close over her like this, so that the rain may not drop in her face.'

'I will,' said Venn earnestly. 'As if I could hurt anything belonging to you ! '

'I only meant accidentally,' said Thomasin.

'The baby is dry enough, but you are pretty wet,' said the reddleman when, in closing the door of his cart to padlock it, he noticed on the floor a ring of water-drops where her cloak had hung from her.

Thomasin followed him as he wound right and left to avoid the larger bushes, stopping occasionally and covering the lantern, while he looked over his shoulder to gain some idea of the position of Rainbarrow above them, which it was necessary to keep directly behind their backs to preserve a proper course.

'You are sure the rain does not fall upon baby ? '

'Quite sure. May I ask how old he is, ma'am ? '

'He ! ' said Thomasin reproachfully. 'Anybody can see better than that in a moment. She is nearly two months old. How far is it now to the inn ? '

'A little over a quarter of a mile.'

'Will you walk a little faster ? '

'I was afraid you could not keep up.'

'I am very anxious to get there. Ah, there is a light from the window ! '

''Tis not from the window. That's a gig-lamp, to the best of my belief.'

'O ! ' said Thomasin in despair. 'I wish I had been there sooner—give me the baby, Diggory—you can go back now.'

'I must go all the way,' said Venn. 'There is a quag between us and that light, and you will walk into it up to your neck unless I take you round.'

'But the light is at the inn, and there is no quag in front of that.'

'No, the light is below the inn some two or three hundred yards.'

'Never mind,' said Thomasin hurriedly. 'Go towards the light, and not towards the inn.'

'Yes,' answered Venn, swerving round in obedience; and, after a pause, 'I wish you would tell me what this great trouble is. I think you have proved that I can be trusted.'

'There are some things that cannot be—cannot be told to——' And then her heart rose into her throat, and she could say no more.

SIGHTS AND SOUNDS DRAW THE WANDERERS TOGETHER

IX

HAVING seen Eustacia's signal from the hill at eight o'clock, Wildeve immediately prepared to assist her in her flight, and, as he hoped, accompany her. He was somewhat perturbed, and his manner of informing Thomasin that he was going on a journey was in itself sufficient to rouse her suspicions. When she had gone to bed he collected the few articles he would require, and went upstairs to the money-chest, whence he took a tolerably bountiful sum in notes, which had been advanced to him on the property he was so soon to have in possession, to defray expenses incidental to the removal.

He then went to the stable and coach-house to assure himself that the horse, gig, and harness were in a fit condition for a long drive. Nearly half an hour was spent thus, and on returning to the house Wildeve had no thought of Thomasin being anywhere but in bed. He had told the stable-lad not to stay up, leading the boy to understand that his departure would be at three or four in the morning; for this, though an exceptional hour, was less strange than midnight, the time actually agreed on, the packet from Budmouth sailing between one and two.

At last all was quiet, and he had nothing to do but to wait. By no effort could he shake off the oppression of spirits which he had experienced ever since his last meeting with Eustacia, but he hoped there was that in his situation which money could cure. He had persuaded himself that to act not ungenerously towards his gentle wife by settling on her the half of his property, and with chivalrous devotion towards another and greater woman by sharing her fate, was possible. And though he meant to adhere to Eustacia's instructions to the letter, to deposit her where she wished and to leave her, should that be her will, the spell that she had cast over him intensified, and his heart was beating fast in the anticipated futility of such commands in the face of a mutual wish that they should throw in their lot together.

He would not allow himself to dwell long upon these conjectures, maxims, and hopes, and at twenty minutes to twelve he again went softly to the stable, harnessed the horse, and lit the lamps; whence, taking the horse by the head, he led him with the covered car out of the yard to a spot by the roadside some quarter of a mile below the inn.

Here Wildeve waited, slightly sheltered from the driving rain by a high bank that had been cast up at this place. Along the surface of the road where lit by the lamps the loosened gravel and small stones scudded and clicked together before the wind, which, leaving them in heaps, plunged into the heath and boomed across the bushes into darkness. Only one sound rose above this din of weather, and that was the roaring of a ten-hatch weir to the southward, from a river in the meads which formed the boundary of the heath in this direction.

He lingered on in perfect stillness till he began to fancy that the midnight hour must have struck. A very strong doubt had arisen in his mind if Eustacia would venture down the hill in such weather; yet knowing her nature he felt that she might. 'Poor thing! 'tis like her ill-luck,' he murmured.

At length he turned to the lamp and looked at his watch.

To his surprise it was nearly a quarter past midnight. He now wished that he had driven up the circuitous road to Mistover, a plan not adopted because of the enormous length of the route in proportion to that of the pedestrian's path down the open hillside, and the consequent increase of labour for the horse.

At this moment a footstep approached; but the light of the lamps being in a different direction the comer was not visible. The step paused, then came on again.

'Eustacia?' said Wildeve.

The person came forward, and the light fell upon the form of Clym, glistening with wet, whom Wildeve immediately recognized; but Wildeve, who stood behind the lamp, was not at once recognized by Yeobright.

He stopped as if in doubt whether this waiting vehicle could have anything to do with the flight of his wife or not. The sight of Yeobright at once banished Wildeve's sober feelings, who saw him again as the deadly rival from whom Eustacia was to be kept at all hazards. Hence Wildeve did not speak, in the hope that Clym would pass by without particular inquiry.

While they both hung thus in hesitation a dull sound became audible above the storm and wind. Its origin was unmistakable—it was the fall of a body into the stream in the adjoining mead, apparently at a point near the weir.

Both started. 'Good God! can it be she?' said Clym.

'Why should it be she?' said Wildeve, in his alarm forgetting that he had hitherto screened himself.

'Ah!—that's you, you traitor, is it?' cried Yeobright. 'Why should it be she? Because last week she would have put an end to her life if she had been able. She ought to have been watched! Take one of the lamps and come with me.'

Yeobright seized the one on his side and hastened on; Wildeve did not wait to unfasten the other, but followed at once along the meadow-track to the weir, a little in the rear of Clym.

Shadwater Weir had at its foot a large circular pool, fifty feet in diameter, into which the water flowed through ten huge hatches, raised and lowered by a winch and cogs in the ordinary manner. The sides of the pool were of masonry, to prevent the water from washing away the bank; but the force of the stream in winter was sometimes such as to undermine the retaining wall and precipitate it into the hole. Clym reached the hatches, the framework of which was shaken to its foundations by the velocity of the current. Nothing but the froth of the waves could be discerned in the pool below. He got upon the plank bridge over the race, and holding to the rail, that the wind might not blow him off, crossed to the other side of the river. There he leant over the wall and lowered the lamp, only to behold the vortex formed at the curl of the returning current.

Wildeve meanwhile had arrived on the former side, and the light from Yeobright's lamp shed a flecked and agitated radiance across the weir-pool, revealing to the ex-engineer the tumbling courses of the currents from the hatches above. Across this gashed and puckered mirror a dark body was slowly borne by one of the backward currents.

'O, my darling!' exclaimed Wildeve in an agonized voice; and, without showing sufficient presence of mind even to throw off his great-coat, he leaped into the boiling caldron.

Yeobright could now also discern the floating body, though but indistinctly; and imagining from Wildeve's plunge that there was life to be saved he was about to leap after. Bethinking himself of a wiser plan he placed the lamp against a post to make it stand upright, and running round to the lower part of the pool, where there was no wall, he sprang in and boldly waded upwards towards the deeper portion. Here he was taken off his legs, and in swimming was carried round into the centre of the basin, where he perceived Wildeve struggling.

While these hasty actions were in progress here, Venn

and Thomasin had been toiling through the lower corner of the heath in the direction of the light. They had not been near enough to the river to hear the plunge, but they saw the removal of the carriage-lamp, and watched its motion into the mead. As soon as they reached the car and horse Venn guessed that something new was amiss, and hastened to follow in the course of the moving light. Venn walked faster than Thomasin, and came to the weir alone.

The lamp placed against the post by Clym still shone across the water, and the reddleman observed something floating motionless. Being encumbered with the infant he ran back to meet Thomasin.

'Take the baby, please, Mrs. Wildeve,' he said hastily. 'Run home with her, call the stable-lad, and make him send down to me any men who may be living near. Somebody has fallen into the weir.'

Thomasin took the child and ran. When she came to the covered car the horse, though fresh from the stable, was standing perfectly still, as if conscious of misfortune. She saw for the first time whose it was. She nearly fainted, and would have been unable to proceed another step but that the necessity of preserving the little girl from harm nerved her to an amazing self-control. In this agony of suspense she entered the house, put the baby in a place of safety, woke the lad and the female domestic, and ran out to give the alarm at the nearest cottage.

Diggory, having returned to the brink of the pool, observed that the small upper hatches or floats were withdrawn. He found one of these lying upon the grass, and taking it under one arm, and with his lantern in his hand, entered at the bottom of the pool as Clym had done. As soon as he began to be in deep water he flung himself across the hatch; thus supported he was able to keep afloat as long as he chose, holding the lantern aloft with his disengaged hand. Propelled by his feet he steered round and round the pool, ascending each time by one of the back streams and descending in the middle of the current.

At first he could see nothing. Then amidst the glistening of the whirlpools and the white clots of foam he distinguished a woman's bonnet floating alone. His search was now under the left wall, when something came to the surface almost close beside him. It was not, as he had expected, a woman, but a man. The reddleman put the ring of the lantern between his teeth, seized the floating man by the collar, and, holding on to the hatch with his remaining arm, struck out into the strongest race, by which the unconscious man, the hatch, and himself were carried down the stream. As soon as Venn found his feet dragging over the pebbles of the shallower part below he secured his footing and waded towards the brink. There, where the water stood at about the height of his waist, he flung away the hatch, and attempted to drag forth the man. This was a matter of great difficulty, and he found as the reason that the legs of the unfortunate stranger were tightly embraced by the arms of another man, who had hitherto been entirely beneath the surface.

At this moment his heart bounded to hear footsteps running towards him, and two men, roused by Thomasin, appeared at the brink above. They ran to where Venn was, and helped him in lifting out the apparently drowned persons, separating them, and laying them out upon the grass. Venn turned the light upon their faces. The one who had been uppermost was Yeobright; he who had been completely submerged was Wildeve.

'Now we must search the hole again,' said Venn. 'A woman is in there somewhere. Get a pole.'

One of the men went to the foot-bridge and tore off the handrail. The reddleman and the two others then entered the water together from below as before, and with their united force probed the pool forwards to where it sloped down to its central depth. Venn was not mistaken in supposing that any person who had sunk for the last time would be washed down to this point, for when they had examined to about half-way across something impeded their thrust.

'Pull it forward,' said Venn, and they raked it in with the pole till it was close to their feet.

Venn vanished under the stream, and came up with an armful of wet drapery enclosing a woman's cold form, which was all that remained of the desperate Eustacia.

When they reached the bank there stood Thomasin, in a stress of grief, bending over the two unconscious ones who already lay there. The horse and car were brought to the nearest point in the road, and it was the work of a few minutes only to place the three in the vehicle. Venn led on the horse, supporting Thomasin upon his arm, and the two men followed, till they reached the inn.

The woman who had been shaken out of her sleep by Thomasin had hastily dressed herself and lighted a fire, the other servant being left to snore on in peace at the back of the house. The insensible forms of Eustacia, Clym, and Wildeve were then brought in and laid on the carpet, with their feet to the fire, when such restorative processes as could be thought of were adopted at once, the stableman being in the meantime sent for a doctor. But there seemed to be not a whiff of life left in either of the bodies. Then Thomasin, whose stupor of grief had been thrust off awhile by frantic action, applied a bottle of hartshorn to Clym's nostrils, having tried it in vain upon the other two. He sighed.

'Clym's alive!' she exclaimed.

He soon breathed distinctly, and again and again did she attempt to revive her husband by the same means; but Wildeve gave no sign. There was too much reason to think that he and Eustacia both were for ever beyond the reach of stimulating perfumes. Their exertions did not relax till the doctor arrived, when, one by one, the senseless three were taken upstairs and put into warm beds.

Venn soon felt himself relieved from further attendance, and went to the door, scarcely able yet to realize the strange catastrophe that had befallen the family in which he took so great an interest. Thomasin surely would be broken down by the sudden and overwhelming nature of this event. No firm and sensible Mrs. Yeobright lived now to support the gentle girl through the ordeal; and, whatever an unimpassioned spectator might think of her loss of such a husband as Wildeve, there could be no doubt that for the moment she was distracted and horrified by the blow. As for himself, not being privileged to go to her and comfort her, he saw no reason for waiting longer in a house where he remained only as a stranger.

He returned across the heath to his van. The fire was not yet out, and everything remained as he had left it. Venn now bethought himself of his clothes, which were saturated with water to the weight of lead. He changed them, spread them before the fire, and lay down to sleep. But it was more than he could do to rest here while excited by a vivid imagination of the turmoil they were in at the house he had quitted, and, blaming himself for coming away, he dressed in another suit, locked up the door, and again hastened across to the inn. Rain was still falling heavily when he entered the kitchen. A bright fire was shining from the hearth, and two women were bustling about, one of whom was Olly Dowden.

'Well, how is it going on now?' said Venn in a whisper.

'Mr. Yeobright is better; but Mrs. Yeobright and Mr. Wildeve are dead and cold. The doctor says they were quite gone before they were out of the water.'

'Ah! I thought as much when I hauled 'em up. And Mrs. Wildeve?'

'She is as well as can be expected. The doctor had her put between blankets, for she was almost as wet as they that had been in the river, poor young thing. You don't seem very dry, reddleman.'

'O, 'tis not much. I have changed my things. This is only a little dampness I've got coming through the rain again.'

'Stand by the fire. Mis'ess says you be to have whatever you want, and she was sorry when she was told that you'd gone away.'

Venn drew near to the fireplace, and looked into the flames in an absent mood. The steam came from his leggings and ascended the chimney with the smoke, while he thought of those who were upstairs. Two were corpses, one had barely escaped the jaws of death, another was sick and a widow. The last occasion on which he had lingered by that fireplace was when the raffle was in progress; when Wildeve was alive and well; Thomasin active and smiling in the next room; Yeobright and Eustacia just made husband and wife, and Mrs. Yeobright living at Blooms-End. It had seemed at that time that the then position of affairs was good for at least twenty years to come. Yet, of all the circle, he himself was the only one whose situation had not materially changed.

While he ruminated a footstep descended the stairs. It was the nurse, who brought in her hand a rolled mass of wet paper. The woman was so engrossed with her occupation that she hardly saw Venn. She took from a cupboard some pieces of twine, which she strained across the fireplace, tying the end of each piece to the firedog, previously pulled forward for the purpose, and, unrolling the wet papers, she began pinning them one by one to the strings in a manner of clothes on a line.

'What be they?' said Venn.

'Poor master's bank-notes,' she answered. 'They were found in his pocket when they undressed him.'

'Then he was not coming back again for some time?' said Venn.

'That we shall never know,' said she.

Venn was loth to depart, for all on earth that interested him lay under this roof. As nobody in the house had any more sleep that night, except the two who slept for ever, there was no reason why he should not remain. So he retired into the niche of the fireplace where he had used to sit, and there he continued, watching the steam from the double row of bank-notes as they waved backwards and forwards in the draught of the chimney till their flaccidity was changed to dry crispness throughout. Then the woman came and unpinned them, and, folding them together, carried the handful upstairs. Presently the doctor appeared from above with the look of a man who could do no more, and, pulling on his gloves, went out of the house, the trotting of his horse soon dying away upon the road.

At four o'clock there was a gentle knock at the door. It was from Charley, who had been sent by Captain Vye to inquire if anything had been heard of Eustacia. The girl who admitted him looked in his face as if she did not know what answer to return, and showed him in to where Venn was seated, saying to the reddleman, 'Will you tell him, please?'

Venn told. Charley's only utterance was a feeble, indistinct sound. He stood quite still; then he burst out spasmodically, 'I shall see her once more?'

'I dare say you may see her,' said Diggory gravely. 'But hadn't you better run and tell Captain Vye?'

'Yes, yes. Only I do hope I shall see her just once again.'

'You shall,' said a low voice behind; and starting round they beheld by the dim light a thin, pallid, almost spectral form, wrapped in a blanket, and looking like Lazarus coming from the tomb.

It was Yeobright. Neither Venn nor Charley spoke, and Clym continued: 'You shall see her. There will be time enough to tell the captain when it gets daylight. You would like to see her too—would you not, Diggory? She looks very beautiful now.'

Venn assented by rising to his feet, and with Charley

he followed Clym to the foot of the staircase, where he took off his boots; Charley did the same. They followed Yeobright upstairs to the landing, where there was a candle burning, which Yeobright took in his hand, and with it led the way into an adjoining room. Here he went to the bedside and folded back the sheet.

They stood silently looking upon Eustacia, who, as she lay there still in death, eclipsed all her living phases. Pallor did not include all the quality of her complexion, which seemed more than whiteness; it was almost light. The expression of her finely carved mouth was pleasant, as if a sense of dignity had just compelled her to leave off speaking. Eternal rigidity had seized upon it in a momentary transition between fervour and resignation. Her black hair was looser now than either of them had ever seen it before, and surrounded her brow like a forest. The stateliness of look which had been almost too marked for a dweller in a country domicile had at last found an artistically happy background.

Nobody spoke, till at length Clym covered her and turned aside. 'Now come here,' he said.

They went to a recess in the same room, and there, on a smaller bed, lay another figure—Wildeve. Less repose was visible in his face than in Eustacia's, but the same luminous youthfulness overspread it, and the least sympathetic observer would have felt at sight of him now that he was born for a higher destiny than this. The only sign upon him of his recent struggle for life was in his finger-tips, which were worn and scarified in his dying endeavours to obtain a hold on the face of the weir-wall.

Yeobright's manner had been so quiet, he had uttered so few syllables since his reappearance, that Venn imagined him resigned. It was only when they had left the room and stood upon the landing that the true state of his mind was apparent. Here he said, with a wild smile, inclining his head towards the chamber in which Eustacia lay,

'She is the second woman I have killed this year. I was a great cause of my mother's death; and I am the chief cause of hers.'

'How?' said Venn.

'I spoke cruel words to her, and she left my house. I did not invite her back till it was too late. It is I who ought to have drowned myself. It would have been a charity to the living had the river overwhelmed me and borne her up. But I cannot die. Those who ought to have lived lie dead; and here am I alive!'

'But you can't charge yourself with crimes in that way,' said Venn. 'You may as well say that the parents be the cause of a murder by the child, for without the parents the child would never have been begot.'

'Yes, Venn, that is very true; but you don't know all the circumstances. If it had pleased God to put an end to me it would have been a good thing for all. But I am getting used to the horror of my existence. They say that a time comes when men laugh at misery through long acquaintance with it. Surely that time will soon come to me!'

'Your aim has always been good,' said Venn. 'Why should you say such desperate things?'

'No, they are not desperate. They are only hopeless; and my great regret is that for what I have done no man or law can punish me!'

BOOK SIXTH

AFTERCOURSES

THE INEVITABLE MOVEMENT ONWARD

I

THE story of the deaths of Eustacia and Wildeve was told throughout Egdon, and far beyond, for many weeks and months. All the known incidents of their love were enlarged, distorted, touched up, and modified, till the original reality bore but a slight resemblance to the counterfeit presentation by surrounding tongues. Yet, upon the whole, neither the man nor the woman lost dignity by sudden death. Misfortune had struck them gracefully, cutting off their erratic histories with a catastrophic dash, instead of, as with many, attenuating each life to an uninteresting meagreness, through long years of wrinkles, neglect, and decay.

On those most nearly concerned the effect was somewhat different. Strangers who had heard of many such cases now merely heard of one more; but immediately where a blow falls no previous imaginings amount to appreciable preparation for it. The very suddenness of her bereavement dulled, to some extent, Thomasin's feelings; yet, irrationally enough, a consciousness that the husband she had lost ought to have been a better man did not lessen her mourning at all. On the contrary, this fact seemed at first to set off the dead husband in his young wife's eyes, and to be the necessary cloud to the rainbow.

But the horrors of the unknown had passed. Vague

misgivings about her future as a deserted wife were at an end. The worst had once been matter of trembling conjecture; it was now matter of reason only, a limited badness. Her chief interest, the little Eustacia, still remained. There was humility in her grief, no defiance in her attitude; and when this is the case a shaken spirit is apt to be stilled.

Could Thomasin's mournfulness now and Eustacia's serenity during life have been reduced to common measure, they would have touched the same mark nearly. But Thomasin's former brightness made shadow of that which in a sombre atmosphere was light itself.

The spring came and calmed her; the summer came and soothed her; the autumn arrived, and she began to be comforted, for her little girl was strong and happy, growing in size and knowledge every day. Outward events flattered Thomasin not a little. Wildeve had died intestate, and she and the child were his only relatives. When administration had been granted, all the debts paid, and the residue of her husband's uncle's property had come into her hands, it was found that the sum waiting to be invested for her own and the child's benefit was little less than ten thousand pounds.

Where should she live? The obvious place was Blooms-End. The old rooms, it is true, were not much higher than the between-decks of a frigate, necessitating a sinking in the floor under the new clock-case she brought from the inn, and the removal of the handsome brass knobs on its head, before there was height for it to stand; but, such as the rooms were, there were plenty of them, and the place was endeared to her by every early recollection. Clym very gladly admitted her as a tenant, confining his own existence to two rooms at the top of the back staircase, where he lived on quietly, shut off from Thomasin and the three servants she had thought fit to indulge in now that she was a mistress of money, going his own ways, and thinking his own thoughts.

His sorrows had made some change in his outward appearance; and yet the alteration was chiefly within. It might have been said that he had a wrinkled mind. He had no enemies, and he could get nobody to reproach him, which was why he so bitterly reproached himself.

He did sometimes think he had been ill-used by fortune, so far as to say that to be born is a palpable dilemma, and that instead of men aiming to advance in life with glory they should calculate how to retreat out of it without shame. But that he and his had been sarcastically and pitilessly handled in having such irons thrust into their souls he did not maintain long. It is usually so, except with the sternest of men. Human beings, in their generous endeavour to construct a hypothesis that shall not degrade a First Cause, have always hesitated to conceive a dominant power of lower moral quality than their own; and, even while they sit down and weep by the waters of Babylon, invent excuses for the oppression which prompts their tears.

Thus, though words of solace were vainly uttered in his presence, he found relief in a direction of his own choosing when left to himself. For a man of his habits the house and the hundred and twenty pounds a year which he had inherited from his mother were enough to supply all worldly needs. Resources do not depend upon gross amounts, but upon the proportion of spendings to takings.

He frequently walked the heath alone, when the past seized upon him with its shadowy hand, and held him there to listen to its tale. His imagination would then people the spot with its ancient inhabitants: forgotten Celtic tribes trod their tracks about him, and he could almost live among them, look in their faces, and see them standing beside the barrows which swelled around, untouched and perfect as at the time of their erection. Those of the dyed barbarians who had chosen the cultivable tracts were, in comparison with those who had left their marks here, as writers on paper beside writers on parchment. Their records had perished long ago by the plough, while the works of these remained. Yet they all had lived and died unconscious of the different fates awaiting their relics. It reminded him that unforeseen factors operate in the evolution of immortality.

Winter again came round, with its winds, frosts, tame robins, and sparkling starlight. The year previous Thomasin had hardly been conscious of the season's advance; this year she laid her heart open to external influences of every kind. The life of this sweet cousin, her baby, and her servants, came to Clym's senses only in the form of sounds through a wood partition as he sat over books of exceptionally large type; but his ear became at last so accustomed to these slight noises from the other part of the house that he almost could witness the scenes they signified. A faint beat of half-seconds conjured up Thomasin rocking the cradle, a wavering hum meant that she was singing the baby to sleep, a crunching of sand as between millstones raised the picture of Humphrey's, Fairway's, or Sam's heavy feet crossing the stone floor of the kitchen; a light boyish step, and a gay tune in a high key, betokened a visit from Grandfer Cantle; a sudden break-off in the Grandfer's utterances implied the application to his lips of a mug of small beer; a bustling and slamming of doors meant starting to go to market; for Thomasin, in spite of her added scope for gentility, led a ludicrously narrow life, to the end that she might save every possible pound for her little daughter.

One summer day Clym was in the garden, immediately outside the parlour-window, which was as usual open. He was looking at the pot-flowers on the sill; they had been revived and restored by Thomasin to the state in which his mother had left them. He heard a slight scream from Thomasin, who was sitting inside the room.

'O, how you frightened me!' she said to some one who had entered. 'I thought you were the ghost of yourself.'

Clym was curious enough to advance a little further and look in at the window. To his astonishment there stood within the room Diggory Venn, no longer a reddleman, but exhibiting the strangely altered hues of an ordinary Christian countenance, white shirt-front, light flowered waistcoat, blue-spotted neckerchief, and bottle-green coat. Nothing in this appearance was at all singular but the fact of its great difference from what he had formerly been. Red, and all approach to red, was carefully excluded from every article of clothes upon him ; for what is there that persons just out of harness dread so much as reminders of the trade which has enriched them ?

Yeobright went round to the door and entered.

'I was so alarmed !' said Thomasin, smiling from one to the other. 'I couldn't believe that he had got white of his own accord ! It seemed supernatural.'

'I gave up dealing in reddle last Christmas,' said Venn. 'It was a profitable trade, and I found that by that time I had made enough to take the dairy of fifty cows that my father had in his lifetime. I always thought of getting to that place again if I changed at all ; and now I am there.'

'How did you manage to become white, Diggory ?' Thomasin asked.

'I turned so by degrees, ma'am.'

'You look much better than ever you did before.'

Venn appeared confused ; and Thomasin, seeing how inadvertently she had spoken to a man who might possibly have tender feelings for her still, blushed a little. Clym saw nothing of this, and added good-humouredly—

'What shall we have to frighten Thomasin's baby with, now you have become a human being again ?'

'Sit down, Diggory,' said Thomasin, 'and stay to tea.'

Venn moved as if he would retire to the kitchen, when Thomasin said with pleasant pertness as she went on with some sewing, 'Of course you must sit down here. And where does your fifty-cow dairy lie, Mr. Venn ?'

'At Stickleford—about two miles to the right of Alderworth, ma'am, where the meads begin. I have thought that if Mr. Yeobright would like to pay me a visit sometimes he shouldn't stay away for want of asking. I'll not bide to tea this afternoon, thank'ee, for I've got something on hand that must be settled. 'Tis Maypole-day to-morrow, and the Shadwater folk have clubbed with a few of your neighbours here to have a pole just outside your palings in the heath, as it is a nice green place.' Venn waved his elbow towards the patch in front of the house. 'I have been talking to Fairway about it,' he continued, 'and I said to him that before we put up the pole it would be as well to ask Mrs. Wildeve.'

'I can say nothing against it,' she answered. 'Our property does not reach an inch further than the white palings.'

'But you might not like to see a lot of folk going crazy round a stick, under your very nose?'

'I shall have no objection at all.'

Venn soon after went away, and in the evening Yeobright strolled as far as Fairway's cottage. It was a lovely May sunset, and the birch trees which grew on this margin of the vast Egdon wilderness had put on their new leaves, delicate as butterflies' wings, and diaphanous as amber. Beside Fairway's dwelling was an open space recessed from the road, and here were now collected all the young people from within a radius of a couple of miles. The pole lay with one end supported on a trestle, and women were engaged in wreathing it from the top downwards with wild-flowers. The instincts of merry England lingered on here with exceptional vitality, and the symbolic customs which tradition has attached to each season of the year were yet a reality on Egdon. Indeed, the impulses of all such outlandish hamlets are pagan still: in these spots homage to nature, self-adoration, frantic gaieties, fragments of Teutonic rites to divinities whose names are forgotten, seem in some way or other to have survived mediæval doctrine.

Yeobright did not interrupt the preparations, and went home again. The next morning, when Thomasin withdrew the curtains of her bedroom window, there stood the Maypole in the middle of the green, its top cutting into the sky. It had sprung up in the night, or rather early morning, like Jack's bean-stalk. She opened the casement to get a better view of the garlands and posies that adorned it. The sweet perfume of the flowers had already spread into the surrounding air, which, being free from every taint, conducted to her lips a full measure of the fragrance received from the spire of blossom in its midst. At the top of the pole were crossed hoops decked with small flowers; beneath these came a milk-white zone of Maybloom; then a zone of bluebells, then of cowslips, then of lilacs, then of ragged-robins, daffodils, and so on, till the lowest stage was reached. Thomasin noticed all these, and was delighted that the May-revel was to be so near.

When afternoon came people began to gather on the green, and Yeobright was interested enough to look out upon them from the open window of his room. Soon after this Thomasin walked out from the door immediately below and turned her eyes up to her cousin's face. She was dressed more gaily than Yeobright had ever seen her dress since the time of Wildeve's death, eighteen months before; since the day of her marriage even she had not exhibited herself to such advantage.

'How pretty you look to-day, Thomasin!' he said. 'Is it because of the Maypole?'

'Not altogether.' And then she blushed and dropped her eyes, which he did not specially observe, though her manner seemed to him to be rather peculiar, considering that she was only addressing himself. Could it be possible that she had put on her summer clothes to please him?

He recalled her conduct towards him throughout the

last few weeks, when they had often been working together in the garden, just as they had formerly done when they were boy and girl under his mother's eye. What if her interest in him were not so entirely that of a relative as it had formerly been? To Yeobright any possibility of this sort was a serious matter; and he almost felt troubled at the thought of it. Every pulse of loverlike feeling which had not been stilled during Eustacia's lifetime had gone into the grave with her. His passion for her had occurred too far on in his manhood to leave fuel enough on hand for another fire of that sort, as may happen with more boyish loves. Even supposing him capable of loving again, that love would be a plant of slow and laboured growth, and in the end only small and sickly, like an autumn-hatched bird.

He was so distressed by this new complexity that when the enthusiastic brass band arrived and struck up, which it did about five o'clock, with apparently wind enough among its members to blow down his house, he withdrew from his rooms by the back door, went down the garden, through the gate in the hedge, and away out of sight. He could not bear to remain in the presence of enjoyment to-day, though he had tried hard.

Nothing was seen of him for four hours. When he came back by the same path it was dusk, and the dews were coating every green thing. The boisterous music had ceased; but, entering the premises as he did from behind, he could not see if the May party had all gone till he had passed through Thomasin's division of the house to the front door. Thomasin was standing within the porch alone.

She looked at him reproachfully. 'You went away just when it began, Clym,' she said.

'Yes. I felt I could not join in. You went out with them, of course?'

'No, I did not.'

'You appeared to be dressed on purpose.'

'Yes, but I could not go out alone; so many people were there. One is there now.'

Yeobright strained his eyes across the dark-green patch beyond the paling, and near the black form of the Maypole he discerned a shadowy figure, sauntering idly up and down. 'Who is it?' he said.

'Mr. Venn,' said Thomasin.

'You might have asked him to come in, I think, Tamsie. He has been very kind to you first and last.'

'I will now,' she said; and, acting on the impulse, went through the wicket to where Venn stood under the Maypole.

'It is Mr. Venn, I think?' she inquired.

Venn started as if he had not seen her—artful man that he was—and said, 'Yes.'

'Will you come in?'

'I am afraid that I——'

'I have seen you dancing this evening, and you had the very best of the girls for your partners. Is it that you won't come in because you wish to stand here, and think over the past hours of enjoyment?'

'Well, that's partly it,' said Mr. Venn, with ostentatious sentiment. 'But the main reason why I am biding here like this is that I want to wait till the moon rises.'

'To see how pretty the Maypole looks in the moonlight?'

'No. To look for a glove that was dropped by one of the maidens.'

Thomasin was speechless with surprise. That a man who had to walk some four or five miles to his home should wait here for such a reason pointed to only one conclusion: the man must be amazingly interested in that glove's owner.

'Were you dancing with her, Diggory?' she asked, in a voice which revealed that he had made himself considerably more interesting to her by this disclosure.

'No,' he sighed.

'And you will not come in, then?'

'Not to-night, thank you, ma'am.'

'Shall I lend you a lantern to look for the young person's glove, Mr. Venn?'

'O no; it is not necessary, Mrs. Wildeve, thank you. The moon will rise in a few minutes.'

Thomasin went back to the porch. 'Is he coming in?' said Clym, who had been waiting where she had left him.

'He would rather not to-night,' she said, and then passed by him into the house; whereupon Clym too retired to his own rooms.

When Clym was gone Thomasin crept upstairs in the dark, and, just listening by the cot, to assure herself that the child was asleep, she went to the window, gently lifted the corner of the white curtain, and looked out. Venn was still there. She watched the growth of the faint radiance appearing in the sky by the eastern hill, till presently the edge of the moon burst upwards and flooded the valley with light. Diggory's form was now distinct on the green; he was moving about in a bowed attitude, evidently scanning the grass for the precious missing article, walking in zigzags right and left till he should have passed over every foot of the ground.

'How very ridiculous!' Thomasin murmured to herself, in a tone which was intended to be satirical. 'To think that a man should be so silly as to go mooning about like that for a girl's glove! A respectable dairyman, too, and a man of money as he is now. What a pity!'

At last Venn appeared to find it; whereupon he stood up and raised it to his lips. Then placing it in his breast-pocket—the nearest receptacle to a man's heart permitted by modern raiment—he ascended the valley in a mathematically direct line towards his distant home in the meadows.

THOMASIN WALKS IN A GREEN PLACE BY THE ROMAN ROAD

II

CLYM saw little of Thomasin for several days after this; and when they met she was more silent than usual. At length he asked her what she was thinking of so intently.

'I am thoroughly perplexed,' she said candidly. 'I cannot for my life think who it is that Diggory Venn is so much in love with. None of the girls at the Maypole were good enough for him, and yet she must have been there.'

Clym tried to imagine Venn's choice for a moment; but ceasing to be interested in the question he went on again with his gardening.

No clearing up of the mystery was granted her for some time. But one afternoon Thomasin was upstairs getting ready for a walk, when she had occasion to come to the landing and call 'Rachel.' Rachel was a girl about thirteen, who carried the baby out for airings; and she came upstairs at the call.

'Have you seen one of my last new gloves about the house, Rachel?' inquired Thomasin. 'It is the fellow to this one.'

Rachel did not reply.

'Why don't you answer?' said her mistress.

'I think it is lost, ma'am.'

'Lost? Who lost it? I have never worn them but once.'

Rachel appeared as one dreadfully troubled, and at last began to cry. 'Please, ma'am, on the day of the Maypole I had none to wear, and I seed yours on the table, and I thought I would borrow 'em. I did not mean to hurt 'em at all, but one of them got lost. Somebody gave me some money to buy another pair for you, but I have not been able to go anywhere to get 'em.'

'Who's somebody?'

'Mr. Venn.'

'Did he know it was my glove?'

'Yes. I told him.'

Thomasin was so surprised by the explanation that she quite forgot to lecture the girl, who glided silently away. Thomasin did not move further than to turn her eyes upon the grass-plat where the Maypole had stood. She remained thinking, then said to herself that she would not go out that afternoon, but would work hard at the baby's unfinished lovely plaid frock, cut on the cross in the newest fashion. How she managed to work hard, and yet do no more than she had done at the end of two hours, would have been a mystery to any one not aware that the recent incident was of a kind likely to divert her industry from a manual to a mental channel.

Next day she went her ways as usual, and continued her custom of walking in the heath with no other companion than little Eustacia, now of the age when it is a matter of doubt with such characters whether they are intended to walk through the world on their hands or on their feet; so that they get into painful complications by trying both. It was very pleasant to Thomasin, when she had carried the child to some lonely place, to give her a little private practice on the green turf and shepherd's-thyme, which formed a soft mat to fall headlong upon when equilibrium was lost.

Once, when engaged in this system of training, and stooping to remove bits of stick, fern-stalks, and other such fragments from the child's path, that the journey might not be brought to an untimely end by some insuperable barrier a quarter of an inch high, she was alarmed by discovering that a man on horseback was almost close beside her, the soft natural carpet having muffled the horse's tread. The rider, who was Venn, waved his hat in the air and bowed gallantly.

'Diggory, give me my glove,' said Thomasin, whose manner it was under any circumstances to plunge into the midst of a subject which engrossed her.

Venn immediately dismounted, put his hand in his breast-pocket, and handed the glove.

'Thank you. It was very good of you to take care of it.'

'It is very good of you to say so.'

'O no. I was quite glad to find you had it. Everybody gets so indifferent that I was surprised to know you thought of me.'

'If you had remembered what I was once you wouldn't have been surprised.'

'Ah, no,' she said quickly. 'But men of your character are mostly so independent.'

'What is my character?' he asked.

'I don't exactly know,' said Thomasin simply, 'except it is to cover up your feelings under a practical manner, and only to show them when you are alone.'

'Ah, how do you know that?' said Venn strategically.

'Because,' said she, stopping to put the little girl, who had managed to get herself upside down, right end up again, 'because I do.'

'You mustn't judge by folks in general,' said Venn. 'Still I don't know much what feelings are now-a-days. I have got so mixed up with business of one sort and t'other that my soft sentiments are gone off in vapour like. Yes, I am given up body and soul to the making of money. Money is all my dream.'

'O Diggory, how wicked!' said Thomasin reproachfully, and looking at him in exact balance between taking his words seriously and judging them as said to tease her.

'Yes, 'tis rather a rum course,' said Venn, in the bland tone of one comfortably resigned to sins he could no longer overcome.

'You, who used to be so nice!'

'Well, that's an argument I rather like, because what a man has once been he may be again.' Thomasin blushed. 'Except that it is rather harder now,' Venn continued.

'Why?' she asked.

'Because you be richer than you were at that time.'

'O no—not much. I have made it nearly all over to the baby, as it was my duty to do, except just enough to live on.'

'I am rather glad of that,' said Venn softly, and regarding her from the corner of his eye, 'for it makes it easier for us to be friendly.'

Thomasin blushed again, and, when a few more words had been said of a not unpleasing kind, Venn mounted his horse and rode on.

This conversation had passed in a hollow of the heath near the old Roman road, a place much frequented by Thomasin. And it might have been observed that she did not in future walk that way less often from having met Venn there now. Whether or not Venn abstained from riding thither because he had met Thomasin in the same place might easily have been guessed from her proceedings about two months later in the same year.

THE SERIOUS DISCOURSE

OF CLYM WITH HIS COUSIN

III

THROUGHOUT this period Yeobright had more or less pondered on his duty to his cousin Thomasin. He could not help feeling that it would be a pitiful waste of sweet material if the tender-natured thing should be doomed from this early stage of her life onwards to dribble away her winsome qualities on lonely gorse and fern. But he felt this as an economist merely, and not as a lover. His passion for Eustacia had been a sort of conserve of his whole life, and he had nothing more of that supreme quality left to bestow. So far the obvious thing was not to entertain any idea of marriage with Thomasin, even to oblige her.

But this was not all. Years ago there had been in his mother's mind a great fancy about Thomasin and himself. It had not positively amounted to a desire, but it had always been a favourite dream. That they should be man and wife in good time, if the happiness of neither were endangered thereby, was the fancy in question. So that what course save one was there now left for any son who reverenced his mother's memory as Yeobright did? It is an unfortunate fact that any particular whim of parents, which might have been dispersed by half an hour's conversation during their lives, becomes sublimated by their deaths into a fiat the most absolute, with such results to conscientious children as those parents, had they lived, would have been the first to decry.

Had only Yeobright's own future been involved he would have proposed to Thomasin with a ready heart. He had nothing to lose by carrying out a dead mother's hope. But he dreaded to contemplate Thomasin wedded to the mere corpse of a lover that he now felt himself to be. He had but three activities alive in him. One was his almost daily walk to the little graveyard wherein his mother lay; another, his just as frequent visits by night to the more distant enclosure which numbered his Eustacia among its dead; the third was self-preparation for a vocation which alone seemed likely to satisfy his cravings —that of an itinerant preacher of the eleventh commandment. It was difficult to believe that Thomasin would be cheered by a husband with such tendencies as these.

Yet he resolved to ask her, and let her decide for herself. It was even with a pleasant sense of doing his duty that he went downstairs to her one evening for this purpose, when the sun was printing on the valley the same long shadow of the housetop that he had seen lying there times out of number while his mother lived.

Thomasin was not in her room, and he found her in the front garden. 'I have long been wanting, Thomasin,' he began, 'to say something about a matter that concerns both our futures.'

'And you are going to say it now?' she remarked quickly, colouring as she met his gaze. 'Do stop a minute, Clym, and let me speak first, for, oddly enough, I have been wanting to say something to you.'

'By all means say on, Tamsie.'

'I suppose nobody can overhear us?' she went on, casting her eyes around and lowering her voice. 'Well, first you will promise me this—that you won't be angry and call me anything harsh if you disagree with what I propose?'

Yeobright promised, and she continued: 'What I want is your advice, for you are my relation—I mean, a sort of guardian to me—aren't you, Clym?'

'Well, yes, I suppose I am; a sort of guardian. In fact, I am, of course,' he said, altogether perplexed as to her drift.

'I am thinking of marrying,' she then observed blandly. 'But I shall not marry unless you assure me that you approve of such a step. Why don't you speak?'

'I was taken rather by surprise. But, nevertheless, I am very glad to hear such news. I shall approve, of course, dear Tamsie. Who can it be? I am quite at a loss to guess. No, I am not—'tis the old doctor!—not that I mean to call him old, for he is not very old after all. Ah—I noticed when he attended you last time!'

'No, no,' she said hastily. ''Tis Mr. Venn.'

Clym's face suddenly became grave.

'There, now, you don't like him, and I wish I hadn't mentioned him!' she exclaimed almost petulantly. 'And I shouldn't have done it, either, only he keeps on bothering me so till I don't know what to do!'

Clym looked at the heath. 'I like Venn well enough,' he answered at last. 'He is a very honest and at the same time astute man. He is clever too, as is proved by his having got you to favour him. But really, Thomasin, he is not quite——'

'Gentleman enough for me? That is just what I feel. I am sorry now that I asked you, and I won't think any more of him. At the same time I must marry him if I marry anybody—that I *will* say!'

'I don't see that,' said Clym, carefully concealing every clue to his own interrupted intention, which she plainly had not guessed. 'You might marry a professional man, or somebody of that sort, by going into the town to live and forming acquaintances there.'

'I am not fit for town life—so very rural and silly

as I always have been. Do not you yourself notice my countrified ways?'

'Well, when I came home from Paris I did, a little; but I don't now.'

'That's because you have got countrified too. O, I couldn't live in a street for the world! Egdon is a ridiculous old place; but I have got used to it, and I couldn't be happy anywhere else at all.'

'Neither could I,' said Clym.

'Then how could you say that I should marry some town man? I am sure, say what you will, that I must marry Diggory, if I marry at all. He has been kinder to me than anybody else, and has helped me in many ways that I don't know of!' Thomasin almost pouted now.

'Yes, he has,' said Clym in a neutral tone. 'Well, I wish with all my heart that I could say, marry him. But I cannot forget what my mother thought on that matter, and it goes rather against me not to respect her opinion. There is too much reason why we should do the little we can to respect it now.'

'Very well, then,' sighed Thomasin. 'I will say no more.'

'But you are not bound to obey my wishes. I merely say what I think.'

'O no—I don't want to be rebellious in that way,' she said sadly. 'I had no business to think of him—I ought to have thought of my family. What dreadfully bad impulses there are in me!' Her lip trembled, and she turned away to hide a tear.

Clym, though vexed at what seemed her unaccountable taste, was in a measure relieved to find that at any rate the marriage question in relation to himself was shelved. Through several succeeding days he saw her at different times from the window of his room moping disconsolately about the garden. He was half angry with her for choosing Venn; then he was grieved at having put himself in the way of Venn's happiness, who was, after all, as honest and persevering a young fellow as any on Egdon, since he had turned over a new leaf. In short, Clym did not know what to do.

When next they met she said abruptly, 'He is much more respectable now than he was then!'

'Who? O yes—Diggory Venn.'

'Aunt only objected because he was a reddleman.'

'Well, Thomasin, perhaps I don't know all the particulars of my mother's wish. So you had better use your own discretion.'

'You will always feel that I slighted your mother's memory.'

'No, I will not. I shall think you are convinced that, had she seen Diggory in his present position, she would have considered him a fitting husband for you. Now, that's my real feeling. Don't consult me any more, but do as you like, Thomasin. I shall be content.'

It is to be supposed that Thomasin was convinced; for a few days after this, when Clym strayed into a part of the heath that he had not lately visited, Humphrey, who was at work there, said to him, 'I am glad to see that Mrs. Wildeve and Venn have made it up again, seemingly.'

'Have they?' said Clym abstractedly.

'Yes; and he do contrive to stumble upon her whenever she walks out on fine days with the chiel. But, Mr. Yeobright, I can't help feeling that your cousin ought to have married you. 'Tis a pity to make two chimley-corners where there need be only one. You could get her away from him now, 'tis my belief, if you were only to set about it.'

'How can I have the conscience to marry after having driven two women to their deaths? Don't think such a thing, Humphrey. After my experience I should consider it too much of a burlesque to go to church and take a wife. In the words of Job, "I have made a covenant with mine eyes; why then should I think upon a maid?"'

'No, Mr. Clym, don't fancy that about driving two women to their deaths. You shouldn't say it.'

'Well, we'll leave that out,' said Yeobright. 'But anyhow God has set a mark upon me which wouldn't look well in a love-making scene. I have two ideas in my head, and no others. I am going to keep a night-school; and I am going to turn preacher. What have you got to say to that, Humphrey?'

'I'll come and hear 'ee with all my heart.'

'Thanks. 'Tis all I wish.'

As Clym descended into the valley Thomasin came down by the other path, and met him at the gate. 'What do you think I have to tell you, Clym?' she said, looking archly over her shoulder at him.

'I can guess,' he replied.

She scrutinized his face. 'Yes, you guess right. It is going to be after all. He thinks I may as well make up my mind, and I have got to think so too. It is to be on the twenty-fifth of next month, if you don't object.'

'Do what you think right, dear. I am only too glad that you see your way clear to happiness again. My sex owes you every amends for the treatment you received in days gone by.' [1]

[1] The writer may state here that the original conception of the story did not design a marriage between Thomasin and Venn. He was to have retained his isolated and weird character to the last, and to have disappeared mysteriously from the heath, nobody knowing whither—Thomasin remaining a widow. But certain circumstances of serial publication led to a change of intent.

Readers can therefore choose between the endings, and those with an austere artistic code can assume the more consistent conclusion to to be the true one.

CHEERFULNESS AGAIN ASSERTS ITSELF AT BLOOMS-END, AND CLYM FINDS HIS VOCATION

IV

ANYBODY who had passed through Blooms-End about eleven o'clock on the morning fixed for the wedding would have found that, while Yeobright's house was comparatively quiet, sounds denoting great activity came from the dwelling of his nearest neighbour, Timothy Fairway. It was chiefly a noise of feet, briskly crunching hither and thither over the sanded floor within. One man only was visible outside, and he seemed to be later at an appointment than he had intended to be, for he hastened up to the door, lifted the latch, and walked in without ceremony.

The scene within was not quite the customary one. Standing about the room was the little knot of men who formed the chief part of the Egdon coterie, there being present Fairway himself, Grandfer Cantle, Humphrey, Christian, and one or two turf-cutters. It was a warm day, and the men were as a matter of course in their shirt-sleeves, except Christian, who had always a nervous fear of parting with a scrap of his clothing when in anybody's house but his own. Across the stout oak table in the middle of the room was thrown a mass of striped linen, which Grandfer Cantle held down on one side, and Humphrey on the other, while Fairway rubbed its surface with a yellow lump, his face being damp and creased with the effort of the labour.

'Waxing a bed-tick, souls ?' said the new-comer.

'Yes, Sam,' said Grandfer Cantle, as a man too busy to waste words. 'Shall I stretch this corner a shade tighter, Timothy ?'

Fairway replied, and the waxing went on with unabated vigour. ''Tis going to be a good bed, by the look o't,' continued Sam, after an interval of silence. 'Who may it be for ?'

''Tis a present for the new folks that's going to set up housekeeping,' said Christian, who stood helpless and overcome by the majesty of the proceedings.

'Ah, to be sure ; and a valuable one, 'a b'lieve.'

'Beds be dear to fokes that don't keep geese, bain't they, Mister Fairway ?' said Christian, as to an omniscient being.

'Yes,' said the furze-dealer, standing up, giving his forehead a thorough mopping, and handing the beeswax to Humphrey, who succeeded at the rubbing forthwith. 'Not that this couple be in want of one, but 'twas well to show 'em a bit of friendliness at this great racketing vagary of their lives. I set up both my own daughters in one when they was married, and there have been feathers enough for another in the house the last twelve months. Now then, neighbours, I think we have laid on enough wax. Grandfer Cantle, you turn the tick the right way outwards, and then I'll begin to shake in the feathers.'

When the bed was in proper trim Fairway and Christian brought forward vast paper bags, stuffed to the full, but light as balloons, and began to turn the contents of each into the receptacle just prepared. As bag after bag was emptied, airy tufts of down and feathers floated about the room in increasing quantity till, through a mishap of Christian's, who shook the contents of one bag outside the tick, the atmosphere of the room became dense with gigantic flakes, which descended upon the workers like a windless snowstorm.

'I never saw such a clumsy chap as you, Christian,' said Grandfer Cantle severely. 'You might have been the son of a man that's never been outside Blooms-End in his life for all the wit you have. Really all the soldiering and smartness in the world in the father seems to count for nothing in forming the nater of the son. As far as that chiel Christian is concerned I might as well have stayed at home and seed nothing, like all the rest of ye here. Though, as far as myself is concerned, a dashing spirit has counted for sommat, to be sure!'

'Don't ye let me down so, father; I feel no bigger than a ninepin after it. I've made but a bruckle hit, I'm afeard.'

'Come, come. Never pitch yerself in such a low key as that, Christian; you should try more,' said Fairway.

'Yes, you should try more,' echoed the Grandfer with insistence, as if he had been the first to make the suggestion. 'In common conscience every man ought either to marry or go for a soldier. 'Tis a scandal to the nation to do neither one nor t'other. I did both, thank God! Neither to raise men nor to lay 'em low—that shows a poor do-nothing spirit indeed.'

'I never had the nerve to stand fire,' faltered Christian. 'But as to marrying, I own I've asked here and there, though without much fruit from it. Yes, there's some house or other that might have had a man for a master—such as he is—that's now ruled by a woman alone. Still it might have been awkward if I had found her; for, d'ye see, neighbours, there'd have been nobody left at home to keep down father's spirits to the decent pitch that becomes a old man.'

'And you've your work cut out to do that, my son,' said Granfer Cantle smartly. 'I wish that the dread of infirmities was not so strong in me!—I'd start the very first thing to-morrow to see the world over again! But seventy-one, though nothing at home, is a high figure for a rover. . . . Ay, seventy-one last Candlemas-day. Gad, I'd sooner have it in guineas than in years!' And the old man sighed.

'Don't you be mournful, Grandfer,' said Fairway. 'Empt some more feathers into the bed-tick, and keep up yer heart. Though rather lean in the stalks you be a green-leaved old man still. There's time enough left to ye yet to fill whole chronicles.'

Begad, I'll go to 'em, Timothy—to the married pair!' said Grandfer Cantle in an encouraged voice, and starting round briskly. 'I'll go to 'em to-night and sing a wedding-song, hey? 'Tis like me to do so, you know; and they'd see it as such. My "Down in Cupid's Gardens" was well liked in four; still, I've got others as good, and even better. What do you say to my

"She cal'-led to' her love'
From the lat'-tice a-bove,
'O, come in' from the fog'-gy fog'-gy dew'.'"

'Twould please 'em well at such a time! Really, now I come to think of it, I haven't turned my tongue in my head to the shape of a real good song since Old Midsummer night, when we had the "Barley Mow" at the Woman; and 'tis a pity to neglect your strong point where there's few that have the compass for such things!'

'So 'tis, so 'tis,' said Fairway. 'Now gie the bed a shake down. We've put in seventy pound of best feathers, and I think that's as many as the tick will fairly hold. A bit and a drap wouldn't be amiss now, I reckon. Christian, maul down the victuals from corner-cupboard if canst reach, man, and I'll draw a drap o' sommat to wet it with.'

They sat down to a lunch in the midst of their work, feathers around, above, and below them; the original owners of which occasionally came to the open door and cackled begrudgingly at sight of such a quantity of their old clothes.

'Upon my soul I shall be chokt,' said Fairway when, having extracted a feather from his mouth, he found several others floating on the mug as it was handed round.

'I've swallered several; and one had a tolerable quill,' said Sam placidly from the corner.

'Hullo—what's that—wheels I hear coming?' Grandfer Cantle exclaimed, jumping up and hastening to the door. 'Why, 'tis they back again: I didn't expect 'em yet this half-hour. To be sure, how quick marrying can be done when you are in the mind for't!'

'O yes, it can soon be *done*,' said Fairway, as if something should be added to make the statement complete.

He arose and followed the Grandfer, and the rest also went to the door. In a moment an open fly was driven past, in which sat Venn and Mrs. Venn, Yeobright, and a grand relative of Venn's who had come from Budmouth for the occasion. The fly had been hired at the nearest town, regardless of distance and cost, there being nothing on Egdon Heath, in Venn's opinion, dignified enough for such an event when such a woman as Thomasin was the bride; and the church was too remote for a walking bridal-party.

As the fly passed the group which had run out from the homestead they shouted 'Hurrah!' and waved their hands; feathers and down floating from their hair, their sleeves, and the folds of their garments at every motion, and Grandfer Cantle's seals dancing merrily in the sunlight as he twirled himself about. The driver of the fly turned a supercilious gaze upon them; he even treated the wedded pair themselves with something like condescension; for in what other state than heathen could people, rich or poor, exist who were doomed to abide in such a world's end as Egdon? Thomasin showed no such superiority to the group at the door, fluttering her hand as quickly as a bird's wing towards them, and asking Diggory, with tears in her eyes, if they ought not to alight and speak to these kind neighbours. Venn, however, suggested that, as they were all coming to the house in the evening, this was hardly necessary.

After this excitement the saluting party returned to their occupation, and the stuffing and sewing was soon afterwards finished, when Fairway harnessed a horse, wrapped up the cumbrous present, and drove off with it in the cart to Venn's house at Stickleford.

Yeobright, having filled the office at the wedding-service which naturally fell to his hands, and afterwards returned to the house with the husband and wife, was indisposed to take part in the feasting and dancing that wound up the evening. Thomasin was disappointed.

'I wish I could be there without dashing your spirits,' he said. 'But I might be too much like the skull at the banquet.'

'No, no.'

'Well, dear, apart from that, if you would excuse me, I should be glad. I know it seems unkind; but, dear Thomasin, I fear I should not be happy in the company—there, that's the truth of it. I shall always be coming to see you at your new home, you know, so that my absence now will not matter.'

'Then I give in. Do whatever will be most comfortable to yourself.'

Clym retired to his lodging at the housetop much relieved, and occupied himself during the afternoon in noting down the heads of a sermon, with which he intended to initiate all that really seemed practicable of the scheme that had originally brought him hither, and that he had so long kept in view under various modifications, and through evil and good report. He had tested and weighed his convictions again and again, and saw no reason to alter them, though he had considerably lessened his plan. His eyesight, by long humouring in his native air, had grown stronger, but not sufficiently strong to warrant his attempting his extensive educational project. Yet he did not repine : there was still more than enough of an unambitious sort to tax all his energies and occupy all his hours.

Evening drew on, and sounds of life and movement in the lower part of the domicile became more pronounced, the gate in the palings clicking incessantly. The party was to be an early one, and all the guests were assembled long before it was dark. Yeobright went down the back staircase and into the heath by another path than that in front, intending to walk in the open air till the party was over, when he would return to wish Thomasin and her husband good-bye as they departed. His steps were insensibly bent towards Mistover by the path that he had followed on that terrible morning when he learnt the strange news from Susan's boy.

He did not turn aside to the cottage, but pushed on to an eminence, whence he could see over the whole quarter that had once been Eustacia's home. While he stood observing the darkening scene somebody came up. Clym, seeing him but dimly, would have let him pass by silently, had not the pedestrian, who was Charley, recognized the young man and spoken to him.

'Charley, I have not seen you for a length of time,' said Yeobright. 'Do you often walk this way ?'

'No,' the lad replied. 'I don't often come outside the bank.'

'You were not at the Maypole.'

'No,' said Charley, in the same listless tone. 'I don't care for that sort of thing now.'

'You rather liked Miss Eustacia, didn't you ?' Yeobright gently asked. Eustacia had frequently told him of Charley's romantic attachment.

'Yes, very much. Ah, I wish——'

'Yes ?'

'I wish, Mr. Yeobright, you could give me something to keep that once belonged to her—if you don't mind.'

'I shall be very happy to. It will give me very great pleasure, Charley. Let me think what I have of hers that you would like. But come with me to the house, and I'll see.'

They walked towards Blooms-End together. When they reached the front it was dark, and the shutters were closed, so that nothing of the interior could be seen.

'Come round this way,' said Clym. 'My entrance is at the back for the present.'

The two went round and ascended the crooked stair in darkness till Clym's sitting-room on the upper floor was reached, where he lit a candle, Charley entering gently behind. Yeobright searched his desk, and taking out a sheet of tissue-paper unfolded from it two or three undulating locks of raven hair, which fell over the paper like black streams. From these he selected one, wrapped it up, and gave it to the lad, whose eyes had filled with tears. He kissed the packet, put it in his pocket, and said in a voice of emotion, 'O, Mr. Clym, how good you are to me!'

'I will go a little way with you,' said Clym. And amid the noise of merriment from below they descended. Their path to the front led them close to a little side-window, whence the rays of candles streamed across the shrubs. The window, being screened from general observation by the bushes, had been left unblinded, so that a person in this private nook could see all that was going on within the room which contained the wedding-guests, except in so far as vision was hindered by the green antiquity of the panes.

'Charley, what are they doing?' said Clym. 'My sight is weaker again to-night, and the glass of this window is not good.'

Charley wiped his own eyes, which were rather blurred with moisture, and stepped closer to the casement. 'Mr. Venn is asking Christian Cantle to sing,' he replied; 'and Christian is moving about in his chair as if he were much frightened at the question, and his father has struck up a stave instead of him.'

'Yes, I can hear the old man's voice,' said Clym. 'So there's to be no dancing, I suppose. And is Thomasin in the room? I see something moving in front of the candles that resembles her shape, I think.'

'Yes. She do seem happy. She is red in the face, and laughing at something Fairway has said to her. O my!'

'What noise was that?' said Clym.

'Mr. Venn is so tall that he has knocked his head against the beam in gieing a skip as he passed under. Mrs. Venn has run up quite frightened and now she's put her hand to his head to feel if there's a lump. And now they be all laughing again as if nothing had happened.'

'Do any of them seem to care about my not being there?' Clym asked.

'No, not a bit in the world. Now they are all holding up their glasses and drinking somebody's health.'

'I wonder if it is mine?'

'No, 'tis Mr. and Mrs. Venn's, because he is making a hearty sort of speech. There—now Mrs. Venn has got up, and is going away to put on her things, I think.'

'Well, they haven't concerned themselves about me, and it is quite right they should not. It is all as it should be, and Thomasin at least is happy. We will not stay any longer now, as they will soon be coming out to go home.'

He accompanied the lad into the heath on his way home, and, returning alone to the house a quarter of an hour later, found Venn and Thomasin ready to start, all the guests having departed in his absence. The wedded pair took their seats in the four-wheeled dogcart which Venn's head milker and handy man had driven from Stickleford to fetch them in; little Eustacia and the nurse were packed securely upon the open flap behind; and the milker, on an ancient overstepping pony, whose shoes clashed like cymbals at every tread, rode in the rear, in the manner of a body-servant of the last century.

'Now we leave you in absolute possession of your own house again,' said Thomasin as she bent down to wish her cousin good-night. 'It will be rather lonely for you, Clym, after the hubbub we have been making.'

'O, that's no inconvenience,' said Clym, smiling rather sadly. And then the party drove off and vanished in the night-shades, and Yeobright entered the house. The ticking of the clock was the only sound that greeted him, for not a soul remained; Christian, who acted as cook, valet, and gardener to Clym, sleeping at his father's house. Yeobright sat down in one of the vacant chairs, and remained in thought a long time. His mother's old chair was opposite; it had been sat in that evening by those who had scarcely remembered that it ever was hers. But to Clym she was almost a presence there, now as always. Whatever she was in other people's memories, in his she was the sublime saint whose radiance even his tenderness for Eustacia could not obscure. But his heart was heavy; that mother had *not* crowned him in the day of his espousals and in the day of the gladness of his heart. And events had borne out the accuracy of her judgment, and proved the devotedness of her care. He should have heeded her for Eustacia's sake even more than for his own. 'It was all my fault,' he whispered. 'O, my mother, my mother! would to God that I could live my life again, and endure for you what you endured for me!'

On the Sunday after this wedding an unusual sight was to be seen on Rainbarrow. From a distance there simply appeared to be a motionless figure standing on the top of the tumulus, just as Eustacia had stood on that lonely summit some two years and a half before. But now it was fine warm weather, with only a summer breeze blowing, and early afternoon instead of dull twilight. Those who ascended to the immediate neighbourhood of the Barrow perceived that the erect form in the centre, piercing the sky, was not really alone. Round him upon the slopes of the Barrow a number of heathmen and women were reclining or sitting at their ease. They listened to the words of the man in their midst, who was preaching, while they abstractedly pulled heather, stripped ferns, or tossed pebbles down the slope. This was the first of a series of moral lectures or Sermons on the Mount, which were to be delivered from the same place every Sunday afternoon as long as the fine weather lasted.

The commanding elevation of Rainbarrow had been chosen for two reasons: first, that it occupied a central position among the remote cottages around; secondly, that the preacher thereon could be seen from all adjacent points as soon as he arrived at his post, the view of him being thus a convenient signal to those stragglers who wished to draw near. The speaker was bareheaded, and the breeze at each waft gently lifted and lowered his hair, somewhat too thin for a man of his years, these still numbering less than thirty-three. He wore a shade over his eyes, and his face was pensive and lined; but, though these bodily features were marked with decay there was no defect in the tones of his voice, which were rich, musical, and stirring. He stated that his discourses to people were to be sometimes secular, and sometimes religious, but never dogmatic: and that his texts would be taken from all kinds of books. This afternoon the words were as follows:—

'"And the king rose up to meet her, and bowed himself unto her, and sat down on his throne, and caused a seat to be set for the king's mother; and she sat on his right hand. Then she said, I desire one small petition of thee; I pray thee say me not nay. And the king said unto her, Ask on, my mother: for I will not say thee nay."'

Yeobright had, in fact, found his vocation in the career of an itinerant open-air preacher and lecturer on morally unimpeachable subjects ; and from this day he laboured incessantly in that office, speaking not only in simple language on Rainbarrow and in the hamlets round, but in a more cultivated strain elsewhere—from the steps and porticoes of town-halls, from market-crosses, from conduits, on esplanades and on wharves, from the parapets of bridges, in barns and outhouses, and all other such places in the neighbouring Wessex towns and villages. He left alone creeds and systems of philosophy, finding enough and more than enough to occupy his tongue in the opinions and actions common to all good men. Some believed him, and some believed not ; some said that his words were commonplace, others complained of his want of theological doctrine ; while others again remarked that it was well enough for a man to take to preaching who could not see to do anything else. But everywhere he was kindly received, for the story of his life had become generally known.

NOTES

By Cyril Aldred

N.B.—The following abbreviations have been used in the notes :—

" E.D.D."—*An English Dialect Dictionary*, by Joseph Wright.

"O.E.D."—*The Oxford English Dictionary.*

The Country of " The Return of the Native "

The action of this story is confined to the neighbourhood of *Egdon Heath* . . . " that vast expanse of moorland which stretches, practically without break, from Dorchester to Bournemouth. Its natural untamable wildness is the charm that makes it so subtly attractive, for it defies all attempts at subjugation. . . . It is unconquered and unconquerable by agriculture, and more immutable in character than any other parts of the Wessex Country " (Hermann Lea, " Thomas Hardy's Wessex ").

Budmouth : " the old watering-place " and Eustacia's native town, is Weymouth.

Rainbarrow : is to be placed probably in the central part of the heath.

Mistover Knap : is the fictitious name given to some houses to the north of Rainbarrow. There is nothing definite to mark the place where Captain Vye's house stood originally, but a pool answering to the description of the pool near Eustacia's house (see page 64) is to be found north of the barrows.

Blooms-End : the home of the Yeobrights, was suggested by a farmhouse called Bhompston on the margin of the heath near Lower Bockhampton.

Alderworth : the name of the cottage which Clym rented after his marriage, probably had its original in a cottage at Affpuddle Heath.

Throop Corner : is the junction of four cross-roads, of which the northern arm leads down to Throop village.

Shadwater Weir: was suggested by the weir in the meadows behind Woodsford Castle.

P. 4, l. 20. *Titanic:* the Titans were the children of Uranus and Ge. Under the leadership of Saturn, they overthrew their father and instituted the Golden Age. They in their turn were overcome by Zeus, the son of Saturn, and flung down to Tartarus (see note on page 77, line 11):

"The Titans fierce, self-hid or prison bound,
Groaned for the old allegiance once more,
And listened in sharp pain for Saturn's voice."
(Keats's "Hyperion.")

P. 5, l. 9. *Tempe:* a beautiful valley in Thessaly watered by the river Peneus. It was celebrated in classical times for its cool shades and its singing-birds.

Thule: the name given by the ancients to an island in the Northern Ocean and considered by them to be the extreme northern limit of the world. Day and night there each lasted for six months and the sea was thick and impenetrable to rowers. Thule is variously identified with Shetland, Iceland, and the coast of Norway.

P. 6, l. 10. *Domesday:* the record of the great survey of the lands of England made by order of William the Conqueror in 1086. It contains a record of the ownership, area, and value of these lands and of the number of tenants, live-stock, etc.

l. 18. *Leland:* (1506–1552) the earliest of modern English antiquaries, was educated at Cambridge and studied at Paris, where he took holy orders. He became library-keeper to Henry VIII before 1530 and the King's antiquary in 1533. He made a tour through England in the following year and his account gives valuable information about the state of the country at the time.

l. 21. *Ishmaelitish:* from Ishmael, the eldest son of Abraham, who together with his mother, Hagar, was expelled to the wilderness of Beersheba. (See Genesis xvi. 12 and xxi. 14.) "And he shall be as a wild ass among men: his hand shall be against every man and every man's hand against him." Hence, Ishmaelite = an outcast.

P. 7, l. 18. *Vicinal:* "a local common way as distinguished from a highway, a by-road or a cross-road," O.E.D.

l. 20. *Ikenild Street:* more commonly Iknield Way, a Roman road running over the downs between Marygreen and Alfredston. To within living memory it has been used for driving cattle to market.

P. 8, ll. 3–4. *Boat-cloak:* "a large cloak worn by officers on duty at sea," O.E.D.

P. 9, l. 11. *Reddleman:* "a digger of, or dealer in, reddle," *i.e.* red-ochre, O.E.D.

P. 13, l. 6. *Barrow:* also called a tumulus, "a mound of earth or stone erected in neolithic and Celtic times over a grave," O.E.D.

l. 9. *Atlantean:* from Atlas, one of the Titans. He was changed into a mountain of stone by Perseus who turned the eyes of the Medusa upon him. The ancients believed that from his immense height he supported the heavens on his shoulders.

P. 16, l. 17. *Mænades:* also known as Bacchantes, are the frenzied priestesses of Bacchus, the Roman god of wine. They are usually represented with dishevelled hair and garlands of ivy, and carry a thyrsus and clashing cymbals.

P. 17, l. 15. *Limbo:* a region, supposed to exist on the border of Hell, the abode of the just who died before Christ's coming, and of unbaptised infants. The word came to be used to mean prison, and later, a place of forgetfulness.

l. 16. *The sublime Florentine:* *i.e.* Dante Alighieri (1265–1321), the greatest of Italian poets, was born at Florence of a Guelf family. He fled from his native city in 1301 and visited Paris. He died at Ravenna. He is really the founder of the Italian language, since his works determined that the Tuscan dialect and not Provençal should become the speech of northern Italy. His most famous poem, the "Divina Commedia," is in three parts, "Inferno," "Purgatario," and "Paradiso." The "Inferno" is a description of Hell, which is described as a conical funnel to the successive circles of which the various categories of sinners are assigned.

"For well I knew
Suspended in that Limbo many a soul
Of mighty worth."
(Canto IV. 11. 40–42; Cary's Translation, 1814.)

l. 27. *Thor:* in Norse mythology the son of Woden, and the god of war. He was also the god of thunder and the protector of the household.

Woden: the Anglo-Saxon form of Odin, the supreme god in the later Scandinavian pantheon. Among his many attributes, he was the god of wisdom, of poetry, and what is more significant in this context, of the dead.

ll. 29–33. *Indeed . . . Gunpowder Plot:* "All over Europe the peasants have been accustomed from time immemorial to kindle bonfires on certain days of the year and to dance round or leap over them. . . . Not uncommonly effigies are burned in these fires, or a pretence is made of burning a living person in them ; and there are grounds for believing that anciently human beings were actually burned on these occasions. . . . Not only among the Celts but throughout Europe, Hallowe'en, the night which marks the transition from autumn to winter, seems to have been of old the time of year when the souls of the departed were supposed to revisit their old homes. . . . But it is not only the souls of the departed who are supposed to be hovering unseen . . . witches then speed on their errands of mischief. . . . The fairies, too, are all let loose, and hobgoblins of every sort roam freely about " (Sir James Frazer, " The Golden Bough ").

l. 37. *Promethean :* from Prometheus, who took pity on the helpless state of mankind and defied Jupiter by stealing fire from heaven. As a punishment for this impiety, Prometheus was chained to a rock on Mount Caucasus, where in the day-time an eagle devoured his liver which was restored each succeeding night. He was eventually liberated by Hercules. From the context, Hardy seems to be referring to the Prometheus of Shelley or of Aeschylus rather than to the figure of classical myth.

P. 18, l. 7. *Dureresque :* from Albrecht Durer (1471–1528), the great German painter and engraver. His work is characterised by accurate draughtsmanship and clean sharp contours ; see for example the " Portrait of the Artist's Father " in the National Gallery. Durer's art is boldly linear and he was for this reason attracted to the drawing of stiff draperies and decisive shadows.

P. 19, ll. 4–11. " *The king . . . may be* " *:* these stanzas are from the ballad " Queen Eleanor's Confession," which was first printed in 1685 in " The Bagford Ballads." Hardy's version follows very closely the version given in Percy's " Reliques ". See Book V. No. 8.

l. 18. *Stave :* " a short song," E.D.D.

l. 19. *Weasand :* " the gullet, throat, windpipe," E.D.D.

P. 20, ll. 11–14. " *Do thou . . . his brother* " *:* the fifth stanza of the ballad mentioned in the note on page 19, ll. 4–11.

P. 21, l. 1. *Vell :* " a film, hide, skin, or a film as one grown over the eye . . . ' I can't zee vell or mark o't,' " (Barnes, " A Glossary of the Dorset Dialect ").

l. 18. *Philistine : i.e.* Goliath, the gigantic Philistine whom David slew with a stone-bolt. See I. Samuel xvii. " And he had greaves of brass upon his legs, and a target of brass between his shoulders" (verse 6).

l. 20. *Nunny-watch*: "a disturbance, excitement . . . a quandary," E.D.D.

l. 22. *Banging*: also "bang-up," a slang synonym for "first-rate," "striking," etc. It is now almost obsolete but was quite common in the last century.

P. 23, l. 36. *Chiel*: "a child of either sex," E.D.D.

P. 25, l. 3. *Zid*: saw.

l. 13. *Strawmote*: "a single straw, a stalk of corn," E.D.D.

l. 17. *Stunpole*: "a stupid fellow, a blockhead," E.D.D.

P. 26, l. 4. *Gallicrow*: a hanged-crow, a scarecrow.

P. 27, l. 16. *Maphrotight*: a corruption of hermaphrodite, *i.e.* a person with characteristics of both sexes.

P. 28, l. 14. *Lammas-tide*: the 1st of August, Lammas, in the early English Church, was observed as a harvest festival at which loaves of bread, made from the first ripe corn, were consecrated.

l. 16. *Rames*: "a skeleton, a carcase . . . frequently applied to a very thin person," E.D.D.

P. 29, l. 26. *Kex*: "the dry, usually hollow, stem of various herbaceous plants," O.E.D.

ll. 27–28. *Nammet-time*: "the time at which the "nammet" was eaten. *Nammet*—a luncheon eaten in the field by farm labourers either in the middle of the morning or of the afternoon," E.D.D.

P. 30, ll. 1–4. "*The king . . . shouldst bee*": the last stanza of the ballad mentioned in the note on page 19, ll. 4–11.

P. 31, l. 23. *Knap*: "a small hill, a mound . . . the brow or top of a hill; rising ground," E.D.D.

l. 27. *Zany*: a fool, a simpleton.

P. 32, l. 13. *Outstep*: "out of the way," E.D.D.

P. 33, l. 1. *Mandy*: "abusive, insolent, saucy," E.D.D.

l. 6. *Vlankers*: "sparks of fire," E.D.D.

l. 9. *Poussette*: "to dance round and round with hands joined," O.E.D.

P. 34, l. 24. *Mommet*: "an image, effigy, a puppet, an odd figure," E.D.D.

P. 35, l. 13. *Nebo*: the mountain from which Moses alone was permitted to view the promised land. See Deuteronomy xxxii. 49–50.

P. 36, l. 14. *Huffle*: "of the wind: to blow unsteadily, to shift, waver; to blow up in sudden gusts," E.D.D.

l. 16. *Pixy-led*: "led astray by pixies, *i.e.* in local folk-lore, a name for supposed supernatural beings akin to fairies," O.E.D.

P. 38, l. 7. *Tartarean:* from Tartarus, the infernal regions of classical mythology. See note on page 77, line 11.

P. 40, l. 1. *Amerigo Vespucci:* (1451–1512) a Florentine merchant who settled at Seville and sailed in 1499 on an expedition to the West and again in 1501 in the service of the King of Portugal. He claimed to have made a voyage in 1497 in which he discovered "Terra Firma," the mainland of South America. His first name was given to the continent of America in virtue of this claim, which was not substantiated by evidence. It was Columbus who first discovered the West Indies in 1492, and the mainland in 1498.

P. 50, l. 21. *Skimmity-riding:* or "skimmington-ride," "a ludicrous procession, formerly common in villages and country districts, usually intended to bring ridicule or odium upon a woman or her husband in cases where the one was unfaithful to, or ill-treated, the other," O.E.D. A woman in the procession was represented as beating her husband with a skimming ladle, and probably the origin of the name is to be found in this circumstance. The procession was always accompanied by noisy music and attracted many rowdy, undesirable characters.

P. 52, l. 27. *Heling:* from hel(l), "to pour out or down," E.D.D.

P. 53, l. 7. *Club:* "a benefit society . . . the members of the club used to walk through the village in procession," E.D.D.

l. 12. *Rozum:* to work away at.

P. 54, l. 20. *Farinelli:* (1705–1782) whose real name was Broschi, was born at Naples. He made his *début* on a concert platform at the age of seventeen and soon became the most famous singer of his age. Among dilettanti, he excited an enthusiastic admiration which culminated in the ejaculation of a female admirer: "One God and one Farinelli!" The allusion here is to his appearance before the family of Philip V of Spain, whom he delighted so much that the monarch insisted on his staying permanently at the court.

ll. 20–21. *Sheridan's . . . Begum Speech:* Richard Brinsley Sheridan (1751–1816), the great playwright and theatre-manager, was also a Member of Parliament and a supporter of Fox. In 1787 he made his great speech of nearly six hours in moving the adoption of the charge against Warren Hastings of extorting money from the begums of Oude.

l. 23. *Tour de force:* a feat of strength, power or skill. (French = turn of force.)

l. 31. *Gown-piece :* " a piece of material sufficient to make a dress," E.D.D.

l. 32. *Slittering :* " gliding thoughtlessly along," E.D.D.

P. 55, l. 3. *Mossel :* morsel.

l. 29. *Fess :* " lively, active, strong," E.D.D.

P. 60, l. 6. *Cæsar :* the great Roman statesman and general made two incursions into Britain. In the first campaign he was obliged to crowd his soldiers hastily into the ships and sail for the Continent as best he could, " lest he might be prevented from sailing by the season of the year, since the equinox was at hand " (ne anni tempore a navigatione excluderetur quod aequinoctium suberat). See "De Bello Gallico," Book V. Ch. 23.

ll. 9–10. *Cimmerian land :* Homer (see note on page 199, line 14) supposes the Cimmerians to dwell in a land beyond the ocean where the sun never shone. At a later date the Cimmerians were known as an historical people inhabiting the regions of the Black Sea. They have given their name to the Crimea.

P. 62, l. 17. *Sappho :* (flourished 611–592 B.C.) the famous Greek poetess of Lesbos, known as " the Tenth Muse." Only a few fragments of her work remain. According to the legend, she threw herself into the sea from the Leucadian promontory when her advances had been rejected by the handsome youth Phaon.

Mrs. Siddons : (1755-1831) the daughter of Roger Kemble, a theatrical-manager, was one of the greatest tragic actresses that Britain has produced. She first attracted attention in Otway's " Venice Preserved," and was subsequently famous for her impersonation of Lady Macbeth and other Shakespearian characters. Hardy probably has here in mind the celebrated portrait of her as " The Tragic Muse," by Joshua Reynolds.

P. 64, l. 29. *Belshazzar :* the last Chaldean ruler of Babylon. While he was feasting with his lords and drinking wine from the sacred vessels taken from the temple of Jerusalem, he was terrified to see a hand appear and write the words of his doom upon the wall. See Daniel v.

P. 66, l. 1. *Parian :* a kind of fine, white marble formerly quarried on the island of Paros and highly valued among the ancients for statuary.

P. 67, l. 4. *Albertus Magnus :* (1193–1280) a native of Swabia, was a Dominican monk and a great scholastic philosopher and an interpreter of Aristotle, whose doctrine he expounded at Cologne and Paris. Thomas Aquinas was among his pupils. His wide learning earned for him the name of "Doctor Universalis." He was notorious for his dabblings in alchemy.

P. 73, l. 6. *Witch of Endor:* the threat of a Philistine invasion drove Saul in despair to Endor where lived a witch who was credited with the power of calling up the dead. Saul requested her to summon up Samuel. The witch, however, recognised him as the king who had put so many of her kind to death. She called up an old man represented to be Samuel who prophesied that Saul and his son should be killed in the coming battle. See I Samuel xxviii. 1–20.

P. 75, l. 2. *Olympus:* in Greek mythology, the home of the gods, where Zeus held his court, a mountain on the confines of Macedonia and Thessaly.

l. 7. *Distaff, spindle, shears:* the Fates were three sister goddesses who presided over the birth and life of men. Clotho presided at the moment of Man's birth and held the distaff; Lachesis with her spindle spun out the events and actions of his life; Atropos cut the thread with her shears. They were held to be inexorable: even the gods could not alter their decrees.

P. 76, l. 1. *Ulex Europæus:* the common furze or gorse.

l. 20. *Ogee:* a sinuous line of two opposite curves as in an S. Ogee mouldings and tracery are a characteristic feature of the Decorated style in English Gothic architecture and of the Flamboyant style in contemporary Continental architecture.

l. 34. *Lotus-eaters:* the lotus was a plant which, according to Homer, produced in those who ate it a state of dreamy forgetfulness and a loss of all desire to return home.

"*Athalie*": in 1843 Mendelssohn wrote incidental music to Racine's tragedy "Athalie." The march, which is popularly known as the "War March of the Priests" is a stirring piece of music, far removed in feeling from the mood of the lotus-eaters.

P. 77, l. 4. *Artemis:* a Greek goddess identified with Diana. She was the goddess of hunting and, as is stressed here, she was also the goddess of the moon.

Athena: the Greek goddess of war, usually represented with a helmet, shield, and spear.

Hera: the sister and consort of Zeus, the goddess of marriage, and presider at child-birth. Her hair was adorned with a crown or diadem.

l. 11. *Hades:* in later classical mythology, the abode of the departed spirits, who flit about in its gloom like bats.

Tartarus was the region of Hades in which the most impious men suffered retribution for their sins. The asphodel meadows were reserved for those who deserved neither bliss nor severe punishment.

l. 24. *Richter:* (1763–1825) a German Romantic novelist who wrote under the name Jean Paul, and for whom Carlyle worked hard to get accepted in England. Reared in humble village surroundings, Richter was at his best in idyllic representations of the life he knew so well.

P. 78, l. 27. *Alcinous:* the prosperous king of Phaeacia and father of Nausicaa who hospitably entertained Ulysses when cast naked upon his shores.

Phæacia: the Phaeaces, as described by Homer, are the inhabitants of Scheria. They were a people of luxurious habits. The ancients identified Scheria with Corcyra which is the modern Corfu. Eustacia's father was a native of this island: see page 77, line 33.

l. 28. *Fitzalan, De Vere:* typical names of noble families.

P. 80, l. 10. *Strafford:* Thomas Wentworth, Earl of Strafford (1593–1641), the efficient Lord Deputy of Ireland who governed the country for Charles I. His methods were characterised by "thoroughness" and the exercise of despotic power for asserting the King's authority. Parliament eventually forced Charles to recall him, and he was impeached on several trumped-up charges, found guilty, and executed.

l. 14. *Saul, Sisera:* types of romantic, but unsuccessful despots who both perished tragically.

l. 15. *Jacob, David:* types of unattractive but successful leaders.

P. 82, l. 9. *Delphian:* from Delphi, the small town in Phocis, celebrated for its oracle of Apollo. The replies were often capable of two interpretations: thus when Croesus, the King of Lydia, sent to ask if he should attack Cyrus, King of Persia; he received the reply that if he did, a great empire would be won. Encouraged by this, Croesus made war on the Persians who defeated him and won his great empire.

l. 10. *Héloïse:* a woman of much learning who was taught by Abelard (1079–1142), a brilliant disputant and lecturer at the schools of St. Geneviève. They fell in love with each other but their love ended in a tragic separation and a famous correspondence. Héloïse died in 1163 and was buried in the same tomb as her lover.

l. 11. *Cleopatra:* the last of the Ptolemaic rulers of Egypt, so captivated Antony, the triumvir, that he allowed the affairs of his empire to go to pieces while he tarried with her. His infatuation led him into war with Octavian, who defeated him at the sea-battle off Actium. It was in this battle that Cleopatra deserted with her contingent and fled to Alexandria where Antony followed. From this point of the struggle his fortunes steadily declined and at length in despair, he committed suicide. Cleopatra attempted to come to terms with Octavian, but when she learnt that he intended to take her captive to Rome, she, too, killed herself.

Cleopatra typifies the voluptuous, passionate lover, whose love debases; Héloïse, the chaste, platonic lover, whose love exalts.

P. 84, l. 25. *Scyllæo-Charybdean :* Scylla was a nymph loved by Glaucus, a sea-deity. Circe became enamoured of Glaucus and in a fit of jealousy turned Scylla into a monster, who in terror flung herself into the sea between Italy and Sicily, opposite Charybdis, and became a danger to mariners.

Charybdis : a dangerous whirlpool in the straits of Messina off the coast of Sicily. Horace says that an author in trying to avoid Scylla drifts into Charybdis.

Thus when I shun, Scylla, your father,
I fall into Charybdis, your mother.
(" Merchant of Venice," III. v. 18–20.)

P. 86, l. 25. *Tilt :* a light canopy or covering (especially one of canvas on a wooden frame) placed over a cart.

P. 89, l. 3. *Mephistophelian :* a word of unknown origin which first appears in the German " Faust-buch " of 1587 as Mephostophiles. It is the name of the evil spirit to whom Faust was said in the legend to have sold his soul. He was traditionally represented as wearing a fiery red cloak and habit.

l. 16. *Cain :* the eldest son of Adam, murdered his brother and for this crime was doomed to become a fugitive. A mark was set upon him so that all should know him. See Genesis iv. 1–16.

P. 93, l. 2. *Ewe-lamb :* a most cherished possession. See II Samuel xii. 1–6.

P. 94, l. 6. *Tantalus :* a Lydian king, highly honoured and prosperous, who divulged the secrets of the gods to mortals. For this impiety, he was plunged up to the chin in a river of Hades which receded when he attempted to drink it. Above him was a bough laden with fruit which was just out of reach. Thus he suffered the tortures of hunger, thirst, and unfulfilled expectation.

P. 100, l. 5. *Ægean:* the Aegean Sea is studded with very many small islands.

P. 101, l. 6. *Franklin:* (1786–1847) Sir John Franklin was the famous Arctic explorer whose final expedition ended disastrously, all the members of the party perishing. Many attempts were made to discover Franklin but did not meet with success and his fate remains a mystery.

ll. 20–21. *Frederick, Archduchess:* Frederick the Great of Prussia, on his accession to the throne in 1740, immediately engaged in prolonged wars with Austria, the dominions of which had passed to the Archduchess Maria Theresa. The cynical disregard of sanctions was as typical of Frederick as his lack of gallantry in making war on a woman.

ll. 21–22. *Napoleon, Queen of Prussia:* after Napoleon had routed the Prussians at Jena in 1806, Louisa their queen attempted to awaken generous impulses in him and to induce him to offer less harsh terms to her defeated countrymen. Her appeals were in vain—the Emperor treated her boorishly and called down the condemnation of Josephine.

P. 105, l. 7. *Withywind:* "the great bind-weed, also the field bind-weed," E.D.D.

l. 27. *Candaules:* the king of Lydia, who according to Herodotus boasted of his wife's beauty to the shepherd Gyges, and allowed him to see her unveiled. Enraged and mortified by this insult, the queen induced Gyges to assassinate her husband. She afterwards married the murderer, who became king and founded a new dynasty.

P. 108, l. 33. *Carthaginian:* Tyrian emigrants built Carthage in a short space of time after their queen, Dido, had purchased as much of the African soil as might be enclosed by an ox-hide. She ordered the hide to be cut into thin strips and with these enclosed a space upon which Carthage rapidly rose.

Tarentine: from Tarentum, an important Greek city in Italy on the Calabrian coast. It was the most powerful and flourishing of the Greek cities of southern Italy. With increase of wealth its citizens became luxurious and effeminate.

l. 34. *Baian:* from Baiae, a town in Campania near Naples. It was situated in beautiful country which abounded in warm natural springs. The baths were the most celebrated in Italy and the town itself was the favourite health-resort of the Romans.

P. 109, l. 27. *Zenobia:* a celebrated princess of Palmyra (a city in an oasis of the Syrian desert), the wife of Odenathus, whom, it was supposed, she assassinated in A.D. 266, afterwards making herself regent for her sons. She later attempted to extend her sway over Syria and Asia, but Aurelian marched against her to repress her insolence and in 273 defeated her. She was taken captive to Rome, where she was treated with humanity.

P. 126, l. 14. *Scroff:* "odds and ends, rubbish, refuse, waste," E.D D.

P. 127, l. 17. "*Castle of Indolence*": an exquisite poem written in imitation of Spenser by James Thomson (1700–1748). The Castle is situated in the land of Drowsiness, where every sense is steeped in enervating delights.

He ceased. But still their trembling ears retained
The deep vibrations of his witching song;
That, by a kind of magic power, constrained
To enter in, pell-mell, the listening throng.
(Canto I. stanza XX.)

P. 136, l. 8. *Dr. Kitto:* (1804–1854) the English writer and Biblical scholar, who at the age of twelve became incurably deaf from injuries received in a fall from a roof. Among his writings is a book called "The Lost Senses" which contains his autobiography and to which Hardy is referring here.

P. 138, l. 5. *Nebuchadnezzar:* the son of Nabopolassar, the Assyrian viceroy of Babylon, who, declaring himself independent, founded the Second Babylonian Empire. In the second year of Nebuchadnezzar's reign Daniel interpreted a dream which had troubled the King and in which he had seen the great idol with the feet of clay. See Daniel ii.

l. 6. *Swaffham tinker:* *i.e.* John Bunyan, "The Immortal Dreamer," whose "Pilgrim's Progress" is said by him to be a dream. The son of a tinsmith, Bunyan (1628–1688) was early set to his father's trade. At the age of 16 he was drafted into the Parliamentary Army. In 1653 he joined a Nonconformist Church in Bedford and preached there. He was imprisoned several times for preaching without a licence, but at length, after spending over twelve years in gaol, was not further molested.

l. 10. *Cretan labyrinth:* a maze constructed by Daedalus, an ingenious Athenian engineer, for Minos, King of Crete, and in which the bull-monster, Minotaur, was confined.

ll. 10–11. *Northern Lights:* the Aurora Borealis, the shifting, coloured lights caused by electrical discharges, which are visible after sundown in the northern polar regions.

ll. 12–13. *Scheherazade:* the mouthpiece of the tales related in the "Arabian Nights' Entertainment," was the wife of the Sultan of the Indies. She diverted him for a thousand and one nights by telling him those stories of fantasy which are now familiar inside the nursery, and at the end of that time her husband revoked his decree whereby he was bound to put her to death.

P. 141, l. 22. *Tussaud:* Madame Tussaud (1760–1850), a Parisian modeller who escaped from France during the Revolution and settled in England. She opened an exhibition of her wax portraits of celebrities in a small hall in Marylebone. The success of this exhibition prompted her to extend it and it has remained a great attraction ever since.

P. 144, l. 1. *Balaam:* the prophet who was summoned by Balak, king of Moab, to curse the invading Israelites, and although warned by God not to do so, yet went on his ass with the princes of Moab. He would have been killed by an angel standing in the way, if his ass had not saved him. When he beat the ass, the Lord opened her mouth, and she reproved him. Finally, Balaam, inspired by God, foretold the happiness of Israel. See Numbers xxii.

l. 7. "*Saint George*": a folk-play evolved from the sword-dance which was widely spread throughout England. The play in its characters and action varies in different localities, but the central incident is doubtless connected with the celebration of the death of the year and its resurrection in the spring.

P. 147, l. 20. *Raffaelle:* (1483–1520) one of the greatest artists of the Italian Renaissance, whose masterpieces are the frescoes he executed in the Vatican. He died at an early age of over-work. In his first works he was influenced by Perugino (1481–1537), the Umbrian painter whose rather cloying pictures are redeemed by a feeling for the atmospheric nature of Umbrian landscapes. This influence is very marked in "The Crucifixion" in the National Gallery (No. 3943).

P. 154, l. 17. *Serpent:* "an obsolete bass wind instrument of deep tone, about eight feet long, made of wood covered with leather and formed with three U-shaped turns," O.E.D.

P. 155, l. 3. *Pyracanth:* "an evergreen thorny shrub, a native of Southern Europe, bearing white flowers and scarlet berries: in England often trained against walls as an ornamental shrub. Also called Christ's, Egyptian, or Evergreen thorn," O.E.D.

P. 159, ll. 16–17. *Present day:* from the end of the eighteenth century, the Turkish Empire, "the sick man of Europe," had been slowly declining. The mutual jealousies of its powerful neighbours, however, saved it from partition. When Hardy wrote this passage the post-war regeneration of Turkey was, of course, unforeseen.

P. 161, l. 15. *Rembrandt:* (1606–1669) the son of a wealthy miller, was the greatest painter of the Dutch school and one of the greatest etchers the world has yet seen. He has been called the "King of Shadows" from his practice of painting subjects illuminated by a limited searching light. For this reason he delighted in portraying the wrinkled faces of old people.

l. 25. *Jared:* an antediluvian patriarch, the father of Enoch. He attained the ripe old age of 962.

Mahalaleel: another patriarch, the father of Jared, who lived 895 years. See Genesis v. 12–20.

P. 164, l. 32. *Scammish:* "rough, awkward, untidy," E.D.D.

P. 166, ll. 35-36. *Lord Lyttleton:* (1744–1779) the time of the death of Thomas, the second Lord Lyttleton, is said to have been announced to him three days before it actually occurred, by means of a dream or vision.

P. 167, l. 10. *Æneas:* Venus, the Queen of Love, was the mother of Aeneas the Trojan hero who, when Troy was falling in flames, escaped with his family and his household gods. His subsequent wanderings are the subject of Virgil's great epic poem. Eventually Aeneas reached Italy, where he settled and founded, according to the legend, the Roman people. The passage referred to is from Virgil's "Aeneid," Book I, ll. 403–404:—

"Ambrosiaeque comae divinum vertice odorem
Spiravere."

(And her ambrosial hair gave forth an immortal fragrance.)

P. 169, l. 4. *Echo:* According to Ovid, Echo was a mountain nymph who, on account of her loquacity, was changed by Juno into an echo—something which cannot speak until someone else has spoken and must repeat the words it hears. She fell in love with Narcissus and pined away for love of him until only her voice remained.

l. 12. *Polly Peachum:* a character in "The Beggar's Opera" by John Gay (see note on page 199, line 17). She loved

Captain Macheath (a fine, gay, dissolute highwayman), married him and remained faithful even when he disclaimed her. After Macheath had been reprieved, he confessed his marriage and vowed to abide with Polly for the rest of his life. The first Polly was Miss Fenton, who became the Duchess of Bolton, and to whom Hardy is probably referring here.

l. 13. *Lydia Languish :* the niece and ward of Mrs. Malaprop, a character in Sheridan's "The Rivals." She was courted by two rivals, Bob Acres and Captain Absolute, whom she knew only as Ensign Beverly. The reconciling of her choice with that of her aunt supplies the subject of the plot. Early in the nineteenth century Harriet Mellon, who later became Duchess of St. Albans, played the part of Lydia in a revival of the play.

P. 174, l. 29. *Israel in Zin :* Zin was the wilderness traversed by the Israelites on their way to Canaan. See Numbers xx. 1.

P. 176, l. 4. *Pis aller :* "the worst that can be or happen, what one accepts when one can do no better ; a last resource" (French = go worst), O.E.D.

P. 179, l. 6. *Ithuriel's spear :* Ithuriel is the angel who in Milton's "Paradise Lost" was commissioned by Gabriel to search for Satan after he had effected his entrance into Paradise. Ithuriel was armed with a spear the slightest touch of which exposed deceit. Hence, when Satan in the guise of a toad squatted close to Eve, Ithuriel made him resume his proper form :

> Him (*i.e.* Satan) thus intent Ithuriel with his spear
> Touched lightly ; for no falsehood can endure
> Touch of celestial temper, but returns
> Of force to its own likeness.
>
> (Milton, "Paradise Lost," IV., 810–813)

P. 197, l. 3. *Pheidias :* (490–432 B.C.) the most celebrated statuary of Athens. He supervised the construction of the Propylaea and the Parthenon and made a statue of Pallas Athene of ivory and gold which was placed in the Parthenon. He is eminent for dignity and breadth of style—his work lacks the suavity of a later age. The Elgin Marbles, which in the last century were considered the greatest treasure of the British Museum, were executed under his supervision.

l. 20. *Æschylus :* (525–456 B.C.) the great Athenian tragic poet. Of his many tragedies, only seven have come down, of which the "Agamemnon" and "Prometheus Bound" are the most popular. Aeschylus may be regarded as the founder of Greek tragedy, having introduced a second actor (where previously there had been only one actor and the chorus) and subordinated the chorus to the dialogue. He was later defeated by his younger rival Sophocles and retired to Syracuse.

P. 199, l. 2. *Gracian :* (1584–1658) a Spanish ecclesiastic, born at Calatayud, who was rector of the Jesuit college at Tarragona. He wrote " Reflections on the Political Conduct of Ferdinand the Catholic," a work entitled " The Hero " which was translated into several languages, and " Criticon," an allegory.

l. 14. *Homer :* the greatest of all epic poets, the alleged author of the " Iliad " and the " Odyssey." There is doubt as to both his birthplace and the date of his birth, the latter being variously placed between 1050 and 850 B.C. Several towns have claimed him as their citizen. It was formerly alleged that the epics were enlargements and remodelling of earlier material by one or more hands ; but recent researches tend to return to the idea of " One Homer."

l. 17. *Clive :* (1725–1774) Robert Clive went to India in 1742 as a clerk in the service of the East India Company. In the war between the French and English, he was given a small command but soon displayed such remarkable military genius that he became Commander-in-Chief of the Company's forces. He was equally successful in his dealings with the native rulers and may be regarded as the virtual founder of the British Empire in India. He returned to England in 1760 and for his services was elevated to the peerage.

Gay : (1688–1732) was apprenticed for some time to a London mercer, but later became secretary to the Duchess of Monmouth, and an intimate of the household of the Duke of Queensberry. His first work to show promise was his " Shepherd's Week " but he also gained considerable success in the libretti of the two light operas, the " Beggar's Opera " and " Polly," and of Handel's " Acis and Galatea." He was buried in Westminster Abbey.

l. 18. *Keats :* (1795–1821) the most gifted of English poets, was the son of a livery-stable keeper in Moorfields. He acquired a knowledge of Latin and French and was apprenticed to an apothecary. Later he became a surgeon, only to desert this profession for writing. His " Odes," his " St. Agnes' Eve " and " Hyperion," are among the best productions of romantic poetry.

P. 201, l. 10. *Mollyhorning:* the word is equivalent to "galivant."

P. 203, l. 16. *John the Baptist:* the forerunner of Christ, who called upon the people to repent. See Matthew iii. 1–2: "In those days came John the Baptist preaching in the wilderness of Judea, and saying, Repent ye: for the kingdom of heaven is at hand."

P. 204, ll. 4–5. *Philip's . . . son: i.e.* Alexander the Great (356–323 B.C.), the son of Philip II of Macedonia, who before he was thirty had conquered Greece, Syria, Phoenicia, Egypt, and Persia, and had penetrated with his soldiers as far as the Ganges.

l. 34. *Rogers:* Samuel Rogers (1763–1855), born at Stoke Newington, was the son of a banker and was himself a man of substance. His "Pleasures of Memory," published in 1792, acquired popularity in an age when the poetical standard was not high. He was offered but declined the laureateship in 1850.

West: Benjamin West (1738–1820), an artist whose true merit lay in portraiture, but whose ambition to be "another Raphael" merely brought him mediocrity. Hazlitt's pronouncement still remains the final comment on his art—"only great by the acre."

l. 35. *North:* Lord North (1733–1792), the undistinguished Prime Minister of George III, whose incompetence was largely responsible for the loss of the American colonies.

Tomline: (1750–1827), an undistinguished prelate who was tutor to the younger Pitt and later became his secretary. He was made Bishop of Lincoln and Dean of St. Paul's. In 1826 he was appointed Bishop of Winchester · among his publications are "The Elements of Christian Theology" and "Refutation of Calvinism."

P. 208, l. 14. *Plato's Socrates:* Plato (428–347 B.C.), the great Greek philosopher, a pupil and admirer of Socrates, spent the later years of his life in teaching and in compiling his "Dialogues," in which Socrates figures as conducting the discussions.

Socrates: (469–399 B.C.) devoted the latter part of his life to philosophy and encouraged the youth of Athens to seek out truth. His method of instruction was to question everything, and to remove all false appearances and conceit of knowledge. His pupils were, in fact, exhorted "to know themselves" by searching self-analysis.

l. 15. *Pontius Pilate:* the Roman governor in Judaea before whom the priests brought Christ. When Christ, questioned upon the nature of his sovereignty, was explaining that his chief function was to bear witness to the truth, Pilate interrupted with, "What is truth?" and would not stay for an answer. See John xviii. 33–38.

P. 223, l. 16. *Blacklock:* Thomas Blacklock (1721–1791), a Scottish divine and poet born in Annan, became blind in his infancy, but in spite of this handicap, acquired a good English education and a considerable knowledge of the Classical and Romance languages. He published some poems and philosophical works.

l. 28. *Sallaert:* (1590–1648?) a little-known painter, born at Brussels, was the friend of Rubens, whose pupil he is supposed to have been. For several years he was dean of the town painters' guild.

Van Alsloot: a portrait and landscape painter who flourished towards the close of the sixteenth century. He was born at Brussels and seems to have been at one time painter to the Archduke Albert of Austria. Two works, "The Procession of St. Gudule," are at Brussels where Hardy probably saw them together with the works of Sallaert.

P. 237, l. 15. *Petrarch, Laura:* Petrarch (1304–1374), Italian poet and humanist, the son of a notary, was born at Arezzo and lived at Florence until he was expelled from that city; when he migrated to Avignon. Here he met Laura, the wife of Count Hugues de Sade. She died in 1348. It was she who inspired the long series of love-poems for which Petrarch is to-day famous.

P. 250, l. 24. *Spade-guineas:* "a guinea coined from 1787 to 1799, in which the shield bearing the arms has the form of a pointed spade," O.E.D.

P. 251, l. 11. *Ulysses:* the mythical Greek hero, King of Ithaca, whose sagacity finally discovered a means of defeating the Trojans. After the ten years war at Troy, he sailed for home, but encountered a series of misfortunes and adventures, recounted in Homer's "Odyssey," which prevented him from reaching Ithaca for twenty years.

P. 254, l. 9. *Rousseau:* Jean Jacques Rousseau (1712–1778), born at Geneva, was the son of a watchmaker. Lacking all moral principle, he led an erratic and sordid existence; sometimes he was taken up and protected by benefactors whose kindness he ill repaid. His life he has described in his posthumously published "Confessions." He came into prominence by the works in which he expounded his revolt against the existing social order. "Le Contrat Social" had a profound effect on French thought and prepared the way for the Revolution. Rousseau attributed evil not to sin but to society. Society is a departure from the natural state in which man is both happy and good. To revert to the desirable conditions, all artificial elements must be banished from life.

P. 262, l. 8. *Caul:* the membrane on the head of some new-born infants, supposed to be a charm against death by drowning. To be born with a caul is the same as the more familiar phrase, "to be born with a silver spoon in the mouth."

l. 14. *Pair-royal:* "a throw of three, all turning up the same number of points, as three twos, three sixes, etc., O.E.D.

P. 271, l. 6. *Raffle:* in dicing, the throwing of three all alike, *i.e.* a triplet. A raffle of aces is a triplet of ones.

P. 295, l. 22. "*Rasselas*": a novel written by Samuel Johnson (1709–1784) to defray the expenses of his mother's funeral. In this story, a prince of Abyssinia escaped from the valley of Amhara, a private paradise surrounded by high mountains, and wandered about to find what condition or rank of life was the most happy. After careful investigation he found no human lot without its drawbacks and decided to return to the "Happy Valley." The reference here is from chapter vi., where an inventor attempts to travel through the air in a flying-machine:

"In a year the wings were finished, and, on a morning appointed, the maker appeared furnished for flight on a little promontory: he waved his pinions a while to gather air, then leaped from his stand, and in an instant dropped into the lake. His wings, which were of no use in the air, sustained him in the water, and the prince drew him to land, half dead with terror and vexation."

P. 297, ll. 19–30. "*Le point du jour*": The sense, but not the beauty, of the verses is contained in the following prose transcription:

"Daybreak touches our thickets with glory. Flora is more beautiful at its return: once more the birds sing softly of love. Everything in nature welcomes the daybreak.

"The daybreak—the cause sometimes of great sadness—how short are the nights for the love-sick shepherd, obliged to leave her whom he loves, at daybreak!"

P. 316, l. 27. *Coup-de-Jarnac:* a treacherous attack, an underhand blow; so called from Baron de Jarnac, who, in 1547, in a duel, killed his adversary by an unexpected blow.

P. 319, l. 12. *Farmer Lynch:* Charles Lynch, who was a justice of the peace in Virginia, was indemnified by an act of the Virginian assembly for having illegally fined and imprisoned certain Tories in 1780. Hence Lynch-law is the practice of inflicting summary punishment on an offender without holding a trial by a properly constituted court.

P. 326, l. 35. *Ahimaaz:* went to and fro to obtain and carry intelligence to David during Absalom's rebellion. When Absalom was defeated, Ahimaaz arrived first with the news: "And the watchman said, Me thinketh the running of the foremost is like the running of Ahimaaz, the son of Zadok. And the king said, He is a good man, and cometh with good tidings." See II Samuel xviii. 19–28.

P. 328, l. 23. *Mary Stuart:* Mary Queen of Scots (1542–1587) was the daughter of James V of Scotland. She married in turn, Francis II of France, Lord Darnley, and Bothwell. Her subjects rose against her and defeated her. She fled to England and was imprisoned by Elizabeth in Fotheringay Castle where she became the centre of plots until her execution.

l. 24. *Château of Hougomont:* a strategic point in the battle of Waterloo. It was resolutely held by the English against desperate attacks and heavy fire.

P. 337, l. 28. *Marnels:* a corruption of "marbles."

l. 34. *Ooser:* "a grotesque mask made of wood with an underjaw open(ed) and closed by pulling a string, and surmounted by a cow's horns and hair. This was made to be worn by a mischievous person to frighten people," E.D.D.

P. 366, l. 18. *Judas Iscariot:* the disciple who betrayed Christ for thirty pieces of silver. He repented, brought back the blood money, and hanged himself. See Matthew xxvi. 14–15 and xxvii. 3.

l. 37. *Black Hole:* the punishment cell of the barracks in Fort William, Calcutta, into which, by order of Suraja Dowlah, 146 Europeans were thrust for a whole night in 1756. Of these prisoners, only 23 survived till morning.

P. 374, l. 5. *Famine, Sword:* see Jeremiah xlii. 16.

P. 380, l. 36. *Black-hearts:* whortleberries.

P. 382, l. 19. *Oedipus:* the most tragic figure of classical myth and drama, was the son of Laius, King of Thebes, and Jocasta. His father, informed by an oracle that he must perish at his son's hands, exposed him at birth, but the child was found by a shepherd who adopted him. Later, in ignorance of his parentage, Oedipus slew his father and obtained Jocasta his mother, for wife. Some years afterwards the facts of his parentage were revealed to Oedipus, who, horrified by his crime, tore out his eyes and went forth from his kingdom as an outcast. Jocasta hanged herself.

P. 419, l. 2. *Last plague:* which slew the first-born of the Egyptians. See Exodus xii. 29.

l. 3. *Sennacherib's host:* According to the story which the Greek historian, Herodotus, had from the Egyptian priests, Sennacherib, King of Assyria, in 701 B.C. advanced towards Egypt and reached Pelusium, where in the night vast numbers of field-mice destroyed the bow-strings of the Assyrians, who were obliged to retire. This defeat is echoed in II Kings xix. 35. "And it came to pass in the night that the angel of the Lord went out and smote in the camp of the Assyrians an hundred and fourscore and five thousand."

Gethsemane: a garden at the foot of the Mount of Olives, a favourite resort with the disciples and the scene of Christ's agony, betrayal, and arrest. See Matthew xxvi. 36–56.

P. 431, l. 6. *Saint Sebastian:* a Roman soldier and Christian martyr, born at Narbonne, who was bound to a tree and shot to death with arrows, about A.D. 288.

P. 445, l. 31. *Lazarus:* the brother of Mary and Martha, whom Christ raised from the tomb where he had been four days buried. See John xi. 39–44.

P. 453, l. 15. *First Cause:* the Creator of the universe.

P. 469, ll. 36–37. "*I have . . . a maid*": see Job xxxi. 1.

P. 473, l. 15. *Bruckle hit:* the expression seems equivalent to "mess of things."

P. 474, l. 30. *Maul:* "to take away roughly," E.D.D.

P. 481, ll. 28–34. "*And . . . nay*": see I Kings ii. 20.

QUESTIONS ON THE TEXT

1. What do you learn from this novel of country life in the latter half of the nineteenth century ?

2. Write a conversation between Clym Yeobright and Christian Cantle, in which Clym attempts to show that all Christian's superstitious fears are unfounded.

3. Criticise Hardy's style, choosing passages which you think illustrate its strength and weakness.

4. Give the meanings of the following dialect words : *rames, nunny-watch, mandy, vlankers, mommet, huffle, heling, slittering, scroff, fess, scammish.*

5. From any evidence in "The Return of the Native," attempt to give a list of those books which you suppose Hardy had in his library.

6. What references in the novel throw light upon Hardy's knowledge of (*a*) the Bible, (*b*) Classical and Norse Mythology, (*c*) folk-lore and superstition ?

7. Give briefly in your own words (*a*) the history of the spade guineas, (*b*) Eustacia's adventures as a mummer.

8. Imagine you are Wildeve on a visit to Paris, and write a letter to Eustacia putting forth the attractions or disillusionments of that city.

9. Give an example from the book, of irony, antithesis, personification, metaphor, alliteration, hyperbole.

10. Draw a picture in pen and ink or colours illustrating any scene which has particularly struck you in the novel.

ESSAY QUESTIONS

1. "The Rousseau of Egdon." Do you think that this description entirely settles the character of Damon Wildeve?
2. "The characters do too exactly what is required of them." Discuss.
3. Compare Gabriel Oak with Diggory Venn as types of patient wooers.
4. Compare Clym Yeobright with Jude Fawley as types of thwarted idealists.
5. How far do you think Hardy was influenced in the creation of the character of Eustacia by contemporary Romantic writers?
6. What is the importance of the rustic characters in the evolution of the story?
7. "The plot as much as passion decides Clym's movements." How far do you think this criticism applies?
8. "It is a novel of contrasts." Discuss this statement with special reference to the characters of Wildeve, Clym, Eustacia, Mrs. Yeobright, Thomasin, and Venn.
9. "An inexorable fate snatches up the protagonists and carries them helpless to their doom." Discuss this statement with reference to "The Return of the Native."
10. "It has the unity of a drama rather than of a novel." Criticise this comment upon "The Return of the Native."
11. Explain what part Egdon Heath plays in the dramatic evolution of the story.
12. Do you consider Hardy's change in the conception of the story (see footnote on page 470) is a strength or weakness?

PRINTED BY R. & R. CLARK, LTD., EDINBURGH